Can Poetry Save the Earth?

Can Poetry Save the Earth?

A Field Guide to Nature Poems

JOHN FELSTINER

Yale University Press   *New Haven & London*

Color gallery courtesy Stanford Institute for Creativity and the Arts.
Published with assistance from the Louis Stern Memorial Fund.

Designed by James J. Johnson and set in Monotype Fournier type
by Duke & Company, Devon, Pennsylvania.
Printed in the United States of America.

Library of Congress Cataloging-in-Publication Data

Felstiner, John.
Can poetry save the earth? : a field guide to nature poems / John Felstiner.
p.   cm.
Includes bibliographical references and index.
ISBN 978-0-300-13750-7 (cloth : alk. paper)
1. American poetry—History and criticism. 2. Nature in literature. 3. Ecology in literature.
4. Conservation of natural resources in literature. 5. Environmental protection in literature.
I. Title.
PS310.N3F45 2009
811.009′36—dc22
2008049729

A catalogue record for this book is available from the British Library.

This paper meets the requirements of ANSI/NISO Z39.48-1992
(Permanence of Paper).
It contains 30 percent postconsumer waste (PCW) and is certified
by the Forest Stewardship Council (FSC).

10   9   8   7   6   5   4   3   2   1

For our next generations

Sarah and Scobie and Brayden

Alek and Camellia

Contents

Illustrations

COLOR

Gallery follows page 210

Preface
The Poetry of Earth Is Never Dead

The young John Keats coined this line in 1816. Since then the poetry of earth has lived up to his claim. Not dead but lively, it's more vital to us than ever.

Poetry has been changing over the centuries, and so has the earth. While poetry thrives, homo sapiens has slowly and not so slowly been abusing the physical world surrounding us. This book opens up a question, a wild notion, an outside— or inside—chance. Can poetry save the earth?

By "earth" I don't so much mean our planet, which will keep spinning till the sun gives out, but the natural world we're both part of and apart from. If poems touch our full humanness, can they quicken awareness and bolster respect for this ravaged resilient earth we live on?

Can poems help, when the times demand environmental science and history, government leadership, corporate and consumer moderation, nonprofit activism, local initiatives? Why call on the pleasures of poetry, when the time has come for an all-out response?

Response starts with individuals, it's individual persons that poems are spoken by and spoken to. One by one, the will to act may rise within us. Because we are what the beauty and force of poems reach toward, we've a chance to recognize and lighten our footprint in a world where all of nature matters vitally. When "the deer freezes" and Robert Hass wants that "moment after / when she flicks her ears & starts to feed again," we too want the deer living its own life undisturbed by humankind.

Simple recognitions like this can awaken us, poem by poem, to urban, suburban, or rural surroundings, east and west, at home or on the road. Walt Whitman watching the sun rise—"Seas of bright juice," Emily Dickinson spotting a snake—"a Whip lash / Unbraiding in the Sun," alert us to a fresh kind of news.

First consciousness then conscience—a passage we all know as single spirits. Stirring the spirit, poetry could prompt new ventures, anything from a thrifty household, frugal vehicle, recycling drive, communal garden, or local business going green, to an active concern for global warming.

Asking only openness, *Can Poetry Save the Earth?* has every sort of reader in mind. Across many centuries, each chapter sites a poet in time and place, and brings out common motifs: sea and land, wilderness and civilization, nature and history, memory and loss, human and other animals.

This field guide to poems takes us through the Anglo-American tradition, beginning with Psalms and Romantic nature poetry. Later we find modern British and American poets engaging with nonhuman nature, cherishing it and sometimes just letting it be. Robert Frost and William Carlos Williams, deeply ingrained with the natural world, were environmentalist before the movement took hold. Then Rachel Carson's 1962 pesticide warning, *Silent Spring*, caught fire astonishingly, triggering the modern environmental movement.

Can Poetry Save the Earth? stops with Gary Snyder (born 1930), the English-speaking world's most striking ecologic poet. In the early Sixties he created a new benchmark of awareness and responsibility. Since then, out of our ongoing legacy, many more recent voices can be heard—Wendell Berry, Scott Momaday, Mary Oliver, and others. These poets, some of them Native American, African American, Canadian, Australian, and Mexican, are working on fresh terrain and deserve a chronicle of their own.

All along the way, poems connecting human experience to a vast nonhuman world share a quality in common with every reader. Samuel Taylor Coleridge called it "My shaping spirit of Imagination." The workings of a poet's imagination show up here with some surprising color and black-and-white images—for instance, the actual "cellar bin" in Frost's dream of "load on load of apples coming in," and an ancient Chinese landscape scroll Snyder lit upon at the age of eleven, which gave him "an eye for the world that I saw as real."

This book's cover is an 1816 engraving of a thundering three-tier waterfall. Keats saw these falls soon after he'd said "The poetry of earth is never dead," and they blew his mind. As he put it, "I shall learn poetry here." In the engraving a small figure gazes at this cascade—not Keats though it could be, and in the pages to come, it could also be ourselves.

Can Poetry Save the Earth? tracks a poetic record rooted in the Bible and British poetry and evolving while America was richly overdeveloping, to the point of environmental crisis. Together the crisis and the tradition make for a time of urgent hope, like the question mark in this book's title. The poems gathered here may end up turning your eye and ear toward a world that is good to live in.

Introduction

Care in Such a World

> My words are tied in one
> With the great mountains
> With the great rocks
> With the great trees
> In one with my body
> And my heart

Around 1900 a tribal shaman chanted that prayer, in the Yokuts tongue:

> *nim yèt·au t·ikexo texal*
> *maiayiu lomto . . .*

An anthropologist transcribed and translated it. With their oral culture the Yokuts people had dwelt in California's San Joaquin Valley since prehistory, numbering in the tens of thousands. Now few if any speakers remain, but there are ways to call on the faith breathing life into that prayer.

"My words are tied in one / With the great mountains." Once upon many times and places, the bonding of words with nature was a given. "Let us make earth, Let us make earth," Apache myth has a creator singing. A Hopi sun god and spider woman sing each tribe to life. Australian aboriginals tell of totemic beings who wandered the continent "singing out the name of everything that crossed their path—birds, animals, plants, rocks, waterholes—and so singing the world into existence."

Another Creation story, in the Hebrew Bible, begins בראשית, *B'reysheet:* "In the beginning" the world was spoken, named into being. "God said, Let there be light, and there was light . . . God called the dry land Earth, and the gathering of the waters God called Seas." The "great whales" and other creatures of earth, sea, and air were brought forth first. Then came the moment for humankind, male and female created alike. God blessed them, that they should "Be fruitful" and not only "replenish the earth" but "subdue" it, "and have dominion over the fish of the sea, and over the fowl of the air, and over every living thing that moveth upon the earth."

Dominion—a fateful gift. It connects us to the earth through natural science, medicine, industry, invention—as in William Blake's Creation scene, where stiff sharp compasses span our world. (plate 1) And dominion also works through naming, the heart of language, making poetry possible. After the seventh day, God brought the birds and beasts "unto Adam to see what he would call them, and whatsoever Adam called every living creature, that was the name thereof." When the Psalms sing out in awe, they also tie their words in one with the earth: "He sendeth the springs into the rivers, which run among the hills. All beasts of the field drink thereof, and the wild asses quench their thirst."

Gusto like this, for the brimful world that words call up, speaks joy more gladly than dominion. Take the vigor in a creation hymn, Psalm 104, wherein the "trees of the Lord are full of sap," Leviathan can "take his pastime" in the wide sea, and plants yield "wine that maketh glad the heart of man." Here earth's fullness comes to mean an interconnected whole, embedding us in its midst. Tied in one and naming things and creatures, words recognize this world—Adam's task, and poetry's too.

We grasp the natural world in poems even when it feels beyond our ken— skyscraper redwoods slowly swaying, deer leaping a high fence seeming paused in air. Think of Helen Keller, deaf and blind from infancy. One landmark day Helen's teacher signed W-A-T-E-R in her palm while pumping water over it, and the girl's whole face lit up. Poems speak that spontaneous sign language, wording our experience of things.

Along with everything else they deal in—memory, desire, joy, fear—poems live on the sensory shock of things: the sight of a circling red-tailed hawk, the taste of just-picked wild blueberries, the sound of rustling fir trees, the smell (and taste, and touch, and gray-green hue) of crushed sage, the cool feel (and sight, taste, sound, washed fragrance) of rushing streamwater.

Alertness to nature other than ourselves has spurred poets in every culture and century. The American William Carlos Williams incited his countrymen in 1923 to "imagine the New World that rises to our windows" every day. His signature poem does just that.

> So much depends
> upon
>
> a red wheel
> barrow

glazed with rain
water

beside the white
chickens

What and how much depends on this barrow, on rain and chickens? "So much depends"—an unending urgency.

That's not a poem! poetry lovers sometimes say. No rhyme, no meter, no message, just a trivial sketch. But look and listen to "wheel / barrow," "rain / water," "white / chickens." For one blazing moment a red wheel spins, rain and whiteness glisten, before a line break turns them mundane. And the stanzas balance on their syllable count, like wheeling a cart. Williams gave his poem no distracting title: what we see is what we get. "No ideas but in things!" he never tired of urging. His poem's saving news? The here-and-now world we seldom really notice.

So much depends on seeing the things of our world afresh by saying them anew. Swamped by commerce and events—markets, movies, Internet, the world's confused alarms—we could do with poetry's exact enlivening touch for nature's common surprises. Shirley Kaufman's falling jacaranda blossoms are "so delicate / even their motion through the air / bruises them." When William Stafford spots "sharp swallows in their swerve / flaring and hesitating / hunting for the final curve" and says, "I place my feet / with care in such a world," we're getting news. An attentiveness to such live detail is a crying need of our time.

"News that stays news"

Poems run deeper than the media's day-in, day-out tidings, and that's just the point: Poetry is "news that stays news" (Ezra Pound). For centuries the nature of poetry has nourished the poetry of nature, fashioning fresh news. An anonymous medieval lyric lets rhymed and measured verse weave weather with longing, nature with humankind.

Western wind, when will thou blow,
The small rain down can rain?
Christ! if my love were in my arms,
And I in my bed again!

Chaucer's *Canterbury Tales* find a rhythm linking the year's season to the spirit's:

When April with its showers sweet
Has pierced March drought down to the root . . .
Then people long to go on pilgrimage.

Shakespeare's sonnet likens the sea to our lives, one line to the next,

> Like as the waves make towards the pebbled shore,
> So do our minutes hasten to their end,

and in this way fastens our mortality to an ongoing seaborne force.

"Earth's most graphic transaction is placed within a syllable," Emily Dickinson wrote a friend. By sleight of mind, our words make nature distinct—clear to us, yet on its own. In the frugal syllables of Bob Hass, translating ancient Japanese haiku, the poet Buson quickens what we see out there:

> Morning breeze
> riffling
> the caterpillar's hair.

"Riffling" is common enough, but on its own line, a find. Bashō fools with us and nature:

> Lightning flash—
> what I thought were faces
> are plumes of pampas grass.

And Issa simply astonishes:

> The man pulling radishes
> pointed my way
> with a radish.

The radish man's working logic shows a traveler and poet the way.

Since the earliest charms, curses, prayers, and songs, through epic and modern lyric, poems have shaped our changing consciousness of the world around us. While earth remembers the balance and harmony sustaining it for so long, even with humans present, what's neglected in a time of crisis are those centuries of poems—the Psalm's "green pastures," Dickinson's "certain Slant of light," Gerard Manley Hopkins's "dearest freshness deep down things," William Blake's "O Earth, return!"—reminding us how connected we are.

Once alerted, our eye and ear find environmental imprint and impetus running through a long legacy. Starting with Native American song, the Bible, Asian haiku, and much else, poetry more than any other kind of speech reveals the vital signs and warning signs of our tenancy on earth.

Poets in industrial England cry out at the loss of rural communities and common land. Romantics such as Wordsworth, Coleridge, and Keats divine a sensuous spiritual resonance between themselves and Nature. Across the ocean, Walt Whitman and Emily Dickinson bend that resonance to their own voice, the first brash and gabby—"The sound of the belch'd words of my voice loos'd to the eddies of the wind"—the other nimble, skeptical: "Touch lightly Nature's sweet Guitar / Unless thou know'st the Tune." Modern poets cover the spectrum from embracing nonhuman nature to respecting its selfhood, with a leaning toward the latter. "You have your language too," Stanley Kunitz tells a finback whale, "an eerie medley of clicks / and hoots and trills." Elizabeth Bishop hooking "a tremendous fish" sees "victory" fill her rented boat, then its "pool of bilge . . . And I let the fish go." "Looking down for miles / Through high still air," Gary Snyder makes out pitch that "glows on the fir-cones / . . . Swarms of new flies."

All too human as we are, we're still dealing with what God granted in Genesis: "Have dominion . . . over all the earth." Today this age-old question persists in more poems than ever, some warmly human-centered, some firmly not, some energized by that tension.

"Not man / Apart"

Although the Bible sets us front and center in our domain, it also tells a story of earth's untamable, unfathomable wildness. Who causes it "to rain on the earth, where no man is?" God humbles Job. "Hast thou entered into the springs of the sea? . . . Canst thou draw out leviathan with an hook?"—whence Herman Melville's white whale, anything but human-centered. D. H. Lawrence in Sicily comes on a snake, who "Writhed like lightning and was gone / Into the black hole" of the earth. George Oppen's ego-free "Psalm" simply says of the wild deer "That they are there!" He ends

> Crying faith
> In this in which the wild deer
> Startle, and stare out.

There's no telling whether they will bolt or stay. Robinson Jeffers looks to the organic wholeness of all things: "Love that, not man / Apart from that." A telling line break!

Homo sapiens, a recent arrival, has to refigure its place on earth, much as the Copernican revolution upset our geocentric universe. Are we a part or apart? The ways we speak of environmental and ecologic concerns reflect these jostling mindsets. Should water and wildland be managed *for* or protected *from* people? The word "Environment" centers our surroundings on the human standpoint, leading to "conservation" or "wise use" of "resources" for our benefit. "Ecology," a more recent term, sees a biosystem of interacting organisms needing "preservation" for the sake of the whole.

Environmental and ecologic thinking, in poems and at large, ranges the ground between what we call civilization and wilderness. For Henry David Thoreau, "in Wildness is the preservation of the World," yet he would leave Walden Pond for his mother's home-cooking and laundrying. Thoreau's successor, Aldo Leopold, says "Think like a mountain," but that's a tall order for us homebodies. Between away and home, there and here, we yearn for one or the other. The wanderer at sea in "Western Wind" longs for "my bed again." W. B. Yeats in London desires "lake water lapping" in western Ireland. Boisterous Dylan Thomas calls up his "green and golden" Welsh boyhood at Fern Hill. So poems keep exploring the universe bearing "nature" and our selves.

Egocentric versus ecocentric: nature poetry lives by the tension. Like science and policy, poetry always proves there's no discounting human presence. After all, a poem of purest notation still has a speaker. "Beauty is nature's fact," says Dickinson, knowing it's our fact as well. "To protect the nature that is all around us," insists the environmental historian William Cronon, "we must think long and hard about the nature we carry inside our heads," whether wild, rural, or urban. Poems do best at tying nature to what's in our heads.

"Love that, not man / Apart from that." It is good to keep remotest events in mind. Two miles up in the Rockies, black Magdalena butterflies do their mating dance, and in Cuba, bee hummingbirds lighter than a dime are courting at two hundred wingbeats per second. (The data alone betray human presence.) Often, misfortune comes of human contact with the wild. A High Sierra bristlecone pine goes on growing after 4,700 years, its location kept secret because a budding geographer once cut one down that was then the oldest living thing. Under global warming, arctic ice floes melt sooner every year, so polar bears strand or drown. Snyder speaks for many poets now, trying "to bring a voice from the wilderness, my constituency."

Such remote events have everything to do with everyday concerns. An ivory-billed woodpecker in Arkansas swampland affects us, as its (possible) 2004 sighting was the first in sixty years, the bird's habitat—and our habitat—having been destroyed by extensive clearing. We can't doubt anymore the great "web of life," which Chief Seattle may have named in 1854. Poems witness to it. Stafford rightly places his feet with care in "such a world," not dictating, not limiting the nature of that world but taking it to heart and mind.

"Making us / look again"

Having seen something once, we may suddenly in double-take *see* it for the first time. Jolted by the delicate blossoms falling from Shirley Kaufman's jacaranda, "the tree making us / look again," we may think twice in a moment of recognition, even act on it.

Old or recent popular and little-known poems will bring such recognitions. "Something I cannot see puts upward libidinous prongs" as Whitman confronts a sunrise. Seeing "a Whip lash / Unbraiding in the Sun," Dickinson takes the snake's measure in her "tighter breathing / And Zero at the Bone—" Seeing, and hearing too. The peasant poet John Clare, around 1830, hears a nightingale's song "Lost in a wilderness of listening leaves." Waiting for pike to rise from a deep pond, Ted Hughes hears "Owls hushing the floating woods." We've heard of owls and woods, but "hushing"? "floating"? Moments like these have stamped English and American poetry, and are there for us now.

Looking again can also mean regarding local ground. Wordsworth was "too tame for the Chippeway" Indians, Thoreau declared. When Missouri-born T. S. Eliot wrote *The Waste Land* (1922) from his adopted England, and famously found April "the cruellest month, stirring / Dull roots with spring rain," this sent Williams to New Jersey stirrings in "Spring and All":

> the stiff curl of wildcarrot leaf
> One by one objects are defined—
> It quickens: clarity, outline of leaf

He'd just started a little magazine calling for "contact between words and the locality that breeds them, in this case America."

Also a lifelong family doctor, Williams felt the responsibility in poetry's crucial quickenings:

> It is difficult
> to get the news from poems
>   yet men die miserably every day
>   for lack
> of what is found there.

A deep claim, and half a century later this wake-up call resounds. Williams lived to look again at his nearby river, fouled by industrial waste: "a pustular scum, a decay, a choking / lifelessness." Now ecologic losses are nearly beyond repair and time is running out. As W. S. Merwin says about vanishing native languages, "the things the words were about / no longer exist."

Realistically, what can poetry say, much less do, about global warming, seas rising, species endangered, water and air polluted, wilderness road-ridden, rainforests razed, along with strip mining and mountaintop removal, clearcutting, overfishing, overeating, overconsumption, overdevelopment, overpopulation, and so on and on? Well, next to nothing. "Poetry" and "policy" make an awkward half-rhyme at best.

Yet next to nothing would still be something. The choices we make now or fail to make, and those foisted on us, determine whether we will subsist on a livable or steadily degraded planet. Occasionally emergencies spark awareness: wildfire, hurricane, earthquake, flood, smog alert, bird flu, oil spill, fuel bust. Preferably we have poets, such as Denise Levertov. Voicing one woman's news of nuclear dread, she gazes on "thistles, nettles, subtle silver / of long-dried cowpads" and gives thanks "that this moment / at least, was not / the last." That startling silver, then the slant rhyme "at least . . . not / the last," and her catch-breath at line breaks all renew our saving touch with the earth.

"Wee may lawfully take the rest"

What on earth have we been doing? How did we get to such a critical pass, where saving our environment becomes a crisis? Since the United States presents a model, with an excessive consumption of goods and resources also seen now in China and elsewhere, some voices and landmarks in this nation's environmental career bear looking into.

In the beginning, early settlers believed "the whole earth is the lords Garden" and blamed "the Natives in New England" for not following God's command to "subdue it." So "if wee leave them sufficient for their use wee may lawfully take the rest." A century later, when Daniel Boone left home for "the country of Kentucky," Nature's "ingenuity and industry" rewarded him with "myriads of trees," flowers, fruits, and "abundance of wild beasts," so he brought his family to possess this "second paradise." Boone's example resounds throughout American experience. At John F. Kennedy's inaugural, Robert Frost recited "The Gift Outright": "The land was ours before we were the land's / . . . the land vaguely realizing westward, / But still unstoried, artless, unenhanced."

Unstoried? The land's first peoples, five hundred tribes with their stories, left little permanent damage for thousands of years. Then harm came so fast that during the decade or two of an American literary renaissance—Emerson and Thoreau, Whitman and Dickinson, Hawthorne and Melville—Manifest Destiny destroyed half of all native inhabitants, their languages and habitats.

Beneath the destruction ran several myths that made it thinkable. To colonists on their quasi-biblical errand into the wilderness, indigenous tribes seemed figures in a tableau awaiting settlement. But their continent was not untouched, or a Christian Eden to be redeemed, nor was it desolate waste. The land had been managed for millennia, mostly well, sometimes ill: canals dug for irrigation, forests burned for grazing, deer and beaver overhunted, herds stampeded over "buffalo jumps." Often Indians cooperated with the white invasion, especially in trade. Still it was invasion. North America had sustained millions before Columbus. By 1620 and the Mayflower, possibly 90 percent had perished from diseases the Europeans carried unknowingly. They thanked God "that he might make room for us," and from then on made more and more room.

They also made sure the next generations would see this land aright. *A Concise School History of the United States,* originating in 1828 and "Adapted to the Capacity of Youth," saw settlers landing in a "New World" of "almost unbroken wilderness" and natives painted "with streaks and with hideous devices." Strangely "They had NO BOOKS," and "Their LANGUAGE being destitute of abstract terms, caused the frequent use of metaphors in speech, such as may be derived from familiar appearances of nature and the habits of animals." Metaphors, nature, animals! No wonder they needed improvement.

Colonists and settlers often learned from these natives how to survive on the continent, but we'd hardly know it from the historical record. One Yankee went on the Gold Rush and complained of salmon-fishing Indians "too lazy to obtain more than will supply their own wants." He also admitted a "war of extermination against the aborigines, commenced in effect at the landing of Columbus." In 1851 California's first governor regretfully predicted a war "until the Indian becomes extinct." Even John Muir, writing for the *Encyclopaedia Britannica* on Yosemite, omitted its ancient inhabitants except to say the valley was "discovered in 1851 by a military company in pursuit of marauding Indians." Soon enough the "way west" had its way.

A young Bostonian, Francis Parkman, made his own summer-long migration, living briefly among the Sioux and crossing midwestern prairies to the Rocky Mountain foothills. In *The Oregon Trail* (1847) he enthused over the wild beauty of it all. A few years later Whitman in *Leaves of Grass* expanded on Parkman, proclaiming himself a "Dweller in Mannahatta" and also "in Dakota's woods," an admirer of "the flowing Missouri" who is "Aware of the buffalo herds grazing the plains." He went on reissuing *Leaves of Grass,* where he "saw the marriage of the trapper in the open air in the far west, the bride was a red girl, / . . . her coarse straight locks descended upon her voluptuous limbs and reached to her feet." Did he come to know of the 1890 massacre at Wounded Knee Creek? He marvels how "herds of buffalo make a crawling spread of the square miles," but those miles had been parceled and scoured. Abetted by government, army, banks, and the Union Pacific, cattle ranchers secured the northern plains for themselves.

Meanwhile Longfellow's *Song of Hiawatha* (1855), steeped in Ojibwa legend, language, and landscape, kept selling in the tens of thousands. Nokomis sang lullabies "By the shores of Gitche Gumee, / By the shining Big-Sea-Water," and her grandson Hiawatha learned the language of the beasts,

> Learned their names and all their secrets,
> How the beavers built their lodges . . .
> Called them "Hiawatha's Brothers."

Longfellow had grand literary genius. In this high romance, it displaced reality. The *New York Times* thanked it for "embalming pleasantly enough the monstrous traditions of . . . a justly exterminated race."

Francis Parkman in 1872 regretted that his fourth edition now "reflects the image of an irrevocable past": no more trappers, and the Indian "an Indian still, but an Indian shorn of the picturesqueness which was his most conspicuous merit." (Picturesque? Conspicuous merit?) By 1892 Parkman's romantic grief for the West and its "savage charms" reached biblical pitch: "The buffalo is gone, and of all his millions nothing is left but bones."

Grieving in a different way, over Wounded Knee, the Sioux shaman Black Elk told Nebraska's poet laureate in 1930: "When I look back now from this high hill of my old age, I can still see the butchered women and children lying heaped and scattered all along the crooked gulch as plain as when I saw them with eyes still young. And I can see that something else died there in the bloody mud, and was buried in the blizzard. A people's dream died there. . . . There is no center any longer, and the sacred tree is dead."

As if to erase such eloquence, for centuries American generations have been bred on slogans such as howling wilderness, virgin land, Manifest Destiny, Westward Movement, march of civilization, frontiersmen, pioneers, territories, Gold Rush, land rush, homesteading, cowboys and Indians, law and order, Daniel Boone, Davy Crockett, Last Mohican, Kit Carson, Custer's Last Stand, Buffalo Bill, "Go West, young man," the Lone Ranger, John Wayne, coonskin, chaps, jeans, the railroad's Golden Spike, and "America! America! / God shed His grace on thee, / . . . From sea to shining sea"—a hymn for its time, with the same beat Dickinson used in her verse.

The difference is, Dickinson's and all the poems in this book are guaranteed to be slogan-free.

"For usufruct alone, not for consumption"

A small-town Vermont lawyer, linguist, diplomat, and traveler spoke out against environmental recklessness a century before Rachel Carson's *Silent Spring* (1962) spurred the modern movement. George Perkins Marsh's *Man and Nature; or, Physical Geography as Modified by Human Action,* considering the biblical command to replenish the earth and subdue it, found that "Man has too long forgotten that the earth was given to him for usufruct alone, not for consumption, still less for profligate waste." Usufruct: an ancient legal right to temporarily use and enjoy the fruits of something not belonging to you, without damaging its substance. But man is "everywhere a disturbing agent. Wherever he plants his foot, the harmonies of nature are turned to discords . . . Indigenous vegetable and animal species are extirpated." Strikingly in 1864, amid civil war, Marsh knew enough to blame heedlessness and avarice for the exhaustion and erosion of soils, for deforestation, for destruction of plants, trees, insects, birds, fish, whales, whole habitats.

For the next hundred years, more headlong than other peoples because of our limitless vistas and inexhaustible resources, America kept gorging the continent as if bent on fulfilling Marsh's premonitions. Hunters extinguished billions of passenger pigeons migrating in mile-wide, 240-mile-long flocks. Loggers stripped old-growth forests. Now we abuse North and South American land to consume a quarter of the world's beef. Oilmen and their political helpers clamor to drill "some remote part of Alaska," the Arctic National Wildlife Refuge, that "empty wilderness" ripe with fossil fuel.

As for "the earth and its cycles," says Alaska's poet John Haines, "Nature has hold of the other end of the string," and sooner or later jerks us up short. He and younger nature poets, compelled by each day's worsening news, cross celebration with loss. In America the Beautiful and elsewhere, carbon-sucking forests and their wildlife have been lost to logging, wildlands to drilling, prairie and grassland to overgrazing, wetland and desert to developers, woods to snowmobiles, dunes to "off-road" and "all-terrain" vehicles, canyons to dams,

Scared Buffalo, Yellowstone National Park.
Natural Trails and Waters Coalition.

soil and aquifers to agribusiness, coral reefs to poison and dynamite fishing, whales and dolphins to military sonar, seabirds to oil spills, pollinating bees to pesticides and development, gorillas to charcoal barons, elephants tigers snow leopards white rhinos hippos to poachers for bushmeat and fur and skins and ivory, brilliant macaw parrots to illegal bird dealers, 38 million sharks a year ("finned" then tossed back to drown) to shark-fin soup, animal and plant species to plunder, to cosmetic, sartorial, culinary, medicinal, and aphrodisiac vanity, and to corporate plus consumerist greed.

All this goes on apace. Turtles, migrating across oceans to lay eggs on the beach where they were born, find a Club Med. On a Florida road between two popular lakes, autos crush thousands of turtles a year. Leatherback tortoises, weighing up to a ton, have existed 230 million years, since before the dinosaurs. One of them, alive when Mozart was composing operas, died in 2006, as did another that Darwin may have found in the Galápagos Islands. Now many die from ingesting plastic bags that look like jellyfish.

Not only predator but endangered species, we have slowed some ruinous trends: smog reduced, rivers cleansed, forests managed, habitats restored, California condors literally snatched from extinction with one breeding pair, wolves and grizzlies reintroduced, bison flourishing, mega-resorts stopped in Puerto Rican wetlands. And public breakthroughs can occur: a crossover vote halting wanton exploitation, big business or a labor union seeing green, bicycles everywhere, an acceptable SUV, wind turbine, leaf blower.

Yet ecologic zeal can backfire. Preserving Yosemite National Park meant first evicting Ahwahnee and Miwok Indians, while Yellowstone got rid of Shoshone and Lakota. Arizona's Black Mesa Mine, shut down for fouling the air, draining the water table and thereby sacred springs, had also provided jobs for Navajo and Hopi Indians. Cleansing the air may itself hasten global warming, because pollution haze absorbs and scatters sunlight. Curtailing ranchers and loggers drives them to sell land to developers. In Canada, the 1980s campaign against slaughtering seals, beaver, and fox for fur coats and scarves left native trappers strapped for a living. They had to turn their land and themselves over to companies building gas pipelines through a pristine valley, flooding the land for a hydroelectric plant, drilling for oil in teeming offshore waters.

Choices pitting nature against jobs, development, or recreation, choices arising every day as environmental awareness grows, can take nasty turns. Using an 1872 law, mining interests buy national forest and federal wildland at $2.50 an acre, then while creating jobs they also sell lush terrain to developers at eight-thousandfold profits. An Arizona ski resort pipes up wastewater to make artificial snow on a peak long sacred to the Hopi. A coal-fired carbon-dioxide-emitting power plant that serves New Mexico Navajo would desecrate and pollute Mother Earth and Father Sky.

The seesaw between ecology and economy has its ironic moments. When "My aspens dear" were felled for railway brakes in 1879, Hopkins cried out,

> O if we but knew what we do
>   when we delve or hew—
> Hack and rack the growing green!

New poplars were planted back then, which are coming to the end of their natural life, and today we'd welcome public transit. For sheer myopia, listen to a California man annoyed by the DDT warning in *Silent Spring:* "We can live without birds and animals, but . . . we cannot live without business." Or take Chrysler's CEO: "We've got to pause and ask ourselves: How much clean air do we need?" At times our entire saga spawns nothing but dismay.

That dire word "Unless" keeps cropping up. Unless China and India and Indonesia along with the industrialized nations make immediate radical changes, our children will be breathing unacceptably dangerous air before they're our age. To drive home dire statistics we summon metaphor, the genius of poetry. Tropical rainforests, home to half the world's species, are perishing, we say, at two football fields per second. Global warming sends immense slabs of berg ice "calving" into the sea.

How to realize that a comeback starts with us, that a moment's mindfulness sends empty beer cans into recycling bins, not shrubbery? The essential choices, ticklish for government and industry, fall to us first as individuals in our eating, housing, clothing, childbearing, transport, recreation, voting. It's a question of human consciousness, poetry's target audience. William Stafford: "We must go back and find a trail on the ground / . . . and lie down whenever there is doubt and sleep there." A thought like this might get us doing something—or doing nothing, just letting animal, vegetable, and mineral alone for once, for good. Poems make us stop, look, and listen long enough for imagination to act, connecting, committing ourselves to the only world we've got.

"Moving / And staying like white water"

A welter of social, economic, and biologic crises confront the news that poems offer. In 1962 Carson's *Silent Spring,* setting a benchmark for environmental awareness, began with an epigraph from John Keats: "The sedge has wither'd from the lake, / And no birds sing . . ." She believed, "The aim of science is to discover and illuminate truth. And that, I take it, is the aim of literature."

Science, policy, and activism point the way toward solutions, but something deeper must draw us there. It can be found in poetry's musical lift, attentive imagery, and shaping force, which stem from prehistory and live on in today's magazines, slim volumes, readings, slams, songs, Web sites, blogs. In country or city, poems make a difference by priming consciousness.

As long ago as we know, poetry has aimed to enlighten and delight. So have the visual arts, honing our perception. John James Audubon in the early 1800s painted five hundred American bird species, vivifying them for the naked eye: an osprey clasping a trout as it takes off, cranes tearing at waterlily roots. (plate 2) After intense observation ("Nature must be seen first alive") he killed many specimens, devising ways of posing them lifelike on a wooden grid. Audubon's art slowed the wholesale slaughter of birds and still helps protect them. Ansel Adams, his purpose sharpened by the granite spirit of Robinson Jeffers, crisply, majestically photographed the soon-to-be-overrun Yosemite valley. When Gary Snyder first saw Chinese scrolls, their mist-blown mountains looked like his northwest Cascades. "The Chinese had an eye for the world that I saw as real."

Artists like poets make us see. Their sheer craft makes things matter by getting them right, like John Constable trying for the shape and flow of clouds on Hampstead Heath, or Winslow Homer painting the endless Maine surf breaking at his feet. And poets have tried their hand: Williams, Lawrence, Moore, Bishop. Hopkins sketches a brook rushing over hollowed rock and that evening notes how "a blade of water played" on the rock and "shaping to it spun off making a bold big white bow coiling its edge over and splaying into ribs." Even his journal can't help charging things with music: "blade . . . played . . . shaping . . . splaying."

Shaping life—that's what makes a poem or picture take hold in us. The early American painter Thomas Cole saw in waterfalls a "beautiful, but apparently incongruous idea, of fixedness and motion—a single existence in which we perceive unceasing change and everlasting duration." A poem like a painting catches life for the ear or eye, stills what's ongoing in human and nonhuman nature.

Motion and stillness, a changing constancy. Coleridge notes a "*white rose* of Eddy-foam, where the stream ran into a scooped or scolloped hollow of the Rock in its channel." This eddy-rose, "overpowered by the Stream," still keeps "blossoming" every moment. Eliot says "we must be still and still moving," Williams senses an "unmoving roar" in Passaic Falls, A. R. Ammons in an "on-breaking wave" finds "immobility in motion." Derek Walcott recalls Caribbean swallows "moving yet motionless." Richard Wilbur spots windblown bedsheets on a clothesline, "moving / And staying like white water."

Here I think we have it. Poetry "moving / And staying" takes after water, flowing yet seeming motionless. That kinship says why nature poetry works so well. Williams felt his poems "transfused with the same forces which transfuse the earth." Poetry, the news from poems, creates a sustainable energy.

A conservation miracle, change renewing order, is ecology in action. No wonder poets fix on a stream's "white bow" or "white rose," the mind's eye finding moment-by-moment permanence in transience. Coleridge in the Alps is struck by "Motionless torrents!" and Wordsworth by "The stationary blasts of waterfalls," Frost swears by a brook whose "white water rode the black forever, / Not gaining but not losing"—that's the miracle. This figure turns up throughout the poetry of nature because it springs from the nature of poetry.

Imagination, momentarily grasping things in flux, admits in the same moment that nature itself is ungraspable. That's as it should be. Likewise metaphors grip us by saying something contrary to fact. A snake is no whiplash, eddy-foam no rose, whitewater no blade or bow or rib, yet those images make us grasp things anew. Poems shaping nature make it at once strange and vital.

"Going into Nature with Poems"

Like handbooks about mushrooms, ferns, flowers, trees, birds, snakes, this book offers a kind of field guide and wake-up call. It's for going *out into* the world with poems in hand or mind, finding things "glazed with rain / water," and for looking closer, going into the nature of Nature. When "the wild asses quench their thirst" in Psalms, and wild deer "Startle, and stare out" in Oppen's "Psalm," we're brought somewhere fresh. If words tie us in one with nature, tying human with nonhuman, and if speech in the beginning brings all into being, maybe the speech of poems will revive our lease on life. We can count on this: the poems we hear have news for us.

PART ONE

"stony rocks for the conies"
Singing Ecology unto the Lord

"And God saw every thing that he had made, and, behold, it was very good." Not just "good," as when "God said, Let there be light: and there was light. And God saw the light, that it was good." Or when "God called the dry land earth; and the gathering together of the waters called he seas: and God saw that it was good." Or when God made two great lights for day and night, and let the waters bring forth living creatures, and made the beasts of the earth, "and God saw that it was good." Not just good but very good, *tov me'od,* and so God rested on the seventh day, the Sabbath.

Strangely enough, after God "created man in his own image ... male and female created he them," the Bible does not add, "God saw that it was good." But something else happened then and still reverberates for humankind. "God said unto them, Be fruitful, and multiply, and replenish the earth, and subdue it: and have dominion over the fish of the sea, and over the fowl of the air, and over every living thing that moveth upon the earth."

Dominion. Long before the Israelites came into a land of milk and honey, Eden may have existed within the Fertile Crescent in Mesopotamia. There Gilgamesh, a Sumerian king "who knew the way things were before the flood," slew the guardian of the Cedar Forest and felled its trees for his city. A dominant Sumerian culture flourished by channeling irrigation from the Euphrates, until overuse and evaporation eventually left the soil poisoned by salt.

Dominion, from the same Hebrew root as "tyrant": an ominous gift, like the command to replenish the earth and "subdue it." That command fed the zeal, so mixed in its effects, of America's Puritan colonists and westward settlers. Governor William Bradford's *Of Plymouth Plantation* shows sensuous affection for an abundant "new" world but a skewed eye for the "hideous and desolate wilderness, full of wild beasts and wild men" in need of subduing. Meanwhile, in England, Francis Bacon, contemporary with Bradford, set out the scientific method and foretold technology's "jurisdiction over the nature of things": "Nature to be commanded, must be obeyed," Bacon said, with an ambiguity that still bedevils us.

Yet Hebraic legacy, while fostering dominion over nature, also ordains stewardship: "And the Lord God took the man, and put him into the garden of Eden to dress it and to keep it," *l'avdah ul'shamra,* to work and to guard. Adam is of the "earth," *adamah,* and the first humans are "given every green herb for meat," then told to let the land rest every seventh year for replenishing.

Just as vital to the Bible scene and story is an everpresent wilderness where momentous events take place. "In the wilderness," God gives water to Hagar and Ishmael, Moses encounters God as the Hebrews wander toward Canaan, Elijah hears the Lord's "still small voice," Isaiah's voice "crieth in the wilderness" preparing a way for Messiah, and Jesus resists temptation.

A mighty litany of wild nature untouched, unknowable by mere man, climaxes the folkloric book of Job. From a whirlwind the Lord demands of Job, "Who hath divided a watercourse for the overflowing of waters, or a way for the lightning of thunder; To cause it to rain on the earth, where no man is; on the wilderness, wherein there is no man?" Nothing in Holy Writ equals the rolling surf of God's questions silencing Job, who has suffered calamity and craves justice. Job's friends tell him, "God thundereth marvelously with his voice," and via the Hebrew poets (and Bible translators) He does just that: "Where wast thou when I laid the foundations of the earth? . . . When the morning stars sang together. . . . Hast thou entered into the springs of the sea? . . . Doth the eagle mount up at thy command, and make her nest on high? . . . Canst thou draw out leviathan with an hook?"

A diving sphere in 1925 descended into the springs of the sea. Given the species-wasting whale-hunting pursued into the twenty-first century, Leviathan's majesty now seems almost crushed. Still that biblical awe of nonhuman nature persists with a modern bent. Henry David Thoreau cursed ravenous fur traders in 1862 and heard the railroad at Walden Pond: "what I have been preparing to say is, that in Wildness is the preservation of the World." That same year, George Perkins Marsh was writing his little-known *Man and Nature,* warning that earth's balanced, harmonious "sustenance of wild animals and wild vegetation" stood at risk from human action. A century later Wallace Stegner fought "the Brave New World of a completely man-controlled environment," urging that "wilderness preserved . . . is good for our spiritual health."

However skewed the biblical sense of our earthly dominion appears today, Scripture does offer one saving grace: a lingo for the natural world. Just as God is deciding to make woman, a helpmeet for Adam, the narrative interrupts: "And out of the ground the Lord God formed every beast of the field, and every fowl of the air; and brought them unto Adam to see what he would call them: and whatsoever Adam called every living creature, that was the name thereof." Then the story resumes with Adam's deep sleep, spare rib, and Eve.

Why, just before womankind comes into being, should the story pause for this event? Because the power of naming, in a patriarchal scheme, is reserved for man not woman? Or because the human couple should culminate all creation? At any rate, the gift of naming sets a benchmark before the Fall: "whatsoever Adam called every living creature, that was the name thereof." (And why not flora along with fauna? Maybe it's our closeness to other creatures.) "The poet is the sayer, the namer," Ralph Waldo Emerson announced, "He is a sovereign" whose American imperative is to "enjoy an original relation to the universe," and "fasten words again to visible things."

Looking for wildness in literature, Thoreau imagines "a poet who could impress the winds and streams into his service, to speak for him; who nailed words to their primitive senses, as farmers drive down stakes in the spring, which the frost has heaved; who derived his words as often as he used them,—transplanted them to his page with earth adhering to their roots." For some time now the sovereignty of words, imperial language, has come into question. This only sharpens the poet's task.

Despite Emerson's "He" and Thoreau's "his" and "him," a woman sixty miles west of Walden Pond was nailing words, enjoying an original relation to the universe. One of Emily Dickinson's canny, uncanny poems spots "A narrow Fellow in the Grass" without ever naming him snake or serpent, describes "a Whip lash / Unbraiding in the Sun," and says she

> never met this Fellow
> Attended, or alone
> Without a tighter breathing
> And Zero at the Bone—

Walt Whitman, unaware of Dickinson though she'd skeptically heard of him, called his naked outdoor exercises "my Adamic air-bath and flesh-brushing from head to foot." "Adamic" has come to mean a poet's firsthand sense of naming things—what John Hollander in "Adam's Task" calls "Gay, first work, ever to be prior, / Not yet sunk to primitive."

God creating the birds sees Adam in His thought.
From Etienne Houvet, *Cathédrale de Chartres;* north portal (thirteenth century)
(Chelles, France, 1919).

A deep current runs from our mythic beginnings, from a world spoken into being—"And God said, Let there be light: and there was light"—into Adam's genius for naming. Made in the image of God, humankind gets an earthly version of that divine creative power. (Apparently Adam never misspoke, otherwise tiny mollusks in spiral shells might be crawling the face of the earth, thinking themselves "whales" not "snails.") Why and how we name the things of our world must stem, like much else good and ill, from the savvy of Homo sapiens. In this sense, we are all poets.

Our primal urge to speak the names of things tallies with a striking trait in the Bible. "O thou, that tellest good tidings to Jerusalem, Lift up thy voice," we hear in Isaiah, "Say unto the cities of Judah, Behold your God!" Throughout the Bible, words and naming make for authenticity—breath and voice and speech and the command to speak, say, talk, tell, call, utter, declare, shout, cry, proclaim, praise, rejoice, sing, and make a joyful noise. Moses complains he is "slow of speech" but the Lord says "I will be with thy mouth." Isaiah is "of unclean lips" but an angel touches a live coal to his mouth. In Jewish mysticism, Kabbalah, "Speech reaches God because it comes from God." No wonder poets feel "called" to speak.

> Who can utter
> the poignance of all that is constantly
> threatened, invaded, expended,

Denise Levertov asks in a psalmlike poem that has already answered her question with "shadow of eucalyptus . . . miner's lettuce, / tender, untasted." No skepticism about the adequacy of words, about their signifying power, undermines biblical poetry. God stands as guarantor for human language.

When it came to translation, a long process renewed this superb Hebrew poetry, especially Psalms in the sixteenth-century Book of Common Prayer. Finally in 1611, when the King James Version emerged, William Shakespeare, George Herbert, Ben Jonson, and John Donne were in force. The poetics of biblical Hebrew found English at its height: "Blessed are those who, going through the vale of misery, use it for a well, and the springs are filled with water. They go from strength to strength." In exile, the poet of Lamentations muses on poetry itself: "What thing shall I liken to thee, O daughter of Jerusalem?"

In Psalms, people have found the Bible's intensest poetry and devotion alike. (*Psalmos* in Greek comes from plucking or twanging the harp, but the Hebrew Psalms, *tehillim*, means "praises.") As far back as David and Solomon, ten centuries before Christ, many of the Psalms were composed by a priestly guild for ritual worship. Yet their personal, often solitary voice gives these songs their hold on us. As does their emotional range, from despair to exaltation, beseeching to thanksgiving—so often couched in nature: "Save me from the lion's mouth . . . in the midst of the congregation will I praise thee." "Deep calleth unto deep at the noise of thy waterspouts: all thy waves and thy billows are gone over me."

Praise and twanging, spirit and music, fuse in the Psalms' charge, their thrust. This force finds its way into modern nature poems, however secular and colloquial, from Dickinson and Whitman to Robert Lowell and Denise Levertov. Take Levertov's book *O Taste and See,* as from Psalm 34, "O taste and see that the Lord is good." Or George Oppen's awestruck "Psalm," beginning "In the small beauty of the forest / The wild deer bedding down— / That they are there!"

Not all Psalms touch on nature, but most do at some point, since the people they speak for existed hard by a harsh if sometimes fruitful landscape. The terrain yields imagery for desolation: "I sink in deep mire, where there is no standing: I am come into deep waters, where the floods overflow me." And for longing: "Like as the hart desireth the water brooks, so longeth my soul after thee, O God." Sometimes, famously, for succor and joy: "He maketh me to lie down in green pastures: he leadeth me beside the still waters."

Naturally, wanting color and grip, the Bible's poets go local. Take the Hebrew maiden in Song of Songs, a "rose of Sharon" and "lily of the valleys": "My beloved is unto me as a cluster of camphire in the vineyards of En-gedi," the wilderness where David the "sweet singer of Israel" hid from Saul "upon the rocks of the wild goats." She says, "the fig-tree putteth forth her green figs, and the vines with the tender grape give a good smell. Arise, my love." Equally besotted by her and nature, he replies, "thou hast dove's eyes within thy locks: thy hair is as a flock of goats, that appear from mount Gilead." Ages before industry and technology as we know them, this grazing, growing, fishing, hunting civilization turned up metaphors rising organically from where and how people lived: "honey and milk are under thy tongue." In fact biblical poetry has roots in earlier cult liturgy and songs reflecting that same landscape.

Sometimes not metaphor but straight proof of earthly sustenance fills a Psalm:

> He sendeth the springs into the rivers: which run among the hills.
> All beasts of the field drink thereof: and the wild asses quench their thirst.

The shaping of such verse, the way it moves and grows, proves that if the natural world reveals divine presence, that presence needs human speech to show it. In the western tradition, at least, much poetry learns from the Psalms.

"The world is charged with the grandeur of God," Gerard Manley Hopkins begins a sonnet, putting earth first while echoing the opening of Psalm 19:

> The heavens declare the glory of God, and the firmament telleth his handiwork.
> Day unto day uttereth speech, and night unto night showeth knowledge.
> There is no speech nor language, where their voice is not heard.

Their sound is gone out through all the earth, and their words to the end of
the world.

The "firmament telleth," the vault of sky. Declare, tell, utter, speech, language,
voice, sound, words: someone wedded to the Hebrew tongue itself must have
composed this Psalm, someone enthused with language and no less enthused
(in + *theos,* god) with physical and animal nature. Even secular nature poetry
lives if not by the grace of God then by the grace of language.

Rolling along as a Creation hymn to God's providence, Psalm 104 at the same
time calls up a brimming, bristling earthly scene. It begins by celebrating Genesis,
the first seven days. Then comes a panorama of wild nature, interdependent bio-
diversity, that exceeds in detail, let alone exuberance, the frugal style of Genesis.

10 He sendeth the springs into the rivers: which run among the hills.
All beasts of the field drink thereof: and the wild asses quench their thirst.
Beside them shall the fowls of the air have their habitation: and sing
among the branches. . . .
He bringeth forth grass for the cattle: and green herb for the service
of men.
15 That he may bring food out of the earth, and wine that maketh glad the
heart of man: and oil to make him a cheerful countenance, and bread
to strengthen man's heart.
The trees of the Lord also are full of sap: even the cedars of Libanus
which he hath planted;
Wherein the birds make their nests: and the fir-trees are a dwelling for
the stork.
The high hills are a refuge for the wild goats: and so are the stony rocks
for the conies.
He appointed the moon for certain seasons: and the sun knoweth his
going down.
20 Thou makest darkness that it may be night: wherein all the beasts of the
forest do move.
The lions roaring after their prey: do seek their meat from God.
The sun ariseth, and they get them away together: and lay them down
in their dens.
Man goeth forth to his work, and to his labour: until the evening.
O Lord, how manifold are thy works: in wisdom hast thou made them all;
the earth is full of thy riches.
25 So is the great and wide sea also: wherein are things creeping innumerable,
both small and great beasts.
There go the ships, and there is that Leviathan: whom thou hast made to
take his pastime therein.
These wait all upon thee: that thou mayest give them meat in due season.
When thou givest it them they gather it: and when thou openest thy hand
they are filled with good.

When thou hidest thy face they are troubled: when thou takest away
   their breath they die, and are turned again to their dust.
30   When thou lettest thy breath go forth they shall be made: and thou shalt
   renew the face of the earth.
The glorious Majesty of the Lord shall endure for ever: the Lord shall
   rejoice in his works.
The earth shall tremble at the look of him: if he do but touch the hills,
   they shall smoke.
I will sing unto the Lord as long as I live: I will praise my God while
   I have my being.
And so shall my words please him: my joy shall be in the Lord.

Always naming, always words galvanizing the things of this world: "The
high hills are a refuge for the wild goats: and so are the stony rocks for the
conies." Here the Book of Common Prayer ekes out extra music, risking re-
dundance ("stony rocks") to load this verse with three resounding *o*-sounds
where the King James Version merely says, "and the rocks for the conies."
You can hear that resonance in young British choristers chanting the Psalm at
evensong. And what of those conies, an English rabbit or Old World sort of
woodchuck (Proverbs calls them "a feeble folk, yet make they their houses in
the rocks"). Even rodents make it into the psalmist's cosmos along with moon
and sun, lion and Leviathan.

When the spirit is willing, poems are too. In Hebrew verse a kind of paral-
lelism helps "declare" God's wildly diverse world. Often the first half-line states
a general truth, then the second specifies it: "All beasts of the field drink thereof:
and the wild asses quench their thirst . . . The trees of the Lord also are full of
sap: even the cedars of Libanus which he hath planted." This turn of thought,
from genus to species, acts out nature's plenty in the same breath with divine
order. Meanwhile the psalmist switches from "he" to "thou": "He appointed
the moon for certain seasons . . . Thou makest darkness that it may be night"—
moving between remote witness and intimate address to God, admiration and
conversation.

God's grandeur in Psalm 104 doesn't at all outshine its lyric brio and ecologic
gusto, upstaging religious awe. The writer's voice, Hebrew and English, feels
livelier going into nature and naming the physical world—Leviathan, "whom
thou hast made to take his pastime" in the sea—than in formulas like "glorious
majesty." With no stain of human dominion, this Psalm plays out joy in God
and nature both.

Culminating an array of nature's God-given world, verse 24 could close the
Psalm well enough with praise: "the earth is full of thy riches." But straightway
we go back into the sea of "things creeping innumerable." Later we follow an-

other formula for Creation—"the Lord shall rejoice in his works"—by plunging back into nature with a breath-stopping image of temblor and fire: "The earth shall tremble at the look of him: if he do but touch the hills, they shall smoke." Then after that cadence, divine duty finally peaks in a poet's credo: "I will sing unto the Lord as long as I live."

"Western wind, when will thou blow"
Anon Was an Environmentalist

Western wind, when will thou blow,
The small rain down can rain?
Christ! if my love were in my arms,
And I in my bed again!

Just hearing and speaking these honest lines is enough. Or better, singing them from this poem's early manuscript. You can hear and see the melody reaching its highest pitch and longest hold at the very thought of "bed," then hastening home on a wavelike cadence, eight notes running through one syllable: "a- gai . . . ai . . . ai . . . ai . . . ai . . . ai . . . ai . . . ain!" (plate 3)

"Western Wind," sixteenth-century manuscript.
The British Library Board. All rights reserved, A601.

Elemental as it is, "Western Wind" opens a way to endure time and circumstance, aloneness and longing, or at least to give them shape, grasp them in rhythmic form, which is poetry's perennial job.

Come at it sharp-eared, clear-eyed, deep-minded, and this late medieval fountainhead of the English lyric tradition shows humankind *conversing* with the physical world. Such verse, brief as the greeting on an answering machine, has a great deal going on: rhythm and meter, sound, rhyme, diction, voice, grammar, metaphor, structure. We can take it as a model of how poems work at their purest.

Yoking nature to human doings, "Western Wind" has also handed down its cadence and four-line format to venerable kinds of verse. In hymns, as in ballads and nursery rhymes, we subconsciously recognize familiar 4-3-4-3-beat lines:

> O *Gód* our *hélp* in *áges pást,*
> Our *hópe* for *yéars* to *cóme.*
> Our *shél*ter *fróm* the *stórmy blást,*
> And *oúr* etérnal *hóme.*

Steeped in that beat, Sundays at Amherst's Congregational church, Emily Dickinson would go home and bend the Protestant hymnal to her own skeptical temper. "The Brain is wider than the Sky," she writes, and more:

> The Brain is deeper than the sea—
> For—hold them—Blue to Blue—
> The one the other will absorb—
> As Sponges—Buckets—do—

Her pleasant rhyming, as in "Western Wind" and countless hymns, beguiles us and disguises a subversive drift, boosting human imagination over God's first creations, sky and sea. Finally, "The Brain is just the weight of God."

A folk spirit moves the four-beat/three-beat ballad Samuel Taylor Coleridge adopted for *Rime of the Ancient Mariner:*

> The fair breeze blew, the white foam flew,
> The furrow followed free;
> We were the first that ever burst
> Into that silent sea.

And a Scots song by Robert Burns:

> Ye flowery banks o' bonnie Doon,
>   How can ye blume sae fair?
> How can ye chant, ye little birds,
>   And I sae full o' care?

More ancient yet, nursery rhymes fall into this pattern, sometimes (just like "Western Wind") dropping the initial unstressed syllable in line one:

> Mary had a little lamb
>> Its fleece was white as snow,
> And everywhere that Mary went
>> The lamb was sure to go.

A primal pulse moves these poems, footfalls from four beats to three, deep in memory.

With its firm pace, our anonymous song has one line prompting the next:

> Western wind, when will thou blow,
> The small rain down can rain?

Then this pair balances with a second:

> Christ! If my love were in my arms,
> And I in my bed again!

Binary like breathing in and out, or outdoors-indoors, nature-humankind, the two couplets weave together through meter and rhyme.

First we absorb the rhythmic energy of "Western Wind" by scanning the verse, noting where its actual spoken stresses fall, getting a sense of its physical body—for a poem acts like an organism. And giving it our own voice, animating it, brings out the play of *spoken* rhythm against a *metrical* norm—life versus art, we might say.

This norm shows up clearly in lines of four "feet" or units, iambic feet. For instance, Dickinson: "The *Bráin* / is *júst* / the *wéight* / of *Gód*." An iamb (sounds like "I am") is two syllables, the second one stressed: "The *smáll* . . . can *ráin*, / . . . And *Í* . . . agáin." In "Western Wind," though, iambs don't become the basic unit right away. It starts with a stress, "*Wés*tern," then five more syllables can all take stresses as the alliteration presses on wavelike. So playing off against the metrical norm, we could actually speak the line this way: "*Wéstern wínd whén wíll thóu blów*."

Early readers bothered by that brusque beginning smoothed the line by adding "O," "O *wéstern wínd*." But the words should seize us abruptly, like "*smáll ráin dówn*" pressing three words together, and "*Christ!*" striking sooner than expected. It's musically syncopated, this play of spoken rhythm against pre-fixed meter. Just as Coleridge's ancient mariner grips his listener, you can't choose but listen to a poem that starts, "*W*estern *w*ind *w*hen *w*ill . . . " While the vowel sounds alternate *eh-ih-eh-ih*, those accented and alliterating *w*'s grab your attention, like infants crying *wah-h-h wah-h-h*.

Not that sound alone has any built-in meaning, only that vocal music, especially vowel music, intensifies whatever it touches, imprints the verse deeper than its mere message. In Coleridge's "Frost at Midnight," snow melting from the eaves creates "*s*ilent *i*cicles, / Qu*i*etly sh*i*ning to the qu*i*et Moon," and *i*-sounds reverberate in Keats's Grecian urn, a "br*i*de of qu*i*etness, / Thou foster-ch*i*ld of s*i*lence and slow t*i*me." Like them, "Western Wind" gathers momentum from five bright vowel-sounds: "Chr*i*st! if *my* love were in *my* arms, / And *I* in *my* bed again!"

Along with vibrant vowels, "Western Wind" gains from its rhymes, especially if "rain" brings out the British pronunciation of "again." "Rhyme" or "rime" has always been a word for poem (though not all poems rhyme). Here rhyming drives home the aim of "Western Wind." Just as rhymes are sounds that come back again, this saga aims at getting back home.

Stanza, rhythm, meter, sound, rhyme: absolutely essential. Now what about the plain (or not so plain) meaning of the words? "Western wind, when will thou blow": "thou" takes only a quick light stress but transforms the whole poem's stance. Nowadays archaic, "thou" has a revealing lineage. Adam, Cain, Abraham, Moses, Elijah, David, Solomon, Job, Jeremiah, the Psalmist all intimately address their Creator. Shelley's "Wild West Wind" he calls "Thou," as Keats does the nightingale and most poignantly, Autumn:

> Where are the songs of Spring? Ay, where are they?
> Think not of them, thou hast thy music too.

Calling the wind "thou," anonymous lines take a personal standpoint, give the wind mythic presence, and bring it close, binding us to nature as language itself always has since Adam, Noah, and all early peoples.

Another small word, the "small" rain, may mean light or slender, a steady drizzle. And oddly in so brief a phrase, "rain" falls twice: "The small rain down can rain." Only in English can a single word, such as "rain" or "stone," double as noun and verb (and adjective too). Here in one breath, "rain" turns active! Matter gains energy, marked by a ringing of final consonants, "rai*n* dow*n* ca*n* rai*n*."

"Christ!," the very next word, carries extra clout. Centuries ago it was no empty profanity. Oaths could still summon a sacred presence onto the scene: "Christ! if my love *were* in my arms." As in the urge for rain, grammar kicks in, a subjunctive verb yearning for what's absent: "Christ! if [only] my love were in my arms, / And I [were] in my bed again!" The rhythm needs both those tightenings, to press toward love and home.

At first glance this poem's halves have nothing to do with each other. The lines on wind and rain occur in nature, with nothing human (though someone must be speaking them). Those on love utter purely human concerns. No transition binds them, their joining's unexpected and unexplained (as in much poetry since T. S. Eliot). Yet despite—and because of—that gap, we make the leap ourselves: wind to longing, rain to loving.

We make it, that is, with a little help from the verse: two halves sharing the same meter, and breathing in and out on the one rhyme sound, "rain / . . . again." In legend as in everyday life, in spiritual and earthly ways, we react to our environment. Weather's doings literally touch on our own in this medieval lyric, thanks to the genius of poetic language, the grace of metaphor: wind and rain turn toward love and home.

Meta-phor, an "across-carrying" from one realm to another, from nature to us, gives both realms new point: windy orator, rain of insults, stormy relationship, stream of consciousness, bear market, and so on. Metaphor is "the great human revolution," Israeli poet Yehuda Amichai has said, "at least on a par with the invention of the wheel." What would hymns, gospel, blues, folk songs from all times and places do without wind, rain, sky, rivers, shores, roads?

Metaphors leap without warning from physical to human nature. And usually, once an image has done its job—wind shows the force of longing, rain the release of tension—we leave that image behind (otherwise Robert Burns's love "like a red, red rose" might sprout thorns). But in "Western Wind" the speaker desires both halves equally, fair weather and a fair friend. Without signaling as much, these lines bind the molecules of metaphor.

Often metaphors move from material to immaterial, from earthly to spiritual: "Thou art my rock and my redeemer." Drawn from nature, they tie humankind in one with that world. Yet they do something else. Analogy (or simile) hedges its bet, saying "like": "Like as the waves make towards the pebbled shore, / So do our minutes hasten to their end." But metaphors shock us, saying outright something that's *not* true. A rain of insults doesn't drop from the sky, a windy orator doesn't ruffle your hair.

So the shock of metaphor, its being not true, can expose nature's otherness as it still arcs between the two realms, physical and human nature: sea of troubles, emotional desert. "Western Wind" connects but doesn't confuse us with weather. There's the poem's crux, environmentally speaking. Since it's we who voice a metaphor or any image, poetry's never pure of human presence. That tension, ourselves attaching to things, can bode ecologic trouble yet bring out human truths.

Not only would an Atlantic westerly blow the (English) voyager shoreward, in an age before steam power, and bring rain to ease drought and grow crops. As far back as we know, seasonal weathers have lent sense to our lives. God chastens Job "out of the whirlwind." The Anglo-Saxon "Seafarer," in Ezra Pound's version, "Weathered the winter, wretched outcast / Deprived of my kinsmen." "When April with its showers sweet / Has pierced March drought down to the root," in the Canterbury Tales, "When Zephyrus [the west wind] with his sweet breath / Has stirred on every wood and heath / The tender sprouts . . . / Then people long to go on pilgrimage." From Chaucer to Bob Dylan, a wind promises change: "The answer, my friend, is blowin' in the wind." And the freshening rain? Perhaps mercy, or sensual release.

Looking into turns of craft keeps us close to a poem—which is good. At some point we step back to look at the structure, even of a four-line lyric. First comes an imploring prayer, a question:

> Western wind, when will thou blow,
> The small rain down can rain?

Then an oath, an exclamation:

> Christ! if my love were in my arms,
> And I in my bed again!

Yoking these two kinds of speech strikes a progression: question answered by exclamation—a drama of its own.

And whose drama? So far we've heard this anonymous lyric without pinpointing the person behind it. Who is saying "Christ! if my love were in my arms"? A straw vote, even nowadays, would elect a man: voyager, rough oath, sexual assertion, claiming a voice. But why so? "Anon was a woman," Virginia Woolf once said, and that might hold for "Western Wind." Setting it to music, Igor Stravinsky brilliantly solves the question by casting the whole poem for not one but two voices, tenor and soprano interweaving "wind" and "rain," "my arms" and "my bed again!" A good way to sing love into nature.

Lasting ten seconds, the simplest words have lasted centuries, joining nature's force to human feeling through a silent metaphor. "Western Wind" holds the germ of much poetry to come.

"The stationary blasts of waterfalls"
Blake, the Wordsworths, and the Dung

"Would to God that all the Lord's people were Prophets." When William Blake (1757–1827) echoed this biblical cry, he might have been thinking of the mad visionary Christopher Smart. Yet Blake had his own revolutionary fix on the world. "One thought fills immensity," he assures us, and "If the doors of perception were cleansed, everything would appear as it is, infinite." And this brash absolute: "Where man is not, nature is barren." Blake believed Innocence meant "To see a World in a Grain of Sand / And a Heaven in a Wild Flower." His vision burns through the natural world. Material, vegetable, corporeal things he turns spiritual, making the spirit's eye, not the body's, his organ of perception.

Blake's spirit reaches into the present, touching Whitman, Yeats, Eliot who felt the force of "Tyger! Tyger! burning bright / In the forests of the night," Britain's Labour Party whose hymn is Blake's "Jerusalem," Pablo Neruda, Aldous Huxley's *The Doors of Perception* on the good of hallucinogens, Allen Ginsberg's entire career, Sixties rebels and rock groups like The Doors.

Crying to "the lapsèd Soul," Blake took on the Hebrew prophets' voice: "O Earth, O Earth, return! / Arise from out the dewy grass." To redeem the Fall meant penetrating our visible world with visionary radiance "Till we have built Jerusalem / In England's green and pleasant land." Abhorring pure Reason, he painted Urizen creating the world with an immense pair of compasses, dominion's measuring tool and the destroyer of imagination. (plate 1)

None of the Romantics matched Blake for fervor. Coming on Wordsworth's perceptive but pedestrian lines—

> How exquisitely the individual Mind
> . . . to the external World
> Is fitted—and how exquisitely, too—. . .
> The external World is fitted to the Mind

—he scribbled in the margin: "You shall not bring me down to believe such fitting & fitted. I know better & please your Lordship." No such passive way of seeing things interested Blake. "Bring me my Bow of burning gold: / Bring me my Arrows of desire: / Bring me my Spear: O clouds unfold! / Bring me my Chariot of Fire."

Yet William Wordsworth himself (1770–1850) had "dizzy raptures":

> My heart leaps up when I behold
> A rainbow in the sky.

His sister Dorothy says that "While I was getting into bed" one night, he composed "Tintern Abbey."

> There was a time when meadow, grove, and stream,
> The earth, and every common sight,
> 　　To me did seem
> 　Apparelled in celestial light.

Since childhood, the "visionary gleam" has "fled." Even his famous daffodils, "Tossing their heads" beside the dancing waves, dance in the past tense. "When on the couch I lie / . . . They flash upon that inward eye."

Those daffodils and Wordsworth's stardom look slightly different in light of the journals of Dorothy Wordsworth (1771–1855), whom William called

> 　　thou my dearest friend,
> My dear, dear friend; and in thy voice I catch
> The language of my former heart, and read
> My former pleasures in the shooting lights
> Of thy wild eyes.

She did have a fine eye and a marvelous pen too, recording their life in England's semi-wild Lake District. Dorothy writes on April 15, 1802: "When we were in the woods beyond Gowbarrow Park we saw a few daffodils . . . But as we went along there were more and yet more . . . I never saw daffodils so beautiful. They grew among the mossy stones about and about them; some rested their heads upon these stones as on a pillow for weariness; and the rest tossed and reeled and danced, and seemed as if they verily laughed with the wind, that blew upon them over the lake." (plate 4)

Dorothy Wordsworth, anonymous silhouette.
Dove Cottage, Wordsworth Trust.

William used to read her journal in the evenings, so his vision—

> I wandered lonely as a Cloud
> That floats on high o'er Vales and Hills,
> When all at once I saw a crowd
> A host of dancing Daffodils;
> Along the lake, beneath the trees,
> Ten thousand dancing in the breeze.

—sounds more like collaboration. And William, we want to ask, "Why *lonely?*"

A fortnight later, having seen a "glorious wild" waterfall, Dorothy and her brother met Coleridge: "Wm and C. repeated and read verses. I drank a little brandy and water and was in Heaven." With or without brandy, she had every bit as vivid a sense of nature as they did. Coleridge calls "her eye watchful in minutest observation of nature." Her journals dazzle with imaginings of light and motion:

> *27th January 1798* . . . while we were in the wood the moon burst through the invisible veil which enveloped her, the shadows of the oaks blackened, and their lines became more strongly marked. The withered leaves were colored with a deeper yellow, a brighter gloss spotted the hollies.
>
> *31st.* The hawthorn hedges, black and pointed, glittering with millions of

diamond drops; the hollies shining with broader patches of light. The road to the village of Holford glittered like another stream. On our return, the wind high—a violent storm of hail and rain at the Castle of Comfort. All the heavens seemed in one perpetual motion when the rain ceased; the moon appearing, now half veiled, and now retired behind heavy clouds, the stars still moving, the roads very dirty.

1st February. . . . The sun shone clear, but all at once a heavy blackness hung over the sea. The trees almost *roared,* and the ground seemed in motion with the multitude of dancing leaves.

The poems seem a division of labor, but not always the household.

March 17, 1802: Mr. O. met us and I went to their house—he offered me manure for the garden. I went and sate with W. and walked backwards and forwards in the orchard till dinner time. He read me his poem. I broiled beefsteaks.

March 19: I went up into the lane to collect a few green mosses to make the chimney gay against my darling's return.

March 23: William worked at *The Cuckow* poem. I sewed beside him.

March 27: A divine morning. At Breakfast Wm. wrote part of an ode ["Intimations of Immortality"]. Mr. Olliff sent the dung and Wm. went to work in the garden. We sate all day in the orchard.

Time passed with William at his desk, Dorothy at her chores, or brother reading aloud and sister listening, then later copying. But it's good to know that when the dung arrived, William made use of it. And good that Virginia Woolf and Elizabeth Hardwick a century later would write gratefully about Dorothy.

In loving symbiosis, William remained the poet—if "Poetry is the breath and finer spirit of all knowledge," as he put it. If so much depends upon the "shaping spirit of Imagination" (Coleridge), then however animated Dorothy's encounter with nature, sheer poetic genius matters too. Take this moment, William suddenly crossing the Alps and entering "a narrow chasm" with one spasm of perception:

> The immeasurable height
> Of woods decaying, never to be decayed,
> The stationary blasts of waterfalls,
> And in the narrow rent at every turn
> Winds thwarting winds, bewildered and forlorn,
> The torrents shooting from the clear blue sky,
> The rocks that muttered close upon our ears,
> Black drizzling crags that spake by the way-side
> As if a voice were in them, the sick sight
> And giddy prospect of the raving stream,
> The unfettered clouds, and region of the Heavens,
> Tumult and peace, the darkness and the light—

Coming down from Simplon Pass (Dorothy was back home), Wordsworth runs for twelve lines without a main verb, the whole scene astir at once. (plate 5) Ongoing participles make the past present—"decaying . . . thwarting . . . shooting . . . drizzling . . . raving"— while "muttered" and "spake" hint at some living presence. Thomas Cole, pioneer American painter, called waterfalls "the voice of the landscape" and saw "fixedness and motion" in them, "unceasing change and everlasting duration."

But "stationary blasts"? Wordsworth is seeing, by saying, something truer than fact: "The stationary blasts of waterfalls." A mind's eye conversing with nature finds and names that dynamic of motion with stillness, energy with design, or call it loss with gain: "The immeasurable height / Of woods decaying, never to be decayed," moving and staying at a line break, suspending and sustaining potential energy.

A few years later, wildness not being all there was to life (and having fathered a child in revolutionary France), he wrote to a friend, "Cataracts and mountains are good occasional society, but they will not do for constant companions." He published a guide to the Lake District and later protested, without success, railway construction in to Lake Windermere. "NIMBY," as such protest is dismissed today—"Not in my back yard"—but this place was also a national treasure threatened by an expanding society.

"The white Eddy-rose . . . obstinate in resurrection"
Coleridge Imagining

> O Lady! we receive but what we give,
> And in our life alone does Nature live:
> Ours is her wedding garment, ours her shroud!

Nature comes alive through human outreach, for Samuel Taylor Coleridge (1772–1834). William Blake is more absolute: "Where man is not, nature is barren." Yet the rapt detail in Coleridge's notebooks gives lakes and streams, hills and woods a life of their own. His conjugal image involves give-and-take, "we receive but what we give," that word "but" meaning "only" and also "just."

Coleridge goes on:

> Ah! from the soul itself must issue forth
> A light, a glory, a fair luminous cloud
> Enveloping the Earth.

Then he gives this light a name:

> Joy, lady! is the spirit and the power,
> Which wedding Nature to us gives in dower
> A new Earth and new Heaven.

So strong is the feeling, it reverses biblical Apocalypse—"And I saw a new heaven and a new earth"—making earth first.

At heart, Coleridge sees Joy "wedding Nature to us" as a poet's calling, that "shaping spirit of Imagination" which serves us all. After the American and French revolutions, he and Wordsworth set about grounding poetry in the common passions of humankind in contact with nature—a fresh declaration of human rights.

Living miles apart, these two souls thought nothing of walking over for a visit, Dorothy Wordsworth usually joining her brother. They would tramp the countryside, and as Coleridge said, Dorothy's journal entries showed "her eye watchful" for nature's fine detail. Day after day in February 1798, her pages abound with frost, night, sky and stars, breeze and wind and blast, stillness and calm, lakes and shores, clouds, sea, hill, woods, and above all the moon.

One night Coleridge sat by the cradle of his son Hartley, musing on all that vivid, shared observation. "Frost at Midnight" begins,

> The Frost performs its secret ministry,
> Unhelped by any wind . . .

After moving from "Sea, and hill, and wood" back to his own childhood pent up "In the great city," he looks ahead for his sleeping child.

> But *thou*, my babe! shalt wander like a breeze
> By lakes and sandy shores, beneath the crags
> Of ancient mountain, and beneath the clouds,
> Which image in their bulk both lakes and shores
> And mountain crags.

Such workings of imagination will grant his child "The lovely shapes and sounds intelligible / Of that eternal language, which thy God / Utters."

Having "Walked with Coleridge over the hills," Dorothy in one note says "The redbreasts sang upon the leafless boughs" (as it happens, a perfect iambic pentameter). You can catch the overland conversation they must have had. Coleridge, bringing "Frost at Midnight" to a close, turns not toward God but nature, blessing his son and circling back to the poem's opening.

> Therefore all seasons shall be sweet to thee,
> Whether the summer clothe the general earth
> With greenness, or the redbreast sit and sing
> Betwixt the tufts of snow on the bare branch
> Of mossy apple-tree, while the nigh thatch
> Smokes in the sun-thaw; whether the eave-drops fall
> Heard only in the trances of the blast,
> Or if the secret ministry of frost
> Shall hang them up in silent icicles,
> Quietly shining to the quiet Moon.

No abstraction here, but earthliness in textured music, *s*-sounds and *th* threading lines one and two. Then what Dorothy saw becomes a seasonal fullness, as we hear "the redbreast sit and sing / Betwixt the tufts of snow on the bare branch / Of mossy apple-tree." And then a moment's run-on—

> while the nigh thatch
> Smokes in the sun-thaw

—gathers *th-* and *s*-alliterations, resonates in "while" and "nigh," and pulses steadily on "nigh thatch / Smokes" and "sun-thaw," giving these "lovely shapes and sounds" to the infant's future.

While Dorothy's keenness kindled to everything around her, Coleridge ends by recalling that "secret ministry of frost" he began with. Beginning at windless midnight, the poem looks to the child's future, then returns home to nighttime quiet. It traces a circular cast of mind, moving out into nature and back, as the verbal music also moves: "silent icicles" chimes with "Quietly shining," then "Quietly" returns in "quiet," joining icicles to the moon. They give back what they receive, moonlight itself reflected from the sun. These icicles shining between earth and sky, like clouds that "image" mountain crags, are what Coleridge promises his son.

It's a fine benediction (the boy did become a decent poet), and if you are S.T.C. you do as well for your next child, blessing him within the local scene.

> If Derwent be innocent, steady, and wise,
> And delight in the things of earth, water, and skies;
> Tender warmth at his heart, with these meters to show it,
> With sound sense in his brains, may make Derwent a poet,—
> May crown him with fame, and must win him the love
> Of his father on earth and his Father above.
>   My dear, dear child!
> Could you stand upon Skiddaw, you would not from its whole ridge
> See a man who so loves you as your fond S.T. COLERIDGE.

The swift three-beat suddenly slows to cherish each accent, "My dear, dear child!," and the voice turns "him" to "you." Finally this father, signing the body of his poem, rhymes himself as well into the landscape.

Just to make sure, Coleridge had actually named Hartley after an English philosopher of the mind and senses, and Derwent for a small lake nearby. When they were six and two, buoyantly he wrote a friend:

> My dear Sir,
>
> The river is full, and Lodore is full, and silver Fillets come out of Clouds, & glitter in every Ravine of all the mountains; and the Hail lies, like Snow, upon their Tops; & the impetuous Gusts from Borrowdale snatch the water up high & continually at the bottom of the Lake; it is not distinguishable from Snow slanting before the wind—and under this seeming Snow-drift the Sunshine *gleams,* & over all the hither Half of the Lake it is *bright,* and *dazzles*—a cauldron of melted Silver boiling! It is in very truth a sunny, misty, cloudy, dazzling, howling, omniform, Day & I have been looking at as pretty

a sight as a Father's eyes could well see—Hartley & little Derwent running in the Green where the Gusts blow most madly—both with their hair floating & tossing, a miniature of the agitated Trees below which they were playing inebriate both with the pleasure—Hartley whirling round for joy, Derwent eddying half-willingly, half by the force of the Gust—driven backward, struggling forward, & shouting his little hymn of Joy.

Thirteen times "and . . . and . . . and . . . ," and verbs galore, throng the canvas with movement and underlined light till these creatures look Pan-like, Dionysian—running, floating, tossing, playing, whirling, eddying, struggling, shouting. Calling them "a miniature of the agitated trees" gets a wild organic at-oneness fresher than any doctrine that nature lives "in our life alone." "Derwent eddying, half-willingly, half by the force of the gust" seems giver and receiver both. The children whirl and shout for *joy*. Coleridge can't do without that word, especially since an illness kept dogging him, and pain addicting him to opium.

Within a few days of this 1802 letter, still "wedding Nature to us," he wrote a short poem that can stand at the center of his work. It has everything: tree and fountainhead, breath and music, gale and quiet, infant and pilgrim, toil and refreshment. Also it blends the ingredients of his craft: rhythm and meter, diction and verbal music, grammar and phrasing, imagery and voice. Like any poem, this "inscription" gains from being spoken aloud.

INSCRIPTION FOR A FOUNTAIN ON A HEATH

This Sycamore, oft musical with bees,—
Such tents the Patriarchs loved! O long unharmed
May all its agèd boughs o'er-canopy
The small round basin, which this jutting stone
Keeps pure from falling leaves! Long may the Spring,
Quietly as a sleeping infant's breath,
Send up cold waters to the traveller
With soft and even pulse! Nor ever cease
Yon tiny cone of sand its soundless dance,
Which at the bottom, like a Fairy's Page,
As merry and no taller, dances still,
Nor wrinkles the smooth surface of the Fount.
Here twilight is and coolness: here is moss,
A soft seat, and a deep and ample shade.
Thou may'st toil far and find no second tree.
Drink, Pilgrim, here; here rest! and if thy heart
Be innocent, here too shalt thou refresh
Thy spirit, listening to some gentle sound,
Or passing gale or hum of murmuring bees!

To hear this poem in time, like music, we can let questions unscroll it line by line.

First, What sort of fountain? Maybe it's close to the Latin *fons*, as in *fons et origo*, source and origin. But why would a spring on a heath call for inscription, especially in the northern Lake District, fairly open and wild? And what will form the actual inscription: the whole poem, or its last seven, or five, or four lines?

Some saving grace must be at stake when a voice cries out three times over: "Such tents . . . ! O long unharmed . . . ! Long may the Spring . . . !" Before any fountain we see "This Sycamore" and its bees, Patriarchs, aged boughs, basin and stone, falling leaves. The ancient tree turns musical organism then biblical refuge. Thanks to a jutting stone the earth basin's pure of fall's dying leaves. Then a Spring wells up, and right away an analogy. Why this suspense, evolving moment by moment a natural, perhaps sacred scene?

Coleridge's first title was "Lines upon a Jutting Stone," as if happy chance (or human hand?) had set a stone there to keep the fountain clear. Did he refine his title? Written at the autumn equinox, full summer verging on winter, his "Inscription" alerts us to a source with music, bees, Patriarchs, and a sleeping infant—signs of harmony, sweetness, faith, and pure promise in rough terrain.

Sometimes poems at their highest pitch act as an *ars poetica*, a test or testament on the art of poetry, like Keats's "Ode on a Grecian Urn." "Inscription for a Fountain on a Heath" has that extra excitement, pulling out all the stops. At one point the verse suffuses with surplus music. In the fountain's "soft and even pulse" and "soundless dance," we're overhearing a praise of poetry's own pulse and sound. Try sounding out those lines,

> With soft and even pulse! Nor ever cease
> Yon tiny cone of sand its soundless dance.

Sibilant *s*-sounds blending with soft *n*'s help "even" slide to "ever cease," then run into the next line, whose varying vowel-sounds each press on *n*: "Yon tiny cone of sand its soundless dance." Subconsciously we sense this music. Coleridge first wrote "noiseless," which is fine, but "soundless" adds that whisper of *s*'s leading "sand" toward "sound" and then into "dance." It's not that "The sound must seem an echo to the sense," as Alexander Pope decreed, but that music intensifies any moment for us.

At the bottom of the spring a cone of sand "dances still"—"still" meaning constantly but also motionless (like Wordsworth's "stationary blasts of waterfalls"). Hearing those *s*-sounds still dancing in "smooth surface" and again in "coolness," "moss," "soft seat," we begin to wonder if Coleridge has lost hold. But it's all so simply spoken:

A soft seat, and a deep and ample shade.
Thou may'st toil far and find no second tree.
Drink, Pilgrim, here; here rest! and if thy heart . . .

Twenty-four single syllables! Their even pulse turns the fountain into a still dance.

Meanwhile what has been moving us from Patriarch to sleeping infant, then from traveler to toiling Pilgrim? Sacred, pure, innocent things, then peace and seeking, draw toward the Spring. And we sense a new presence, someone almost biblically saying "Thou." This speaker's been present all along, offering a hand, pointing out very present things: "*This* Sycamore . . . *Such* tents . . . *this* jutting stone . . . *Yon* tiny cone . . . *Here* Twilight is . . . *here* is moss." Through these lines a benevolent kind of Ancient Mariner holds us with "Thou . . . thy . . . thou . . . Thy."

How evenly, how slowly the voice says "Drink, Pilgrim, here; here rest!" After the warning in a natural beat, "and *fínd* no *sécond trée*," we're directed, spiritually upgraded, and held where the rhythm compresses: ". . . *hére; hére* . . ." This heath holds holy ground. Drink at the source and any sound, whether gale or hum, makes a fresh beginning.

The voyager in an anonymous medieval quatrain, "Western Wind," craves rain. T. S. Eliot's *The Waste Land* conjures an oasis, "A spring / A pool among the rock." His poem "Little Gidding" arrives "At the source of the longest river / The voice of the hidden waterfall." Robert Frost's "Directive" sends us back to "a spring as yet so near its source" and ends, "Drink and be whole again beyond confusion."

Coleridge's "Inscription" belongs in this company. It ends on a casual exclamation: "or hum of murmuring bees!" Like human imagination, bees go out gathering and come back, making honey and wax, sweetness and light. So the "hum of murmuring bees" goes round to the first line "musical with bees," shaping this poem like a basin, offering not only an inscription for the fountain but the fountain itself, at once origin and goal. What could be simpler?

Along with William Wordsworth, Coleridge made his first walking tour of the Lake Country in 1799, taking notes on what impressed him. Watching river water rush over hollowed stone, he notes

> The white Eddy-rose that blossom'd up against the Stream in the scollop, by fits and starts, obstinate in resurrection.

Four years later he rewrites it from memory among several "Images":

> The *white rose* of Eddy-foam, where the stream ran into a scooped or scolloped hollow of the Rock in its channel—this Shape, an exact white rose, was for

ever overpowered by the Stream rushing down in upon it, and still obstinate in resurrection it spread up into the Scollop, by fits & starts, *blossoming* in a moment into a full flower.

The verbs bear the force—ran, overpowered, rushing, spread up, blossoming. The nouns—Eddy-foam, Shape, Stream, Scollop, flower—give it form. It takes the mind's eye to see a white rose blossoming: energy taking shape, exact yet full of the stream's momentum, spent yet contained.

A robust climber, Coleridge in the Alps had recently called glacial falls "Motionless torrents!" Others, such as Wordsworth at Simplon Pass, have found this paradox compelling. One morning the *Pequod*'s crew watch Moby-Dick powerfully breach—he "hovered for a moment in the rainbowed air"—and Melville calls this "a mighty mildness of repose in swiftness." In his last poem, "Crossing the Bar," Tennyson imagines "such a tide as moving seems asleep." For Yeats the Easter 1916 revolt or resurrection is a stone that must "trouble the living stream" until "a terrible beauty is born." Clearly this flux taking form answers a human need.

Is it true that "we receive but what we give, / And in our life alone does Nature live"? Nature has its own life, often lending us images of private or public struggle, "obstinate in resurrection."

Wedding nature to us, his "shaping spirit of Imagination" seeks a spring on a heath. His inner eye creates a "Shape, an exact white rose" out of river water breaking up. Suffering pain as he did, Coleridge couldn't help adding a final thought to this notebook entry, "*It is the life* that we live," as if anything human or poetic might have its obstinate blossoming rose.

"last oozings hours by hours"
John Keats Eking It Out

He wishes instead "to look into some beautiful Scenery—for poetical purposes," says John Keats (1795–1821), declining a weekend invitation. Soon afterward, less flip, he begins a sonnet on the song of grasshoppers and crickets, "The poetry of earth is never dead," and after several lines tries again: "The poetry of earth is ceasing never."

Two years later, having nursed him devotedly for months, Keats lost his younger brother Tom to consumption. The death jolted his attempts to square poetry with "a World of Pains and troubles." In "Ode to a Nightingale," an aching heart starts from the world "Where youth grows pale, and spectre-thin, and dies," then flees on the "wings of Poesy" toward "Country-green" and the nightingale—"Already with Thee! tender is the night."

> I cannot see what flowers are at my feet,
>   Nor what soft incense hangs upon the boughs,
> But, in embalmèd darkness, guess each sweet
>   Wherewith the seasonable month endows
> The grass, the thicket, and the fruit-tree wild.

Bird's song, botanic bliss, all their sensuousness cannot hold up: "Fled is that music."

We think of Keats as weakly, yet for a brief spell the poet had been hardy as Coleridge and the Wordsworths. During the summer of 1818, with his friend Charles Brown he took a walking tour of England's Lake District and the Scottish highlands. In rugged and already Romantically picturesque landscape, Keats saw, really saw, things he'd never seen. Walking westward over hilly country toward Windermere, they stopped when the lake came into view with mountains beyond in mist and clouds. "How can I believe in that?" Keats exclaimed, "surely it cannot be!" Nothing in the world could equal it. Then a hundred yards further: "more and more wonderfully beautiful!"

Up at dawn, they didn't mind walking eight to ten miles before breakfast. "We arose this morning at six, because we call it a day of rest, having to call on Wordsworth who lives only two miles hence," Keats writes to Tom. But Lord Wordsworth (as he calls him) was away campaigning for a Tory candidate, so "before breakfast we went to see the Ambleside water fall." This "first waterfall I ever saw" struck Keats to the core. His journal-letter to Tom shows him "open-lidded," exuberant at the fall's energy and design.

> The morning beautiful—the walk easy among the hills. We, I may say, fortunately, missed the direct path, and after wandering a little, found it out by the noise—for, mark you, it is buried in trees, in the bottom of the valley—the stream itself is interesting throughout with "mazy error over pendant shades." Milton meant a smooth river—this is buffeting all the way on a rocky bed ever various—but the waterfall itself, which I came suddenly upon, gave me a pleasant twinge. First we stood a little below the head about halfway down the first fall, buried deep in trees, and saw it streaming down two more descents to the depth of near fifty feet—then we went on a jut of rock nearly level with the second fall-head, where the first fall was above us, and the third below our feet still—at the same time we saw that the water was divided by a sort of cataract island on whose other side burst out a glorious stream—then the thunder and the freshness. At the same time the different falls have as different characters; the first darting down the slate-rock like an arrow; the second spreading out like a fan—the third dashed into a mist—and the one on the other side of the rock a sort of mixture of all these. We afterwards moved away a space, and saw nearly the whole more mild, streaming silverly through the trees. What astonishes me more than any thing is the tone, the coloring, the slate, the stone, the moss, the rock-weed; or, if I may so say, the intellect, the countenance of such places. The space, the magnitude of mountains and waterfalls are well imagined before one sees them; but this countenance or intellectual tone must surpass every imagination and defy any remembrance. I shall learn poetry here.

In memory's knapsack Keats carries the "mazy" river of Milton's *Paradise Lost*. But this Eden has no "smooth river—this is buffeting all the way on a rocky bed." A painter who'd gone there decades earlier found the stream too "overgrown with wood" to approach easily, "but if a path could be carried through," it "might be made very beautiful." Keats liked it "buried deep in trees."

Then suddenly the waterfall grips him. They descend halfway, "grasping the

Joseph Farington, Waterfall at Ambleside.
From T. H. Horne, *The Lakes of Lancashire, Westmoreland and Cumberland, delineated in forty-three engravings, from drawings by Joseph Farington, R.A.* (London, 1816).
Division of Rare and Manuscript Collections, Cornell University.

trees and edges of rock to prevent our tumbling headlong," Brown says. He feels unsteady, but "Keats scrambled down lightly and quickly." They station themselves on a jut of rock beside the falls, and Keats is buffeted by the all-at-once action above and below him: "at the same time we saw that the water was divided by a sort of cataract island on whose other side burst out a glorious stream—then the thunder and the freshness."

So much sight and sound cascading around him almost quashes speech: "I live in the eye." Giving Tom the falls' different "characters," Keats watches one darting down "like an arrow," another spreading "like a fan." It's a rush of force that shapes the sharp arrow and fan he sees.

Something marvelous in this event fascinates Keats, the way moment by moment the flux holds still. This way too, life becomes art, like Shakespeare's "never-resting time" resting for fourteen lines in a sonnet, a brief grip on life's wasting force. Wordsworth in the Alps sees "The stationary blasts of water-falls," and Coleridge, their "Motionless torrents!" In a Swiss waterfall, Gerard Manley Hopkins spots "branchings and water-spandrils . . . quills . . . fans . . . jostling foam-bags." Keats himself is "affected . . . extremely" by a "wave" of wind "billowing through a tree." So it is with the falls' "thunder and the fresh-ness" at Ambleside. Seeking the shape of his vision, Keats finds a darting arrow, a spreading fan. "I shall learn poetry here."

Curiously enough, his words from the Lake Country might be unknown today had they not been published in Kentucky, then a frontier region. During his walking tour, he would ask Tom to forward letters to their brother George, who'd just emigrated to America. Years later George loaned this letter to an edi-tor who ran it in Louisville's *Western Messenger,* saying these sentences "touch upon the deepest veins of truth." He's proud to publish Keats's Ambleside rapture here "at the Falls of the Ohio."

When Tom perished of consumption in late 1818, Keats's exposure had al-ready damaged him, and the poetry shows this. He'd been overwhelmed by marble sculptures from the Parthenon in Athens, a friend notes, "and would sit for an hour or more at a time beside them rapt in revery." His "Ode on a Gre-cian Urn" enters a scene on the urn's carved face, freezing its forever-yearning lovers beneath undying trees.

> Ah, happy, happy boughs! that cannot shed
> Your leaves, nor ever bid the spring adieu;
> And, happy melodist, unwearied,
> Forever piping songs forever new;
> More happy love! more happy, happy love!
> Forever warm and still to be enjoy'd,
> Forever panting, and forever young.

Crying "happy" and chanting "ever," six times over, masks a fear that our lives can't live up to art. Then Keats calls the urn "Cold Pastoral!" and stiff artifice —a long way from what nature gave him, the falls "streaming silverly," their "thunder and the freshness."

That autumn, in crisis, "Now I find I must buffet it—I must take my stand upon some vantage ground and begin to fight—I must choose between despair & Energy—I choose the latter." Rooting his choice in the year's natural rhythms, Keats composes "To Autumn," giving the season that "greeting of the Spirit" he said certain things "require . . . to make them wholly exist."

"Season of mists and mellow fruitfulness." Merging weather with crops, the ode calls to a human figure of fullness.

> Season of mists and mellow fruitfulness,
>   Close bosom-friend of the maturing sun:
> Conspiring with him how to load and bless
>   With fruit the vines that round the thatch-eaves run;
> To bend with apples the moss'd cottage-trees,
>   And fill all fruits with sweetness to the core;
>   To swell the gourd, and plump the hazel shells
>   With a white kernel; to set budding more,
> And still more, later flowers for the bees,
> Until they think warm days will never cease,
>   For Summer has o'erbrimm'd their clammy cells.

At first we could be witnessing some agricultural birth rite of female-male fruitfulness. But who's the speaker? Stanza one keeps summoning Autumn, moving through limitless process, a present participle ("Conspiring . . . ") plus seven infinitives ("to load . . . bless . . . bend . . . fill . . . swell . . . plump . . . set budding"). No main verb seals this process.

The earliest surviving manuscript, luckily preserved for two centuries through many hands, shows no second thoughts here, and rapid writing—"furuits with sweeness," "wam days with never cease." "To Autumn" brims with so much life, you want to be everywhere at once. In a way, the poem needs no commentary, only voicings and a glance back, with Keats, to Coleridge's "Frost at Midnight" where "all seasons shall be sweet to thee," and to his never-ceasing autumn fountain on a heath.

Still this poem reveals more the more we dwell in it—in the weather behind it, for instance. Because September 1819 found Keats beset by tuberculosis, he hails "the Weather I adore fine Weather as the greatest blessing I can have." Jonathan Bate in *The Song of the Earth* notes that after three frigid European autumns and poor harvests, 1819 saw the sunny days so vital to a consumptive. "How beautiful the season is now—How fine the air. A temperate sharpness

Season of Mists and mellow fruitfulness,
Close bosom-friend of the maturing sun;
Conspiring with him how to load and bless
The Vines with fruit that round the thatch eves run;
To bend with apples the moss'd Cottage trees
And fill all fruits with ripeness to the core
To swell the gourd, and plump the hazle shells
With a white kernel; to set budding more
And still more later flowers for the bees
Until they think warm days with never cease
For summer has o'erbrimm'd their clammy cells —

Who hath not seen thee? for thy haunts are many
Sometimes whoever seeks abroad may find
Thee sitting careless on a granary floom
Thy hair soft lifted by the winnowing wind
While bright the sun slants through the husk
or on a half reap'd furrow sound asleep
Dos'd with red poppies: while thy reaping hook
Spares from some slumberous
or on a half reap'd furrow sound asleep
Dos'd with the fume of poppies, while thy hook
Spares the next swath, and all its twined flowers

And sometimes like a gleaner thou dost keep
Steady thy laden head across the brook;
Or by a Cyder-press with patient look
Thou watchest the last oozing hours by hours

John Keats, "To Autumn" manuscript.

about it," Keats writes a friend. And to his brother George that same day: "Now the time is beautiful. I take a walk every day for an hour before dinner." It's the autumn equinox, summer verging on fall, when a newly cropped grain field "struck me so much in my sunday's walk that I composed upon it."

That greeting of the spirit, "Season of mists and mellow fruitfulness," involves no human footprint or anxious self as in the nightingale ode, no "Wordsworthian or egotistical sublime" (Keats's phrase), or Coleridge's "in our life alone does Nature live." Nothing like Shelley's autumn 1819 West Wind ode: "I fall upon the thorns of life! I bleed!" Free of any "I," Keats's stanza does what autumn does: bend, fill, swell the season's process in "o'er-brimming" language. After "my sunday's walk" he revised "sweetness" in line six: "And fill all fruit with *ripeness* to the core." Now Shakespeare's *King Lear* can be heard, "Men must endure / Their going hence, even as their coming hither: / Ripeness is all," balancing Keats's mortal fears while day still equals night.

Choosing energy over despair, loading his verse with ripeness, Keats lets a line break act out abundance: "to set budding more, / And still more . . ." And still it grows,

> to set budding more,
> And still more, later flowers for the bees.

And now he actually brims the stanza with one line more than in the Nightingale and Urn odes. Those ten-line stanzas had a sonnetlike quatrain (rhymed a-b-a-b) and sestet (c-d-e c-d-e). Now the added line tucks in a fresh rhyme—on "never cease"!—just before the end:

> to set budding more,
> And still more, later flowers for the bees,
> Until they think warm days will never cease,
> For Summer has o'er-brimm'd their clammy cells.

This extra verse, this increase, prolongs late summer with still more richness. Think of Rainer Maria Rilke's marvelous "Herbsttag" (Autumn Day), written at the 1902 equinox:

> Command the last fruits to be full in time;
> grant them even two more southerly days,
> press them toward fulfillment soon and chase
> the last sweetness into the heavy wine.

At least in his ode, consumptive Keats could "think warm days will never cease."

"To Autumn" now speaks straight to the season, intimate in nearly every line: "thee . . . thy . . . Thee . . . Thy . . . thy . . . thou . . . thy . . . Thou."

Who hath not seen thee oft amid thy store?
 Sometimes whoever seeks abroad may find
Thee sitting careless on a granary floor,
 Thy hair soft-lifted by the winnowing wind;
Or on a half-reaped furrow sound asleep,
Drowsed with the fume of poppies, while thy hook
 Spares the next swath and all its twinéd flowers:
And sometimes like a gleaner thou dost keep
 Steady thy laden head across a brook;
 Or by a cider-press, with patient look,
  Thou watchest the last oozings hours by hours.

Autumn the sun's bosom-friend becomes a person, "Thy hair soft-lifted by the winnowing wind." And what a metaphor! Since "winnowing" derives from "wind" that fans chaff from grain, the echo follows nature, just as this image itself does, drawn from the harvesting that's going on.

Unlike the germinal bustle in stanza one, what's going on has reached a poise, whatever stage the harvest's at. If in the granary with threshed grain, Autumn sits easy, only her hair moving. If a reaper, then sleeping "Drowsed," his scythe stilled. If gleaning, then keeping steady over a brook. If pressing cider, then patient, watching. Three times a run-on line shifts gear to hold this poise by spanning, balancing two accented words across the break: "whoever seeks abroad may *find* / *Thee* sitting careless"; "while thy *hook* / *Spares* the next swath"; "thou dost *keep* / *Steady* thy laden head." Steadfast Keats himself means to hold out.

Moving and staying at the same time, Keats (or Autumn) does it again as the stanza ends. At first he wrote, "Thou watchest the last oozing hours by hours." Two days later he made it "oozings," squeezing out still more sweetness, much as the flowers have not just "hours" to rhyme with but "hours by hours."

Pressing out those last oozings, "To Autumn" brings the Nightingale's eight and the Urn's five stanzas down to three. Like the season's turn, the hours verge on evening.

Where are the songs of Spring? Aye, where are they?
 Think not of them, thou hast thy music too—
While barred clouds bloom the soft-dying day,
 And touch the stubble-plains with rosy hue;
Then in a wailful choir the small gnats mourn
 Among the river sallows, borne aloft
  Or sinking as the light wind lives or dies;
And full-grown lambs loud bleat from hilly bourn;
 Hedge crickets sing; and now with treble soft

The redbreast whistles from a garden croft;
        And gathering swallows twitter in the skies.

First asking about loss, Keats then deflects his question—to "bloom the soft-dying day":

Where are the songs of Spring? Aye, where are they?
        Think not of them, thou hast thy music too—
While barred clouds bloom the soft-dying day . . .

Having found Autumn "amid thy store," now he opens up the full nature of things, an ecosystem with humankind only hinted in stubble, lambs, garden.

Music fills the scene in Keats's closing stanza, trying as when Tom died to square poetry with "a World of Pains and troubles." Gnats wail but crickets sing, lambs bleat but redbreasts whistle, balancing mortal life. The gnats' choir is "borne aloft / *Or* sinking," they mourn on wind that "lives *or* dies." Lambs bleating can't sound wholly innocent, yet music, whatever its burden, lifts the spirit. Keats savors the mixed weather itself—a "temperate sharpness," he calls it. "I never liked stubble fields so much as now—Aye better than the chilly green of the spring. Somehow a stubble plain looks warm." Somehow.

A stubble plain, the crop cut and gone, has its music too. Keats first wrote: "While a gold cloud gilds the soft-dying day." Then dropping the redundant "gold . . . gilds," he says: "While barred clouds bloom the soft-dying day." Those firm stresses, "barred clouds bloom," borrow a metaphor from the fertile landscape itself, making "bloom" an active verb and lending warm color. As it happens, the century's great landscape artist, John Constable, had taken a cottage that summer in Keats's beloved Hampstead and was painting just such glowing cloud-forms above the Heath. (plate 6)

A deft hand closes this poem. After "the small gnats mourn / Among the river sallows" (willows), Keats anticipates a rhyme by having them "*borne* aloft / Or sinking"—an extra, o'er-brimming echo of "mourn" well before the "lambs loud bleat from hilly bourn" (border). And there he has Hamlet in mind, on death "from whose bourn / No traveller returns." Then still his wording overflows. As the wind "lives or dies," "borne" and "bourn" sprout a bonus rhyme, a poignant pun on "born."

What's more, having changed "gathering" to "gather'd swallows," Keats goes right back to "gathering swallows," maybe to keep them twittering—"now," he says—to hold the energy of their gathering before they migrate. The signs, sounds, rhythms in this ode create a fullness of organisms at one and at home. Like earth itself with the bees' "warm days," "The poetry of earth is never dead . . . is never ceasing."

A fullness of nature with no "I," no ego, though Keats had anxiety enough, choosing "between despair & Energy." What puns do is finesse a dire choice, so that bonus play of "born" against "dies" was anything but frivolous. "As for Pun-making, I wish it was as good a trade as pin-making," he writes a few days after "To Autumn." And "at my worst," says his deathbed letter from Rome a year later, Keats "summoned up more puns, in a sort of desperation, in one week than in any year of my life." Call it escape, or call it revival.

John Keats made up an epitaph for his tombstone: "Here lies one whose name was writ in water." Yes, and no. Truer to think of him scrambling sure-footed down the rock flank of Ambleside waterfall, stunned by its sudden thunder and freshness, then seeing "the whole more mild, streaming silverly through the trees. . . . I shall learn poetry here."

"Its only bondage was the circling sky"
John Clare at Home in Helpston

> I grew so much into the quiet love of nature's preserves that I was
> never easy but when I was in the fields passing my sabbaths and
> leisure with the shepherds & herdboys as fancys prompted
> sometimes playing at marbles on the smooth-beaten sheeptracks
> or leapfrog among the thymy molehills sometimes running among
> the corn to get the red & blue flowers for cockades to play at
> soldiers or running into the woods to hunt strawberries or stealing
> peas in churchtime when the owners were safe to boil at the
> gypseys fire who went half-shares at our stolen luxury we heard
> the bells chime but the field was our church

Running everywhere here, John Clare (1793–1864) tells his children about his own childhood in the village of Helpston and East Anglia's fen country. His early teens saw country landowners just beginning to mark out "preserves" for (hunting) game, so Clare says "nature's" preserves with some force. "In a strange stillness watching for hours the little insects climb up & down the tall stems of the wood grass," this son of a farm laborer and an illiterate mother learned lively loving attentiveness—we might be hearing a psalmist's praise of God's plenty. Victorian England would soon sponsor books like *Earth Lore for Children* to prime their Anglican faith. For Clare, "we heard the bells chime but the field was our church."

Rolling through a whole countryside with all his senses, he leaves his children what legacy he can.

> I often pulld my hat over my eyes to watch the rising of the lark or to see
> the hawk hang in the summer sky & the kite take its circle round the wood I
> often lingered a minute on the woodland stile to hear the woodpigeons clap-
> ping their wings among the dark oaks I hunted curious flowers in rapture &
> muttered thoughts in their praise I lovd the pasture with its rushes & thistles
> & sheep tracks I adored the wild marshy fen with its solitary hernshaw swee-
> ing [heron swinging] along in its mellancholy sky I wandered the heath in
> raptures among the rabbit burrows & golden blossomd furze I dropt down
> on the thymy molehill or mossy eminence to survey the summer landscape
> as full of rapture as now

Clare's vigor, finesse, integrity, surprise, and joy have charmed Nobel laureate Seamus Heaney, and for Pulitzer Prize winner Carolyn Kizer he's "without doubt the most neglected great poet in our language." Edward Thomas, Galway Kinnell, Ted Hughes, Derek Walcott, and Robert Hass single him out. What sort of writer is this, still scarcely noticed, who outsold Wordsworth, Coleridge, and Keats for a time?

At first laughed at by his parents, he "hit upon a harmless deception by repeating my poems over a book as though I was reading it this had the desird effect they often praisd them & said if I coud write as good I shoud do." His father had a horde of songs by heart, so there was much singing at home. Eventually his mother stopped lighting the fire with scraps of paper she found stuffed in crannies, and encouraged his writing.

With little schooling but greatly self-taught, Clare worked around Helpston as a thresher with his father, as plowboy, or potboy in an inn, or weeding, tending horses, gardening, shoemaking, lime-burning. He was an avid botanist and ornithologist, learned fiddling from the gypsies, and collected hundreds of local folk tunes. By husbanding a few shillings, at thirteen he purchased James Thomson's popular *The Seasons,* which inspired some poems of his own. When a local bookseller showed them to Keats's publisher, this led to a first book, *Poems Descriptive of Rural Life and Scenery* (1820). An instant hit, reprinted three times within the year, here was what Wordsworth had called for, "the real language of men in a state of vivid sensation," though Clare was seen more as a rustic wonder. He met the literati in London and aristocrats sponsored him, sometimes arriving in carriages at his cottage to call him in from the fields where he was busy reaping wheat. This cost him wages.

Though they never met, Clare had doubts about Keats, finding too many dryads and naiads in his woods: "In spite of all this his descriptions of scenery are often very fine but as it is the case with other inhabitants of great cities he often described nature as she appeared to his fancies & not as he would have described her had he witnessed the things he described." Clare must have liked the "last oozings hours by hours" of Keats's cider press, though, and his "stubble-plains." About Clare's verses, Keats said: "Images from Nature are too much introduced without being called for by a particular Sentiment." Clare's publisher wanted him to "speak of the Appearances of Nature . . . more philosophically."

More sentiment, more philosophy? That's just the point. Feeling and thought fuse in sheer description when Clare pulls his hat over his eyes to watch "the hawk hang in the summer sky" or drops down rapt "on the thymy molehill." It's true, his fine poems to autumn and the nightingale don't o'er-brim with tension like Keats's odes. But Clare has his music too, plus a unique firsthand energy.

Even an early unpublished poem, recalling childhood winter mornings, gets that energy into a loosely woven sonnet.

> The schoolboys still their morning rambles take
> To neighboring village school with playing speed
> Loitering with pastimes leisure till they quake
> Oft looking up the wild geese droves to heed
> Watching the letters which their journeys make
> Or plucking awes on which the fieldfares feed
> And hips and sloes—and on each shallow lake
> Making glib slides where they like shadows go
> Till some fresh pastimes in their minds awake
> And off they start anew and hasty blow
> Their numbed and clumpsing fingers till they glow
> Then races with their shadows wildly run
> That stride, huge giants, o'er the shining snow
> In the pale splendour of the winter sun.

Along with awkward inversions and rhymes, we get an indelible memory, "letters" made by "wild geese droves," while "awes" (hawthorn berries) and "fieldfares" (thrushes) hold onto native English. So do "glib"—not flippant, as nowadays, but the original dialect for slippery—and "clumpsing," numb with cold. (Clare added glossaries to his books.) When the schoolboys "races with their shadows wildly run," that clumsy inversion lets Clare's clumpsing fingers dazzle us endlessly "In the pale splendour of the winter sun."

Country sights merit the same care as celestial vision: "I usd to drop down under a bush & scribble the fresh thoughts on the crown of my hat as I found nature then" (if only that hat were in the British Museum). "I found the poems in the fields / And only wrote them down." Instead of cheapening his craft, Clare's humbleness deepens it. "The Nightingale's Nest" leads us through seventy-five lines of seasonal change, boyhood excursions, and something beyond Keats's ken: birdsong "Lost in a wilderness of listening leaves"!

Through branches and brambles and nearby alarms we find the nest:

> no other bird
> Uses such loose materials or weaves
> Its dwelling in such spots—dead oaken leaves
> Are placed without and velvet moss within
> And little scraps of grass and, scant and spare,
> What scarcely seem materials, down and hair.

Verifying a poet's Eden, he actually counts the eggs and corrects his sense of their color:

Sutherings, heavy sighings.

Swail, shade.

Swingle, a flail.

Swopping, pouncing.

Teem, pour out.

Toltering, hobbling.

Twilly-willy, woollen or stuff gown.

Water-blobs, the meadow-bught, or marsh-marigold.

Weals, stripes.

Whopstraws, a contemptuous appellation for countrymen.

Wood seers.—" Insects that lie in little white knots of spittle on the backs of leaves and flowers. How they come I don't know, but they are always seen plentiful in moist weather, and are one of the shepherd's weather-glasses. When the head of the insect is seen turned upward, it is said to betoken fine weather; when downward, on the contrary, wet may be expected. I think they turn to grasshoppers, and am almost certain, for I have watched them minutely." J. C.

John Clare, Glossary.

From John Clare, *The Village Minstrel and Other Poems*, vol. 2 (London, 1820).

> Snug lie her curious eggs in number five
> Of deadened green or rather olive-brown,
> And the old prickly thorn-bush guards them well.
> So here we'll leave them, still unknown to wrong,
> As the old woodland's legacy of song.

One thought carries those eggs and a thorn bush into the woodland's "legacy of song."

Clare had cause to look back longingly on "nature's preserves" where he grew up, "the lonely nooks in the fields & woods & my favorite spots . . . before enclosure destroyed them." When he was sixteen, Parliament passed an Act for the Enclosure of Helpston and neighboring parishes. For centuries the village had lain among huge fields, woods, heath, and wasteland whose talismanic names spot Clare's prose and poems: Lolham Bridges, Oxey Woods, Woodcroft Field, Emmonsales Heath, Round Oak Spring, Swordy Well. Now barriers of all sorts enclosed the open common lands for private use, setting rectangular

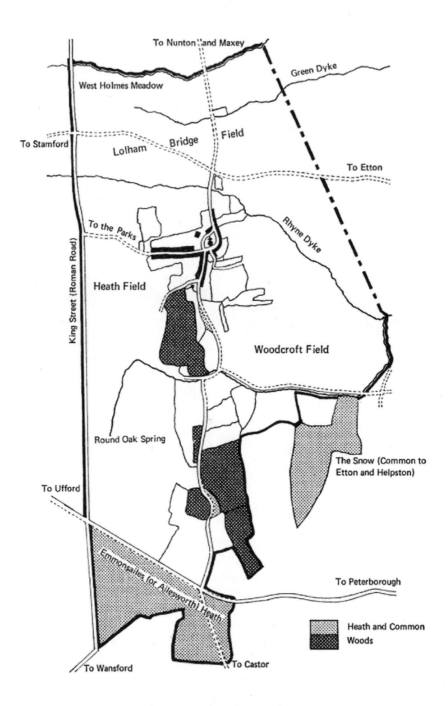

Helpston parish, before Enclosure.
Courtesy of John Barrell, from John Barrell, *The Idea of Landscape and the Sense of Place, 1730–1840: An Approach to the Poetry of John Clare* (Cambridge University Press, 1972).

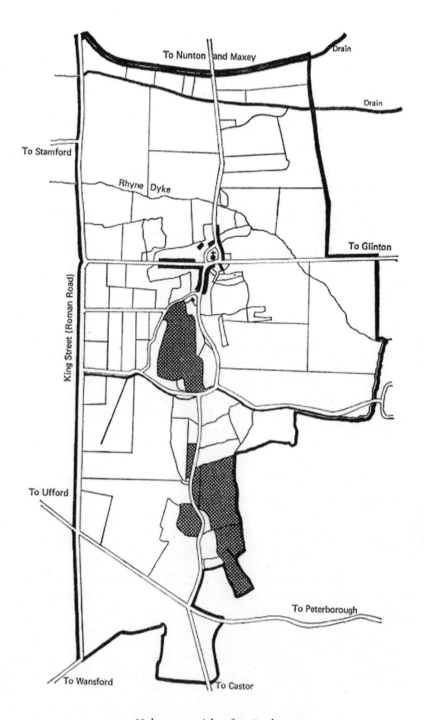

Helpston parish, after Enclosure.
Courtesy of John Barrell, from John Barrell, *The Idea of Landscape and the Sense of Place, 1730–1840: An Approach to the Poetry of John Clare* (Cambridge University Press, 1972).

bounds on a world that once centered in Helpston and ranged out freely in the circle of a child's roving. That "wandering scene" is gone, Clare says in "The Moors," "Its only bondage was the circling sky." The "wild pasture," the "commons wild and gay" of "my boyish hours / Free as spring clouds and wild as summer flowers," the "brook that dribbled on," the "sky-bound moors" are all blocked where "Fence now meets fence in owners' little bounds." Where "the field was our church" and there were

> paths to freedom and to childhood dear
> A board sticks up to notice "no road here,"

blocking body and spirit both. Wordsworth's seedtime when he "bounded o'er the mountains" may have fled, but he can still revisit the "wild secluded" cliffs above Tintern Abbey. Inspired by Oliver Goldsmith's *The Deserted Village,* Clare feels politically as well as personally threatened:

> Enclosure came and trampled on the grave
> Of labour's rights and left the poor a slave.

It also closed off an encircling world that only "the horison's edge surrounds."

A circle of wild intimate terrain, like a bird's rounded nest, both belong to that loss, and Clare knew his birds. His ongoing natural history of Helpston records scores of species, many of them first sightings in his county. Again and again in his bird's-nest poems the word "snug" occurs, along with "safe" and "sheltered": "how snug" the lark's nest "in a horse's footing [footprint] fixed!" In "The Pettichap's Nest," featured by Jonathan Bate in *The Song of the Earth,* Clare finds this tiny warbler building "close by the rut-gulled waggon road," with no grass clump or thistle spears or prickly bush to shield it from sheep, horses, oxen. Lined with feathers and pea-sized eggs so delicate a "green grasshopper's jump might break the shells," her nest speaks for the Helpston poet, vulnerable, surviving, seeking a safe center.

Other animals inhabit the circle John Clare flourished in. A grunting badger hunted by "dogs and men" turns and fights for hours, "tries to reach the woods," "sticks and cudgels" beat him,

> He falls as dead and kicked by boys and men
> Then starts and grins and drives the crowd again
> Till kicked and torn and beaten out he lies
> And leaves his hold and cackles, groans and dies.

Any moralizing would only weaken the spate of verbs driven by "and . . . and . . . and," by the shock of "grins" and "cackles" and that last line's falling cadence.

Turning thirty, Clare had bouts of depression on top of poverty, seven children to feed, publishing troubles, anguish at enclosure, and an unwanted move from his birthplace. Though only three miles away, this displacement meant a loss of place, "Green fields and every pleasant place," "places known so long":

> I miss the heath, its yellow furze
> Molehills and rabbit tracks that lead
> Through besom ling and teasel burrs
> That spread a wilderness indeed

Hallucinations and depression send him to an asylum near London. Four years later he walks off the grounds one July morning and in cracked old shoes makes his way back home, over eighty miles in four days, lying down in sheds "with my head towards the north to show myself the steering point in the morning," living on grass, a tobacco chaw, and a pint of ale when someone tosses him a few pennies. At St. Ives he rests on a flint heap, at Stilton "I was compleatly foot-foundered & broken down."

After a few months, "homeless at home," he's confined to the Northampton General Lunatic Asylum for his last twenty-four years. His wife never visits, but the asylum steward, William Knight, transcribes Clare's poems. All told, he wrote over 3,500. Those published during his lifetime were tidied up for the gentry, in grammar, spelling, punctuation, dialect. The keenest of them still tingle with detail and strike unforgettable notes: the moorland, whose "only bondage was the circling sky," the nightingale's song "Lost in a wilderness of listening leaves."

"Nature was naked, and I was also"
Adamic Walt Whitman

"Of pure American breed, large and lusty —age thirty-six years," an early review of *Leaves of Grass* depicts its author, "never once using medicine—never dressed in black, always dressed freely and clean in strong clothes—neck open, shirt collar flat and broad, countenance tawny transparent red, beard well mottled with white, hair like hay after it has been mowed in the field and lies tossed and streaked." This unsigned 1855 article in the *Brooklyn Daily Times* hails "A rude child of the people!—No imitation— No foreigner—but a growth and idiom of America. . . . The effects he produces in his poems are no effects of artists or of arts, but effects of the original eye or arm, or the actual atmosphere, or tree, or bird."

A rousing salvo, as promising as any writer could desire for a first book, self-published and anonymous. The thing is, he himself wrote it, Walt Whitman (1819–1892). And went on ringing his own bell. The Sage of Concord, Ralph Waldo Emerson, had sent a letter of thanks for "the most extraordinary piece of wit and wisdom that America has contributed." Without asking permission, Whitman had the letter published in the *New York Tribune*. Then after a year, giving *Leaves of Grass* a second edition, he not only included Emerson's letter (again without authorization), but printed a salute from it in gilt letters on the spine of this dark green volume: "I Greet You at the / Beginning of A / Great Career / R. W. Emerson."

Then Whitman added an "open letter" to Emerson, "dear Friend and Master,"

Walt Whitman, *Leaves of Grass* frontispiece, 1855.
Archives, Beeghly Library, courtesy of the Bayley/Whitman Collection of
Ohio Wesleyan University.

deploring the state of American literature—"Its costumes and jewelry prove how little it knows Nature. . . . it shows less and less of the indefinable hard something that is Nature"—and urging an "avowed, empowered, unabashed development of sex." He prophesies that "American-blooded" poems will complete the "physical continent" by celebrating "These States" with their "ever-satisfying and ever-unsurveyable seas and shores," which are, he assures Emerson, "Those shores you found."

Behind Whitman's festive embrace of Emerson stand the English Romantic poets who inspired them both. "One impulse from a vernal wood" had taught Wordsworth more "than all the sages can." His heart leapt up at "A rainbow in the sky" and "A host of dancing daffodils" in verse that reached the States during Emerson's childhood. Against the "mechanic" quality of much eighteenth-century poetry, its predetermined form, Coleridge heeded "Nature, the prime genial artist." A poem should mimic nature's "organic form": "it shapes, as it develops, itself from within. . . . Such as the life is, such is the form." Just so, "organic" and "energy" share the same root.

This green thinking liberated Emerson. *Nature* (1836), his first book, declared that poets must "expand and live in the warm day like corn and melons." Thoreau echoes this in his own first book: "As naturally as the oak bears an acorn, and the vine a gourd, man bears a poem." So does Whitman: "perfect poems show the free growth of metrical laws and bud from them as unerringly and loosely as lilacs or roses on a bush, and take shapes as compact as the shapes of chestnuts and oranges and melons and pears"—though for him the Guinness record for pumpkins would sometimes be more like it.

Emerson himself sounded primal. "Adam in the garden, I am to new-name all the beasts in the field." *Nature* looked to "fasten words again to visible things"—"again" because in Eden we were at one with physical and animal nature. Thoreau wanted poets "who nailed words to their primitive senses, as farmers drive down stakes in the spring, which the frost has heaved." Whitman's bard would "make every word he speaks draw blood . . . with the perfect rectitude and insouciance of the movements of animals and the unimpeachableness of the sentiment of trees in the woods and grass by the roadside."

Americans revered their British forebears—"We think this man stands above all poets," Whitman said of Coleridge, "he was like Adam in Paradise, and almost as free from artificiality"—but took their cue from Emerson. Walt's "open letter" called him Moses leading to the Promised Land, and Columbus. Reading *Nature* at Harvard, Thoreau felt that "In [Emerson's] world . . . Man and Nature would harmonize."

So Adam, Moses, Columbus, and Emerson severed us from Europe. Britons dwelling in domesticated terrain, Thoreau insisted, could not speak for "Vast,

Titanic, inhuman Nature" on Maine's Mount Katahdin, or the Algonquin version he preferred, Ktaadn, "primeval, untamed, and forever untamable." At eighteen, thinking of Shelley and Keats, he frowned on Americans "prone to sing of skylarks and nightingales, perched on hedges, to the neglect of the homely robin redbreast, and the straggling rail-fence of their own native land." England's poets had "not seen the west side of any mountain," Wordsworth was "too tame for the Chippeway."

As if heeding these voices, a Scotsman who'd come to the United States during the Gold Rush went on to explore California's Sierra forests, "the most beautiful on the face of the earth." John Muir one gleeful day in 1874 clung to the top of a hundred-foot spruce swaying through thirty degrees in a winter windstorm. Showing Emerson Yosemite, he was dismayed at the aging philosopher's reluctance to spend "one good wild memorable night around a Sequoia camp-fire." Even Wordsworth dazzled by an Alpine waterfall, Keats in the Lake District, Hopkins in Switzerland, pale beside Muir running for an open meadow to witness "Fifty-six new-born falls" and an "outgush of snowy cascades" thronging the upper Yosemite valley.

Emerson soon backed off from his first flush welcoming Whitman, and Walt eventually found him artificial. Though *Nature* says "radical correspondence" connects man to the world, and "In the presence of nature, a wild delight" verging on fear runs through him, Emerson finally sees that "beauty in nature is not ultimate." It serves the "wants," "needs," "uses" of man. Prophesying "the kingdom of man over nature," and "subordinating nature for the purposes of expression," the Master smacks of Genesis and man's dominion. Whitman dissents: Emerson's speech "is always a *make*, never an unconscious *growth*." He's not there when we need the "vitalizing influences of abysmic nature," Whitman coins a word to tell us.

Finding vital flow in himself as in nature, Whitman prefaced *Leaves of Grass* with a manifesto, nine thousand words mapping turf for the new American poet. "On him rise solid growths that offset the growths of pine and cedar and . . ."—here follow fifteen trees our native poet will embody, along with his "flights and songs and screams that answer those of the wildpigeon and . . ."—here nineteen birds are named.

Bonding wild nature to American voices makes a tall order (à la Paul Bunyan's tall tales). A "bard . . . commensurate with a people . . . incarnates its geography and natural life and rivers and lakes. Mississippi and Columbia and Ohio and Saint Lawrence with the falls and beautiful masculine Hudson, do not embouchure where they spend themselves more than they embouchure into him." That "embouchure" is not a verb doesn't hinder Whitman from claiming that the country's spirit flows into this bard. "Walt" would be his name, rather than a nobler Ralph Waldo, Henry David, Henry Wadsworth, along with William Cullen Bryant and John Greenleaf Whittier, fine poets in their way and citizens. This man must "attract his own land body and soul to himself and hang on its neck with incomparable love and plunge his semitic muscle into its merits and demerits." In his excitement Whitman means "seminal," for a new American poetry must seed the body of the land together with its people.

So much happens in this prose, it's a wonder anything's left for the poems. Yet something is, above all what's oddly absent from his Preface, the word "I."

> I will go to the bank by the wood and become undisguised and naked,
> I am mad for it to be in contact with me.

"Song of Myself," the core of *Leaves of Grass*, starts on "I" and moves through earth and sky, animal and human, humor and pathos, to end after fifty-two sections on "you."

More boisterous than Emerson, Whitman takes over Eden:

> I harbor for good or bad, I permit to speak at every hazard,
> Nature without check with original energy.

From this baseline a sunrise breaks out:

> To behold the day-break!
> The little light fades the immense and diaphanous shadows,
> The air tastes good to my palate.

As if our poet were the first to see such an event:

> The heav'd challenge from the east that moment over my head,
> The mocking taunt, See then whether you shall be master! . . .
> Dazzling and tremendous how quick the sun-rise would kill me,
> If I could not now and always send sun-rise out of me.

A mutual force, not dominion, yokes us to nature—though that force may equal the sun.

"Walt Whitman, a kosmos" begins section 24, and how does a cosmos begin?

> Unscrew the locks from the doors!
> Unscrew the doors themselves from their jambs!

A stimulating fellow but you wouldn't want him dropping in often. Whitman was derided for haphazard enumeration, but "Through me" his prophet-like Hebraic breath lines marshal a motley crowd, make up a universe:

> Through me many long dumb voices,
> Voices of the interminable generations of prisoners and slaves,
> Voices of the diseas'd and despairing and of thieves and dwarfs,
> Voices of cycles of preparation and accretion,

> And of the threads that connect the stars, and of wombs
>   and of the father-stuff,
> And of the rights of them the others are down upon,
> Of the deform'd, trivial, flat, foolish, despised,
> Fog in the air, beetles rolling balls of dung.

One cycle arcs all the way from "long dumb voices" to "balls of dung," from suffering humanity to nature persisting. In staggered ranks as they enter, generation by generation, Whitman unscrolls a cosmos of sundry voices by phasing them: "Through me many . . . voices," then "Voices of . . . and of," then "And of," then "Of," then simply "Fog . . . beetles." Everything interdepends—to use a verb coined during his prime.

Walt speaks for the despised and rejected, like Isaiah, for the poor and meek, like Jesus. "I give the sign of democracy," says he, and the lingo proves this, blending high speech with low, philosophic "cycles of . . . accretion" with American slang, "down upon." The human condition melds with nature: prisoners and slaves phase into fog, the diseased and despairing into beetles. Those mean specimens, scarab beetles "rolling balls of dung," were sacred symbols of renewal in ancient Egypt. Everywhere they feed on dung, lay their eggs in it, and recycle its nutrients underground thus cleansing the land.

Whitman felt right and jaunty in the world:

> I find I incorporate gneiss, coal, long-threaded moss, fruits, grains,
>   esculent roots,
> And am stucco'd with quadrupeds and birds all over,

and his own voice felt right with nature:

> I lean and loafe at my ease observing a spear of summer grass.
> My tongue, every atom of my blood, form'd from this soil, this air.

A "spear of summer grass" grafts right onto "My tongue," giving it sexual and botanic thrust. Likewise "The sound of the belch'd words of my voice loos'd to the eddies of the wind" pleased him immensely, made him one with the elements.

This much was good, but not enough. Whitman's song of himself celebrates spirit along with flesh, especially his own flesh:

> Divine am I inside and out, and I make holy whatever I touch
>   or am touch'd from,
> The scent of these arm-pits aroma finer than prayer,
> This head more than churches, bibles, and all the creeds.

Imagine Emily Dickinson reading this in Amherst at twenty-five, and trying her own bold voice: "The Brain—is wider than the Sky" and "deeper than the

Sea," she wrote, but "just the weight of God." She'd have backed "This head more than churches," but the rest was more than she needed to know.

Another profane passage mixing spirit into earthliness would have gotten Whitman tarred and feathered by the Puritan fathers:

> If I worship one thing more than another it shall be the spread
>   of my own body, or any part of it . . .
> Firm masculine colter it shall be you!
> Whatever goes to the tilth of me it shall be you!
> You my rich blood! Your milky stream pale strippings of my life!
> Breast that presses against other breasts it shall be you!
> My brain it shall be your occult convolutions!
> Root of wash'd sweet-flag! timorous pond-snipe! nest of guarded
>   duplicate eggs! It shall be you!
> Mix'd tussled hay of head, beard, brawn, it shall be you!

A wavelike surge intoning "you!" and "You" binds "worship" into his own body. So do the unexpected images. With Adam's birthright, Whitman loved naming country things from a Long Island landscape he knew well—"colter" a prong sending the plow-blade into the "tilth" or tilled earth, sweet-flag's root, a snipe's long beak, duplicate eggs—and he wanted their sexual energy too. His litany of worship comes to a flagrant close:

> Winds whose soft-tickling genitals rub against me it shall be you!
> Broad muscular fields, branches of live oak, loving lounger in my
>   winding paths, it shall be you!

It's a great deal more than Robinson Jeffers meant, guarding nature's wholeness: "Love that, not man / Apart from that."

"I dote on myself, there is that lot of me and all so luscious," "Song of Myself" lets us know. When Longfellow and Whittier were setting the tone in 1855, Walt's carnal openness took nerve, just as his language did. A sunrise sends him over the top:

> To behold the day-break! . . .
> Hefts of the moving world at innocent gambols silently rising
>   freshly exuding,
> Scooting obliquely high and low.

Like daylight heaving up, his verbs are gamboling, freshly exuding, scooting obliquely. No one before or since has seen or said things this way:

> Something I cannot see puts upward libidinous prongs,
> Seas of bright juice suffuse heaven.

"Something I cannot see," mystical though he can speak it: bare sunrise, the day's orange orgasm.

Whitman was never tarred and feathered, but in Washington, having tended gently to Civil War wounded from both sides, his "indecent" book got him dismissed from a government job. The Secretary of the Interior didn't have far to look in *Leaves of Grass*: "Loafe with me on the grass, loose the stop from your throat," Walt asks his soul, "Only the lull I like, the hum of your valvèd voice." Yet that music alone, tuning "lull" with "hum" between *l*'s and *v*'s, should have absolved him.

One summer morning "you settled your head athwart my hips," he goes on to his soul-mate, "And parted the shirt from my bosom-bone, and plunged your tongue to my bare-stript heart." Brazenness then finds a biblical cadence, not debasing but sanctifying earth:

> Swiftly arose and spread around me the peace and knowledge that pass
>   all the argument of the earth,
> And I know that the hand of God is the promise of my own,
> And I know that the spirit of God is the brother of my own,
> And that all the men ever born are also my brothers, and the women
>   my sisters and lovers,
> And that a kelson of the creation is love,
> And limitless are leaves stiff or drooping in the fields,
> And brown ants in the little wells beneath them,
> And mossy scabs of the worm fence, heap'd stones, elder, mullein
>   and poke-weed.

We've felt this pulse before, shaping a new world in Genesis:

> And the earth was without form and void;
> and darkness was upon the face of the deep.
> And the spirit of God moved upon the face of the waters.

The wonder is, without meter or rhyme we're borne by natural breath lines through a chain of being from divine peace to human love and down through "kelson," for a ship's keel, to "brown ants," "mossy scabs," and commonplace "elder, mullein and poke-weed"—poke-weed!

"He combined the contemplation of nature and of civilization, which are apparently entirely contradictory, into a single intoxicating vision of life," said—of all people—Franz Kafka, long before most of Whitman's compatriots had seen as much. "I admire in him the reconciliation of art and nature."

Contradiction came handily to Whitman. While rejecting "bibles, and all the creeds," he still drew from the prophets and Psalms. Listen to Psalm 104:

> The earth shall tremble at the look of him: if he do but touch the hills,
>   they shall smoke.
> I will sing unto the Lord as long as I live: I will praise my God while I have
>   my being.

Except for "Lord" and "God," "Song of Myself" could be thrilling at nature's force. What does Whitman sound like in Hebrew? "Ezekiel," says his Israeli translator.

Sometimes he overdid his strength—"Who goes there? hankering, gross, mystical, nude; / How is it I extract strength from the beef I eat?"—leaving himself open to parody, such as Ezra Pound's "Whitman Is the Voice of One Who Saith":

> Lo, behold, I eat water melons. When I eat water melons the world eats
> water melons through me.
> When the world eats water melons,
> I partake of the world's water melons.

Yet Whitman at his nerviest outstrips his parodists, as "Song of Myself" closes:

> The spotted hawk swoops by and accuses me, he complains of my gab
> and my loitering.
> I too am not a bit tamed, I too am untranslatable,
> I sound my barbaric yawp over the roofs of the world.

Gab or yawp or Long Island shaman, his words are tied in one with nature's rhythms:

> The last scud of day holds back for me,
> It flings my likeness after the rest and true as any on the shadow'd wilds,
> It coaxes me to the vapor and the dusk.

The last scud of wind-driven mist, vague shadowed wilds, vapor and dusk, signal a passing away, but even that surges with outlandish exuberance—nature's and his own:

> I depart as air, I shake my white locks at the runaway sun,
> I effuse my flesh in eddies, and drift it in lacy jags.

Then he returns to the soil and grass of section one:

> I bequeath myself to the dirt to grow from the grass I love,
> If you want me again look for me under your boot-soles.

Finally his rolling rhythm carries Whitman's song from himself to ourselves:

> Failing to fetch me at first keep encouraged,
> Missing me one place search another,
> I stop somewhere waiting for you.

And yes, he does still wait for us, where humankind melds with the earth.

A glimpse at Walt Whitman's life shows the same motives that drove his poetry. Decades after its publication, he kept on growing *Leaves of Grass*, adding and revising through eight more editions until the year he died. Put in *"American things*," he tells himself, "*minerals, vegetables, animals etc*," and he calls this life's work his "Great Construction of the New Bible," then late in life wonders if *Leaves of Grass* was perhaps "only a language experiment."

It was all these at once: organic whole, American anthem, new Scripture, and more, with its sexual candor and democratic zeal. And his groundbreaking language tries just about everything human and nonhuman nature will bear.

As did Whitman's own life. His early years on New York's Long Island (which he gave its Indian name Paumanok, "fish-shaped") meant spearing eels under the ice, gathering seagull eggs, sailing around Montauk Point, fraternizing with fishermen and herdsmen, walking the plains and woods and shores. *Specimen Days in America*, a "huddle of diary-jottings, war memoranda of 1862–'65, Nature-notes of 1877–'81," details the life behind *Leaves of Grass*. In Brooklyn during the 1840s, for instance, he often went to Coney Island, "a long, bare unfrequented shore, which I had all to myself, and where I loved, after bathing, to race up and down the hard sand, and declaim Homer or Shakspere to the surf and sea-gulls by the hour." ("Unfrequented" will daze anyone who knew Coney Island a century later, mackerel-crowded with sunbathing bodies.)

"Even as a boy, I had the fancy, the wish, to write a piece, perhaps a poem, about the sea-shore," says *Specimen Days*, "the solid marrying the liquid." The seashore meant "an invisible *influence*, a pervading gauge and tally for me, in my composition": "a stretch of interminable white-brown sand, hard and smooth and broad, with the ocean perpetually, grandly, rolling in upon it, with slow-measured sweep, with rustle and hiss and foam." A century later, William Carlos Williams would date "the American poem" from Whitman on the sands, gazing out to sea. That "slow-measured sweep" of ocean onto land keeps his verse lines swelling and reforming in changeless change. Crossing the East River on ferries between Brooklyn and Manhattan, he feels a "still excitement," that sensation "as you stand and lean on the rail, yet hurry with the swift current."

Whatever else may be true of Walt Whitman, he sensed all things connected —poems, surroundings, doings of his body and spirit. After his Civil War years with the wounded in Washington, comforting, writing and reading letters, bringing gifts, speaking poems, or simply sitting at bedside, Lincoln's assassination evoked a very long elegy with an American dooryard grounding its title. "When Lilacs Last in the Door-yard Bloom'd" follows the coffin across this country, always in earshot of a hermit-thrush warbling with "bleeding throat . . . And the voice of my spirit tallied the song of the bird."

A paralytic stroke hit Whitman in 1873, and two years later another. Unwell and depressed, he spent long periods at a New Jersey farm, outdoors and alert to sights, sounds, smells, trees, flowers, fruit, birds and birdsong, bees, night sky—"no talk, no bonds, no dress, no books, no *manners*." He'd walk down the farm lane and wrestle with a hickory sapling "to get into my old sinews some of its elastic fibre and clear sap."

One August day, Walt makes his way to a secluded dell "fill'd with bushes, trees, grass, a group of willows, a straggling bank, and a spring of delicious water running right through the middle of it, with two or three little cascades."

> A light south-west wind was blowing through the tree-tops. It was just the place and time for my Adamic air-bath and flesh-brushing from head to foot. So hanging clothes on a rail near by, keeping old broadbrim straw on head and easy shoes on feet, havn't I had a good time the last two hours! First with the stiff-elastic bristles rasping arms, breast, sides, till they turn'd scarlet—then partially bathing in the clear waters of the running brook . . . stepping about barefooted every few minutes now and then in some neighbouring black ooze, for unctuous mud-bath to my feet . . .
>
> As I walk'd slowly over the grass, the sun shone out enough to show the shadow moving with me. Somehow I seem'd to get identity with each and every thing around me, in its condition. Nature was naked, and I was also.

"Earth's most graphic transaction"
Syllables of Emily Dickinson

"If I read a book and it makes my whole body so cold no fire ever can warm me I know *that* is poetry. If I feel physically as if the top of my head were taken off, I know *that* is poetry. These are the only way I know it. Is there any other way." This is the "Belle of Amherst," as she once jokingly called herself, Emily Dickinson (1830–1886), writing to Thomas Wentworth Higginson, man of letters, former Unitarian minister, champion of women's rights, gun-running abolitionist who'd led the Union Army's first Negro regiment. After meeting the poet, the Civil War hero told his wife: "I never was with any one who drained my nerve power so much."

Years before, Dickinson had sent him four poems out of the blue. "Are you too deeply occupied to say if my Verse is alive?" she asked. "Should you think it breathed . . . I should feel quick gratitude." Higginson wrote back asking for a picture, and she let him see an uncommon spirit: "I had no portrait, now, but am small, like the wren, and my Hair is bold, like the Chestnut bur—and my eyes, like the Sherry in the Glass, that the guest leaves—Would this do just as well?" A wren's quickness, burr-like hair, sherry eyes sound a rare note. But sherry "that the guest leaves"? This is something else.

There really were fine pictures of Emily, but her sister and brother disliked them, for lacking "the play of light and shade" in her "startling" face. Again elusively, giving Higginson a career update, she slips into her habitual 4-3 beat: "I made no verse, but one or two—until this winter—Sir." In fact she'd written almost three hundred lyrics by then, including lines relaying the Holy Trinity to her garden plot: "In the name of the Bee— / And of the Butterfly—And of the Breeze—Amen!" Dickinson tells him her family are all religious "except me—and address an Eclipse, every morning—whom they call their 'Father.'" And this too: "You speak of Mr Whitman. I never read his Book—but was told that he was disgraceful."

Before striking up this correspondence, she'd seen Higginson's judgment on poetic eccentricity: "It is no discredit to Walt Whitman that he wrote 'Leaves of Grass,' only that he did not burn it afterwards. A young writer must commonly plough in his first crop." She herself was nothing if not eccentric, and Higginson was unequipped to see how these two mid-century poets, like Hawthorne and Melville in the novel and Thoreau in the essay, were breaking new ground for American writing.

Emily Dickinson in Amherst could well have missed *Leaves of Grass* by "Walt Whitman, a kosmos, of Manhattan the son," which hardly sold at first. But one poem she likely encountered. Her household took the recently founded *Atlantic Monthly*, whose February and May 1860 issues it's known she read. That April the magazine published Whitman's "As I Ebb'd with the Ocean of Life."

> Nature here in sight of the sea taking advantage of me to dart upon me
> and sting me,
> Because I have dared to open my mouth to sing at all. . . .
> Ebb, ocean of life, (the flow will return,)
> Cease not your moaning you fierce old mother,
> Endlessly cry for your castaways, but fear not, deny not me,
> Rustle not up so hoarse and angry against my feet as I touch you or
> gather from you.

Too gabby for her, but Dickinson felt Nature's dart and sting, and by 1860 she'd "dared . . . to sing," sounding her own depths in "I taste a liquor never brewed":

> Inebriate of Air—am I—
> And Debauchee of Dew—
> Reeling—thro endless summer days—
> From inns of Molten Blue—

While it's easier to picture Walt tramping Long Island shoreline than Emily staggering home soused, that's not the point. Her reeling speech gets unheard-of reach from summer's "Molten Blue."

In the popular view, Dickinson seems a wraith in white, seldom descending from her small wooden desk in the upstairs corner bedroom. Yet she had intense friendships, and knew uncultivated nature around Amherst. "When much in the Woods, as a little Girl, I was told that the Snake would bite me, that I might

Emily Dickinson, ca. 1855.
Collection of Philip and Leslie Gura.

pick a poisonous flower, or Goblins kidnap me, but I went along and met no one but Angels, who were far shyer of me, than I could be of them."

Liking the names of things, she kept a herbarium as a girl, a booklet with dried flowers labeled in English and Latin. At age nine for a photo, she's holding an illustrated book with a cut flower in it, and at sixteen, a flower's in one hand a book near the other. Later she writes to young cousins about discovering a witch hazel shrub: "I had never seen it but once before, and it haunted me like childhood's Indian pipe, or ecstatic puff-balls, or that mysterious apple that sometimes comes on river-pinks." Puffballs, a mushroom-like fungus, burst at the touch and discharge brown powder. But "ecstatic"? That sprouted from her own nature. "I have long been a Lunatic on bulbs." One day in her conservatory she showed someone a chrysalis that "had burst its bonds, and floating about in the sunshine was a gorgeous butterfly," says the neighbor. "I did not understand all she said about it, but it was beautiful to see her delight and to hear her talk."

At ease in the natural world, Dickinson was less forward than Whitman. A photo shows the Bard on whose upraised fingers a butterfly has alighted; after his death a pasteboard butterfly was found among his things. He spoke readily for "beetles rolling balls of dung" and "threads that connect the stars," but she was not so sure.

> Touch lightly Nature's sweet Guitar
> Unless thou know'st the Tune
> Or every Bird will point at thee
> Because a Bard too soon—

Like slant-rhyming "Bard" with "Bird," her touch for nature was light, whatever the overtones.

Dickinson's glancing touch graces a riddle she sent to friends from 1879 on, known by an opening line as ungraspable as the creature itself:

> A Route of Evanescence
> With a revolving Wheel—
> A Resonance of Emerald—
> A Rush of Cochineal—
> And every Blossom on the Bush
> Adjusts its tumbled Head—
> The mail from Tunis, probably,
> An easy Morning's Ride—

For "revolving" she'd tried alternatives: "delusive," "dissembling," "dissolving." The simplest word catches wingbeats so rapid they blur like wheel spokes in a four-line whir of r's. Evanescence has left us floating amid motion, color, sound: a precious bright green humming, a scarlet or ruby-throated rush. Then with no notice the hummingbird—if that's what it was—is gone.

What's left is every blossom astir, adjusting itself in the wake of a quick visit. Then a witness fancies how fast this happened. Whereas (in Shakespeare's *Tempest*) Tunis lies so far from Naples that no letter can arrive "unless the sun were

Walt Whitman, with butterfly, 1877.
Charles E. Feinberg Collection, Library of Congress.

post," here the bird's sheer speed makes "An easy Morning's Ride." Flippancy tips the poem's angle of vision, ousting any human dominion over nature.

Intimate with flora and some fauna in her environs, Dickinson still doubted they were hers by poetic right. On Nature:

> We pass, and She abides.
> We conjugate her Skill
> While She creates and federates
> Without a syllable.

Still the speaker brings uncommon skill, as in one syllable, "raw," of another poem:

> A Bird came down the Walk—
> He did not know I saw—
> He bit an Angleworm in halves
> And ate the fellow, raw,

And then he drank a Dew
From a convenient Grass—
And then hopped sidewise to the Wall
To let a Beetle pass—

He glanced with rapid eyes
That hurried all around—
They looked like frightened Beads, I thought—
He stirred his Velvet Head

Like one in danger, Cautious,
I offered him a Crumb
And he unrolled his feathers
And rowed him softer home—

Than Oars divide the Ocean,
Too silver for a seam—
Or Butterflies, off Banks of Noon
Leap, plashless as they swim.

Granted, Dickinson's bird "came down the Walk" close to home, not in wildness where Muir and Thoreau found the truth of things. This Bird (she capitalized words she liked) dwells far from Jonah's or Melville's whale, Beowulf's monster, Jack London's wolf, Ted Hughes's crow, though not far from Whitman's beetles. Dickinson, who'd read Darwin on the survival of the fittest and probably Tennyson on "Nature, red in tooth and claw," found nature fierce and strange enough on her own turf.

Usually it's humans who come down a walk, so that phrase magnifies the bird as he bites a worm "in halves" and eats it—comma—"raw" (how else?). A bluff rhyme, "He did not know I saw— /. . . And ate the fellow, raw," links her covert self to a bestial species. Again she intervenes, with a surreal take on his "rapid eyes": "They looked like frightened Beads, I thought." Tacking on "I thought" admits that by adorning we add little to Nature, however apt that "Velvet" head. She acts "Without a syllable."

Now things turn ambiguous. Does stanza three run on to four—"He stirred his Velvet Head / / Like one in danger, Cautious . . ."—or does four begin a new gesture: "Like one in danger, Cautious, / I offered him a Crumb . . ."? Is the Bird or the speaker "in danger, Cautious"? Both are quite possible, thanks to odd syntax and punctuation. Indifferent or not, the animal "unrolled his feathers / And rowed him softer home" on a quiet off-rhyme with "Crumb."

Softer even "Than Oars divide the Ocean /. . . Or Butterflies, off Banks of Noon / Leap, plashless as they swim." Instead of ending with the bird, Dickinson goes somewhere out of mind and to a mystic river. Do butterflies actually leap from riverbanks and swim, with or without splashing? In any event, "Banks of Noon" snaps our synapses, leaves us blinking into midday sun.

Birds, butterflies, and most often bees seize Dickinson's attention, acting out everything under the sun: "Buccaneers of buzz," "Baronial bees," "the goblin bee," "the lover bee," "When landlords turn the drunken bee / Out of the foxglove's door." She's in fine company here: Coleridge's "Sycamore, oft musical with bees," Keats's Autumn flowers "And still more, later flowers for the bees," and Yeats calling "honey bees / Come build" in his crumbling tower. Maybe Plato swayed her, likening the imagination to bees—they fetch abroad, then return and make honey.

Still she looks askance at all things great and small, including herself.

> To make a prairie it takes a clover and one bee,
> One clover, and a bee,
> And revery.
> The revery alone will do,
> If bees are few.

She doubts human sovereignty and Adam's gift of naming.

> "Nature" is what we see—
> The Hill—the Afternoon—
> Squirrel—Eclipse—the Bumble bee— . . .
> Nature is what we know—
> Yet have no art to say—
> So impotent Our Wisdom is
> To her Simplicity.

What would she have made of a recent discovery in Burma, a hundred-million-year-old bee found in amber along with four tiny flowers it was sipping?

Questioning "Nature" so often makes Dickinson's doubts even more penetrating:

> But Nature is a stranger yet;
> The ones that cite her most
> Have never passed her haunted house,
> Nor simplified her ghost.

Never simple, Nature is too mysterious for lyric beauty and too actual, in this double negative:

> Where melody is not
> Is the unknown peninsula.
> Beauty is nature's fact.

"Beauty is nature's fact": six syllables subverting ages of human presumption.

Nature's oldest fact occasioned an animal poem that boggles mind and body both. One day Dickinson's friend Samuel Bowles, editor of the Springfield, Massachusetts *Republican,* put on his front page "The Snake"—which was not her title, because she never gave any. We learn she "met Him," this so-called recluse "met this Fellow." Her Amherst home had thirteen acres, with a meadow opposite her window. As a girl she was told a snake might bite her, "but I went along and met no one but Angels."

Known by its first line, this poem snares our primal fear in a riddle.

> A narrow Fellow in the Grass
> Occasionally rides—
> You may have met Him—did you not
> His notice sudden is—
>
> The Grass divides as with a Comb—
> A spotted shaft is seen—
> And then it closes at your feet
> And opens further on—
>
> He likes a Boggy Acre
> A Floor too cool for Corn—
> Yet when a Boy, and Barefoot—
> I more than once at Noon
> Have passed, I thought, a Whip lash
> Unbraiding in the Sun
> When stooping to secure it
> It wrinkled, and was gone—
>
> Several of Nature's People
> I know, and they know me—
> I feel for them a transport
> Of cordiality—
>
> But never met this Fellow
> Attended, or alone
> Without a tighter breathing
> And Zero at the Bone—

Unnerving from A to Z, "A narrow Fellow" down to "Zero at the Bone," *that* is poetry when "it makes my whole body so cold no fire ever can warm me."

It took someone whose "Verse is alive," as she wrote Higginson, to come alert yet vulnerable upon "A narrow Fellow in the Grass"—"narrow," i.e., slim but also mean and confining, plus "Fellow," a comrade but also an ill-bred male. Then startlingly he "rides," a cavalier not a reptile, and the next line jars us with an unmarked question: "You may have met Him—did you not." This Fellow's "notice sudden is," strangely giving notice or noticing *us,* as the inverted "sudden is" scrapes its rhyme against "rides."

Now a sexual hint emerges like Original Sin, as the grass divides and "A spotted shaft is seen." No creature is named, though she knows him well enough:

> He likes a Boggy Acre
> A Floor too cool for Corn—

Sam Bowles exclaimed, "How did that girl ever know that a boggy field wasn't good for corn?" Her memory then turns to childhood shock:

> Yet when a Boy, and Barefoot—
> I more than once at Noon
> Have passed, I thought, a Whip lash
> Unbraiding in the sun.

Her later editor-relatives thought "Child" more seemly than "Boy," and changed "Noon" to "Morn," smoothing the rhyme with "Corn." But they couldn't tame Emily's wildness. This "Whip lash / Unbraiding" is no mere figure of speech but visionary menace: "It wrinkled, and was gone." Compare her calmer poem—"Sweet is the swamp with its secrets, / Until we meet a snake; / 'Tis then we sigh for houses . . . "

Dickinson unsettles her Sunday hymnal meter too, shifting from an 8-6-8-6 syllable count to 7-6-7-6, every other line hanging on an unstressed syllable: *Bare*foot, *Whip* lash. This odd-even pace keeps us off balance and expectant, though again reassured for a moment, relaxed:

> Several of Nature's People
> I know, and they know me—
> I feel for them a transport
> Of cordiality—

Against the whiplash and her sense of unknown nature, Dickinson risks a casual tone on "Several" and on "People I know," such as squirrels and deer. Likewise her "transport" or rapture gets lightened by genteel "cordiality"—Now Emily, be cordial to our guests! Except that the heart (Latin *cor*) at the root of "cordiality" will come back to end this tale on a kind of cardiac arrest.

Pointing toward a close, that word "But" rebuts cordiality:

> But never met this Fellow
> Attended, or alone

The lout and somehow fellow creature's still not named. One syllable in this species standoff, "*or* alone," turns dire when finally "alone" gets locked in by its rhyme:

> But never met this Fellow
> Attended, or alone

Have passed
I thought a
Whip lash
Unbraiding in the
Sun
When stooping
to secure it
It wrinkled
And was gone

Several of
nature's People
I know and they
know me
I feel for
them a transport
of Cordiality

Emily Dickinson, "A narrow Fellow in the Grass" manuscript.
By permission of The Houghton Library, Harvard University MS Am 1118.5 (B193)
© The President and Fellows of Harvard College.

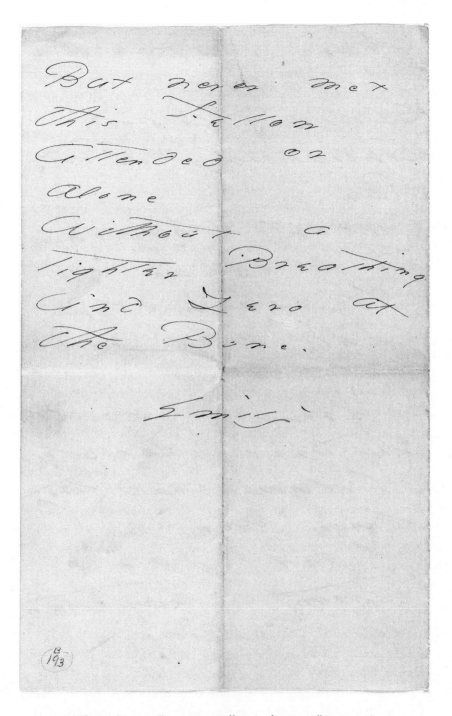

Emily Dickinson, "A narrow Fellow in the Grass" manuscript.
By permission of The Houghton Library, Harvard University MS Am 1118.5 (B193)
© The President and Fellows of Harvard College.

> Without a tighter breathing
> And Zero at the Bone—

Cordiality gives way to anguish (*angst* as in narrow, constricted), when tighter breathing cramps the chest. Dickinson's handwriting, often expressive, has a ripcord stroke across both *t*'s in "*Transport* of cordiality" and again in "*tighter breathing.*"

"And Zero at the Bone": her most stunning line. After "breathing" catches at the break, this final line feels absolute, fastening "alone" to "Bone" in the poem's only perfect rhyme. Frozen at sight of a cold-blooded creature, the marrow goes null, "Zero at the Bone." At this depth opposites fuse, pure recognition with blank dread.

Another chilling Dickinson lyric comes to mind, "After great pain, a formal feeling comes," where "Nerves" and "stiff Heart" have grown "like a stone." It ends,

> As Freezing persons, recollect the Snow—
> First—Chill—then Stupor—then the letting go—

"Snow" sinks into "letting go," like "alone" into "Bone." Such moments are not some reportage after the event. "In a poem, what's real *happens*," says her German translator Paul Celan.

Dickinson wrote about choosing words, "as I can take but few and each must be the chiefest . . . Earth's most graphic transaction is placed within a syllable, nay, even a gaze." Transaction—between Earth and her? Her own syllables act on us: "His notice sudden *is* . . . And Zero at the *Bone*."

Spasmodic, uncontrolled, wayward, T. W. Higginson called Dickinson's verse. Yes, her genius was wayward and she'd the strength to tell him so: "Myself the only Kangaroo among the Beauty." To herself she says, "Tell all the Truth but tell it slant," which means omitting, disjoining, perplexing words, syntax, knowledge. Unknowing can rivet her, or it can amuse, so that facing caprice in nature she goes jocular:

> Apparently with no surprise
> To any happy Flower
> The Frost beheads it at its play—

Or not so jocular, since "an Approving God" likes that "blonde Assassin," she says. Dickinson (in her words) "keeps Believing nimble."

The young woman who told Higginson her family worships "an Eclipse, every morning" was not likely to share nineteenth-century sacramental ideas of nature, of skylark and sycamore and daffodil embodying divine spirit. Our ignorance and mortality, she said, make us "as exempt from Exultation as the Stones." Yet "A Word that breathes distinctly / Has not the power to die," so we keep turning to her finely tuned and timed lines.

> A Pit—but Heaven over it—
> And Heaven beside, and Heaven abroad,
> And yet a Pit—
> With Heaven over it . . .
> The depth is all my thought—

That Pit would be mortal Earth, but again she refrains from labeling, and we're drawn beyond our depth.

Reclusive and a spinster, as they say, but not sheltered, Emily Dickinson knew death close up: women dying in childbirth, children from disease, Amherst's casualties throughout Civil War. Yet 1862 drew more poems from her than any other year. The general "anguish," she said at the end of that year, increases "what we have the power to be."

Losses studded her days: friends and mentors, Sam Bowles, her mother, her father, and painfullest of all, her eight-year-old nephew Gilbert. She wrote a friend: "'Open the Door, open the Door, they are waiting for me,' was Gilbert's sweet command in delirium. *Who* were waiting for him, all we possess we would give to know." But "*is* there more?" she added. "Then tell me its name!"

In illness Dickinson said, "I write in the midst of Sweet-Peas and by the side of Orioles, and could put my Hand on a Butterfly, only he withdraws." At her death in May 1886, her sister-in-law Susan prepared the body for burial, putting violets and a pink orchid at her throat and flowers and boughs over the white coffin. An old family retainer remembers Emily's funeral wish: "She asked to be carried out the back door, around through the garden, through the opened barn from front to back, and then through the grassy fields." Through the garden, through grassy fields, a little like the carriage in her best-known poem, "Because I could not stop for Death": "We passed the Fields of Gazing Grain."

Passing fields of grain, yes. But *gazing* grain?

"sick leaves . . . storm-birds . . . rotten rose . . . rain-drop"
Nature Shadowing Thomas Hardy

"**D**own their carved names the rain-drop ploughs." They're not only dead and buried, but nature's eroding their very names, their loving memory. Something less bleak than this, from Thomas Hardy (1840–1928), might be preferred, but listen to its relentless pulse. Usually an eight-syllable line has three or four accents. Lewis Carroll's "Jabberwocky":

> 'Twas *brill*ig and the *slith*y *toves*
> Did *gyre* and *gim*ble in the *wabe.*

W. B. Yeats:

> And *lift* your *ten*der *eye*lids, *maid,*
> And *brood* on *hopes* and *fears* no *more.*

A. E. Housman:

> But *oh,* good *Lord,* the *verse* you *make,*
> It *gives* a *chap* the *bel*ly-*ache.*

Hardy's line bears seven stresses, driving nearly every syllable:

> *Down their carved names* the *rain-drop ploughs.*

We'll come back to this landmark poem.

Thomas Hardy was born of yeoman stock, as they say, in southern England's Dorset, a region his novels call Wessex, its medieval name. Those stories of human and rural circumstance are still loved as books and films: *Far from the Madding Crowd, The Return of the Native, The Mayor of Casterbridge, The Wood-landers, Tess of the Durbervilles, Jude the Obscure.* But when his last novel was dubbed Jude the Obscene, Hardy turned to verse, publishing eight hundred old and new poems up to his death. The Victorian novelist became a modern poet, revered by Robert Frost, W. H. Auden, Dylan Thomas, Philip Larkin, Derek Walcott, and countless others.

Hardy's novels feel no more upbeat than his verse, though sometimes they end in weddings. One of them tells us, "happiness was but the occasional episode in a general drama of pain." In these books, weather and landscape touch every page, nature not simply echoing but looming over human destiny.

"Novels of Character and Environment," Hardy called them, joining two sides of life. Even before we meet Diggory Venn, who peddles red pigment to sheep farmers, *The Return of the Native* opens on Egdon Heath, a "heathy, furzy, briary wilderness . . . the untameable, Ishmaelitish thing." Ishmael we know—son of Abraham and Hagar, cast out in the wilderness (and the survivor in Melville's *Moby-Dick*). Through Hardy, American readers come to know furze, or gorse, a spiny yellow-flowered shrub cut for fodder, bedding, winter fuel, as we're drawn back into a pre-Christian landscape of pagan ritual.

Egdon, a huge Wessex heath that may once have housed King Lear, has a Druidic and Saxon past and goes deeper than human time. Hardy paints it as "somber," "embrowned," "waste," "gloom," "obscurity," "unenclosed wild," "exhaling darkness." Key events take place there, shaped and then absorbed by the implacable terrain.

Nature shadows if not actually determining the human condition in Hardy's poems too. "We stood by a pond that winter day," he'll say,

> And the sun was white, as though chidden of God,
> And a few leaves lay on the starving sod;
> —They had fallen from an ash, and were gray.

Instead of *ver perpetuum*, Eden's and Arcadia's perpetual green, winter is seldom far from Wessex, and any God there is, scolds humanity and nature both.

"The Darkling Thrush," written on the last day of the nineteenth century, starts this way:

> I leant upon a coppice gate,
> > When Frost was spectre-gray,
> And Winter's dregs made desolate
> > The weakening eye of day.

Even when a bird's "full-hearted evensong" bursts through "bleak twigs overhead," it's an "aged thrush, frail, gaunt, and small, / In blast-beruffled plume" that greets "the growing gloom." While Coleridge's "Frost at Midnight" has a "redbreast sit and sing / Betwixt the tufts of snow on the bare branch / Of mossy apple-tree," Hardy's mind of winter gave him listless breezes and leaden skies.

Behind this outlook a private ache matched his surroundings. In Cornwall in 1870, on the cliff-hung, sea-struck western coast near legendary Camelot, he fell in love with Emma Gifford. Eventually their marriage went askew, as she became withdrawn then deranged. Yet her death in 1912 provoked his finest poems, landscapes of remorse and loss impassioning memory.

Their forthright speech, rhythm, and rhyme save Hardy's lyrics from morbidness. "The Going," written just weeks after Emma died, wanders

> Where so often at dusk you used to be;
> Till in darkening dankness
> The yawning blankness
> Of the perspective sickens me!

Rhymes ending on an unstressed syllable already tweak the ear: "dankness / blankness." Leaving the last two syllables unstressed, "*used* to be / . . . *sick*ens me," can sound grotesque or comical. In this lament, where comical won't do but awkward will, Hardy takes that risk. We feel blank dusk spawning his haplessness.

However steeped in landscape and weather, these nostalgia-driven poems always foreground the human scene. "I Found Her Out There" tells how Emma could not be buried on the Cornish shore where they passionately met, but inland instead, in Dorset. Hardy's stanzas start with the much-missed woman, veer toward coastal scenes, then return to her.

> . . . I brought her here,
> And have laid her to rest
> In a noiseless nest
> No sea beats near.
> She will never be stirred
> In her loamy cell
> By the waves long heard
> And loved so well.
>
> So she does not sleep
> By those haunted heights
> The Atlantic smites
> And the blind gales sweep,
> Whence she often would gaze
> At Dundagel's famed head,
> While the dipping blaze
> Dyed her face fire-red.

Short lines drive home a stark seascape, as ocean "smites" the "heights" and three stresses make "blind gales sweep."

Why then "blind"? Indifferent to us, oblivious to her? A marine force in each stanza seems to moor the sundered couple: salt-edged air, beating sea, sweeping gales, flailing wind, throbbing swell. Hardy knew well the ocean of Matthew Arnold's "Dover Beach," "the grating roar / Of pebbles which the waves draw back, and fling, / At their return, up the high strand"—a wave-worn world holding no "certitude, nor peace, nor help for pain."

His sorrowing imagination contradicts Emma's own words for their first Cornwall meetings "at this very remote spot, with beautiful sea-coast, and the wild Atlantic ocean rolling in with its magnificent waves and spray, its white gulls and black choughs and grey puffins, its cliffs and rocks and gorgeous sun settings sparkling redness in a track widening from the horizon to the shore." She has a keen eye for the wintry scene, but "beautiful," "magnificent," "gorgeous" don't match "those haunted heights" where "blind gales sweep." His stark tone makes the lost moment true, makes it matter.

Estranged from his wife before she died, Hardy had met Florence, whom he would later marry. Of course she was hurt to hear his reaction to Emma's death: "Woman much missed, how you call to me, call to me." "Let me view you, then," he cries in "The Voice," "yes, as I knew you then, / Even to the original air-blue gown!" Published the year Florence married him, this poem ends

> faltering forward,
> Leaves around me falling,
> Wind oozing thin through the thorn from norward,
> And the woman calling.

Those falling rhythms, "*fal*tering . . . *fall*ing . . . *nor*ward . . . *call*ing," and cold wind "oozing thin" through a thorn tree, sink us in the poet's turf, where landscape presses on memory.

In body and spirit both, Hardy revisited his prime love's landscape. "After a Journey" opens on a perfect line that Hamlet could have uttered, "Hereto I come to view a voiceless ghost." Then come Hardy's bizarrest cadences and couplings:

> Whither, O whither will its whim now draw me?
> Up the cliff, down, till I'm lonely, lost,
> And the unseen waters' ejaculations awe me.

Emma's ghost has drawn him to Pentargan Bay, where creaturely life ignores them: "The waked birds preen and the seals flop lazily." Then his rhyme buckles present to past, assuring her that "though Life lours"—darkens, threatens—he'll always come back to where "Our days were a joy, and our paths through flowers."

Hardy's weather and terrain didn't fill notebooks of minute detail, as with Gerard Manley Hopkins. Chance and change in human affairs fascinated him more than the curve of a bluebell or watercourse. Nature looms and cuts into our lives. In one poem it literally undercuts a family's doings, as the title bodes.

"During Wind and Rain" deals with youthful Emma's happy, talented family.

> They sing their dearest songs—
> He, she, all of them—yea,
> Treble and tenor and bass,
>   And one to play;
> With the candles mooning each face. . . .
>   Ah, no; the years O!
> How the sick leaves reel down in throngs!
>
> They clear the creeping moss—
> Elders and juniors—aye,
> Making the pathways neat
>   And the garden gay;
> And they build a shady seat. . . .
>   Ah, no; the years, the years;
> See, the white storm-birds wing across!
>
> They are blithely breakfasting all—
> Men and maidens—yea,
> Under the summer tree,
>   With a glimpse of the bay,
> While pet fowl come to the knee. . . .
>   Ah, no; the years O!
> And the rotten rose is ript from the wall.
>
> They change to a high new house,
> He, she, all of them—aye,
> Clocks and carpets and chairs
>   On the lawn all day,
> And brightest things that are theirs. . . .
>   Ah, no; the years, the years;
> Down their carved names the rain-drop ploughs.

Emma's musical, convivial, privileged family is given lucid, easygoing verse. Nothing darkens the storytelling . . . until each stanza's ominous dots. Ellipsis marks something left out or leaving off. We're not told what, but it ruptures the fable, as his speech mutates from domestic idiom to classical lament.

"Ah, no; the years O!" Refrains in a ballad resound deeper than its narrative stanzas. Like a Greek chorus, they distill what's just been told or take it askew. Usually they close each stanza, so Hardy could have left off with "Ah, no; the years O!" and "Ah, no; the years, the years," jolting us into silence with Time's derision. But he doesn't. An earthbound force besets this family.

As the stanzas set out singing "songs," then clearing "moss," breakfasting "all," and changing "house," each of those words will need its rhyming mate. Yet by the time we reach the refrain, "Ah, no," there's still no rhyme and we've stopped listening for it. Only then does a final line, longer than the story lines or the refrain, fasten "throngs" onto "songs," "ript from the wall" onto "breakfasting all." Here as ever a poem's shaping, its body language, reveals something deeper than storytelling.

Hardy's title, "During Wind and Rain," makes each bottom line return with news from nature. Do you wonder how long this family aglow in candlelight will sing its songs? See "How the sick leaves reel down in throngs!" Whether a neat gay garden will keep back the creeping moss? "See, the white storm-birds wing across!" In gusting wind and rain, Coleridge found "Joy . . . wedding nature to us." Not Hardy. "Western wind when will thou blow, / The small rain down can rain?": this anonymous wind and rain slake the soil and bring voyagers home. Hardy sees no such luck. Sick leaves, storm birds bring winter violence, ripping our espaliered roses from the wall.

Meanwhile his music harshens. In the opening stanzas, three or four pleasing accents per line give way abruptly to six: "*How* the *sick leaves reel down* in *throngs*! . . . *See,* the *white storm-birds wing* a*cross*!" The next refrain quickens with triple alliteration: "And the *rotten rose* is *ript* from the *wall*." Finally the poem's last line, no further to go, starts with the adverb of catastrophe, "Down." Seven stresses drill through our human attempt to carve out permanence, even in death. They end on "ploughs," hinting at growth but grating rhymewise on the high new "house," eroding joy and memory itself—can a single raindrop do so much? "Down their carved names the rain-drop ploughs."

"freshness deep down things"
The World Charged by Gerard Manley Hopkins

Quoin, groin, veins, lobes, cusp, comb, cornice, sheath, spike,
spray, skeined, sleeve-pieces, shard-covered, shires of snow,
shoaling colors . . .

The poet-priest Gerard Manley Hopkins
(1844–1889) loved naming the things of earth and sea and air, pinpointing,
likening them to other things, and playing with names:

shallowing shore, crispings, cross-harrowed, grotted, whorled, wimpling,
ricked and sharply inscaped, flaked or foiled like fungus, zigzag brooks ravelled out and shining, the huddling and gnarls of the water, the dance and
swagging of the light green tongues or ripples of waves, the backdraught
shrugging the stones together.

All these are culled from his journals, where one day's entry can hold as many
as fifteen such items, the honeycomb cells of his imagination.

"Pied Beauty" goes into the world wild and wide-eyed, naming motley jostling life while packing all this earthliness within a pious frame.

Glory be to God for dappled things—
    For skies of couple-colour as a brinded cow;
        For rose-moles all in stipple upon trout that swim;
Fresh-firecoal chestnut-falls; finches' wings;
    Landscape plotted and pieced—fold, fallow, and plough;
        And all trades, their gear and tackle and trim.
All things counter, original, spare, strange;
    Whatever is fickle, freckled (who knows how?)
        With swift, slow; sweet, sour; adazzle, dim;

He fathers-forth whose beauty is past change:
                    Praise him.

Maybe "dappled" is familiar enough, and "couple-colour" will make sense, but much else sounds odd. The best Hopkins anthology explains only one word, "brinded" as archaic for "brindled" (a cow's tawny coat flecked with darker color). But "stipple," small dots, or "pied," meaning speckled? For an orthodox believer bound to religious rule, Hopkins nourishes an unorthodox love of what's idiosyncratic. His poetry wrestles language into fresh revealings.

Not only the pied, dappled, brindled, stippled particulars of the created world arouse Hopkins, but speaking them does too. He treasured the word hoard English inherits from its native Anglo-Saxon rather than its Latin base. He'll charge a line with seven stresses: "*Frésh-firecóal chést*nut-*fálls; fínches' wíngs*," or interweave their rhymes: "things/cow/swim, wings/plough/trim, strange/how/dim, change/him." He'll set vowels resonating and consonants ticking. All this music, as Hopkins said of the composer Henry Purcell, "throngs the ear."

Now what—to borrow his question about Spring—"What is all this juice and all this joy," this revel in earthly beauty, doing in the mouth of a priest who vows fleshly abstinence? Is it all AMDG, as the Jesuits say, *ad majorem Dei gloriam*, for the greater glory of God? After all, "Pied Beauty" frames the natural scene between "Glory" and "Praise." But to sense only sacral energy in him reduces Hopkins. Before converting to Catholicism, at age eighteen he was composing Keatsian verse about Summer's "lusty hands, in gusts of scented wind / Swirling out bloom till all the air is blind," verse thirsting for sweetness: "Plum-purple was the west." Later this avid spirit would have him fusing nature's earthly and divine radiance.

When Hopkins entered Oxford University in 1863, the Austrian botanist and Catholic priest Gregor Mendel's cross-breeding of peas was starting up modern genetics, and Darwin's *Origin of Species* exciting the Oxford debate between science and religion. God's presence in nature Hopkins certainly held dear, and why shouldn't that belief support a passionate naturalist, even an environmentalist?

Turning Catholic at twenty-two, then Jesuit, Hopkins committed to an ascetic existence. He burned his early poems (so he thought) as too worldly, yet nothing quenched his gusto for earth's material glories. Britain's finest religious poet was also the "finest of English poets of nature," as Robert Lowell called him. That mix, which later spurred Denise Levertov among others, fuels the sonnet "God's Grandeur," written when Hopkins broke a long poetic silence. Its first line echoes Psalm 19, "The heavens declare the glory of God," but shifts that focus from heaven to earth:

The world is charged with the grandeur of God.
  It will flame out, like shining from shook foil;
  It gathers to a greatness, like the ooze of oil
Crushed. Why do men then now not reck his rod?
Generations have trod, have trod, have trod;
  And all is seared with trade; bleared, smeared with toil;
  And wears man's smudge and shares man's smell: the soil
Is bare now, nor can foot feel, being shod.

And for all this, nature is never spent;
  There lives the dearest freshness deep down things;
And though the last lights off the black West went
  Oh, morning, at the brown brink eastward, springs—
Because the Holy Ghost over the bent
  World broods with warm breast and with ah! bright wings.

Framing makes some but not all the difference, as in "Pied Beauty." Beginning and ending, God and the Holy Ghost embrace a threatened world.

This world is "charged," like the word itself: stored with electric energy, loaded, entrusted, assailed. To his friend Robert Bridges, Hopkins explained "shining from shook foil" in a letter no less crackling with energy: "I mean foil in its sense of leaf or tinsel. . . . Shaken goldfoil gives off broad glares like sheet lightning and also, and this is true of nothing else, owing to its zigzag dints and creasings and network of small many cornered facets, a sort of fork lightning too."

He sounds drunk on the tone, taste, texture of words, and the way they move. An olive press stresses all ten syllables—"Crushed. Why do men then now not reck his rod?"—and not for wordplay alone. Failure to heed divine will was wasting his world, as Hopkins looked around him. In 1877, the year of "God's Grandeur," agricultural depression was setting in, farmhands leaving for the city, technology breeding brutality, poverty, misery, and railways enmeshing the land. Anglo-Saxon "trod," overriding its rhyme word "God," acts out this wasting process, as does the grinding of "seared . . . bleared, smeared."

Then by grace of a sonnet's form, the weighty eight-line octave gives way to a sestet of fresh perception. After those industrially crowded monosyllables,

And all is seared with trade: bleared, smeared with toil;
  And wears man's smudge, and shares man's smell: the soil
Is bare now, nor can foot feel, being shod,

the breath turns limber for a promise, a blessing: "nature is never spent; / There lives the dearest freshness deep down things."

Now the prime example we humans have drawn from nature, night turning to day, brings a spiritual lift. Out of blackness arises morning

Because the Holy Ghost over the bent
　World broods with warm breast and with bright wings.

Why bent? With toil, humility, ruin of God's creation? The last line alone works wonders. Earlier accents on *w* and *b*, "West went" and "brown brink," return threefold and interwoven: the "World broods with warm breast and with bright wings."

But wait! One syllable's missing, so Hopkins adds a stress to fill out the line: "with warm breast and with *ah!* bright wings." Sheer craft makes this happen. An astonished indrawn breath turns meter into revelation.

You can hear that breath when the American poet Stanley Kunitz, at ninety-five, reads aloud "God's Grandeur" because in his twenties he'd found it "so fierce and eloquent. . . . I knew that it was speaking directly to me and giving me a hint of the kind of poetry that I would be dedicated to for the rest of my life."

Can we subtract divinity and still feel the full charge, in Hopkins's world? "Spring," another sonnet, starts "all in a rush / With richness":

Nothing is so beautiful as Spring—
　When weeds, in wheels, shoot long and lovely and lush;
　Thrush's eggs look little low heavens, and thrush
Through the echoing timber does so rinse and wring
The ear, it strikes like lightnings to hear him sing.

Pure mundane ecstasy, though more slips through: "thrush's eggs look little low heavens." They don't just look *like* blue sky, the eggs *look* little low heavens, we see heaven *through* them.

Especially while Hopkins was abstaining from poetry, the journals teem with his surroundings. He never tires of spotting, and often sketching, the "horned waves" of a glacier, "spray-end" of an ash stem, "silver bellies" of flouncing fresh-caught mackerel, noticing then noting the organic shape, pattern, color, sound, movement of things, now and then exalting them. One fall night, the Northern Lights' "soft pulses" rising upward "wholly independent of the earth" in space and time gave "a new witness to God and filled me with delightful fear." Yet even then he thrives on detail.

Steaming across the Irish Sea from Isle of Man to Liverpool, only Hopkins on board could have seen crests "ravelled up by the wind into the air in arching whips and straps of glassy spray and higher broken into clouds of white and blown away. Under the curl shone a bright juice of beautiful green. The foam exploding and smouldering under water makes a chrysoprase green"— chrysoprase being a semiprecious quartz. Or take the opening of a brilliant sonnet,

As kingfishers catch fire, dragonflies draw flame;
As tumbled over rim in roundy wells
Stones ring; like each tucked string tells, each hung bell's
Bow swung finds tongue to fling out broad its name,

where each person and thing

Deals out that being indoors each one dwells;
Selves—goes itself; *myself* it speaks and spells.

Light glinting off birds and insects, stones resounding down a well, tense violin strings, a bell's clapper, animate and so-called inanimate nature sing out their names. Their *anima* or soul so seizes Hopkins he invents the verb "selve."

Right here, in the idea of selving, his concerns unite: nature, divinity, poetry. Each mortal thing's singular vitality gives it divine charge. "There lives the dearest freshness deep down things." That freshness, like poetry, speaks and spells God. For the unique, indwelling design of a thing he coined the term inscape, while the force sustaining an inscape and impressing it on us he called instress. In other words, form and energy. And form and energy, fused "like shining from shook foil," means ecstasy: "kingfishers catch fire, dragonflies draw flame."

Call it sacred or profane, Hopkins craved ecstasy, what Lowell called his "inebriating exuberance." Poetry gave him a discipline for that, harnessing energy, shaping rhythmic and verbal exuberance. "This morning I saw a hawk," we would say. "The Windhover" says,

I caught this morning morning's minion, King-
   dom of daylight's dauphin, dapple-dawn-drawn Falcon, in his riding
Of the rolling level underneath him steady air, and striding
High there, how he wrung upon the rein of a wimpling wing
In his ecstasy!

However these syncopations behave—"read it with the ears," Hopkins hopefully said, "and my verse becomes all right"—the speaker's ecstasy fuels the hawk's.

Ecstasy over a bird. Not surprisingly, Hopkins felt a lifelong closeness to John Keats. "My grandfather was a surgeon, a fellow-student of Keats," he told Bridges, and recalled that his schoolmaster "would praise Keats by the hour." Hopkins prized "To Autumn" and held up Keats as one (like himself) whose "beautiful works have been almost unknown and then have gained fame at last."

When trees near Keats's house in Hampstead were threatened with cutting down, Hopkins's father published some protesting verse. Later, hurt by "the decline of wild nature," Hopkins writes a sonnet deploring Oxford's growth into a manufacturing hub: "Thou hast a base and brackish skirt. . . . Thou hast confounded / Rural, rural keeping—folk, flocks, and flowers." He liked walking to a village across the Thames River where aspens in a double row hung over the towpath. One letter reports, "I am sorry to say that the aspens that lined the river are everyone felled." Why? For use as "shoes," locomotive brake blocks for the Great Western Railway penetrating the Thames valley.

"Binsey Poplars" has this note: "felled 1879."

> My aspens dear, whose airy cages quelled,
> Quelled or quenched in leaves the leaping sun,
> All felled, felled, are all felled;
>   Of a fresh and following folded rank
>   Not spared, not one
>   That dandled a sandalled
>   Shadow that swam or sank
> On meadow and river and wind-wandering weed-winding bank.
>
> O if we but knew what we do
>   When we delve or hew—
>   Hack and rack the growing green! . . .
> After-comers cannot guess the beauty been.
>   Ten or twelve, only ten or twelve
>   Strokes of havoc unselve
>   The sweet especial scene,
>   Rural scene, a rural scene,
>   Sweet especial rural scene.

Nowadays we'd welcome public transit. Back then, his anguish pulls out all the stops: repeating sounds, rhythmic surprise, rare wording. These lines have often been set to music, and Hopkins himself loved composing. Once he put some eighteenth-century pastoral verse to music: "I groped in my soul's very viscera for the tune and thrummed the sweetest and most secret catgut of the mind." His poems live on this word music, though few with the environmental fervor of "Binsey Poplars."

What's more, he was a draftsman who early on hoped to become a painter. Visually, nothing fascinated Hopkins more than rushing water. Writing about a swift brook "roaring down" into Loch Lomond, he asks,

> What would the world be, once bereft
> Of wet and wildness? Let them be left,
> O let them be left, wildness and wet;
> Long live the weeds and the wilderness yet.

Ted Hughes called this one of those poems that "are better . . . than actual landscapes." Even Hopkins's peace-seeking "Heaven-Haven," subtitled "A nun takes the veil," goes to the sea for elemental force:

> And I have asked to be
> > Where no storms come,
> Where the green swell is in the havens dumb,
> > And out of the swing of the sea.

Longing for quiet, he still can't keep the sea's rolling cadence out of his final line.

Why did water so grip Hopkins? His journals abound with cloud, rain, rainbow, pool, brook, river, sea, surf, gorge, glacier, and waterfall in the British Isles and continental Europe.

> July 20 [1873]—Water high at Hodder Roughs; where lit from within looking like pale gold, elsewhere velvety brown like ginger syrop; heavy locks or brushes like shaggy rope-ends rolling from a corner of the falls and one huddling over another; below the rock the bubble-jostled skirt of foam jumping back against the fall, which cuts its way clean and will not let it through, and there spitting up in long white ragged shots and bushes like a mess of thongs of bramble, and I saw by looking over nearer that those looping watersprigs that lace and dance and jockey in the air are strung of single drops, the end one, like a tassel or a heavier bead, the biggest; they look like bubbles in a quill.

Just one sentence, shot through with six similes (gold, syrup, rope-ends . . .) and six metaphors (velvet, brushes, skirt . . .). A rage for figures of speech grasps what's ungraspable: water like syrup, foam as a skirt. And look nearer, how these images momentarily "catch" something liquid without snagging it, to see it as stable shape. Falling, rolling, jumping, spitting water becomes bushes, bramble, "looping watersprigs," that is, twigs of water—a paradox resolved, a sort of miracle.

Hiking in the Swiss Alps, Hopkins grumbles that having a companion dilutes his ecstasy. He got that ecstasy in waterfalls, whose explosive flux also excited Wordsworth, Coleridge, Keats, Muir, plus countless artists and photographers. At Reichenbach Falls it took "discharges of rice . . . falling vandykes [trim beards]" to capture, for the mind's eye, races and rills and blown vapor cascading among the rocks.

The next day "We saw Handeck waterfall . . . the greatest fall we have seen," Hopkins writes. "I watched the great bushes of foam-water, the texture of branchings and water-spandrils which makes them up. At their outsides nearest the rock they gave off showers of drops strung together into little quills which sprang out in fans," and later "in jostling foam-bags." Of course there were no bags, quills, or fans, no bushes, branches, or spandrils—architectural triangles. Only attentiveness shapes and stays the falls that aren't really staying at all.

Something it is about waterfalls! Though no Darwinian, Hopkins would have thrilled at a chimpanzee in Tanzania's Gombe Stream National Park, swinging wildly in front of a waterfall, dipping his hand and rolling rocks down its face, then sitting and staring at the falls for minutes on end.

A small water-born event rivets Hopkins on the Isle of Man, between England and Ireland, and also prompts a notebook sketch. "We passed the beautiful little mill-hamlet of Balaglas in the glen and started a shining flight of doves," his account begins. They climb up a forceful brook where

> Round holes are scooped in the rocks smooth and true like turning: they look like the hollow of a vault or bowl. I saw and sketched as well as in the rain I could one of them that was in the making: a blade of water played on it and shaping to it spun off making a bold big white bow coiling its edge over and splaying into ribs.

Hopkins had "jumped into one of the pools above knee deep," so when he got home in heavy rain, "Mr. Sidgreaves covered me under his plaid."

Those round scooped holes catch his gaze, they're "smooth and true like turning," as if turned on a lathe. In his sketch, Hopkins is looking downstream at a "blade" of rushing water playing against the hollow and the "bold big white bow coiling its edge." Again and again his verbs enliven nouns, force animates form, proving "nature is never spent." His sketching hand works hardest on the rock's scooped bowl, especially how its dark hue shows through the spun-off coil of spray, a constant bow shape formed from flow. We've all spotted such events in a creek, brook, stream, or river—Coleridge saw a "*white rose* of Eddy-foam" in the River Greta—but seldom with such exact passion for their inscape and instress, design and energy. Nature lives this way, and so does poetry.

All this is not to say that Gerard Manley Hopkins spent his days exploring. Wed to the Society of Jesus, he studied, taught, preached, and ministered in England, Wales, Scotland, and Ireland. His duties and sometimes his doubts, on top of poor health, wore on him, and in 1885 what are known as the Terrible Sonnets emerged. They deal with agony, wrestling: "No worst, there is none. Pitched past pitch of grief." Despite—and because of—despair, he reaches for what language can do, risking a rich pun on "pitch" (throw, slope, height or depth, black tar). The same verve Hopkins gave to God's grandeur and the windhover's ecstasy takes the Alps as psychic terrain:

> O the mind, mind has mountains; cliffs of fall
> Frightful, sheer, no-man-fathomed. Hold them cheap
> May who ne'er hung there. Nor does long our small
> Durance deal with that steep or deep. Here! creep,
> Wretch, under a comfort serves in a whirlwind: all
> Life death does end and each day dies with sleep.

Two lines here strain endurance by drumming on ten monosyllables. And words get cramped in "mind, mind . . . Life death," like a tense snare about to be sprung.

Gerard Manley Hopkins, Balaglas, Isle of Man. Aug. 12, '73.
From *Journals and Papers* by Gerard Manley Hopkins (1937), copyright by permission of Oxford University Press on behalf of The British Province of the Society of Jesus.

The deep-down freshness even in painful turns of speech helped Hopkins pass through this agony: "leave comfort root-room," he tells himself, and his next poems touch on workingmen and the unemployed. One sonnet he liked particularly praises Harry Ploughman:

> Hard as hurdle arms, with a broth of goldish flue
> Breathed round.

Plowmen were growing scarce even in Hopkins's day, and anyway we've forgotten his metaphors' rural sense: "hurdle," a wood frame used in fences, and "flue," a light down or fluff. But he had misgivings in evoking Harry's

> rack of ribs; the scooped flank; lank
> Rope-over thigh; knee-nave; and barrelled shank—

These bodily shapings, tracing the inscape of God's creature—do they get too intimate, touching the plowman's "barrowy brawn"?

> He leans to it, Harry bends, look. Back, elbow, and liquid waist
> In him.

"I always knew in my heart Walt Whitman's mind to be more like my own than any other man's living," Hopkins said once. "As he is a very great scoundrel this is not a pleasant confession."

What else there was of Whitman in him, Hopkins needn't have regretted either: a fearless way with words that broke and sowed new ground for modern poetry. Though the American's long breath lines and ceaseless democratic "Song of Myself" have little in common with the Briton's taut sonnets and God-struck humility, they do share a mortal love and vital touch for even the meanest earthly matter. "And what is Earth's eye, tongue, or heart else, where / Else, but in dear and dogged man?" Hopkins, but it could be Whitman speaking. Both poets owned great nerve, "Crying *What I do is me: for that I came*" and sounding "the dearest freshness deep down things."

Like Emily Dickinson, who had that nerve and oddness too, Hopkins honed earthbound things to a spiritual edge. And like her, he published almost no poems during his lifetime. Dying of typhoid at forty-four, he composed a psalmlike lament: "See," the thickets are rife with crisp green herbage "and fresh wind shakes / Them; birds build—but not I build." Yet he did, in spading language to pray this way: "Mine, O thou lord of life, send my roots rain." Eventually the poems came out, and their wakening, their delight-delivering force is never spent.

"O honey bees, / Come build in the empty house of the stare"

Nature Versus History in W. B. Yeats

"I had still the ambition, formed in Sligo in my teens, of living in imitation of Thoreau on Innisfree." Born in 1865, rooted in west Ireland's County Galway, William Butler Yeats died shortly before World War II broke out in 1939. Spanning the decades from Victorian to modern, his poems took on every question: love, sexuality, transience, age, death, local place and legend, mythic past and visionary future, nobility vis-à-vis common folk, country and city, dreams and responsibilities, private as against public, spiritual and earthly life, nature versus history. All this mattered in the world at large and vitally in his craft. "Out of the quarrel with others we make rhetoric," he said, "of the quarrel with ourselves, poetry."

One day in London, feeling homesick, Yeats suddenly remembered a small island in a lake near Sligo, and Thoreau at Walden Pond. Published in 1892 (the year John Muir founded California's Sierra Club), "The Lake Isle of Innisfree" springs from that Romantic yearning toward a distant mythic place.

> I will arise and go now, and go to Innisfree,
> And a small cabin build there, of clay and wattles made;
> Nine bean rows will I have there, a hive for the honey bee,
> And live alone in the bee-loud glade.
>
> And I shall have some peace there, for peace comes dropping slow,
> Dropping from the veils of the morning to where the cricket sings;

There midnight's all a glimmer, and noon a purple glow,
And evening full of the linnet's wings.

I will arise and go now, for always night and day
I hear lake water lapping with low sounds by the shore;
While I stand on the roadway, or on the pavements gray,
I hear it in the deep heart's core.

Though Yeats's yen for Innisfree (pronounced "Innishfree," meaning Heather Island) hasn't much in common with the cabin Thoreau actually built on a pond near Boston, he feels a kindred impulse to get away from society and revive the spirit. As Thoreau says in *Walden,* "The mass of men lead lives of quiet desperation."

"I will arise and go now." Knowingly or not, Yeats is echoing Robert Louis Stevenson. In *A Child's Garden of Verses,* "Travel" begins, "I should like to rise and go / . . . Where below another sky / Parrot islands anchored lie." Stevenson himself had gone to Samoa in the South Seas, whence he wrote praising Yeats's "artful simplicity" in "The Lake Isle of Innisfree." He doesn't mention the borrowing. In any case, Yeats reaching toward an island "below another sky" taps into childlike genius.

About poetry we often wonder, Does style drive content or vice-versa? The answer is yes. "Innisfree" was Yeats's first lyric with "my own music," for music means every bit as much as meaning here. An early draft even has noontide not midnight "all a glimmer," and midnight not noon "a purple glow" of heather! Evidently the facts of nature must yield, to get him from "pavements gray" to "lake water lapping."

Happily for the music, Yeats recited "The Lake Isle of Innisfree" on the BBC, an old man voicing a young man's poem. "I am going to read my poems with great *em*phasis upon the *rhythm*," he announces. "It gave me a devil of a lot of trouble to get [them] into verse, and that is why I *will* not read them as if they were prose." We then hear a throaty resonant chant of weighted cadences and Irish inflections: "Oy will uh*roy-y-se* ond go now, ond *go-o-o* to Innish*free-e-e* . . ." Each stanza gets a startling music on the last word, raising the pitch for "bee-loud *gla-a-ade*" and "linnet's *wi-i-ings*." Then three stressed syllables close the poem, "deep heart's core," rising from a profundo "*deep hahrt's*" to a higher drawn-out tone on "*caw-w-wr*." Poetry is not ordinary speech, it partakes of inspiration, vision, oracle, carrying us from humdrum *here* to a mythic *there*. Yeats's "there" itself resounds four times in six lines.

Civilization's dream is to get away from it all to another place, classical Arcadia, Coleridge's Xanadu, the "Country-green" of Keats's nightingale. Yeats goes into Celtic woods:

Who will go drive with Fergus now,
And pierce the deep wood's woven shade,
And dance upon the level shore?
Young man, lift up your russet brow,
And lift your tender eyelids, maid,
And brood on hopes and fears no more.

And no more turn aside and brood
Upon love's bitter mystery;
For Fergus rules the brazen cars,
And rules the shadows of the wood,
And the white breast of the dim sea
And all dishevelled wandering stars.

Shadowy, dim, disheveled may unnerve us, but Yeats had more in mind. King
Fergus of ancient Ulster, a hero and poet as well, abdicated to live in the woods.
That gesture seized Yeats from early on. He cherished Irish myth, legend, folk
imagination, and a tension was already pulling on him, between poetry and
power, intellect and action, country and city. So he sets it all to music, entrust-
ing life and nature to well-woven four-beat verse.

Celtic folk tradition never let Yeats go. At twenty-three he edited *Irish Fairy
and Folk Tales*, to breed popular consciousness. Fairies, ghosts, legendary he-
roes—he takes this fabulous world at face value. His entry on banshees, female
spirits whose wild wailing portends a death, reports confidently that "at Dullahan" one of them hurled a bucket of blood in a peasant's face. He adds a sort
of proof: "Mr. and Mrs. S. C. Hall give the following notation of the banshee's
cry," and there on a treble staff is a spine-chilling cry!

Throughout his half-century career, Irish places and place-names bind Yeats
to the landscape. In this ballad, "salley" is a willow tree:

Down by the salley gardens my love and I did meet;
She passed the salley gardens with little snow-white feet.
She bid me take love easy, as the leaves grow on the tree;
But I, being young and foolish, with her would not agree.

First Yeats called this "An Old Song Resung," as it was "an extension of three
lines sung to me by an old woman at Ballisodare." Enlisting in the tradition,
he weaves his own words into a lilting Irish melody. What counts is popular
lineage, re-rooting him in native soil: "an old woman" sang "to me . . . at Ballisodare," a village near Sligo.

Place names—Sligo, Innisfree, Dullahan, Ballisodare, Coole, Ballylee, Drum-
cliff, Ben Bulben—charmed him no less than the natural scene behind them.
Whereas Gerard Manley Hopkins fastened on organic detail, with Yeats our
senses don't feel alerted to wind, moon, stream, lake, seashore, rock, woodland,

tree, flower, bird. Instead, like Blake (whose poems he published) and Hardy, he makes them symbols. Crickets singing and lake water lapping at Innisfree betoken peace, Fergus rules the sea and stars.

Nature served to offset politics, history, personal experience, especially after the Easter Rebellion when Irish nationalists revolted in Dublin. Britain executed the leaders, throwing Yeats into doubt over bravery and rashness, action and decorum. "All changed, changed utterly: / A terrible beauty is born," runs the refrain in "Easter 1916." The poem asks if historic emergency ennobles or coarsens men and women, if zeal and fanaticism sacrifice human fineness. Yet one surprising stanza shifts away from politics. With brief lines turning on idiomatic rhymes, Yeats simply depicts "the living stream" and "birds that range / From cloud to tumbling cloud."

> Minute by minute they change;
> A shadow of cloud on the stream
> Changes minute by minute;
> A horse-hoof slides on the brim,
> And a horse plashes within it;
> The long-legged moor-hens dive,
> And hens to moor-cocks call;
> Minute by minute they live:
> The stone's in the midst of all.

Because the stone of political monomania can only momentarily "trouble the living stream" of natural change, this one stanza needs no refrain claiming that "A terrible beauty is born." Hearty play between moorcocks and moorhens, changing yet unchanged, survives the convulsion that brought forth independent Eire.

Soon after Easter 1916, Yeats visited his friend Lady Gregory's Coole Park estate. The place reminds him how years before, when he was young, wild swans would

> All suddenly mount
> And scatter wheeling in great broken rings
> Upon their clamorous wings. . . .
> Unwearied still, lover by lover,
> They paddle in the cold
> Companionable streams or climb the air.

The words catch a wild avian energy—"suddenly mount . . . scatter wheeling . . . clamorous wings . . . paddle in the cold . . . climb the air"—but the swans drive home a poet's loneliness: "I have looked upon those brilliant creatures, / And now my heart is sore." Years later, again remembering "sudden thunder of the mounting swan," Yeats finds "Another emblem there!"—"Nature's . . . a mirror of my mood."

Another brilliant bird turns emblem in Yeats's apocalypse "The Second Coming":

> Turning and turning in the widening gyre
> The falcon cannot hear the falconer;
> Things fall apart; the centre cannot hold.

He never practiced the noble sport of falconry, but if it offers such recognitions—

> The best lack all conviction, while the worst
> Are full of passionate intensity

—so much the better. At any time, those words may apply.

Once, during the unrest provoked by Irish rebellion, Yeats composed a perfect poem, "The Stare's Nest by My Window," balancing nature with history, birds and bees with firsthand human experience. "In the west of Ireland," he notes, "we call a starling a stare, and during the civil war, one built a nest in a hole in the masonry by my bedroom window." This time his refrain rounds off all four stanzas, moving from "honey-bees" through political mayhem toward a cry for regeneration, "O honey-bees, / Come build . . ."

> The bees build in the crevices
> Of loosening masonry, and there
> The mother bird brings grubs and flies.
> My wall is loosening; honey-bees,
> Come build in the empty house of the stare.
>
> We are closed in, and the key is turned
> On our uncertainty; somewhere
> A man is killed, or a house burned.
> Yet no clear fact to be discerned:
> Come build in the empty house of the stare.
>
> A barricade of stone or of wood;
> Some fourteen days of civil war:
> Last night they trundled down the road
> That dead young soldier in his blood:
> Come build in the empty house of the stare.
>
> We had fed the heart on fantasies,
> The heart's grown brutal from the fare,
> More substance in our enmities
> Than in our love; O honey-bees,
> Come build in the empty house of the stare.

Lines of terse idiom ending on a refrain, two rhymes per stanza with one of them always on "stare," telling detail ("loosening masonry," "grubs and flies") and anecdote (a "house burned," a soldier "trundled down the road") blending with broad confessional truths ("We are closed in . . .," "We had fed the heart on fantasies . . ."), and finally that stark cry: "O honey-bees, / Come build in the empty house of the stare"—only a poet's lifelong quarrel with himself could bring it off.

As long as Yeats struggled to unite private, public, and visionary experience within a poem, he had to be questioning art itself. "Sailing to Byzantium" tests the saving grace of art against a touchstone of natural process not yet spoiled by human action:

> The salmon-falls, the mackerel-crowded seas,
> Fish, flesh, or fowl, commend all summer long
> Whatever is begotten, born, and dies.

Art, art takes a lasting shape that flesh can't deliver:

> Once out of nature I shall never take
> My bodily form from any natural thing,
> But such a form as Grecian goldsmiths make
> Of hammered gold and gold enamelling.

Somewhere he'd read of artisans setting a golden bird "upon a golden bough," nature transformed into art. Yet once there they sing

> To lords and ladies of Byzantium
> Of what is past, or passing, or to come.

Great art, yes, but still it sings of mortal nature, the changing stream of what's begotten, born, and dies—those spawning "salmon-falls," like the moorhens calling moorcocks in "Easter 1916."

Yeats's sense of mortality led to ever-stronger writing. In July 1936, with war looming, he wrote "Lapis Lazuli," prompted by the eighteenth-century Chinese stone a young poet had given him. (plates 7 and 8) First Yeats looks to tragic Hamlet and Lear for blazing joy. Then he turns to this deep-blue gemstone, a mountain scene with three men climbing, carved into lapis lazuli so that

> Every discoloration of the stone,
> Every accidental crack or dent,
> Seems a water-course or an avalanche,
> Or lofty slope where it still snows
> Though doubtless plum or cherry-branch
> Sweetens the little half-way house
> Those Chinamen climb towards.

It's no small feat, turning accident into art and nature both. It takes guessing, imagining into the stone: "doubtless plum or cherry-branch . . ." Then Yeats

Lapis lazuli stone, Chinese, eighteenth century.
Courtesy of David Parker, and of A. P. Watt Ltd. on behalf of Gráinne Yeats.

Lapis lazuli stone, back.
Courtesy of A. P. Watt Ltd. and the National Library of Ireland.

moves deeper than possible into this carved lapis. One man "Carries a musical instrument," which is true, but another, we're told, "asks for mournful melodies," and "Their ancient, glittering eyes, are gay."

Writing his own epitaph, W. B. Yeats turned death into art on the ground of a long-lived landscape. "Under Ben Bulben" takes its title from a mountain near Sligo where he spent his childhood. Embedding place-names in verse, the poem ends:

> Under bare Ben Bulben's head
> In Drumcliff churchyard Yeats is laid.
> An ancestor was rector there
> Long years ago, a church stands near,
> By the road an ancient cross.
> No marble, no conventional phrase;
> On limestone quarried near the spot
> By his command these words are cut:
>> *Cast a cold eye*
>> *On life, on death.*
>> *Horseman, pass by!*

His own words—and "On limestone quarried near the spot."

PART TWO

"strangeness from my sight"
Robert Frost and the Fun in How You Say a Thing

"Go forth, under the open sky, and list / To Nature's teachings." Though the advice and the meter fit, Robert Frost (1874–1963) could never have penned this, with its clichés and archaic "list" for "listen." William Cullen Bryant, the popular nineteenth-century poet and journalist, was musing on mortality and coined this antidote that Frost's mother, herself a mystically inclined poet, would quote at home. She also recited Bryant's "To a Waterfowl" so often that one day at thirteen, cutting leather in a shoemaker's shed, Robbie found he could say the whole poem by heart. When Frost later went forth under the open sky, Nature's teachings caught his eye and ear, but in quite another idiom:

> Speaking of contraries, see how the brook
> In that white wave runs counter to itself.
> It is from that in water we were from
> Long, long before we were from any creature.

How he arrived at shaping such sentences shows American poetry evolving into twentieth-century speech.

Born in San Francisco when Emerson and Whitman were flourishing, Frost lived to speak a poem at John F. Kennedy's 1961 inaugural. This homespun poet, however, had uneven beginnings. While his mother lavished attention, his father was given to unstable employment, political adventuring, gambling, drinking, "dalliance," and brutality mixed with fervor toward his son. During the boy's early years his home moved constantly. Yet the still-young city and environs of San Francisco held plenty to grow on: the peninsula's neighborhoods, hills, surrounding waters and islands, ocean dunes, tides, Seal Rocks, and across the as-yet-unbridged Golden Gate, Sausalito's harbor, Mount Tamalpais, hills and woods around Nicasio, Napa Valley fields. An after-dinner family walk below the city's Cliff House around 1880 led to his first lines on nature, "Song of the Wave," and much later to the "shattered water," battered shore, and "night of dark intent" in "Once by the Pacific."

Frost's West Coast genesis ended at eleven when his father died and his mother took him and his sister east for good. Yankee terrain and temper seemed cold at first, but Rob and Jeanie came to know southeast New Hampshire: farm, wood, meadowland, thickets, streams, dirt roads, stone walls, apple orchards, berry-picking, first snowfall. One winter day Rob filled a thimble with water and put it on the windowsill overnight. Next morning he tapped out the mold of ice, set it on a wood stove, and watched it melt. Decades later this gave him "the figure a poem makes": "It begins in delight and ends in wisdom. . . . Like a piece of ice on a hot stove the poem must ride on its own melting."

Swinging birches, tracking animals, scything grass, tossing hay, becoming "versed in country things" went along with a passion for reading, history, Latin, and Frost's ventures as editor of his high school paper. He absorbed Emerson on self-reliance and a poet's cheerfulness, which comes from sunlight, air, water, Emerson said, and "from every pine-stump and half-imbedded stone, on which the dull March sun shines." Frost later recalled "first thinking about my own language" via Emerson: "'Cut these sentences and they bleed,' he says . . . he had me there."

Thoreau primed him too: "A true account of the actual is the rarest poetry." In one of Frost's teenage poems, "Clear and Colder," Boston Common looks

> bright with the light of day,
> For the wind and rain had swept the leaves
> And the shadow of summer away.
> The walks were all fresh-blacked with rain.

That "fresh-blacked with rain" smacks of Thoreau's "actual." As a senior, Frost bought the first two volumes of Dickinson's poems and read them to his sweetheart Elinor.

> I reason, Earth is short—
> And Anguish—absolute—
> And many hurt—
> But, what of that?

Dickinson's dry, terse, spoken idiom and slant rhymes hit home, along with her troublings over mortality and divinity. Shakespeare's plays gave him the vigor, the rightness of getting human speech into blank verse, iambic pentameter. Also Hardy's novels "taught me the good use of a few words."

What drove Frost was the absolute value of making poems matter, and fueling that drive was personal pain: his father's death, his grandparents' sternness, his mother's hard times as a teacher. Since childhood he'd felt insecure about his own worth, sensitive to affront, jealous of anyone who might outdo him, even of his betrothed, who also wrote poems and was his co-valedictorian. After school she kept putting off marrying him, until in 1894 he did something desperate. In one day, by train and steamer and foot, he got himself south to the Virginia–North Carolina border and started walking mud roads near a canal into the jungly, snake-infested Dismal Swamp, trying to throw his life away. Toward midnight he stumbled on a canal boat, and for a dollar they took him out of the swamp. Walking, hopping freight cars, taking a night in jail and working for a few days, eventually he wrote his mother for rail fare and returned home after twenty-four days. A year later he and Elinor married.

With his wife pregnant in rural New Hampshire, Frost would wander in search of flowers for her. Botanizing started, that summer of 1896, with a poem called "The Quest of the Orchis": "I skirted the margin alders for miles and miles" until "putting the boughs aside," he found "The far-sought flower." Reverence, a keen eye, plus a knack for getting the name and nature of things into verse, stamped his work from then on.

A decisive turn, the road taken, occurred in October 1900 when Frost moved to a thirty-acre farm near Derry, New Hampshire, with Elinor and a baby daughter. Their son had just died from infant cholera. That loss, plus the death of his mother and a long rough winter, dropped him into despair and worse. But the farm had everything—woodlot, hayfield, stone walls, pasture spring, apple trees, wild flowers, berry bushes, paths to cut, west-running brook— and come spring, his mood picked up. "To the Thawing Wind" says "Find the brown beneath the white" and "Turn the poet out of door." "Mowing" catches "my long scythe whispering to the ground." Three more children came during the Derry years. "We were showing the country things to the children as they came along. We had apples pears peaches plums cherries grapes blackberries raspberries cranberries and blueberries of our own." "A Prayer in Spring," celebrating orchard, bees, and hummingbirds, concludes: "For this is love and nothing else is love."

Even the dreaded onset of autumn prompts a genial prayer, "October," weaving slow supple lines with simple and surprising rhymes.

O hushed October morning mild,
Thy leaves have ripened to the fall;

Tomorrow's wind, if it be wild,
Should waste them all.
The crows above the forest call;
Tomorrow they may form and go.
O hushed October morning mild,
Begin the hours of this day slow.
Make the day seem to us less brief.
Hearts not averse to being beguiled,
Beguile us in the way you know.
Release one leaf at break of day;
At noon release another leaf;
One from our trees, one far away.
Retard the sun with gentle mist;
Enchant the land with amethyst.
Slow, slow!
For the grapes' sake, if they were all,
Whose leaves already are burnt with frost,
Whose clustered fruit must else be lost—
For the grapes' sake along the wall.

Keats's autumn ode is not far away. Delaying the seasonal change with six stresses, "Make the day seem to us less brief," and balancing loss, "one leaf at break of day; / At noon . . . another leaf; / One from our trees, one far away," Frost has left Dismal Swamp behind.

The moral of his Derry experience occurs in "The Pasture," with its hopeful gesture toward Elinor and us:

I'm going out to clean the pasture spring;
I'll only stop to clear the leaves away
(And wait to watch the water clear, I may):
I shan't be gone long.—You come too.

I'm going out to fetch the little calf
That's standing by the mother. It's so young
It totters when she licks it with her tongue.
I shan't be gone long.—You come too.

He made this the prologue of later books.

Frost would look back on the Derry years as a sacred source of his vocation. Yet they were not idyllic. Hard put as a poultry farmer, and selling few poems, he fell into self-doubt, depression, occasional rage—his "inner weather," as he put it. Disabling hayfever and pneumonia afflicted him. He and Elinor lost another child at birth, meanwhile his sister suffered in body and mind. Yet with all this, an "ache of memory" kept him attached to the New Hampshire farm where indoors and out, he'd shown the children "sheer morning freshness at the brim."

There he read more Thoreau: "I went to the woods because I wanted to live deliberately, to front only the essential facts of life." Frost had his students at a local academy read *Walden* aloud, and he seconded Thoreau's hope for "a poet who could impress the winds and streams into his service, to speak for him; who nailed words to their primitive senses, as farmers drive down stakes in the spring, which the frost has heaved." At Derry he found what his poems would need, the "sound of sense," ingraining measured verse with natural speech. Chopping wood in his yard one day, he feels someone behind him who "caught my ax expertly on the rise." His neighbor, denouncing machine-made handles, offers one he himself has hewn:

> He showed me that the lines of a good helve
> Were native to the grain before the knife
> Expressed them, and its curves were no false curves
> Put on it from without. And there its strength lay
> For the hard work.

There, with no false curves, lay the strength of Frost's writing in the American grain.

Surprisingly, or maybe not, he nailed down his American idiom after moving to England, where he'd broken away with his family in 1912. To release "the vitality of our speech" (Frost wrote his favorite Derry student), a poet "must learn to get cadences by skillfully breaking the sounds of sense with all their irregularity of accent across the regular beat of the metre." A few months later: "The living part of a poem is the intonation entangled somehow in the syntax idiom and meaning of a sentence." And yet again: There is the "regular pre-established accent and measure of verse," and the "irregular accent and measure of speaking intonation," natural rhythm. "I am never more pleased than when I can get these into strained relation."

It sounds as if a wild pony's being lassoed: "breaking," "entangled," "strained." Such is the sound of sense, for Frost. "If it is a wild tune, it is a poem"—wild, yet a tune. Neither loose freedom nor tight form will do, for American speech. Clearly the poet's as taken with the task of saying as with what gets said. "But all the fun's in how you say a thing," he says, and we always almost believe him.

In England Frost wrote out of homesickness for New England. "Mending Wall" sets sound and sense against restriction, letting colloquial phrasing accent the first syllable, then easing into an iambic beat: "*Some*thing there *is* that *does*n't *love* a *wall*." Against his neighbor's "Good fences make good neighbors," a casual rhythm breaks iambic pattern, freeing up the poet's tongue:

Spring is the mischief in me, and I wonder
If I could put a notion in his head:
Why do they make good neighbors? Isn't it
Where there are cows?

We're hearing the cadence of self-reliance.

Or take "Birches," recalling a boy who climbed a slender tree "Up to the brim, and even above the brim."

Then he flung outward, feet first, with a swish,
Kicking his way down through the air to the ground.

Impulsive phrasings barely contain their ten syllables, then the next line pours over, until the speaker fancies climbing "*Toward* heaven" but not too far:

Earth's the right place for love:
I don't know where it's likely to go better.

A solid maxim, loosened a little by mischief.

"The language is appropriate to the virtues I celebrate," Frost wrote from England to an American publisher, aiming like Wordsworth to catch what's heroic and spiritual in common speech. T. S. Eliot, leaving Harvard for England at the time, was practicing with Anglo-European models. But not Frost. His next book, *North of Boston* (1914), opens with "Mending Wall" and runs to rustic narrative and dialogue. Only "one poem in the book will intone," Frost said. "The rest talk."

"After Apple-Picking" doesn't lack talk, but its voice strikes dark fantastic tones.

My long two-pointed ladder's sticking through a tree
Toward heaven still,
And there's a barrel that I didn't fill
Beside it, and there may be two or three
Apples I didn't pick upon some bough.
But I am done with apple-picking now.

Extra-long then short lines startle at first, with one leaning word after another: *Aft*er, *Ap*ple, *Pick*ing, *point*ed, *lad*der, *stick*ing. Even "*heav*en" (not just sky) keeps us off balance. At least the rhyming seems familiar: abbacc. But that won't last. No one before had tried such colloquial rhymes: noun with number ("tree . . . three"), adverb with verb ("still . . . fill"), noun with adverb ("bough . . . now"). This is not cooked-up rhyming, but common words tuned to rhyme, and not just single sounds but whole phrases rhyming rhythmically: "through a tree . . . two or three," "Toward heaven still . . . I didn't fill," "pick upon some bough . . . apple-picking now." And Frost's run-ons can be momentous or mundane: "through a tree / Toward heaven"; "two or three / Apples." Just so, American folk art blends beauty with local use.

A fall poem—not a happy season for Frost, or Keats—with apples falling smacks of Eden's apple that brought toil, seasons, death into the world. It's *after* the harvest, life is lapsing. And why a two-pointed ladder, unless this poem has in store some doubleness, ambiguity, contradiction? A ladder left pointing, an unfilled barrel, an unpicked bough trouble his resolute "*But* I am done with apple-picking now."

Now we learn it's nighttime, toward winter. Rough-joined syntax brings on a fitful recollection of his morning's vision.

> Essence of winter sleep is on the night,
> The scent of apples: I am drowsing off.
> I cannot rub the strangeness from my sight
> I got from looking through a pane of glass
> I skimmed this morning from the drinking trough
> And held against the world of hoary grass.
> It melted, and I let it fall and break.

"Essence," "scent," "drowsing": a dreamlike drift. Then a run-on sentence drifts across the breaks—"sight [that] I got," "glass [that] I skimmed"—in a spellbound replay: "I cannot rub . . . I got from looking . . . I skimmed . . . And held . . . and I let it fall." He sees darkly through "a pane of glass" (or film of ice), his strange window on things before it falls and breaks. Not one of your crisp New England Thanksgivings, but a moment of strange deep vision.

We lapse into an uneasy dream of nature's plenty driven by short lines, erratic rhymes, surreal detail.

> But I was well
> Upon my way to sleep before it fell,
> And I could tell
> What form my dreaming was about to take.
> Magnified apples appear and disappear,
> Stem end and blossom end,
> And every fleck of russet showing clear.
> My instep arch not only keeps the ache,
> It keeps the pressure of a ladder-round.
> I feel the ladder sway as the boughs bend.

A dream's keenness touches flecks of russet and the ladder rung, yet things sway and bend in hypnotic pulse: "appear and disappear, / Stem end and blossom end." He's half asleep before the pane has fallen.

From that drowse, the next passage turns subterranean, foreboding.

And I keep hearing from the cellar bin
The rumbling sound
Of load on load of apples coming in.
For I have had too much
Of apple-picking: I am overtired
Of the great harvest I myself desired.
There were ten thousand thousand fruit to touch,
Cherish in hand, lift down, and not let fall.

Dream has verged on trauma, "The rumbling sound / Of load on load of apples coming in," but gets a homey touch when "coming in" finds its "cellar bin." (plate 9) A great harvest, yes, but now gone underground from heaven "ten thousand thousand" times. Even Paul Bunyan would balk at ten million apples to "not let fall."

Some did fall, thanks to a sudden rhyme:

For all
That struck the earth,
No matter if not bruised or spiked with stubble,
Went surely to the cider-apple heap
As of no worth.
One can see what will trouble
This sleep of mine, whatever sleep it is.
Were he not gone,
The woodchuck could say whether it's like his
Long sleep, as I describe its coming on,
Or just some human sleep.

On a late recording, Frost's gravelly voice speaking a younger man's lines gets their weary, ominous drift. Painstakingly he says "One-can-see-what-will-trouble / This-sleep-of-mine . . ." Who knows? Is death a human animal's long sleep after the Fall, do we awake from it? Was that strange morning sight of icy grass a mortal hint, despite the harvest? Frost's fun in "how you say a thing" lets trouble sound whimsical as it chimes with "stubble," and "winter sleep" has passed through "cider-apple heap" into "just some human sleep."

"white water rode the black forever"
Frost and the Necessity of Metaphor

Summer 1914 saw war looming, as Frost's *North of Boston* came out in London to enthusiastic reviews. No less than three of these came from Edward Thomas, a younger Welsh writer deciding whether to enlist. The two men found personal and literary sympathies, and both loved plant life. Their friendship quickly became intense. Meanwhile *North of Boston*'s popularity in America opened up Frost's reach. He bought a farm near New Hampshire's White Mountains, then later moved to another in the Green Mountains of southern Vermont. Besides poetry, he pursued teaching and lecturing that flourished for the next half-century. "Barding around," he called it.

On one such occasion in May 1953, a small high school group had the fortune to sit at Frost's feet. The venerable poet spoke about aspiring poets. "You know, I get lots of letters," he said. "I open them up and if the poems haven't any rhyme I toss them right in the trash. Now if they're rhymed, and one word belongs there for the sense while the other's dragged in to make a rhyme, I throw *them* away too. But if I can't tell which is which, if both rhyme words belong, why those are the poems I read!"

Of course there's more to it all than rhyming. Frost told an Oxford audience "about poetry—it's the ultimate. The nearest thing to it is penultimate, even religion." What rhymes can do happens in "Fire and Ice," where nature's metaphors converse about passion and catastrophe. Best memorized, these lines get their clout from tempo and one jolting rhyme.

Some say the world will end in fire,
Some say in ice.
From what I've tasted of desire
I hold with those who favor fire.
But if it had to perish twice,
I think I know enough of hate
To say that for destruction ice
Is also great
And would suffice.

The country-store cracker-barrel lingo (with hints of Emily Dickinson) can fool us into missing that rude halving from line one to two, plus the sly rhymes. Having gotten used to "fire" and "ice," then "perish twice," rhymewise we think we know enough to expect "mice" or "lice," or "mire" or "ire," when out of nowhere comes—"hate." Wondering *Where does "hate" come from?* we're looking deep into rhyme and beyond. Again the rhyme resumes, on "ice," but then "hate" abruptly echoes with chilling banality in "also great," while "ice" prompts the picky, killing formality of "would suffice." A few lines and the sermon's done, ice is it.

Another wisdom poem from the same year, "Dust of Snow," pleased Frost for its curt lines and plain rhyme.

The way a crow
Shook down on me
The dust of snow
From a hemlock tree

Has given my heart
A change of mood
And saved some part
Of a day I had rued.

From the local scene a fluent sentence draws black and white and green toward a small but saving epiphany. You could convert this into haiku:

Crow in a hemlock
shakes down dust of snow on me
—this day saved, in part.

But "Poetry is what gets lost in translation," Frost once remarked. He hasn't put "some" there just to fill out the line, hasn't dragged in "mood" or "rued" just for the rhyme. And if "rued" sounds forced, remember an old usage, "Oh, you'll rue the day . . . ," which gives this saving moment a home truth.

Frost's most notorious rhyme is really a repetition, closing a rhyme-spurred musing on landscape and weather. Having spent all one summer night on a long satiric poem, at dawn he gave up and wrote on the winter solstice. He liked to say that "Stopping by Woods on a Snowy Evening" came in one go, and his voice does start naturally here.

> Whose woods these are I think I know.
> His house is in the village though;
> He will not see me stopping here
> To watch his woods fill up with snow.
>
> My little horse must think it queer
> To stop without a farmhouse near
> Between the woods and frozen lake
> The darkest evening of the year.
>
> He gives his harness bells a shake
> To ask if there is some mistake.
> The only other sound's the sweep
> Of easy wind and downy flake.
>
> The woods are lovely, dark and deep,
> But I have promises to keep,
> And miles to go before I sleep,
> And miles to go before I sleep.

The overlapping rhymes move like Dante's in the *Divine Comedy* (which begins, "Midway through the journey of our life / I found myself in a dark wood"). Frost's ongoing scheme, in this poem about stopping, makes the final stanza all the more perplexing.

Something more than a Currier and Ives twilight idyll is in the making. Whose woods these are I only *think* I know, I'm almost trespassing, and watching woods sublimely fill with snow can feel somber too. It's queer to stop in an isolated spot, freezing and dark, it may even be a mistake.

Another voice pulls dark and deep on this poem. The Frost children used to recite a traditional (if grim) bedtime prayer from the eighteenth-century *New England Primer*:

> Now I lay me down to sleep,
> Pray the Lord my soul to keep.
> And if I die before I wake,
> I pray the Lord my soul to take.

A striking coincidence: this prayer's four-beat lines and rhyme sounds tally with Frost's, while "keep" and "sleep" turn up to silence his voice.

Endless questions trouble sleep in the closing stanza. Its first line, "The woods are lovely, dark and deep," often gets a standard comma added after "dark," even in authorized editions. But no comma belongs there. Nature must be lovely because it's *both* "dark and deep." So what keeps the journeyer from keeping promises? Lovely or deeply tempting woods? Perhaps open-ended "promises" helped make this poem Frost's favorite, "my best bid for remembrance." Are these promises driven by love for his wife and family, so hard to fulfill? Or sacred promises to give his all—he loved the saying "You bet your sweet life!"—so his work will be "acceptable in Thy sight, O Lord" (he liked this from Psalm 19)? Or promises to himself, to become America's leading poet?

Frost didn't write "Stopping by Woods . . ." quite in one go. In draft, his last stanza said

> But I have promises to keep
> That bid me on, and there are miles . . .

Given his regenerative scheme, that new word "miles" would ask for yet another stanza when he "didn't have another stanza in me, but with great presence of mind and a sense of what a good boy I was I instantly struck the line out and made my exit with a repeat end." And that, as he says in "The Road Not Taken," has made all the difference. He never conceded that these closing lines,

> And miles to go before I sleep,
> And miles to go before I sleep,

hint a death wish. Yet even without the Primer's "if I die," we hear more than drowsy mumbling. Repeating "sleep" sends it down or up to another level, like the "long sleep" in "After Apple-Picking." For all we know, he's stopping there to this day.

New Hampshire (1923), containing "Stopping by Woods on a Snowy Evening," "Dust of Snow," "Fire and Ice," and "The Ax-Helve," won the Pulitzer Prize, first of four he would receive. The poet kept up farm labor, walking, hiking, botanizing, and more writing, yet never ceased worrying over his literary stature. On top of this, family matters impinged: his sister's dementia, his wife's heart trouble and weariness from births, miscarriages, and infant death, his son's suicide, his daughters' physical and mental disorders. The snow a crow shook down from a tree could not redeem all that. Instead Frost wrote an autumn poem, "Bereft," letting weather say what it could: "Somber clouds in the west were massed . . . leaves got up in a coil and hissed."

With some pluck, Frost finished the title poem of his next book, "West-Running Brook." Near Derry a husband and wife talk over the contraries wedding them. "Look, look,"

> (The black stream, catching on a sunken rock,
> Flung backward on itself in one white wave,
> And the white water rode the black forever,
> Not gaining but not losing . . .)

Coleridge in England's Lake District fastened on a scooped rock throwing up a ceaseless white wave, an exact "Shape . . . forever overpowered by the stream rushing down in upon it, and still obstinate in resurrection." Like Coleridge and countless others, Frost fastens on flux taking form, motion holding still—in effect, loss regaining.

Here again nature offers an image of life, and of poetry too, going and staying at every line break. Summing up existence as "The stream of everything that runs away," "The universal cataract of death / That spends to nothingness," Frost finds an energy for "not losing" in the brook near his home:

> It is this backward motion toward the source,
> Against the stream, that most we see ourselves in,
> The tribute of the current to the source.
> It is from this in nature we are from.
> It is most us.

The tribute of the current to the source: as sacred a creed as Frost was likely to hold.

He dearly needed one in March 1938 when Elinor died, his friend and wife of forty-six years. She'd wanted her ashes scattered among the alders along Hyla Brook at Derry, where the children grew up and so much goodness and pain transpired. But when Frost went back there, the grounds seemed too derelict for that act. He foundered for months until a friend, Kathleen Morrison, became his savior and secretary-manager. Frost's perfect sonnet for her, "The Silken Tent," begins "She is . . ."—and that's gently all we hear of her, as metaphor takes over:

> She is as in a field a silken tent
> At midday when a sunny summer breeze
> Has dried the dew and all its ropes relent,
> So that in guys it gently sways at ease,
> And its supporting central cedar pole,
> Which is its pinnacle to heavenward
> And signifies the sureness of the soul,
> Seems to owe naught to any single cord,
> But strictly held by none, is loosely bound
> By countless silken ties of love and thought
> To everything on earth the compass round,
> And only by one's going slightly taut
> In the capriciousness of summer air
> Is of the slightest bondage made aware.

After speaking this Frost once said, "It's a one-sentence sonnet," turned quizzical, and asked, "But what if there isn't any pole?" A dozen teenage boys, dazed by then, couldn't gauge such questions of the soul or of woman's grace, or know how this man's need was anything but capricious and slight. We could, though, hear "pole" link to "soul," "summer breeze" lead to "ease," "summer air" make us "aware," sounding out the world around us for news of the human condition.

World War II did not alter Frost's stance. In nature he'd long been imagining historical or private accident and terror: "fire and ice," the Pacific's "shattered water," a spider's "design of darkness" on a moth, and something crashing "as a great buck" into the lake across from you. You'd thought the universe was there to reflect human love, but this counterforce came

> Pushing the crumpled water up ahead,
> And landed pouring like a waterfall,
> And stumbled through the rocks with horny tread,
> And forced the underbrush—and that was all.

Nothing could swerve Frost from fronting the world's worst with pentameter and rhyme. For his 1939 *Collected Poems* he wrote a preface, "The Figure a Poem Makes," saying that a poem "ends in a clarification of life—not necessarily a great clarification, such as sects and cults are founded on, but in a momentary stay against confusion."

Shortly after atomic bombs were dropped on Hiroshima and Nagasaki in August 1945, Frost sought a stay against confusion and then some. "Back out of all this now too much for us," his breathtaking "Directive" starts—ten staccato syllables pacing us back toward Derry and the brook where their children played and Elinor wanted her ashes: "a farm that is no more a farm" and a "children's house of make-believe."

> Your destination and your destiny's
> A brook that was the water of the house,
> Cold as a spring as yet so near its source.

Nearby, your guide has hidden "A broken drinking goblet like the Grail." The poem ends,

> Here are your waters and your watering place.
> Drink and be whole again beyond confusion.

Bracing, symbolic, and religious, yes, but the goblet's broken, and only *like* a holy grail, for "the key word in the whole poem is source," Frost said, "—whatever source it is."

He might or might not have blanched to hear that "Directive" is akin to T. S. Eliot's wartime *Four Quartets,* where a hidden source,

the last of earth left to discover
Is that which was the beginning;
At the source of the longest river
The voice of the hidden waterfall
And the children in the apple-tree.

"Directive" and "West-Running Brook," with its "backward motion toward the source," part from Eliot in Frost's reliance (like Thoreau and Whitman) on American idiom and terrain. He found personal and national sources in a more rustic vein than did William Carlos Williams (also Eliot's antagonist). All these poets meant to save us somehow.

"But all the fun's in how you say a thing." Frost really meant "all," everything poetry does to save some part of a day. From his deathbed in January 1963, a last letter said: "Metaphor is it and the freshness thereof." October grapes, ax-helve, apples coming in, summer air, dust of snow, woods, brook.

"Larks singing over No Man's Land"
England Thanks to Edward Thomas, 1914–1917

"He reminds us that words are alive, and not only alive but still half-wild and imperfectly domesticated." Edward Thomas (1878–1917) might have been speaking for himself and "those who love all life so well that they do not kill even the slender words but let them play on." As it happens, he meant the peasant poet John Clare, a century earlier, who loved "tracking wild searches through the meadow grass." Like Clare, Thomas owned close knowledge of animals and plants, of "what life is, how our own is related to theirs," our "responsibilities and debts among the other inhabitants of the earth."

"Birds' Nests," echoing Clare's poem of that name, spots summer nests "torn" by wind and it ends on a meadow search:

> And most I like the winter nest deep-hid
> That leaves and berries fell into;
> Once a dormouse dined there on hazel nuts;
> And grass and goose-grass seeds found soil and grew.

Seeming simple, like much in Edward Thomas, this opens to change and chance, then promise of life.

"Tall Nettles" bears the darker touch that would mark his war poems.

> Tall nettles cover up, as they have done
> These many springs, the rusty harrow, the plough

Long worn out, and the roller made of stone:
Only the elm butt tops the nettles now.

This corner of the farmyard I like most:
As well as any bloom upon a flower
I like the dust on the nettles, never lost
Except to prove the sweetness of a shower.

Like the birds' nest berries, nuts, and seeds, even the wear of time—rusty harrow, worn-out plow, overgrown nettles, dust—is given a keen eye and cheering turn.

Thomas was born in London in 1878, of Welsh parents. His early memories are of "wild unconscious play" in the fields, then "the time of collecting eggs, flowers and insects," and later "when we read poetry out of doors." A school friend recalls "Talking, and looking at the earth and the sky, we just walked about until it was dark," attending to "the general life of the common birds and animals, and to the appearances of trees and clouds and everything upon the surface that showed itself to the naked eye."

An older friend called "Dad," a sunburned sinewy gamekeeper-poacher who climbed trees for nests and dug into thorn bushes, could imitate "the hollow note of the bullfinch . . . the chiding of a sparrow hawk at its prey . . . a young rook's cry whilst gobbling a worm: it was perfectly true to nature." Dad knew the curative power of every herb—a knowledge "fast decaying," Thomas wrote in 1895.

Already at nineteen, learning from "my favorite—Thoreau," he published *The Woodland Life*, sketches of southern English countryside. "Still the pewits move uneasily in the open, always facing the wind and the thin wall of snow bearing down upon them." When it came to nature, his love fed his literacy. They both show a zeal, long before this was in vogue, to respect wildness for its own sake and ours as well. He went on to write *Beautiful Wales, The Heart of England, The South Country, The Country,* and *In Pursuit of Spring*.

Shuttling between landscape and literature, Thomas by 1913 had produced twenty-five books, plus essays and reviews, but no poetry. Then one encounter released a new voice. Robert Frost, feeling stymied in America, had taken his family to England. In October the two met and took to each other, Frost feeling Thomas's marital and literary anxieties, Thomas deepening Frost's botanical savvy. One night in rural Gloucestershire they hunted rare ferns by matchlight. Just days before war broke out in August 1914, the friends returning from one of their long rambles witnessed "A wonder!" that Frost recalled in "Iris by Night": a watery moon-made rainbow whose "two mote-swimming many-colored ends" gathered into a ring, "And we stood in it softly circled round."

Reading Thomas's account of a biking journey, Frost saw his friend had poems to write, drawn from passages such as this about pewits on Salisbury Plain near Stonehenge:

> His Winter and twilight cry expresses for most men both the sadness and the wildness of these solitudes. When his Spring cry breaks every now and then, as it does to-day, through the songs of the larks, when the rooks caw in low flight or perched on their elm tops, and the lambs bleat, and the sun shines, and the couch [grassy weed] fires burn well, and the wind blows their smoke about, the plain is genial. . . . But let the rain fall and the wind whirl it, or let the sun shine too mightily,

and the Plain becomes "a sublime, inhospitable wilderness. It makes us feel the age of the earth." Thoreau had called English poetry "tame and civilized," but Thomas's wintry plain proves otherwise, that "the earth does not belong to man, but man to the earth."

Frost heard what he liked, a lyric spirit in natural speech. When *North of Boston* came out in 1914, their kinship led Thomas to review it not twice but three times. "This is one of the most revolutionary books of modern times . . . It speaks, and it is poetry." Now he began finding verse rhythms in his own countryside prose. "I am in it now & no mistake," he wrote Frost, and in December sent him his first poems.

With the European war only miles away, Thomas, aged thirty-six with three children, debated whether to enlist or accept Frost's invitation to come farm and write in New England. "Something, I felt, had to be done before I could look again composedly at English landscape, at the elms and poplars about the houses." Seeing a moonrise and wondering about "those who could see it" in France if they were "not blinded by smoke, pain, or excitement," he's pierced by willingness to die for England. When asked what he was fighting for, "He stooped, and picked up a pinch of earth. 'Literally, for this.' He crumbled it between finger and thumb, and let it fall." Thomas enlisted in July 1915, training and teaching map-reading in the south of England until January 1917. By then he'd written the 143 poems upon which his reputation rests.

But what could wartime poems do if "Literature," as Thomas said, "sends us to Nature principally for Joy"? In "Haymaking," written when he enlisted, "night's thunder far away" yields to a cold sweet morning of "perfect blue." Ease and harmony seldom come simply for Thomas, but through paradox or balancing. (No wonder Frost's "The Wood-Pile" struck him, its cordwood left "To warm the frozen swamp as best it could / With the slow smokeless burning of decay.") "Haymaking" settles into a scene, as from Breughel or Constable, of laborers at rest after mowing:

> The tosser lay forsook
> Out in the sun; and the long waggon stood

Without its team; it seemed it never would
Move from the shadow of that single yew.

A peaceable "morning time" poised against change like that "long waggon":

The men leaned on their rakes, about to begin,
But still. And all were silent.

On Keats's Grecian Urn—the "calmest . . . stillest" ode, Thomas thought—
lovers are "still" and "silent," they "cannot fade" and never "can those leaves
be bare." In "To Autumn" the sleeping reaper's hook "Spares the next swath."
Thomas ends "Haymaking" on such a note: "All of us gone out of the reach of
change." But change was still to come.

"The sun used to shine," from 1916, recalls his forest walks with Frost, prospect-
ing for flowers and talking of everything. "We turned from men or poetry"

To rumours of the war remote
Only till both stood disinclined
For aught but the yellow flavorous coat
Of an apple wasps had undermined.

They couldn't help speaking of war, and then savoring the present moment
they spotted that perished apple, with undertones from Frost's "After Apple-
Picking." "Edward's poems do not directly discuss the war," said his wife Helen,
"but they do mention it and the war *gave point* to what he was describing." The
point is, Thomas cannot suppress his outdoors gusto or inward concern. They
interact, sparely.

The war
Came back to mind with the moonrise
Which soldiers in the east afar
Beheld then.

No escapism here. War wedges its terse irony into a summer evening saunter.

Thomas volunteered to serve overseas and on January 30, 1917, at 4 A.M.
disembarked in France with an artillery unit. For three months at Arras near the
Belgian border he kept a diary: cold, raw days, shelling at night, letters to and
from home, strafing, reading Shakespeare ten minutes per night, weather, landscape, owls, moles, hares, foxes, and throughout, the birds—partridge, black-
bird, thrush, magpie, sparrow, "Black-headed buntings talk, rooks caw," "Lin-
nets and chaffinches sing in waste trenched ground," "Larks singing over No
Man's Land." Of course nature persists in time of war, and above all birdsong.
Thomas took on that bittersweet persistence, much as Isaac Rosenberg not far
away heard "night ringing with unseen larks" though "Death could drop from
the dark / As easily as song." A year later Rosenberg was killed.

For Thomas, no poems at all were possible in France. In March 1917, though, an anthology appeared in London with poems of his from 1915–16. When the *Times Literary Supplement* called his naturalism absurd vis-à-vis "the tremendous life of the last three years," Thomas wrote a friend: "Must I only use [my eyes] as field-glasses and must I see only Huns in these beautiful hills eastward . . . ?" Anyway, he really had registered that dire life. Poems such as "The Owl" are

> Salted and sobered, too, by the bird's voice
> Speaking for all who lay under the stars,
> Soldiers and poor, unable to rejoice.

Yeats too sampled nature in wartime, but for Thomas, birds and plantlife were his day-in day-out life. In "Rain," a wild midnight downfall put him in mind of others lying alone

> Like a cold water among broken reeds,
> Myriads of broken reeds all still and stiff.

Amid shells going out and coming in, he writes to Frost: "I should like to be a poet, just as I should like to live, but I know as much about my chances in either case, and I don't really trouble about either. Only I want to come back more or less complete."

April 1917 saw Thomas, now a second lieutenant, preparing for the major British offensive at Arras, peering out through a hedge where "larks hover above the dry grass just in front." Twenty years earlier he'd sent his wife letters delineating weather, hills, rivers, hedgerows, birds, and flowers. Now from an observation post he writes, "I simply watched the shells changing the landscape." A nearby village "is now just ruins among violated stark tree trunks. But the sun shone and larks and partridge and magpies and hedgesparrows made love and the trench was being made passable for the wounded that will be harvested in a day or two." April—too early a harvest.

The next day, Easter Sunday April 8, a German shell fell two yards from him, a dud. About that time, Thomas's wife Helen wrote Frost describing his battlefield behavior: "In a pause in the shooting he turns his wonderful field glasses on to a hovering kestrel & sees him descend & pounce & bring up a mouse." Weeks later, when the letter came back from a censor because she'd included photos, she adds a postscript: "He was killed on Easter Monday by a shell." A few hours before that moment, his last diary note says, "The light of the new moon and every star / And no more singing for the bird." A copy of Frost's 1916 *Mountain Interval* was found in Thomas's kit-bag.

Still stinging from this loss, Frost wrote (but never published) "War Thoughts at Home." Behind a weathered house, blue jays are squabbling with crows. Inside, "A little bent over with care," a woman rises from her knitting to look out at this "bird war." "She thinks of a winter camp / Where soldiers for France are made," and the poem ends,

> On that old side of the house
> The uneven sheds stretch back
> Shed behind shed in train
> Like cars that long have lain
> Dead on a side track.

Here Frost at home, finding blue jay and crow at war, imagines the woman's house now backing on a railroad wasteyard. Thomas, abroad, sees sunny larks and magpies mating near a shell-torn French village.

His American friend, who'd written "The Road Not Taken" about him and called Thomas "the only brother I ever had," never got over losing him. "I don't suppose there is anything for us to do to show our admiration but to love him forever," Frost wrote to Thomas's widow. And to another English friend: "His concern to the last was what it had always been, to touch earthly things and come as near them in words as words would come."

"the necessary angel of earth"
Wings of Wallace Stevens

"I have seen cowboys; I have seen prairie dogs; hundreds of wild ducks, Indians in camp with smoke coming through their discolored tent-tops; I have seen mountains swimming in clouds and basking in snow; and cascades, and gulches," says a marveling Wallace Stevens (1879–1955). Three days pulling past farms, prairies, and mountains on Canadian Pacific Railroad in 1903 took him to British Columbia, the Rockies—fresh from Harvard College and New York Law School and "particularly taken by . . . the rock character of mountains above the timber-line." This six-week hunting trip stayed with him even to his deathbed—the virile poet vis-à-vis reality. "We use nails to stir the tea."

The mind, for Stevens, confronts nature, "pressing back against the pressure of reality." Besides their campfire, his Canadian journal records two fires burning: "One, the moon, lights mountainous camels moving, without bells, to the wide North; another, the twilight, lights the pine tops and the flaring patches of snow." Mountainous camels or camel-like mountains, Stevens in later career might have given them bells after all. And those pine tops, the flaring patches of snow, could have qualified for his poem of earthly beauty, "Sunday Morning," where "Deer walk upon our mountains, and the quail / Whistle about us their spontaneous cries."

After only a few days in British Columbia, he's exerting what Coleridge called "my shaping spirit of Imagination." Thus, "There are certain areas of spruce and fir in the forests that take on the appearance of everglades." (This vision is a bit uncanny. Twenty years later he began following his imagination to Florida.) Though hunting is "bloody difficult," pushing through swamp and slash and burned timber, his mind's eye keeps reaching: "The peaks to the South shelve off into the heavens. . . . And the blue distances merge mountain and sky into one."

Responding to the wild North's snow and endless forests, "I have seen" mountains swimming in clouds, "I have seen" hundreds of wild ducks. Peaks shelving off, blue distances merging, already act out his lifelong aim, "the great poem of the earth": to stretch our sense of the actual world, finding fresh faith in a time when religious faith has faded.

Like Frost, Jeffers, Marianne Moore, and W. S. Merwin, Stevens had religious roots, in his case the Pennsylvania Dutch community. He never lost touch with that Puritan ethic and never stopped answering it with poems of earthly richness. Most vibrant of all are the eight stanzas of "Sunday Morning." They begin not in church but in a woman's bedroom:

> Coffee and oranges in a sunny chair,
> And the green freedom of a cockatoo
> Upon a rug . . .

A sensuous sunniness and droll parrot's "green freedom" promote "any balm or beauty of the earth" over divine dogma, releasing us from "blood and sepulchre." Because conflicts of earth and paradise, death and rebirth have lost their grip, "Sunday Morning" steps in for the "silent shadows" of divinity, the "cloudy palm / Remote on heaven's hill."

Stevens reconnects the created world—"April's green," "the swallow's wings," "echoing hills"—to pagan humankind, with their "chant in orgy on a summer morn." Only when it's clear that "We live in an old chaos of the sun," not amid God's plenty but in an "island solitude, unsponsored, free," does he end this poem with Nature's plenty.

> Deer walk upon our mountains, and the quail
> Whistle about us their spontaneous cries;
> Sweet berries ripen in the wilderness;
> And, in the isolation of the sky,
> At evening, casual flocks of pigeons make
> Ambiguous undulations as they sink,
> Downward to darkness, on extended wings.

There you have it, abundant as Psalms—"The trees of the Lord also are full of sap. . . . The high hills are a refuge for the wild goats"—but now "unsponsored," free of divine dependence.

Breathing into these lines, their verbal music feels devotional. A vocal excitement, a sibilance as "the quail / Whistle about us their spontaneous cries," leads to psalmlike testimony: "Sweet berries ripen in the wilderness." But that's it, a perfect sentence as if grafted from Keats's ode to Autumn, who comes to bless the vines "And fill all fruits with sweetness to the core." It was Keats Stevens reckoned on, not our Lord rejoicing in His works.

In "Sunday Morning" Nature's varieties flourish with the lines' inward variety. No two have the same shape, so pauses come after one syllable ("And,"), three ("At evening,"), five, or seven odd-numbered syllables reaching toward the next strong beat while the sentence evolves. Familiar subject-verb events— deer walk . . . quail whistle . . . berries ripen—give way to a slower movement as the pigeons sink wavelike to darkness. Whether by chance or the poet's gift doesn't matter, when the only ripples of an extra syllable in these lines belong to "spontaneous," "casual," "ambiguous"—signs of how little dominion we have, how unknowing we are, though we speak of "our" mountains and quail whistling "about us."

The poet's long final sentence unscrolls a natural event, evening flocks of pigeons, that ultimately sinks out of our ken:

> And, in the isolation of the sky,
> At evening, casual flocks of pigeons make
> Ambiguous undulations as they sink,
> Downward to darkness, on extended wings.

"Isolation," by what gauge? Evening sky can be simply that, empty of any transcendent presence. These undulations are "casual" and "ambiguous" in our sight but not the pigeons', certainly. And not, in a way, the poet's.

As the lines descend, their phrasings vary with the birds' own movement along a trail of crisp consonants—the *k*-sound in "sky" passing through "casual," "flocks," and "make" toward "sink," surer than any outright rhyme. The pigeons as they "sink, / Downward to darkness" carry that *k* heard finally in "extended." And as "sink" nearly sings to rhyme the poem's last word, those extended wings hold up, slow up for the mind's eye, an otherwise vanishing beauty.

Like Keats in autumn, when "barred clouds bloom the soft-dying day" and "gathering swallows twitter in the sky," Stevens finds for life and death an earthly music, the extended wings of sound and rhythm—his response to "the verve of earth."

A trio of mettlesome poets, born within a few years of each other, fought from the 1920s onward for an American imagination "creating or finding and revealing" new reality, "a part of unprecedented experience." Stevens praised Marianne Moore with these words, speaking for his own aims as well. Likewise

Moore admired William Carlos Williams's imaginative "power over the actual." It takes what Stevens calls "The poem of the act of the mind" to reveal the verve of earth in pigeons sinking "on extended wings," or in a "cold wind" above "tufted rock / Massively rising high and bare / Beyond all trees."

Late in life Stevens published "Essays on Reality and the Imagination" under a title, *The Necessary Angel,* drawn from a recent poem:

> Yet I am the necessary angel of earth,
> Since, in my sight, you see the earth again.

This claim never faded. Poetry, for Stevens, offers the "supreme fictions" that let us think of life. Through him we "see the earth again," as in Dickinson's snaky "Whip lash / Unbraiding in the sun," Frost's "Magnified apples . . . And every fleck of russet showing clear." Not that he wants us foisting our feelings on things, but instead, imagining nature such as never before, like those "flaring patches of snow" he first saw in the Rockies.

Pennsylvania-born and an insurance executive in Hartford, Connecticut, he'd anticipated tropical richness in the "pungent fruit and bright, green wings" of "Sunday Morning." Later, Florida fired his imagination of earth and sea. "The Idea of Order at Key West" features a woman singing and "It was her voice that made / The sky acutest at its vanishing." Tell me, he asks a companion there,

> tell why the glassy lights,
> The lights in the fishing boats at anchor there,
> As the night descended, tilting in the air,
> Mastered the night and portioned out the sea.

In other words—but enough of other words, Stevens has already spoken them!

Given his tropical bent, what will he make of a snow man's bare imaginings?

> THE SNOW MAN
> One must have a mind of winter
> To regard the frost and the boughs
> Of the pine-trees crusted with snow;
>
> And have been cold a long time
> To behold the junipers shagged with ice,
> The spruces rough in the distant glitter
>
> Of the January sun; and not to think
> Of any misery in the sound of the wind,
> In the sound of a few leaves,
>
> Which is the sound of the land
> Full of the same wind
> That is blowing in the same bare place

For the listener, who listens in the snow,
And, nothing himself, beholds
Nothing that is not there and the nothing that is.

Baffling as it is, this intricately linked sentence traces just about all we can know.

"One must . . ." We go more than two stanzas into the poem before realizing that "must" is not insisting ("You must try snowshoeing some day") but inferring ("You must be dull-witted to go snowshoeing and not love it"). So, an inert mind can sense only an inert world—is that the poem's drift? Stevens seems to regret such loss of feeling, yet before hearing of misery we really do "regard the frost and the boughs" in his crisp language, we do "behold the junipers shagged" or rough with ice, the pines "crusted" with snow. Anyone in a cold climate will "see the earth again" with Stevens, that "distant glitter / / of the January sun."

Now we can listen again for another possibility. "One must have a mind of winter . . . To behold the junipers . . . and not to think / Of any misery in the sound of the wind." Maybe one really must, and not slobber sentiment. A Zen Buddhist listener will be clear-minded, "nothing himself," and yet keenly sense "the nothing that is": elemental wind, a few leaves, and sometimes those moonlit camel "mountains swimming in clouds and basking in snow" that Wallace Stevens saw in the Rockies at twenty-two.

"broken / seedhusks"

Reviving America with William Carlos Williams

"Things would really grow for him," Flossie said about her husband of fifty years, William Carlos Williams (1883–1963). He remembered "once when the boys were small taking them in along an old wood road in our boots from Paterson Avenue among the trees to dig up a wild azalea. I found a bush and carried it out, the roots and a good hunk of wet sod resting, in a burlap bag, across my shoulders."

Unlike Frost, Williams came to style himself an urban pastoral poet, a local of Rutherford, New Jersey, just across the Hudson River from Manhattan. During his boyhood and on through World War II, though, Rutherford was more rural than urban, a small town surrounded by field, farm, marsh, and woodland. "Imagine!" he says of his early years, "No sewers, no water supply, no gas, even. Certainly no electricity; no telephone, not even a trolley car. The sidewalks were of wood . . . cesspools in the back yard and outhouses . . . Our drinking water was rain water collected from the roof." Willie got a dime an hour for pumping water down from a wooden tank in the attic.

The poet's earliest "thronging memories" preserve his beginnings, his genesis. From his first year: "Pop was chopping down a small tree. Each time he'd swing the axe and I heard it wham into the wood, I'd let out a wild cackle of delight." He recalls his uncle shooting a squirrel that fell "bloody, at our feet" from a pine tree, and unforgettably, a cow running wild that they chased "over the fence, the milk flying out behind her in our faces." That sensation alone could breed a budding poet.

"Kipp's woods, just over the back fence, was our wilderness"—"my magic forest," says Williams. "I knew every tree in that wood, from the hickory where a squirrel had its hole to the last dogwood where in the fall the robins would gather for the red berries they are so fond of." Alert to the names and behavior of things, "What I learned was the way the moss climbed about a tree's roots, what growing dogwood and iron wood looked like; the way rotten leaves will mat down in a hole—and their smell when turned over."

He collected insects and butterflies, "but flowers and trees were my peculiar interest. To touch a tree, to climb it especially, but just to know the flowers was all I wanted." Williams went on to compose two hundred flower poems. "The slender neck of the anemone particularly haunts me for some reason and the various sorts of violets—the tall blue ones, those with furry stems and the large, scarce, branching yellow ones, stars of Bethlehem, spring beauties, wild geranium, hepaticas with three-lobed leaves." Sent to school in Switzerland, fifty years later he recalls how the "green-flowered asphodel made a tremendous impression on me."

Of course hindsight is not transparent but filtered, sifted. Early impressions that end up as memories first took root subliminally and then persisted for good cause. The moments Williams recollects had all along been shaping his sense of himself, only later to confirm it. "There is a long history in each of us that comes as not only a reawakening but a repossession when confronted by this world." A child's response to kaleidoscopic nature feeds into the poet's designs on "this world." "The tassels of the chestnut—young and old trees, beggar's lice, spiders, shining insects—all these things were as much part of my expanding existence as breathing. I was comforted by them. It was an unconscious triumph all day long just to be able to get out of doors and into my personal wild world." And that thought could easily be John Clare's.

The child's "personal wild world" underwrites the poet's key moments, such as "cheeping birds" resting and feeding on "harsh weedstalks" in "To Waken an Old Lady." Williams's "expanding existence" in childhood would lead to "the stiff curl of wildcarrot leaf" in "Spring and All," where "It quickens: clarity, outline of leaf," and plant life enters the world: "rooted, they / grip down and begin to awaken." Simply the crisped energy in that "stiff curl of wildcarrot leaf," new growth taking form, has bred a strain of possibility in modern poetry.

Born to a half-Sephardic Puerto Rican mother and an English father from Santo Domingo, Williams came by poetical leanings on his own, knowing from the outset he'd need gainful employment. High school thoughts of an athletic career shattered when he collapsed after a hard race, yet this provoked a poem.

A black, black cloud
flew over the sun
driven by fierce flying
rain.

Though he realized rain doesn't drive clouds, this instinctual beginning gave
Williams joy, crystallized his calling.

For a livelihood he took up medicine, working over forty years as an expert
and beloved general practitioner, tending to all sorts of people in Rutherford
homes and schools and in Passaic Hospital, delivering thousands of babies, leading community organizations. During the flu epidemic of 1918 he made sixty
house calls a day. Amid all this, over the years, he scrounged time to write—in
his office between patients and at home late at night: poetry collections, novels,
stories, translations, essays, plays, reviews, autobiography, and always letters.
"My family is prostrated—my patients are dying—I have not kissed my mother
for three weeks." Zealous to regenerate American poetry, he wrote for many
magazines and started several.

"Make it new!" his comrade Ezra Pound declared, and Williams never tired
of doing so.

"Waken! my people, to the boughs green
With ripening fruit within you!
Waken to the myriad cinquefoil
In the waving grass of your minds!
Waken to the silent phoebe nest
Under the eaves of your spirit!"

cries "The Wanderer" (1914), intoxicated with everything "so new now / To
my marveling eyes." This youth merges with "The Passaic, that filthy river"
bearing him beneath its mud and stench "Into the crystal beginning of its days."
A little later, T. S. Eliot would seek renewal in *The Waste Land* by setting off
London's fouled river with a fluent verse from Spenser, "Sweet Thames, run
softly till I end my song." The difference is that American-born Eliot went
back to Europe and a classic source, whereas Williams stayed local, in Walt
Whitman's footsteps.

"To me especially it struck like a sardonic bullet," *The Waste Land*, "the great
catastrophe to our letters." Williams felt "we were on the point of . . . a new art
form itself—rooted in the locality which should give it fruit," when Eliot expa-
triated. Though he himself had fed on Keats's verbal music along with Shakespeare's plays and sonnets, Williams drove his own agenda: to deal in American
material and idiom with homegrown rather than inherited wordcraft.

Emily Dickinson, "my patron saint," had "succeeded by hammering her
form obstinately into some kind of homespun irregularity," such as her "un-

rhymes." She "followed the American idiom." As for the bard who claimed "I hear America singing, her varied carols," Williams thanked Whitman for breaking from European models—rhyme, stanza, pentameter—toward freer rhythms, the ocean's "measured sweep" at Coney Island in Brooklyn. "The greatest moment in the history / of the American poem was when / Walt Whitman stood looking to sea / from the shelving sands." But Whitman, whose free verse could turn flaccid and garrulous, "to me is one broom stroke and that is all." The same letter dismissed Robert Frost's "bucolic simplicity"—which is a gross simplification. Not that Frost, who twice snubbed Williams in Vermont, wasn't also vying for the inside lane in American poetry.

When *The Waste Land* came out in 1922, giving poetry "back to the academics" and sowing disillusion, Williams was already writing in his own vein. *Al Que Quiere*, he titled an early book, "To whoever wants it," thinking of a soccer pass. Like Whitman and unlike Eliot, he caught the ordinary grace of people he doctored, the young housewife "tucking in / stray ends of hair." And of flowers too. "Blueflags" takes his children to "where the streets end / in the sun / at the marsh edge," and among reeds they pluck fistfuls of wild iris

> till in the air
> there comes the smell
> of calamus
> from wet, gummy stalks.

—calamus, whose bladelike leaves meant sexuality for Whitman. More and more flowers show up in Williams's verse, with the common vernacular names he cherished: star-of-Bethlehem, spring beauty, Indian tobacco, heal-all, boneset. He wrote poems called "Primrose," "Queen-Ann's-Lace," "Great Mullen," and "Daisy":

> The dayseye hugging the earth
> in August, ha!

whose "crisp petals remain / brief, translucent, greenfastened."

That fresh eye animates a 1920 wake-up call for American verse that even Williams's detractors love. "To Waken an Old Lady" salutes his mother, then seventy-three.

> Old age is
> a flight of small
> cheeping birds
> skimming
> bare trees
> above a snow glaze.
> Gaining and failing

they are buffeted
by a dark wind—
But what?
On harsh weedstalks
the flock has rested,
the snow
is covered with broken
seedhusks
and the wind tempered
by a shrill
piping of plenty.

Eighteen lines and at the fulcrum a startle—"But what?"

We enter a process of discovery: "Old age is / . . ." What we can't know is that this definition-like beginning will be the last we hear of old age. From then on a landscape unscrolls, of birds, trees, snow, wind, weeds, seeds, and shrill piping. Like a baking recipe—TO RAISE A SOUFFLÉ—or a medical procedure, "To Waken an Old Lady" notes each step, leaves us groping, eager for the next— "But what?" Like a catch breath in singing, each line break at once pauses and proceeds, stays and goes.

Something *happens* here, enacting not recalling. Ear and eye switchback down the page through an event. Hating what's hackneyed, shunning elaboration, the poem doesn't COPY reality (Williams liked thumping capitals) but IMITATES, becomes the mind's new reality, the only kind we can grasp inside ourselves. He jostles us into seeing and hearing with fresh immediacy by jagging his line endings, playing his own pauses off against habitual speech. "Old age is" should right away tell us what old age is—but we're stopped by a break. Verbs usually fasten onto their objects—but the birds are held for a moment, "skimming / bare trees."

So far, things seem bleak: small, skimming, bare, failing, buffeted, dark. Then midway through, suddenly "But what?" occurs in a brief time-lapse between present ("they are buffeted") and past ("the flock has rested"). Now "the snow / is covered with broken / "—But what? Seedhusks! Because in one moment the flock has stripped those husks and fed on seeds. Bare Anglo-Saxon (not Latinate) syllables, "weedstalks" and "seedhusks" sound dry but tally rhythmically and nearly rhyme, as "seedhusks" save the day in a tongue-crisping, one-word line of their own. Nature plays out her vicissitudes: wind, yes, but tempered; tempered, but shrill; shrill, then "piping of plenty," offering relief while echoing the falling cadence of "gaining and failing."

By the end (more like a new beginning) we've all but forgotten the bluff statement that started this poem. Medically speaking, Dr. Williams's "Old age is" turns up a bizarre definition, with seedhusks instead of creaking joints. His

William Carlos Williams.
Reprinted courtesy of New Directions Publishing Corporation.

exercise in metaphor jumps straight from old age to nature—a feat of imagination. Usually figures of speech go back and touch base with what they're figures for. Take Shakespeare:

> Like as the waves make towards the pebbled shore,
> So do our minutes hasten to their end.

"To Waken an Old Lady" finesses old age to immerse in an ecologic drama of small birds surviving harsh weather. Immersing in nature's doings turns out to be the real prescription, after all. His mother lived to one hundred and two.

Springtime in the northeast is welcome but slow in coming, since "April is the cruellest month," Eliot says, "stirring dull roots with spring rain." Echoing Chaucer, Shakespeare, Baudelaire, Dante, Milton, Spenser, et al., *The Waste Land* mightily spurred Williams to compose an American antidote, *Spring and All*, part prose manifesto and part poem sequence. "There is a constant barrier between the reader and his consciousness of immediate contact with the world," so Williams urges us to "imagine the New World that rises to our windows" every day.

Where *The Waste Land* intones "dead land . . . dull roots . . . dried tubers . . . dead tree," Williams's title poem "Spring and All" relocates that landscape just where, as a physician, he often found himself.

> By the road to the contagious hospital
> under the surge of the blue
> mottled clouds driven from the
> northeast—a cold wind. Beyond, the
> waste of broad, muddy fields
> brown with dried weeds, standing and fallen
>
> patches of standing water
> the scattering of tall trees
>
> All along the road the reddish
> purplish, forked, upstanding, twiggy
> stuff of bushes and small trees
> with dead, brown leaves under them
> leafless vines—
>
> Lifeless in appearance, sluggish
> dazed spring approaches—
>
> They enter the new world naked,
> cold, uncertain of all
> save that they enter. All about them
> the cold, familiar wind—
>
> Now the grass, tomorrow
> the stiff curl of wildcarrot leaf
> One by one objects are defined—
> It quickens: clarity, outline of leaf
>
> But now the stark dignity of
> entrance—Still, the profound change
> has come upon them: rooted, they
> grip down and begin to awaken

As he was about to present this poem at Harvard in 1951, Williams stopped and joshed his academic audience: "Now you notice what I said: there is *no* subject that the modern poem cannot approach, there is no selected material. It's what you *do* with a work of art, it's what you *put* on the canvas and *how* you put it on that makes the picture. It's how the words *fit in*—poems are not made of *thought*, beautiful *thoughts*, it's made of *words! pigment! put on! here! there! made! actually!*" Williams himself loved painting, like Hopkins, Lawrence, Elizabeth Bishop, Derek Walcott. His "Spring and All" reads like a kinetic landscape-in-words.

"In the composition," he says, "the artist does exactly what every eye must do with life." Sketching in his canvas—"By the road . . . under the surge . . . All along the road . . . under them"—Williams adds daubs of shape, color, texture, and even smell, rank "muddy fields" and "standing water." Under wind-driven clouds the land appears inert, poor "stuff," yet bristling with the ways adjectives can take form: "purplish, forked, upstanding, twiggy." Most telling of all: among jagged phrasings for fifteen lines, no main verb snags the viewer's eye until "leafless" modulates to "Lifeless" and midway through the time of this poem, "sluggish / dazed spring approaches—"

"They enter the new world naked," so raw we can't tell whether "They" are plant life or newborn infants. A translation by Octavio Paz reads *Entran en el mundo desnudos,* "They enter the world naked." Was Mexico's spokespoet, on behalf of the continent's indigenous peoples, doubting this "*new* world"? Williams had another priority: "at last SPRING is approaching" after our dead-time spent copying the European past, he says in *Spring and All.* "THE WORLD IS NEW."

Organic uprising rings like revolutionary speech:

> Now the grass, tomorrow
> the stiff curl of wildcarrot leaf

We've seen that stiff curl of Queen Anne's lace in the ground or the flower shop, but have we *said* it so as to *see* it afresh? What grips the mind's eye is a tension between "curl" and "stiff" (he added that adjective later), a charged energy caught in momentary stillness, growth taking shape, plus the compression of "wildcarrot" in one word. "One by one objects are defined," says the poet, getting a double sense from "defined": identified and outlined, by nature and the poet both.

The sixty-eight-year-old speaking this younger man's lyric still bubbles with excitement. After the poem's fifth alerting dash we hear "It quickens," which fuses poetry's with nature's work of quickening. Life around us quickens in several ways: it warms up, pulsing more rapidly; the core or "quick" of things wakens from death to life, as in "the quick and the dead"; new life stirs, the fetus "quickens."

Toward the end, through expectant line breaks, momentum still gathers with each verb. Answering Eliot's feverish "What are the roots that clutch," "Spring and All" sees nature's renewable energy reaching deep into local ground with no stop in sight: "rooted, they . . . ," "rooted, they . . . ,"

> rooted, they
> grip down and begin to awaken

"source then a blue as"
Williams and the Environmental News

"There is a constant barrier between the reader and his consciousness of immediate contact with the world," says William Carlos Williams in *Spring and All* (1923). He'd just helped start a little magazine, *Contact*, calling for "contact between words and the locality that breeds them, in this case America." Local, the native environs—which is why Eliot's defection in *The Waste Land* "struck like a sardonic bullet." Nothing so marks Williams, over five decades, as this urge to cleanse our consciousness.

> so much depends
> upon
>
> a red wheel
> barrow
>
> glazed with rain
> water
>
> beside the white
> chickens

Just *how* much depends upon the barrow, the water, the chickens? And *what* exactly depends on them?

Try removing the first pair of lines. Without them it's a pleasant sort of haiku. With them, a crying need, as the poem's one fancy word, "depends," literally hangs over this scene. "*So* much": with no limit, maybe everything depends on a wheelbarrow and rainwater and white chickens—or on "wheel / barrow" and "rain / water" and "white / chickens," words as musical pulses, daubs of paint disclosing everyday things.

Whatever depends depends on seeing those things afresh by saying them anew. "When we name it, life exists," in *Spring and All*, a claim exceeded only by Blake's "Where man is not, nature is barren." Williams knew that Life, reality, nature, however we call what's not our sole private selves, does possess "independent existence." We can't know things themselves, we can only awaken a sense of them. Name "the stiff curl of wildcarrot leaf" and "It quickens."

As for "The Red Wheelbarrow," these seven or eight seconds have garnered proverbial force because and in spite of easy access. Seen farmwise, the barrow, water, and chickens matter a good deal. But "red"? "glazed"? "white"? That excitement springs the new world to our windows. Williams prized early English words and the roughhewn compounds he coined, like "weedstalks" and "seedhusks" in "To Waken an Old Lady." Breaking "wheel / barrow" and "rain / water" turns what's familiar into something strange and fresh, with a "red wheel" spinning radiant for a moment while "rain" and "white" glisten before going commonplace.

Call this poem mundane, unadorned, simply reporting what's out there. But even its stance on the page, those shaped stanzas, shiver with extra purpose. Four times running we see four or three syllables over two, maybe wheelbarrow-shaped. And take "glazed," a word of many uses: doughnuts and pie, pottery and fine majolica, oil paintings, snow, eyes. Williams liked this word. Elsewhere *Spring and All* features a "broken plate / glazed with a rose," and an old lady wakens to birds "skimming / bare trees / above a snow glaze." Translating "The Red Wheelbarrow," Latin American poets enhance the scene: Ernesto Cardenal's glazed wheelbarrow is *reluciente,* shining like a halo or the family silver, while Octavio Paz's is *barniẓada,* varnished. For Williams the barrow's deceptively simple: shining, yes, in the light this poem draws onto itself, yet it's a common light, as on frozen snow or fresh-baked pie. "Glazed" belongs to a thriving old Indo-European family: glass, gloss, gleam, glow, glare, glint, glitter, glisten, glimpse, glance, glide, glee, glad, gold. In this moment, this wheelbarrow stands radiantly for itself.

Williams does not like "like," the simile for knowing ourselves via nature. Likening emotions "such as anger with lightning, flowers with love," he thought an empty effort.

—Say it, no ideas but in things—

A poet foisting passion onto wind and rain, let's say, "makes nature an accessory . . . it blinds him to his world." Anon knew this centuries ago, leaving the link unspoken:

> Western wind when will thou blow,
> The small rain down can rain?
> Christ! if my love were in my arms,
> And I in my bed again!

Freeing poetry this way frees nature as well. Without fusing or confusing us with the world outside, Williams brings it alive to us: "reality needs no personal support but exists free from human action" (except, alas, as humankind weighs in more and more). Behold, the work of imagination is "not 'like' anything but transfused with the same forces which transfuse the earth." His bravest claim!

Like Coleridge, he never lost faith in the priming force of imagination. It's no surprise that "The Pot of Flowers"—

> Pink confused with white
> flowers and flowers reversed
> take and spill the shaded flame
> darting it back
> into the lamp's horn . . .

—stems not from flowers but a friend's painting. Years later his last book celebrates Breughel, "The living quality of / the man's mind" and the painter's "covert assertions / for art, art, art!" Poetic Imagination, capitalized by Coleridge, mimicked divine Creation, and with secular American zeal, Williams claimed as much. So much, even human survival, depends upon cleansing the way we see and say things, wakening to the glisten of a red wheelbarrow.

Renewing contact with our world also meant declaring American independence. As *Spring and All* came out, Williams began a year's sabbatical from medical practice to recover the continent's founding spirits: Eric the Red, Columbus, Ponce de Leon, Cortez, De Soto, Cotton Mather, on through Daniel Boone, Sam Houston, Edgar Allan Poe, and Abraham Lincoln. Days on days in the New York Public Library gave access to their words and deeds, reshaped in his own voice. The point was to "re-name the things seen . . . to draw from every source one thing, the strange phosphorus of the life, nameless under an old misappellation." This book would be *In the American Grain*.

So he took his family for a six-month sojourn in Europe, personally encountering Joyce, Duchamp, Brancusi, Man Ray, Cocteau, also Pound and Hemingway and H.D., pagan and Catholic Italy, monuments and ruins, architecture, art, wine, ravishing countrysides. Enthralled by the Old World, Williams went on writing about the New.

He maneuvers his Columbus chapter so as to end with the 1492 beginning, the Admiral's years of storm-ridden sailing and human treachery culminating in that first astonished October morning. "Bright green trees, the whole land so green it is a pleasure to look on it," *árboles muy verdes . . . y toda ella verde, qu'es plazer de mirarla*. As if encountering Eden's *primavera*, its "first green" or Eternal Spring, Columbus marvels at the greenness of the land (which he named San Salvador), but with a European grasp: "The nightingale was singing" (though America has none), fish "so unlike ours that it is wonderful," *maravilla*, unheard-of wild-branching trees "the greatest wonder in the world," dugout canoes "wonderfully worked." All this means to persuade the Admiral's Spanish sponsors, but he's also striving to say what moves him. On shore he sends men for water, and *en este tiempo anduve así por aquellos árboles*, "During that time I walked among the trees which was the most beautiful thing which I had ever seen," *que eran la cosa más fermosa de ver*.

Among these green fertile wonders, *In the American Grain* omits passages that taint the discoverer's purity. Columbus assures Ferdinand and Isabella that he's looking out for gold, that these unspoiled natives "could easily be made Christians," that the islands would supply "as much of aloes wood, and as many slaves for the navy, as their Majesties will wish to demand." Of course it's a given that Spain may claim this land, this "ravished" Eden, as Williams puts it.

Once past the "miraculous first voyage," he doesn't overlook "the crassness of the discoverers" driven like Cortez, "the slaughterers" such as Ponce de Leon, the Puritans' mean and "vigorous hypocrisy," and he could have no inkling of ecologic devastation to come. Still, he cherishes an eighteenth-century French Jesuit in Maine, Père Sebastian Rasles, who shares life among the Abnaki Indians, "TOUCHING them every day," struggling to learn their energetic language, respecting their culture. Williams scorns any view of an Indian ceremonial as unrelated to us—"unrelated, that is, except to the sand, the corn, the birds, the beasts, the periodic drought, and the mountain sights and colors."

To recover what we need, he settles on the legendary Daniel Boone (ignoring his role as land speculator): woodsman, huntsman pushing ever farther into the wilderness, "filled with the wild beauty of the New World to overbrimming," seeing "the truth of the Red Man, not an aberrant type, treacherous and anti-white to be feared and exterminated, but as a natural expression of the place." In this vein he praises Sam Houston too, who lived among Cherokees to touch the ground of American being. "It is imperative that we sink," says Williams, "we must go back to the beginning."

Back home, Williams kept at *In the American Grain* "which I MUST MUST MUST

MUST finish before I can be young again." His book's "dynamic energy" roused D. H. Lawrence and others. Meanwhile the fight against Eliot's Eurocentrism went on. "The Source" goes to rural America upon which so much depends, a morning pasture

> On whose green three maples
> are distinctly pressed
> beside a red barn
>
> with new shingles in the old . . .

Those maples "are distinctly pressed" between green and red by a poet-painter, while his bias for beginnings spots "new shingles in the old." In rustling spring-water over uneven stones,

> An edge of bubbles stirs
> swiftness is molded

Like Frost's "West-Running Brook," where "white water rode the black for-ever," this "Source" or spring shows energy finding its own shape—a demo-cratic American virtue.

In nature as in poems, Williams aims to find the vital form of things, how "the stiff curl of wildcarrot leaf . . . quickens." His little-known "Young Sycamore" pulses with that barely contained energy.

> I must tell you
> this young tree
> whose round and firm trunk
> between the wet
>
> pavement and the gutter
> (where water
> is trickling) rises
> bodily
>
> into the air with
> one undulant
> thrust half its height—
> and then
>
> dividing and waning
> sending out
> young branches on
> all sides—
>
> hung with cocoons
> it thins
> till nothing is left of it
> but two

eccentric knotted
twigs
bending forward
hornlike at the top

A priming gesture—"I must tell you," "So much depends"—gets life going here, sends sap rising through six cognate bunchings up into "this young tree."

Up, and of course down the page, as we read. This tree "rises / bodily" through the body of its poem. Tracing the shape, the growth itself of a young sycamore, old-fashioned grammar and syntax come into play. First of all, does "I must tell you" take "this young tree" as its object, as in "tell you" a story? Or after "I must tell you" do we pause, to begin a sentence of which "this young tree" is the subject? Or maybe both?

Greeting each line in time, right away we're deflected by a subordinate clause: "this young tree / whose round and firm trunk . . ." Then, expecting "trunk" to take its own verb, instead we get a prepositional phrase: "between the wet / pavement and the gutter." And then again, a parenthesis abuts the gutter, "(where water is trickling)." Eventually our original tree seems to find its verb:

this young tree
whose round and firm trunk
. . . rises
bodily

But on close inspection it's the trunk that "rises bodily," not the tree.

Wait as we will, no verb for "this young tree" comes along. What matters is process. We watch the trunk rising "with one undulant thrust half its height," whether wave- or snake- or phallus-like. Halfway through, the poem takes on present participles, "dividing and waning / sending out," and then adds a past participle, "hung with cocoons"—branchings aplenty, both arboreal and grammatical. Whitman celebrated the "free growth" of poems as they "bud . . . unerringly" like "lilacs or roses on a bush." For Williams the trunk "rises bodily . . . and then . . . it thins." By this time a generic "tree" has found its "round and firm" body, the poem's form organic to its substance.

Even now, with almost nothing left of it, "Young Sycamore" still surprises. Its bottom lines sprout its treetop, and these hints of old age—eccentric, knotted, bending forward, hornlike—must actually be young buds, holding new life like the hanging cocoons. Tendril lines with no comma or period, crisp edgings "knotted" and "hornlike," thrust the tree close, alive to sight and touch. We feel firsthand, present, the poem's body language "transfused with the same forces which transfuse the earth."

Yet Williams never saw this tree. His sycamore rises bodily from an Alfred Stieglitz photograph made in New York City, "Spring Showers" (1901). So the poet wasn't scribbling words on paper while embracing a tree trunk, *en plein air* like Van Gogh in a wheat field daubing chrome yellow, cobalt blue, crow black marks. But does this disillusion us—that art should intervene between a sensuous urban sapling and its vivid written counterpart? In both arts, visual and verbal, what counts is making it new, as with Cézanne, Matisse, Joyce, Woolf, Stieglitz. "The objective is not to copy nature," which is already there, says Williams, "but to imitate nature" in livening words. Since apathy toward the physical world is not an option, his young sycamore goes "undulant . . . waning . . . hung with cocoons . . . bending" to an unstopping end.

Commonplace human nature as well, especially during the Depression years, can stir with new life. A kind of phased repetition gives the savor of plums

> To a Poor Old Woman
> munching a plum on
> the street a paper bag
> of them in her hand
>
> They taste good to her
> They taste good
> to her. They taste
> good to her . . .

"In a poem," said Paul Celan, "what's real *happens*."

What's real *happens* in "Iris," where a willful momentum plays off against oddly uniform stanzas.

> a burst of iris so that
> come down for
> breakfast
>
> we searched through the
> rooms for
> that
>
> sweetest odor and at
> first could not
> find its
>
> source then a blue as
> of the sea
> struck
>
> startling us from among
> those trumpeting
> petals

Alfred Stieglitz, *Spring Showers, 1901*.
Photogravure, 30.8 × 12.6 cm, Alfred Stieglitz Collection, 1949.849,
Art Institute of Chicago.

If all poems are quest poems, few home in on their goal so winningly, each tapered cluster focusing in on an action, an event.

"Iris" wants gradual unscrolling, line-by-line seeking, like "To Waken an Old Lady" with its pivotal "But what?" Below a title that gives nothing away, Williams explodes "a burst of iris so that / . . . "—so that *what?* Leaning into the line break we look for what happens now, but the next line tucks in a time-frame: "a burst of iris so that / [having] come down for / breakfast . . ." Before breakfasting "we searched through the / . . . ," and every run-on line keeps the search open—"But what?"

> through the / rooms
> rooms for / that
> that / sweetest odor
> and at / first
> could not / find
> its / source
> then a blue as / of the sea

Urging us on by staying and going at every moment, Williams reinvents the lyric poem, much as Eadweard Muybridge invented the motion picture at Stanford by making frame-by-frame stills of a trotting horse.

Narrowing the quest, each triplet in "Iris" draws eye and ear across stanza breaks by echoing their opening words: "searched . . . sweetest . . . source . . . startling." And rightly, "source" touches off the poem's strangest verse, a wild fragment, a painter's daub:

> source then a blue as

Williams wasn't given to simile-mongering, but his

> source then a blue as
> of the sea

abruptly opens this event to something oceanic, primordial. Then a triple stress spanning three lines—sea / struck / / startling—shocks us deeper than words. Sweet smell has led to a sight of blue that blooms trumpeting petals, a shape and sound of overnight-bursting iris, the origin now the goal.

"His only decent poems," Yvor Winters brusquely rebuked a first-year professor in 1965, "are very early and very short!" But aren't there fine short later poems by Williams, such as "Iris," and early long poems too, all fed by a lifelong current?

In "The Wanderer" a young poet merged with "The Passaic, that filthy river" (well before the "empty bottles, sandwich papers" in Eliot's Thames river), as it bore him "Eddying back cool and limpid / Into the crystal beginning of its days." Decades later that same New Jersey source impels *Paterson*, the five-book epic Williams worked on for twenty years, trying like Thoreau and Whitman to turn up fertile soil for American consciousness and conscience.

Paterson opens where Passaic Falls originates from

> oozy fields
> abandoned to grey beds of dead grass,
> black sumac, withered weed-stalks,
> mud and thickets cluttered with dead leaves

—originates, that is, from a wasteland, like *Spring and All*'s road to the contagious hospital. But instead of Eliot's "dry stone" and "thunder without rain," here the falls pour down their gorge "in a recoil of spray and rainbow mist" into a page-long torrent of verse. At the brink these waters, "glass-smooth with their swiftness, / quiet or seem to quiet." Then, fusing violence and quiescence, they

> fall, fall in air! as if
> floating, relieved of their weight,
> split apart, ribbons; dazed, drunk
> with the catastrophe of the descent
> floating unsupported
> to hit the rocks: to a thunder,
> as if lightning had struck

Watching waterfalls at a distance, that sense we get of massive force simply floating downward has brought this spellbound potency out of oozy fields and dead grass.

Passaic Falls' raw energy speaks for chosen ground, the local place turned universal through a poet's deep regard. The family doctor thinks of Paterson's decaying families:

> The language, the language
>   fails them . . .
> They may look at the torrent in
>   their minds
> and it is foreign to them.

He lends his mind's eye to catch life aflow but not lost, held in the Falls'

> unmoving roar, fastened
> there: the rocks silent
> but the water, married to the stone,
> voluble, though frozen.

Whatever became of those families, Williams's *Autobiography* closes with him taking his grandson to hear the Falls "let out a roar as it crashed upon the rocks at its base. In the imagination this roar is a speech or a voice. . . . It is the poem itself that is the answer."

Alongside his radical bent, as with nature's firstlings in *Spring and All,*

> rooted, they
> grip down and begin to awaken

—along with that biologic revolution, Williams felt political incitement too. Sacco and Vanzetti's execution outraged him, and especially the Spanish Civil War, García Lorca's murder, then Guernica, so that he chaired his local Committee for Medical Help to Loyalist Spain. Williams loved García Lorca "stemming exclusively from Iberian sources," not northern European, and the Chilean Pablo Neruda "who collected / seashells on his / native beaches."

The native stimulus always grabbed him, so when in 1950 a Paterson twenty-three-year-old came seeking "some kind of new speech," Williams put Allen Ginsberg's letter right into *Paterson.* When Robert Lowell applauded *Paterson,* Williams congratulated him on finding "a way to mention local place names" in poems such as "The Quaker Graveyard in Nantucket." Later Lowell went to Europe. Williams wrote: "Come back enriched in experience but come back . . . The trend has always been toward denial of origins, assertion of origins is the more fertile basis for thought—and technique."

All his life he dwelt in one place and spent thousands of days traversing the region on house calls. Before World War II and long before environment became a catchword, with suburban sprawl wiping out the semiwild countryside he loved, Williams put his flexible lines to use in "The Defective Record." Developers are cutting a riverbank, "killing whatever was / there before," craving land

> to build a house
> on to build a
> house on to build a house on
> to build a house
> on to build a house on to . . .

This worsened during and after the war. Travelling the Northwest in 1948, he saw how much "this beast man has devastated." Near home, highways destroyed the woods and industrial waste fouled the rivers. A "pustular scum, a decay, a choking / lifelessness," he notes in *Paterson,* "An acrid, a revolting stench," though maybe just once

> Where the dredge dumped the fill,
> something, a white hop-clover
> with cordy roots (of iron) gripped
> the sand in its claws—and blossomed
> massively

Something, at least, can "grip down and begin to awaken."

Turning seventy, disabled by a heart attack and harsh strokes, Williams worked on a long love poem, "Asphodel, That Greeny Flower." For a boy in Switzerland, the "green-flowered asphodel made a tremendous impression on me," so he pressed it in a book with other flowers, and much later found it growing in New Jersey too. Now this mortal man's poem entreats Flossie, his wife, "Listen while I talk on / against time."

> Of asphodel, that greeny flower,
>> like a buttercup
>>> upon its branching stem—
> save that it's green and wooden—
>> I come, my sweet,
>>> To sing to you.

Threefold pacing opens a way to move and breathe. Denise Levertov, whom Williams valued, calls it a swift yet stately pace "to express formally a hard-earned wisdom."

Storm and sea, "sea wrack / and weeds" enter this poem, and "starfish / stiffened by the sun,"

> But the sea
>> which no one tends
>>> is also a garden
> when the sun strikes it
>> and the waves
>>> are wakened.

Still the atom bomb pervades several pages, while

> Every drill
>> driven into the earth
> for oil enters my side
>> also.
>>> Waste, waste!

Yet flowers crop up that the man and woman have loved over the years: apple blossom, pink mallow, wild plum, lily, honeysuckle, daisy, violet. "Only the imagination is real!" he cries once again, and (like Coleridge): "But love and the imagination / are of a piece." Williams died in 1963, five weeks after Frost and just as Rachel Carson's *Silent Spring* was awakening modern environmental consciousness.

"Poetry is news that stays news," his buddy Ezra Pound had said. Here then are his lines that stay freshest in mind, reviving whenever human spirit needs them:

Of asphodel, that greeny flower,
       I come, my sweet,
              to sing to you!
My heart rouses
       thinking to bring you news
           of something
that concerns you
       and concerns many men. Look at
           what passes for the new.
You will not find it there but in
       despised poems.
           It is difficult
to get the news from poems
       yet men die miserably every day
           for lack
of what is found there.

"room for me and a mountain lion"
D. H. Lawrence in Taormina and Taos

*H*ermoso es! (She's beautiful!). In New Mexico D. H. Lawrence (1885–1930), meeting two hunters with a mountain lion they've killed, gives his sense of her, the "fine rays in the brilliant frost of her face. / Beautiful dead eyes."

From his birthplace in the mining and farming terrain of Midlands England, Lawrence ranged the world seeking a place to fuse spiritual with bodily life. His native country gave him that in the novels, but lush Tuscany and torrid Sicily fired his poetry. Meanwhile he took on the New World—Mexico and fervently the Southwest, "the rounded sides of the squatting Rockies, / Tigress-brindled with aspen, / Jaguar-splashed, puma-yellow, leopard-livid slopes of America."

Birds, Beasts and Flowers! (1923), a gallery of piercing, raving poems, came out first in the United States, with that exclamation mark occurring only on the cover he himself designed, not on the title page. (plate 10) Along with Taos, Santa Fe, Española, and Lobo in New Mexico, the poems stem from Italy, Germany, Austria, Australia, Ceylon, and not from jolly old England. In Tuscany pomegranate and peach, the "bursten" fig, "fruit of the female mystery, covert and inward . . . showing her crimson through the purple slit / Like a wound," the grape and dark Etruscan cypress all make his mythic mind run wild. In Sicily the almond tree under "Etna's snow-edged wind," the "ruddy-muzzled cyclamens / In little bunches like bunches of wild hares," the mosquito with its "small, high, hateful bugle in my ear . . . / Obscenely ecstasied / Sucking live blood, / My blood," and stunningly a snake at his water trough all draw Lawrence into a vortex of selfhood wrestling with the indifferent ravishing nature of things.

Several seasons near Taormina in Sicily spawned poems on the mosquito, ass, he-goat, she-goat, and "Snake"—that generic monosyllable facing us like a totem.

> A snake came to my water-trough
> On a hot, hot day, and I in pyjamas for the heat,
> To drink there. . . .
>
> He reached down from a fissure in the earth-wall in the gloom
> And trailed his yellow-brown slackness soft-bellied down, over
>   the edge of the stone trough
> And rested his throat upon the stone bottom,
> And where the water had dripped from the tap, in a small clearness,
> He sipped with his straight mouth,
> Softly drank through his straight gums, into his slack long body,
> Silently.

Right away there's no objectivity, no feigning an invisible naturalist's discreet notation. It's a "hot, hot" day at "my" water-trough, and doubtful whether "I" in pajamas can get a sane sense of any creature. Loaded language thrusts this reptile on us: "a fissure . . . in the gloom," "slackness soft-bellied," "his slack long body, / Silently." Something biblical and phallic deepens a primal human fear, yet the snake simply rests and sips softly and silently.

The storyteller's narrative touch plus his Whitmanesque lines build a scene not open to the taut voice of Dickinson's "A narrow Fellow in the Grass."

> He lifted his head from his drinking, as cattle do,
> And looked at me vaguely, as drinking cattle do,
> And flickered his two-forked tongue from his lips, and mused a moment,
> And stooped and drank a little more,
> Being earth-brown, earth-golden from the burning bowels of the earth
> On the day of Sicilian July, with Etna smoking.
>
> The voice of my education said to me
> He must be killed,
> For in Sicily the black black snakes are innocent, the gold are venomous.
>
> And voices in me said, If you were a man
> You would take a stick and break him now, and finish him off.

That he "looked at me vaguely" makes sense, but "mused a moment" lends him the poet's own muse. And his sex too. "He" owes less to volcanic Etna's burning bowels than to D. H. Lawrence's. Still, "a man" lives vulnerable on earth, while the snake, "Being earth-brown, earth-golden," springs from a deeper source.

However weak, we with our education wield much might over this fragile resilient planet. Lawrence bares a streak of manly violence, then a disarming candor.

> But must I confess how I liked him,
> How glad I was he had come like a guest in quiet, to drink
>   at my water-trough
> And depart peaceful, pacified, and thankless
> Into the burning bowels of this earth?
>
> And truly I was afraid, I was most afraid,
> But even so, honoured still more
> That he should seek my hospitality
> From out the dark door of the secret earth.

Confession, fear, honor, plus verboseness: refreshing traits in the modern poetry of nature, compared to the 1920s' spare rural truths of Frost and Williams's bracing botany.

In this to-and-fro drama, there's no knowing which is protagonist, which antagonist.

> He drank enough
> And lifted his head, dreamily, as one who has drunken,
> And flickered his tongue like a forked night on the air, so black,
> Seeming to lick his lips,
> And looked around like a god, unseeing, into the air,
> And slowly turned his head,
> And slowly, very slowly, as if thrice adream
> Proceeded to draw his slow length curving round
> And climb again the broken bank of my wall-face.
>
> And as he put his head into that dreadful hole,
> And as he slowly drew up, snake-easing his shoulders, and entered further,
> A sort of horror, a sort of protest against his withdrawing into that
>   horrid black hole,
> Deliberately going into the blackness, and slowly drawing himself after,
> Overcame me now his back was turned.

Rendering what's physical—flickering tongue, head lifting and turning, "slow length curving" and climbing—Lawrence at the same time makes it mythic: "a forked night," whatever that means, a godlike snake "unseeing" and "thrice adream."

Again the human mind sinks from honor to horror as the snake deserts him into earth's unknowable blackness. Humility gives way to confounding.

I looked round, I put down my pitcher,
I picked up a clumsy log
And threw it at the water-trough with a clatter.

I think it did not hit him;
But suddenly that part of him that was left behind convulsed in
    undignified haste,
Writhed like lightning, and was gone
Into the black hole, the earth-lipped fissure in the wall-front
At which, in the intense still noon, I stared with fascination.

Something "earth-golden . . . like a god" gives way to "clumsy . . . clatter . . .
convulsed," words that set off a sinuous, silent, slow epiphany and leave us
staring into earth's dark door.

"Snake" might have left off here, in fascination (and still no noonday drink).
But Lawrence feels a curse he felt too in Melville's *Moby-Dick*, "the maniacal
fanaticism of our white mental consciousness." His unguarded, likable gab suffers a final spasm of loss after the violence.

And immediately I regretted it.
I thought how paltry, how vulgar, what a mean act!
I despised myself and the voices of my accursed human education.

And I thought of the albatross,
And I wished he would come back, my snake.

The notion of "my" snake sounds petty, as against the creature's self-sufficient
purity of purpose. Still these lines tap into human conscience. Coleridge's Ancient Mariner must wear around his neck the albatross he killed, until one day
he spots water-snakes swimming alongside the ship:

Blue, glossy green, and velvet black
They coil'd and swam, and every track
    Was a flash of golden fire. . . .
A spring of love gusht from my heart,
    And I bless'd them unaware!

The albatross falls from his neck into the sea, but Lawrence has "missed my
chance with one of the lords / Of life."

Coping with the animate world around him, Lawrence joins an entire tradition. Since 30,000 years ago in France's Lascaux cave, drawings of stags,
wild goats and asses, bears, horses, and bulls stand as vibrant and stylized as
Picasso's. Millennia before the American continent was "discovered," native
peoples carved and painted animals as intimate totems on remote desert rocks.
Much later, Psalms praise the Lord for "things creeping innumerable" in "the
great and wide sea": "There is that Leviathan, whom thou hast made to take his

pastime therein." And God awes Job: "Canst thou draw out leviathan with an hook?" Moby-Dick's pastime in the Atlantic, flailing whaleboats and drowning Ahab, seems supernatural—whether malevolent, indifferent, or unknowable.

Though Lawrence could make free with "the blue deep bed of the sea" where "enormous mother whales lie dreaming," he put his sense of unknowing into "Fish."

> They are beyond me, are fishes.
> I stand at the pale of my being
> And look beyond.

A "slim young pike" goes beyond this poet's limits, "Slouching along away below, half out of sight," even as its human-like "slouching" keeps the pike within verbal sight.

> But watching closer
> That motionless deadly motion,
> That unnatural barrel body, that long ghoul nose . . .
> I left off hailing him.

That "motionless deadly motion" catches something uncanny, like the "repose in swiftness" of Melville's breaching whale. So does "unnatural," while betraying a stubborn human sense of what's natural.

This fish gets the poet's best shot, in wildly empathic writing:

> Your life a sluice of sensation along your sides,
> A flush at the flails of your fins, down the whorl of your tail.

Suddenly he's caught a "gold-and-greenish" one,

> Unhooked his gorping, water-horny mouth,
> And seen his horror-tilted eye,
> His red-gold, water-precious, mirror-flat bright eye;
> And felt him beat in my hand, with his mucous, leaping lifethrob.

Lawrence's words have a lifethrob of their own. Never mind "water-horny"— what's "gorping"? In Midlands dialect they're gaping, gawking. Roiling language paints this creature's death throes at once close and strange,

> But I, I only wonder
> And don't know.
> I don't know fishes.

You've got to love a poet who comes down to this.

Much as he cherished Italy and England too, Lawrence nursed a love-hate for America, a sharp but skewed notion of the paleface country's boundless democratic benevolence, its greed and prosperity. He decried our eagle perched over the world, "The pioneering brute invasion of the West, crime-tinged!"

Despite all this, "your demonish New World nature" somehow breeds "will . . . endurance . . . desperateness . . . generosity."

A generation before most Americans, Lawrence found "life surging itself at its very wellhead" in Whitman, "pioneering into the wilderness of unopened life." *Birds, Beasts and Flowers!* shows what he shared with Walt: himself as a benchmark, tied in sympathy to the life stirring about him; a sensual yet wildly fanciful touch for that life; rangy verse lines surging up, down, sideways, and back upon themselves, colored by flagrant turns of speech; always bodily, always spiritual risings of consciousness; ardor for physical nature crossed with skepticism about its human visitor.

Britons yearn southward toward Mediterranean lands, and Lawrence also needed the dryly flourishing high desert and mountains north of Santa Fe. Aspen, cedar, cottonwood, spruce, balsam, piñon pine, and red rock crop up in his poems, in "my hearth-rug of desert." Like Robinson Jeffers, who visited Taos about when he was there, Lawrence revered the hawk and "scorched breast" eagle, "Sun-breaster," "sun-starer," "foot-fierce" with the "god-thrust entering you steadily from below." His book's cover features an eagle clasping a snake, drawn by him in Southwest-Indian style. Lawrence adored the hummingbird too—primeval, huge, a "jabbing, terrifying monster." Given a 160-acre ranch northwest of Taos, at 8,600 feet on Lobo Mountain, he even tried to form a utopian community. His ashes ended up there.

"Mountain Lion," one of his least known but most striking poems, has him

> Climbing through the January snow, into the Lobo canyon
> Dark grow the spruce trees, blue is the balsam, water sounds still
> unfrozen, and the trail is still evident.

He meets "Two Mexicans, strangers"—"Men! The only animal in the world to fear!" What are they doing here, what are they carrying?

> Something yellow.
> A deer?
>
> *Qué tiene, amigo?*—
> *León*— . . .
>
> It is a mountain lion,
> A long, slim cat, yellow like a lioness.
> Dead.
>
> He trapped her this morning, he says, smiling foolishly.
>
> Lift up her face,
> Her round, bright face, bright as frost.
> Her round, fine-fashioned head, with two dead ears:

And stripes on the brilliant frost of her face, sharp, fine dark rays,
Dark, keen, fine rays in the brilliant frost of her face.
Beautiful dead eyes.

Hermoso es!

They go out towards the open;
We go on into the gloom of Lobo.

Ecstasy drives his rave for her "face, / Her round, bright face, bright as frost. / . . . the brilliant frost of her face, sharp, fine dark rays, / Dark, keen, fine rays in the brilliant frost of her face." Too much incantatory energy has built up to end here.

As in "Snake," Lawrence presses toward the source he always sought, whether in nature or humankind.

And above the trees I found her lair,
A hole in the blood-orange brilliant rocks that stick up, a little cave.
And bones, and twigs, and a perilous ascent.
So, she will never leap up that way again, with the yellow flash of a
    mountain lion's long shoot!
And her bright striped frost-face will never watch any more,
    out of the shadow of the cave in the blood-orange rock,
Above the trees of the Lobo dark valley-mouth.

In a dark hole like the snake's, fascinating, secret, the sexual richness of "blood-orange" twice over and "the yellow flash" signal some sort of revelation, akin to Blake's "Tyger, tyger burning bright, / In the forests of the night!"

Strangely enough, not even looking into the cave,

Instead, I look out.
And out to the dim of the desert, like a dream, never real,

to the Sangre de Cristo range, snow-covered year round, and Picoris, an Indian pueblo, and "green trees motionless standing in snow." Unlike Hemingway, Lawrence was no hunter, so the death of a singular puma rakes his mind, like the snake's retreat.

And I think in this empty world there was room for me and a
    mountain lion.
And I think in the world beyond, how easily we might spare a million
    or two of humans
And never miss them.
Yet what a gap in the world, the missing white-frost face of that
    slim yellow mountain lion!

A fifth time now he calls up her frost face. Think of Hemingway's "Snows of Kilimanjaro," wondering "what the leopard was seeking at that altitude." Or

Peter Matthiessen decades later: "That the snow leopard is, that it is there, that its frosty eyes watch us from the mountain—that is enough."

Today there are four billion more humans than when Lawrence wrote his poem, and countless fewer pumas. We're living in that world beyond. Once "there was room for me and a mountain lion." There may not be much longer.

"not man / Apart"
Ocean, Rock, Hawk, and Robinson Jeffers

Not Man Apart. For a 1965 Sierra Club photo book, the environmental activist David Brower took this title from Robinson Jeffers (1887–1962). A mind-cleansing rightness strikes home if we hear those three spare words the way they actually occur in his poem. Praising "Organic wholeness, the wholeness of life and things," Jeffers then says: "Love that, not man / Apart from that"—a loaded line break! (plate 11)

Ansel Adams found Jeffers "a strange presence with his rugged features and relentless glance" when they met in 1926. Later he told Alfred Stieglitz he hoped "to call attention to the simplicities of environment . . . to 'the enormous beauty of the world,' as Jeffers writes. Pray for me." His photographs of California's Big Sur coast are featured in *Not Man Apart*, and Adams mostly turned his lens on the nonhuman world.

Jeffers deplores the "contagion" of selfish humanity on our planet,

> But who is our judge? It is likely the enormous
> Beauty of the world requires for completion our ghostly increment.

Less hangs on "Beauty" here than on "enormous," the cosmos in which humanity is a late and transient addition. Not "man / Apart," he wrote, and this too:

> The coast hills at Sovranes Creek;
> No trees, but dark scant pasture drawn thin
> Over rock shaped like flame;

> The old ocean at the land's foot, the vast
> Gray extension beyond the long white violence;
> A herd of cows and the bull
> Far distant, hardly apparent up the dark slope;
> And the gray air haunted with hawks.

With no main verb, these notings begin "The Place for No Story." But any scene requires a seer, seeing "rock shaped like flame." And whose pasture and herd?—though they're barely there. Jeffers could have ended tellingly on "gray air haunted with hawks," but a he adds a comment:

> No imaginable
> Human presence here could do anything
> But dilute the lonely self-watchful passion.

—much as in a later poem, he encounters "pure naked rock" and ends having "Felt its intense reality with love and wonder, this lonely rock."

Prophetic arrogance has been the charge against him, and misanthropy, something sharper than Frost's "I had a lover's quarrel with the world." Yet the bitterness Jeffers felt at human wastage—the "year's filth," "the power-shovels"—always sprang from loving awe of the earth he dwelled on.

His family, strict Calvinists, had moved from Pennsylvania to California in 1902. At seventeen, in *The Youth's Companion,* Jeffers published "The Condor," whose rhyme and meter he'd soon abandon but not its austere stance: "My wings can dare / All loneliest hanging heights of air." California condors had thrived for tens of thousands of years, until whaling and sealing deprived them of marine carcasses. Then thanks to power lines, pleasure shooting, and lead from eating hunters' kills, Jeffers saw them decline from six hundred to about fifty in the wild. By 1985 one breeding pair remained. Then an astonishing recovery program literally snatched them from extinction. They're now back in their hundreds, though still plagued by lead poisoning.

After college in southern California, Jeffers in 1914 moved north with his new wife, Una. Traveling by stagecoach they "looked down through pines and sea-fogs on Carmel Bay"—"our inevitable place." Una describes Big Sur, south of Carmel, with the verve of a Dorothy Wordsworth transplanted to the Pacific rim: "Canyons, gushing springs and streams, are thickly wooded with redwoods and pines, laurels, tan-oak, maples and sycamores, and, high up, the rosy-barked madrones. . . . Lashing waves roll in, incredibly green and blue beyond the foam, menacing and gray in storm," wildflowers of every sort, "Flashing bird-wings . . . And high above, arrogant hawks hover, marsh hawks and sparrow hawks, redtails and peregrine falcons. Vultures too peering down, and a rare pair of eagles." In "Lashing," "Flashing," "peering," you can feel the bent of mind she shared with her husband.

"I'd sooner, except the penalties, kill a man than a hawk." This rude thought, from "Hurt Hawks," might turn one off Jeffers, but listen to the end. Having fed the broken-winged redtail for six weeks,

> I gave him the lead gift in the twilight.
>   What fell was relaxed,
> Owl-downy, soft feminine feathers; but what
> Soared: the fierce rush: the night-herons by the flooded river
>   cried fear at its rising
> Before it was quite unsheathed from reality.

No false sentiment, no sentiment at all, spoonfeeds these lines. "Soared . . . fierce . . . fear" identify with animate life, while "rising . . . unsheathed from reality" discovers a raw spirit-bound beauty.

Along with hawks, Jeffers bonded with gray rock, the "granite sea-boulders" he hauled up "wind and wave-worn" to help construct Tor House on a stone outcrop fifty yards above the Pacific. Digging for a fireplace foundation he found bedrock blackened by ancient Indian campfires, and from a disused Spanish mission brought home a discarded boulder with an Indian mortar hole in it. A few years later, with his twin boys, he built Hawk Tower (setting into it a piece from Yeats's old stone tower in Ireland). Again and again his verse comes back to "living rock," "lonely rock," "water-darkened . . . lovely rock," "pure naked rock." His poem "Rock and Hawk" calls these two presences, bird and stone, "Fierce consciousness joined with final / Disinterestedness." No American poet had bound together such starkness and passion, speaking from "this granite edge of the continent."

Jeffers first caught East Coast attention in a 1925 California anthology whose title poem, "Continent's End," stands where the ocean "beat its boundary, the groundswell shook the beds of granite." Like the Yokuts shaman—"My words are tied in one / . . . With the great rocks"—a western Whitman feels the continent's pulse: "my song's measure is like your surf-beat's ancient rhythm." Here was a voice akin to Thoreau confronting "vast, terrific . . . inhuman Nature" at Maine's Mount Katahdin.

From his own standpoint, Jeffers spoke of "Inhumanism," based on "the astonishing beauty of things" and "the fact that mankind is neither central nor important in the universe." What he felt as pure nobleness doesn't always sit well. In one of many poems looking deep into her place on earth, "Yom Kippur 1984," Adrienne Rich (b. 1929) has just moved from the East Coast to Santa Cruz County, near Carmel. Jeffers-like, she meets the "grey Pacific unrolling its scrolls of surf." Searching for some lines she remembers, "something to bind me to this coast . . . / I find the hatred in the poet's heart." She cites a poem of his: "the hateful-eyed and human-bodied are all about me: you that love multi-

Horace Lyon, Tor House and Hawk Tower, ca. 1930.
Tor House Foundation.

tude may have them." Rich responds for migrant workers' multitude as against his solitude, "the poet's tower facing the western ocean." Loving the biblical "stranger that dwelleth among you," she questions her own separateness as Jew, woman, lesbian. When winter flood tides "crumble the prophet's headland," she asks, "when leviathan is endangered," what will solitude mean then?

As he aged and his voice grew faint against the noise of progress, Jeffers dug in, "Mourning the broken balance, the hopeless prostration of the earth / Under men's hands and their minds . . . my own coast's obscene future." Nowadays California coastal dwellers, watching their bluffs and beaches erode, build cement "sea walls, because we don't put waves before the homes of people." This may seem necessary, but it masks a puzzling idea of waves.

A certain pain arises from photos of Tor House and Hawk Tower solitary on a wild bluff in 1919, '23, '27, before "suburban houses" crowded round. And from Jeffers recalling how he and Una once watched a puma stride along a nearby ridge. In 1936 the carving of a coast road, Highway 1, brought acute dismay, yet "the great bronze gorge-cut sides of the mountains" remain "Not the least hurt," "Beautiful beyond belief."

That summer Jeffers hiked with his son up "the pathless gorge of Ventana Creek" near Big Sur and recounted this event in "Oh, Lovely Rock." Introducing his lucid, level reading of the poem at the Library of Congress, he says, "You must understand that this is not southern California. There are no orange groves and no oil wells." Instead there's "forest on forest above our heads." Past midnight the fire's flame "Lighted my sleeping son's face . . . and the vertical face of the great gorge-wall / Across the stream." There was "no fern or lichen, pure naked rock . . . as if I were / Seeing rock for the first time." Those silent dots of his trace a movement of mind from the visual into the visionary. They occur again as he sees

> the real and bodily
> And living rock. Nothing strange . . . I cannot
> Tell you how strange.

It's "living" rock, he reminds us. And strange, though rock would seem familiar. In it he sees a "fate going on / Outside our fates." He and his son will die, "this age will die," but "this rock will be here,"

> the energies
> That are its atoms will still be bearing the whole mountain above.

Ending this memory of a "lovely rock," he "Felt its intense reality with love and wonder, this lonely rock." Emotion doesn't belie his severe creed, the integrity of humankind's organic wholeness with our earth. It takes openness to sense those atomic energies, and humility to move from "lovely" to "lonely," speaking for himself in speaking for pure naked rock.

Seventy years later to the day, a group with Jeffers's grandson clambered two days up the still pathless gorge and found the rock, now spread with ferns and moss. Or was there green growth even back then in 1936, and the nighttime force of his vision made Jeffers see "pure naked rock"? (Plate 12)

Turning fifty and struck by Europe's imminent barbarism, in other poems he draws on the oracles of W. B. Yeats, for whom "The falcon cannot hear the falconer; / Things fall apart; the centre cannot hold." Where catastrophe for Yeats was cultural, Jeffers imagines the sun combusting like a nova:

> The earth would share it; these tall
> Green trees would become a moment's torches and vanish, the oceans
> Would explode into invisible steam.

And where Yeats hoped an aristocracy rooted in folk tradition could save civilization, Jeffers relies on a lonely rock and our true selves, no more changed "in ten thousand years than the beaks of eagles."

Often a stubborn love for primordial nature vies with disdain in his writing. In "Orca," written just after World War II, he again feels the "surf-beat's ancient rhythm" just below his home. "Sea-lions loafed in the swinging tide in the inlet," and offshore rocks

> Bristled with quiet birds, gulls, cormorants, pelicans, hundreds
>   and thousands
> Standing thick as grass on a cut of turf. Beyond these, blue,
>   gray, green, wind-straked, the ocean
> Looked vacant.

Then "two black triangles, tacking and veering," killer-whale fins, drove in panicking the seals. "The water boiled for a moment," while below "a screaming / And wheeling sky . . . brown blood and foam / Striped the water of the inlet." Terror, death, "yet it looked clean and bright, it was beautiful. / Why? Because there was nothing human involved . . . no smirk and no malice," only the raw trend of things.

Riveted to a lovely, lonely rock "Smooth-polished by the endless attrition of slides and floods," Jeffers waives any affection for "man / Apart" (and for himself too), in favor of a deeper, necessary love.

"submerged shafts of the / / sun, / split like spun / glass"
Marianne Moore's Fantastic Reverence

"In England," she said in 1943 when the war's outcome stood in doubt, "One pays a fine for throwing away a used bus ticket that could have been preserved as waste paper, and the grocer is not expected to furnish a bag with what he sells but to put it into the basket or shopping bag brought by the purchaser." It's surprising, this indignation, coming from Marianne Moore (1887–1972), our idiosyncratic poet of tapestry oceans and lapis lazuli seagulls and Brooklyn Dodgers. But there she is railing at "slumbering civic indifference," decades early. "One of the most eloquent phases of savage resourcefulness is thrift," she said, "involving as it does responsibility to nature." Moore was moved back then by Native American economies (some of which have since been questioned): "After removing a plant, the Indian was careful to drop a seed in the hole."

Thrift, in fact, marks Moore's every move. "To a Snail":

> If 'compression is the first grace of style',
> you have it

Why is a snail like Athenian rhetoric? Her few syllables graft human language onto animal nature, recycle available wisdom, identify a primitive creature, and give it respect with intimacy. Relishing "the curious phenomenon of your occipital horn," she gets threefold use from "curious": exotic, intricate, exciting curiosity. When Marianne Moore reached American readers—first a knowing few during the 1920s and 1930s, eventually a wide public—her oddness struck first: cockeyed but consistent stanzas and rhyming, an oblique specific take on any animal, artifact, and idea under the sun, and a habit of sowing poems with authoritative citations. About quotation Moore pled simple economy: "I've always felt that if a thing has been said in the very best way, how can you say it better?" Though sensible enough, this doesn't do justice to her novelty.

We're not dealing here with T. S. Eliot's quotations in *The Waste Land*, those notorious fragments—"This music crept by me upon the waters"—meant to shore up our paltry present with past richness. Moore's quotes blend into the poem, as we hear when she reads aloud. Whimsical, like her own phrases, they can also seem finicky. And that she was, prizing exactitude (plus concision, clarity, surprise), preferring attentiveness to vague sentiment.

These qualities served Moore when she went climbing on Washington's Mount Rainier. John Muir had found it "so fine and so beautiful it might well fire the dullest observer to desperate enthusiasm." A generation later our keenest observer made a long poem on that "Octopus / of ice" with tentacle glaciers. Borrowing with "relentless accuracy" from a National Parks pamphlet, she describes rock "'stained transversely by iron where the water drips down.'" After all, poetry should be no less "genuine," she said, than science. She describes "the hard mountain 'planed by ice and polished by the wind'," fancying the pamphlet's well-turned phrase for nature's artisanry on Rainier's upper slopes.

Sometimes poets must "set down an unbearable accuracy." She means the shock of metaphor, impossible yet true perception. When Gerard Manley Hopkins notes lambs frolicking in a field "as though it was the ground that tossed them," Moore marvels how "precision is a thing of the imagination." Her knack was conscientious exactness.

Moore's best-liked poem began this way when Eliot published it in 1918:

> THE FISH
> Wade through black jade.
> Of the crow blue mussel-shells, one
> Keeps adjusting the ash-heaps;
> Opening and shutting itself like

Each quatrain had the same syllable count. A year later she changed everything but the words themselves.

> THE FISH
> wade
> through black jade.
>   Of the crow-blue mussel-shells, one keeps
>   adjusting the ash-heaps;
>   opening and shutting itself like

Marianne Moore, 1920–1925.
The Rosenbach Museum and Library, Moore XII:E:05.

Marianne Moore (third from right), Mount Rainier, 1922.
The Rosenbach Museum and Library, Moore XII 28.06.

Her title wades into the body of the poem. No longer half-hidden like mussels, the rhymes—"wade . . . jade," "keeps . . . heaps"—stud five-line stanzas with staggered margins and syllables, one, three, nine, six, eight. Instead of squared quatrains, wavelines keep making move after move, stanzas go on exposing rhyme after crisp rhyme.

Moore wants us "galvanized against inertia," each phrase creating an "unbearable accuracy," a fresh perception contrary to fact. The fish "wade"—but no, it's humans who struggle through water. As they wade through jade, that quick rhyme deludes us, for seawater is anything but hard gemstone, and anyway jade comes in green, not black. But crows come in black. We enter some dark element as "crow-blue" color drags a land bird undersea, a raucous predator lending submarine sheen to sluggish shells.

One of them keeps "adjusting . . . ash-heaps," which bring on a mortal mood though ash stands for slow-stirring sea bottom. This shell then pauses at a stanza break, "opening and shutting itself like / / . . ." We're left hanging on this simile-in-the-making until "like / / an / injured fan" adds unlikely injury and unbalanced rhyme to an oddly genteel image. All this contrariness makes

"The Fish" no marine document but, as Moore said of precision, "a thing of the imagination."

No wonder the contemporaries she swore by were Wallace Stevens and William Carlos Williams. Note Stevens's motto: "Things as they are / Are changed upon the blue guitar." And the poets' admiration was mutual. Stevens found Moore "radiant with imagination" in the "sensitive handling" of reality, and Williams welcomed "a blasting aside, a dynamization" in verse.

"The Fish" moves on among hard surfaces—barnacles, crevices, cliff, chasm—turning up things we do and don't expect in the ocean: jellyfish and rice grains, crabs and toadstools, even spun glass, iron wedges, stars, burns, hatchet strokes. We can take it as pure whimsy, though we're headed for where "the submerged shafts of the sun" will spotlight cliff and sea, endlessly combating.

THE FISH
wade
through black jade.
      Of the crow-blue mussel-shapes, one keeps
      adjusting the ash-heaps;
            opening and shutting itself like

an
injured fan.
      The barnacles which encrust the side
      of the wave, cannot hide
            there for the submerged shafts of the

sun,
split like spun
      glass, move themselves with spotlight swiftness
      into the crevices—
            in and out, illuminating

the
turquoise sea
      of bodies. The water drives a wedge
      of iron through the iron edge
            of the cliff; whereupon the stars,

pink
rice-grains, ink-
      bespattered jelly-fish, crabs like green
      lilies, and submarine
            toadstools, slide each on the other.

All
external
      marks of abuse are present on this

```
                    defiant edifice—
                        all the physical features of

ac-
cident—lack
                    of cornice, dynamite grooves, burns, and
                    hatchet strokes, these things stand
                            out on it; the chasm-side is

dead.
Repeated
                    evidence has proved that it can live
                    on what can not revive
                            its youth. The sea grows old in it.
```

What are we to make of her whimsical wading fish, barnacles encrusting a wave, spun glass sunbeams, water's iron wedge? Much anthologized, these lines still guard their dreamlike eccentricities.

The poem's barely begun when its fish have vanished, giving way to menacing changes: an ash-heaped mussel shell, an injured fan, a wave's "side" whose barnacles can't "hide / there." Uncanny vision penetrates the dark deep along a swish of *s*-sounds passing along wavelike indents:

```
                        the submerged shafts of the

sun,
split like spun
                    glass, move themselves with spotlight swiftness
                    into the crevices—
                            in and out . . .
```

Precise imagination fuses nature with art, "sun, / split like spun / glass."

Once we buy that fusion, Moore's verbal leaps present enigmas—fish in jade, a mussel fan, glasslike sun, illuminating yet vaguely ominous spectacles. This oceanscape can turn turquoise to iron. And while "the iron edge / of the cliff" seems graspable, how (except through rhyme) does water drive "a wedge / of iron" into it? Before our eyes the starfish and

```
pink
rice-grains, ink-
                    bespattered jelly-fish, crabs like green
                    lilies, and submarine
                            toadstools, slide each on the other.
```

So do Moore's slabs of sound, like her friend Alexander Calder's mobiles. It's as if her verbal fantasia, in 1918, foresaw today's surreal color films of underwater life.

A riot of metamorphosis, "The Fish" takes after Shakespeare's song from *The Tempest*:

> Full fathom five thy father lies;
> Of his bones are coral made;
> Those are pearls that were his eyes:
> Nothing of him that doth fade,
> But doth suffer a sea change
> Into something rich and strange.

And her marvel, her sea change, turns metaphor-making into a naturalist's revel.

Moore's last three stanzas go beyond human limits, beyond even the sun's illumining reach. No fish remain, no spun glass or turquoise sea but a "defiant edifice," that sea-buffeted cliff. Stanza form, the poem's hold on order, persists perfectly, as its rhyming skews: oblique rhymes on unaccented syllables —"All / external," "this / . . . edifice," "dead. / Repeated"—and a key word hyphen-cracked, "ac- / cident—lack." For all her love of exactitude, Moore verges on chaos: abuse, accident, chasm, death. Somehow dynamite, burns, hatchets have ravaged the ocean cliffs of their cornice or architectural crown. The "chasm-side" fronting the sea is dead—chasm, perhaps, as from geologic time, when earth and waters split. Solid land is dead yet "can live / on," living on the sea that batters it.

At bottom, these stanzas forge a human struggle with raw nature, playing on color, shape, texture, motion, and naming to expose a wild system in the natural world. Like all metaphors, this grand one gets doubled energy, thrift at work.

Was Marianne Moore an environmentalist? It takes all kinds to make a (better) world. She can't boast the outdoors immersion of Frost, Jeffers, May Swenson, John Haines, Maxine Kumin, and others, but always bends her curiosity on the natural world, like Emily Dickinson whose "Japanesely fantastic reverence for tree, insect, and toadstool" Moore admired. The house she grew up in, "The Wren's Nest," housed birds and cats, and she had a pet alligator. Her first ambition, to be a visual artist, had her sketching plants and animals throughout her life. "I took pictures of nearly everything," Moore writes from the mountains, "logs sunk in the earth and two out of five fringed gilled newts that I caught in a spring. . . . I saw a falling star which looked like a sheet of paper on fire and a bat so close that I could see light through its wings—a kind of amber."

She relished natural history from libraries, museums, films, and lectures, and her poems make up a bestiary of common, rare, and mythical animals: basilisk, bear, buffalo, bug, chameleon, crow, dragon, dragonfly, elephant, ermine, fish, fox, frog, giraffe, jellyfish, jerboa, lion, mongoose, monkey, mouse, nautilus, octopus, ostrich, pangolin, peacock, reindeer, snail, snake, swan, tiger, unicorn, whale, wood-weasel. These critters don't challenge her, as in D. H. Lawrence's

"Snake" or her friend Elizabeth Bishop's "The Fish," Galway Kinnell's "The Bear," Ted Hughes's "Pike." Instead they snap us to attention. "A live snake is worth feeling," she says, like "a fine gold mesh bag with nothing in it and is silky like a poppy petal—dry and warm."

Moore couldn't stop linking nature and art: at night the stars "glittered like cut silver." Along with bat wings, snakeskin, gilled newts, and stars themselves, Moore's touch for amber, gold mesh, and cut silver, her jade sea and spun glass sun, do what art does best, what brushwork does for Audubon's osprey, Constable's clouds, what focus and contrast do for the redwoods of Ansel Adams.

When Miss Moore came upon a curious fact about the Estridge (ostrich) in a sixteenth-century account, she looked into the natural and folkloric history of this creature and composed her witty, gaudy, motley, fact-studded poem "He 'Digesteth Harde Yron'," because to her astonishment he does. For Stevens this pinpoints Moore: "she has the faculty of digesting the 'harde yron' of appearance," she can "confront fact in its total bleakness" with art that gains "a revelation of reality."

Williams saw a "porcelain garden" in Moore's poetry, meaning pleasure in cleanness, color, precision, design. She saw natural things through the lens of art and culture. (And vice-versa. When Ford invited her to name new automobile models, she suggested Mongoose, Civique, and Utopian Turtletop— much catchier than the Edsel they decided on.) "A sea gull / / Of lapis lazuli" delighted her, decades before Yeats's "Lapis Lazuli" saw waterfalls in a carved stone's "accidental crack." Yet her love of artifice fed an acute respect and awareness for things, from ocean cliffs to a mussel's motions.

Moore liked to cite Thoreau, "A true account of the actual is the rarest poetry," where "true," for her, means precisely imagined. In "Poetry," her syllables seek

> the genuine.
> Hands that can grasp, eyes
> that can dilate, hair that can rise
> if it must

when confronted with wildness:

> the bat
> holding on upside down or in quest of something to
> eat, elephants pushing, a wild horse taking a roll, a tireless
> wolf under
> a tree.

We shall "have it," she says, "the genuine," when "the poets among us can be 'literalists of the imagination'," creating "imaginary gardens with real toads in them."

"There, there where those black spruces crowd"
To Steepletop and Ragged Island
with Edna St. Vincent Millay

It is a hot summer afternoon. The air is drowsy with the sweetness
of the tiny trumpet-shaped flowers above my head, and, save for
the monotonous droning of many bees, there is no sound anywhere.

A girl of eighteen on the Maine coast is
fetching back to early childhood—Edna St. Vincent Millay (1892–1950).

Beside me are two long, slender white wands from which I have been peeling
the bark for ribbons (with primitive implements of sharp teeth and nails). I
taste again the sweetness of the smooth round stick in my mouth. I see again
the moist, delicate green of the bark's lining. And into my nostrils I breathe
the hot spicy fragrance until my very soul is steeped in it.

Instinctively she goes into present tense to bring past time and place alive,
overlaying that memory with the moment of writing: "I taste *again* . . . I see
again."

As she verges on adulthood, this journal journey takes her back "Through
a meadow where at every step I had to pick the violets to clear a place for my
feet," and up a "path to a secret spot where fox-berries grew bigger, sweeter and
more plentifully than anywhere else in the world" (she *knew* that, did she?). "I
liked the old white house and the vivid grass around it. I loved the blackberries
and the hill." On finding this once-loved place, "I caught my breath in an ecstasy
of recognition." This is the woman now remembered as a 1920s Greenwich
Village libertine.

Nineteenth-century Camden, Maine, on Penobscot Bay, held plenty for any
child: the sea for sailing, rowing, canoeing, swimming, Megunticook River and
Lake, woods and fields rife with trees, flowers, berries, all ringed by hills that

once attracted Thoreau venturing into Maine wilderness. What's rare is her touching memory for it all.

"All my childhood is in those bayberry-bushes, & queen-of-the-meadow, or maybe you call it hardhack, & rose-hips. And cranberries—I remember a swamp of them." When the river near her house ran over and there was no heat, the kitchen floor flooded and froze, so the sisters skated on it. "Another joy in the tall grasses was when it was raining hard," their mother recalls, the girls "leaping about in the rain, letting the summer showers soak them." "Earth-ecstatic," Edna calls herself. Traveling north of Bangor once, she saw "a big snowy mountain" forty miles off and was told it's Katahdin, Maine's highest. "Yes sir," she writes home, "I've seen it! Beautiful!"

Long after she'd moved to Manhattan and later settled upstate as a much-prized love poet, the ocean still drew this "girl who had lived all her life at the very tide-line of the sea." "Exiled" is astir with surf, spray, tide, sand, seaweed, driftwood, fog, gulls, mussels, shells, "green piles groaning . . . windy wooden piers." "Inland" calls up "water sucking the hollow ledges, / Tons of water striking the shore," and asks for "One salt smell of the sea once more."

Of course no childhood is purely idyllic. The eldest of three sisters whose single mother was an ill-paid visiting nurse often away from home, Millay had constant chores on top of schoolwork. "The color—Oh—. . . I want to climb Megunticook before the leaves are all gone. But I can't. I've got to work—all the time." Yet her mother published poems in *The Maine Farmer*, taught her to read via Shakespeare and Shelley, to sing and play piano. Edna loved Latin poetry, edited her school magazine, and was a passionate actress with flaming red hair and green eyes, red lips, white skin. "She had lots of spark and spunk," a school friend remembers, and was a "spitfire" against any injustice.

Too poor for college, Millay stayed home to work, and began "Renascence."

> All I could see from where I stood
> Was three long mountains and a wood;
> I turned and looked another way,
> And saw three islands in a bay.

Winter anguish presses down, then another hundred lines surge under cool rain,

> And as I looked a quickening gust
> Of wind blew up to me and thrust
> Into my face a miracle
> Of orchard-breath.

> God, I can push the grass apart
> And lay my finger on Thy heart!

One E. Vincent Millay submitted this poem in 1912 to a prestigious New York competition. When the judges ranked it high but not among the prizewinners, an outcry arose and her career took off. The literati lionized (and courted) her, benefactors sent her to Vassar, her celebrity exploded with a quatrain.

> My candle burns at both ends;
>   It will not last the night;
> But ah, my foes, and oh, my friends—
>   It gives a lovely light!

Along with irony, her passion and womanly pride sent slim volumes into tens of thousands of hands.

"I shall forget you presently, my dear," one sonnet begins, and another, "Oh, oh, you will be sorry for that word!" The form lent itself, and she bent it, to her own wryness.

> I, being born a woman and distressed
> By all the needs and notions of my kind . . .

Seasonal transience weaves into her mood.

> Pity me not because the light of day
> At close of day no longer walks the sky;
> Pity me not for beauties passed away
> From field and thicket as the year goes by.

This bifocal view, nature and human loss, dates far back in our civilization, as with François Villon's "Ballad of the Ladies of Bygone Times": *Où sont les neiges d'antan?* "Where are the snows of yore?" Or Shakespeare's "Sap checked with frost and lusty leaves quite gone, / Beauty o'ersnowed and bareness every where." Millay writes,

>   Love is no more
> Than the wide blossom which the wind assails,
> Than the great tide that treads the shifting shore,
> Strewing fresh wreckage gathered in the gales.

While traditional meter marks her off from the Californian Robinson Jeffers, whom she thought America's best poet, Millay's voice resounds on her own seacoast: "tide that treads," "Strewing fresh wreckage."

At their finest, her sonnets join Millay with Shakespeare and Keats.

> What lips my lips have kissed, and where, and why,
> I have forgotten, and what arms have lain
> Under my head till morning; but the rain
> Is full of ghosts tonight, that tap and sigh
> Upon the glass and listen for reply,

And in my heart there stirs a quiet pain
For unremembered lads that not again
Will turn to me at midnight with a cry.
Thus in the winter stands the lonely tree,
Nor knows what birds have vanished one by one,
Yet knows its boughs more silent than before;
I cannot say what loves have come and gone,
I only know that summer sang in me
A little while, that in me sings no more.

Instead of Shakespeare's three quatrains capped by a couplet, the Italian sonnet form rhymes eight lines then six. An octave's worth of chagrin, running on with only two rhyme sounds, turns toward the season, bolstering her story: "Thus in the winter . . ." Nature certifies her pain, and we can see why Thomas Hardy admired her so.

Meanwhile it's Shakespeare, as ever, at bottom. Not imitation but homage ripens Millay's lines, remembering *his* bare tree, boughs, and birds:

That time of year thou mayst in me behold,
When yellow leaves, or none, or few, do hang
Upon those boughs which shake against the cold,
Bare ruin'd choirs where late the sweet birds sang.

Nothing could match that astonishing metaphor, "Bare ruin'd choirs." Skeptics tax Millay's diction and syntax as antiquated thus sentimental. But "What lips my lips have kissed" ends on two perfect lines fusing her voice with the lost season:

I only know that summer sang in me
A little while, that in me sings no more.

Stretching "summer" over the break "A little while," then inverting "sang in me" to "in me sings," she turns up the fateful rhyme "no more."

Much depends on tact and skill. Nothing antique, sentimental, or beautified adorns a later poem, touching Millay's most vexed affair. After a bluff, breathtaking start, Maine's rockbound windbound scene takes over, filling up twelve of fourteen lines in her staunchest sonnet.

Hearing your words, and not a word among them
Tuned to my liking, on a salty day
When inland woods were pushed by winds that flung them
Hissing to leeward like a ton of spray,
I thought how off Matinicus the tide
Came pounding in, came running through the Gut,
While from the Rock the warning whistle cried,

And children whimpered, and the doors blew shut;
There in the autumn when the men go forth,
With slapping skirts the island women stand
In gardens stripped and scattered, peering north,
With dahlia tubers dripping from the hand:
The wind of their endurance, driving south,
Flattened your words against your speaking mouth.

Romance frames but barely contains a maritime saga. Once her opening rakes the air clean, line two gives way to a throbbing island seascape, a Maine way of marine life, women's life, lasting till the end.

Millay's lines course so strongly, we hardly notice their deft turns: "a salty day" for the salt of skepticism, and "like a ton of spray," as figures of speech carry the Atlantic northeaster into inland woods. No misused lover but someone rooted in one place is calling up its roughened ways. Matinicus Island lies twenty-five miles off Camden. Maybe the violent sea and hard fishing life reflect her youth—strapped, no father at home, a game mother. Before the word occurs, we sense "their endurance" obliquely in the women's "slapping" skirts, their gardens "stripped and scattered" as they "stand," planted against the wind.

An island starkness stretches Millay's poetics. Coastal rhythms rhyming locally ("through the Gut" / "doors blew shut," "men go forth" / "peering north"), wavelike cadences, local lingo toughened by long use, all drive a single sentence. She moves from the present ("a salty day") to the past (a "whistle cried") and on into a perennial present (the "women stand"). And throughout, ongoing verbs animate an old weather-centered story: "Hissing . . . pounding . . . running . . . warning . . . slapping . . . peering . . . dripping . . . driving." Set between "Hearing your words" and "your speaking mouth," a drama of place and people offsets romance with survival—getting the news from poems, as William Carlos Williams put it.

By 1923 Millay really had burned her candle at both ends, as turbulent affairs vied with illness, drinking, nervous breakdown. Still, she won a Pulitzer Prize that year, the first woman poet to do so, and married a fine Dutchman, Eugen Boissevain, widower of an American suffragist she'd admired in college. The couple bought a dilapidated dairy farm on seven hundred hilly acres in upstate New York and named it Steepletop, after a local wildflower, the steeplebush (or queen-of-the-meadow). They set about renovating the house, discovering a second brook, keeping birdfeeders full, cultivating fruits and herbs and vegetables, crating huckleberries for sale, picking "overwhelming blueberries" and "heavily bearing pear trees," snowshoeing miles for the mail. Millay's knowledge of flowers expanded, and of birds. One summer she noted fourteen species nesting on the ground, and rejoiced at a Bohemian waxwing, "Oh, at last I have seen one! (Seen two!)"

Near Santa Fe, New Mexico, in the winter of 1926, a western bird triggered something new in Millay. The Grand Canyon, Petrified Forest, Painted Desert, and Enchanted Mesa charmed her, and an Indian dance at Zuni pueblo. But what spurred a poem, "Pueblo Pot," was a "red-shafted flicker and his bride"—"two Navajos enchanted," she calls them. They appeared on a housetop,

> flashing the wonder of their underwings;
> There stood, mysterious and harsh and sleek,
> Wrenching the indigo berry from the shedding woodbine with strong
> ebony beak.

Condors and hawks in Jeffers's poems had recently astonished East Coast readers, and later when Millay visited him, "She questioned me about the local hawks." In "Pueblo Pot" her rangy lines take after him (and D. H. Lawrence, with his New Mexico eagle's "heavy black beak"). She kindles to a new bird. While the eastern flicker is a yellow-shafted race, the western, her first spotting, is red-shafted—"the wonder of their underwings."

A rapture heats this December desert scene and her own style too.

> The black new moon was crescent on the breast of each;
> From the bodies of both a visible heat beat down,
> And from the motion of their necks a shadow would fly and fall,
> Skimming the court and in the yellow adobe wall
> Cleaving a blue breach.
>
> Powerful was the beauty of these birds.
> It boomed like a struck bell in the silence deep and hot.

No such charge emanates from birds Millay prized at Steepletop—bobolink, waxwing, cuckoo, and scores of others. These flickers,

> The scarlet shaft on the grey cheek,
> The purple berry in the ebony beak,

met some craving in her, "the fierce light of the birds" akin to her own ardor.

As for the bond with Jeffers, what made it work? "I don't live near the sea," Millay told him, as his rocky home recalled her youth on the Maine coast, its "Tons of water striking the shore." "The beach where you went swimming," he wrote after her first visit, "is piled with stormy brown sea-weed." Jeffers called Millay "the once-a-century poet" who could manage "flamelike & powerful & very sweet" sonnets. She kept a picture of him on her desk.

Meanwhile political events roused her temper. The Massachusetts case of Sacco and Vanzetti, anarchist immigrants falsely accused of murder, came to a boil with their death sentence in 1927. Millay demonstrated wearing a placard,

Robinson Jeffers and Edna St. Vincent Millay at Hawk Tower, 1930.
Photo by Una Jeffers. Courtesy of Special Collections, Occidental College Library,
and Jeffers Literary Properties.

was arrested, went to the governor, wrote "I cry to you with a million voices,"
and published a last-minute poem.

> Let us abandon our gardens and go home
> And sit in the sitting-room.
> Shall the larkspur blossom or the corn grow under this cloud?
> Sour to the fruitful seed
> Is the cold earth under this cloud,
> Fostering quack and weed, we have marched upon but cannot conquer;
> We have bent the blades of our hoes against the stalks of them.

Edna St. Vincent Millay, Sacco and Vanzetti protest, 1927, "Free Them and
Save Massachusetts! American Honor Dies With Sacco and Vanzetti!"
Special Collections, Vassar College Libraries.

Nature speaks for human trouble—this ancient thought draws her close to home. The sun will no longer rise for us "Out of the glittering bay, / And the warm winds be blown inward from the sea." Anguished, her voice turns medieval in its animism of nature:

> See now the slug and the mildew plunder.
> Evil does overwhelm
> The larkspur and the corn;
> We have seen them go under.

Sacco and Vanzetti, electrocuted the next night, leave us "a blighted earth to till / With a broken hoe."

Away from the world, at Steepletop, Millay's herbs and flowers could still gladden her, despite rains and untimely frost. Wanting a further retreat, she and Boissevain bought Ragged Island, eighty rocky acres with a fisherman's shack and no electricity, approachable only at high tide, four miles offshore in Casco Bay, Maine. "Ragged Island, where we shall be entirely alone," she wrote a friend, "to gather driftwood, and haul our lobster-traps, and make fish-chowder, and sail, and read, and sit on the rocks." A visitor in 1945 watched Edna waving her arms as she came down the path to the dock, three seagulls circling round her head. At fifty-three and not at all robust, here "She was glowing with health and spirits; her red hair was blown free and her green eyes were shining."

Later when they went swimming, she let them know what the environment itself required. "We think bathing dress of any sort is indecent, and so do the waves and so do the sea gulls and so does the wind." She was in her element, floating for hours on end. "There, there where those black spruces crowd / To the edge of the precipitous cliff," runs her 1946 poem "Ragged Island." "There, thought unbraids itself, and the mind becomes single"—"you only look; you scarcely feel," and she incants the utopian adverb, "Oh, to be *there*."

World War II had fired Millay's sense of injustice, already honed by love and mortality. When the Nazis destroyed a Czech village, she wrote a thirty-two-page rhymed narrative, *The Murder of Lidice*, heard on radio all over America. But she was taking morphine hourly, and though Ragged Island helped her recover for a while, not much hope remained. Eugen died in 1949, and late one night the next year, Edna alone at home fell down the stairs and broke her neck.

Along the woodland path to their gravestones at Steepletop, poems of the place are now set on cedar posts, including her "Counting-out Rhyme" (as in *eeny, meeny, miny, moe*). What's the environmental news here? Only finding supple rhythms and rhymes tilting like leaves in her nearby trees, in the names of nearby trees. (plate 13)

Silver bark of beech, and sallow
Bark of yellow birch and yellow
   Twig of willow.

Stripe of green in moosewood maple,
Colour seen in leaf of apple,
   Bark of popple.

Wood of popple pale as moonbeam,
Wood of oak for yoke and barn-beam,
   Wood of hornbeam.

Silver bark of beech, and hollow
Stem of elder, tall and yellow
   Twig of willow.

"Gale sustained on a slope"
Pablo Neruda at Machu Picchu

*P*ertene*ʒ*co a un peda*ʒ*o de pobre tierra austral
hacia Araucanía, "I belong to a piece of poor austral earth verging on Araucania," he writes, giving Chile's southern provinces their Indian name,

> my doings have been timed from far away, as if that wooded and perpetually
> rainy land held a secret of mine that I do not understand, that I ignore and
> must come to know, and that I search for desperately, blindly, examining long
> rivers, fantastic plantlife, heaps of wood, the seas of the south, plunging myself
> into botany and the rain without ever reaching that precious spume the waves
> lay down and break up, without reaching that span of special earth, without
> touching my true soil,

sin llegar a ese metro de tierra especial, sin tocar mi verdadera arena. Yet this sentence does touch it, priming an act of memory by our most celebrated twentieth-
century poet, Pablo Neruda (1904–1973). Word waves carry him back and
down in time and space, earth and sea, each verb pressing further: "I search
. . . examining," "plunging . . . without reaching . . . without touching." Time
past gathers the *tierra, madera, vegetación, mares, olas, lluvia* making up this
landscape: earth, wood, plant life, seas, waves, rain. Truly his sense of things
stems from nature in that "span of special earth."

Neruda took to memory when his father and stepmother died in 1938. His
mother had died two months after he was born, which sharpened the poet's urge to
root himself. Desolate, he seeks his origin in "the tangled Chilean forest," a damp

landscape teeming with life—giant bristling rauli trees, dripping ferns, scents of wild herbs, an enormous red spider, a golden beetle, red copihues (bellflowers), butterflies, a decaying tree trunk encrusted with blue and black mushrooms.

"Nature gave me a kind of *embriaguez*"—intoxication, euphoria—as in some profuse paradise. But she wasn't always benign. "Summer is scorching in Cautín," he remembers from age ten, settling into the present tense.

> I go through the countryside in search of my poetry, walking and walking. Around Ñielol hill I get lost, *me pierdo. Estoy solo,* I'm alone, my pocket filled with scarab beetles. In a box I've got the hairy spider I just caught. Overhead the sky's blocked out. The forest is always damp, I slip, suddenly a bird cries out, the weird cry of the chucao. It comes up from under my feet like a terrifying omen. The copihues look like drops of blood, barely visible. Passing under giant ferns I feel tiny. A ringdove flies past my mouth, the dry sound of wingbeats. Higher up other birds are mocking me with harsh laughter. I can hardly find my way.

Solo, perdido stamp his childhood memories.

Immersing in germinal nature, Neruda brings a son's and lover's need, just as he would find a "mother of stone" and "sunken bride" at the Incas' hidden city of Machu Picchu. Add to this twofold need the image of his father, a trainman opening up Chile's southern frontier, his "golden beard," "his engine's / whistle / piercing the rain." Along with endemic machismo, Neruda's robust voice stems from *fuerte tierra virgen,* in his words, the south's strong virgin earth.

From the boy who gathered gaudy spiders, one vowel-rich image catches Neruda's ambivalence at nineteen: *Las arañas oscuras del pubis en reposo,* "The darksome spiders of the pubis at rest." By the time he published *Twenty Love Poems and a Despairing Song* (1924), destined as a breviary for countless Latin American lovers, Neruda's stance had firmed up, though he was no less struck by woman's earthly presence. *Ah, las rosas del pubis!* "My rough peasant's body digs down in you / and makes a son leap from deep in earth." This rough peasant was studying French in Santiago by then.

Like the Bible's Song of Songs, he yokes his beloved to nature: "your hands are soft as grapes." More often she's fused by a primitive magic: she "is" the twilight, the rivers sing "in her." At times it's both.

> *Cuerpo de mujer, blancas colinas, muslos blancos,*
> *te pareces al mundo en tu actitud de entrega.*
> Body of woman, white hills, white thighs,
> you look like the world spread out in surrender.

Surrender is problematic enough, while Neruda's bravado lets commas tie "woman" to "body" and "hills." But do feminist ethics clash with ecology here? Aren't we part of nature, rather than not?

"The color of poppies sits on your brow," "sweet toads rush trembling from your footsteps," says Neruda, gazing at "your eyes' full lids / gold as oxen, while plump doves / build their white nests in you." Potent praise, but with poppies on her brow, toads underfoot, oxen in her eyes, doves' nests somewhere else, she's not likely to do much or get anywhere at all. Kenneth Rexroth renders Neruda's "Serenata":

> So, nameless, vague as life, turbid
> As the burgeoning mud and vegetation,
> You awake in my breast whenever I shut my eyes.
> When I lie on the earth you come into being
> Like the flowing dust, the river deepening its bed.

Since Eden revives here, or some Amerindian Creation story, maybe censure by hindsight has its limits? Besides, such earth-bent energy drives Neruda's benchmark poems of the 1920s and 1930s, and his epic *Alturas de Macchu Picchu* (Heights of Macchu Picchu).

The poet's long path to this ruinous forgotten city in the Peruvian Andes leads through nature as well as history. An early poem sees "plums rolling to earth / that rot in time, endlessly green." That wasting and sustaining could fit a city reclaimed from oblivion after four centuries. Later in Madrid during the Spanish Republic, Federico García Lorca and others published Neruda's "*Entrada a la madera*" (Entrance into Wood), from his book *Residence on Earth*:

> clasp me to your life, to your death,
> to your beaten matter,

he pleads to the wood, as if it held his mother lost in infancy (*madera* is cognate with *madre*) and eventually those beaten-down native workers who built Machu Picchu.

Back home in Chile he wrote "*Inundaciones*." Here is no metaphor, floods subject humankind to nature.

> The poor live on low ground waiting for the river
> to rise one night and sweep them out to sea.
> I've seen small cradles floating by, the wrecks
> of houses, chairs, and a great rage of ash-
> pale water draining terror from the sky:
> this is all yours, poor man, for your wife and crop,
> your dog and tools, so you can learn to beg.
> No water climbs to the homes of gentlemen
> whose snowy collars flutter on the line.
> It feeds on this rolling mire, these ruins winding
> their idle course to the sea with your dead,

among roughcut tables and the luckless trees
that bob and tumble turning up bare root.

You'd think nature impartial, but no. Gentlemen's "snowy collars flutter on the line," pristine privileged collars, while "on low ground" the poor undergo forces of rain and river—their "roughcut tables" rolling past at flood level and "the luckless trees." These "bob and tumble," which sounds playful for only a moment. Luckless like the trees, and "turning up bare root," the poor are basic, vital, exposed.

Binding history to nature, Neruda was ready for Machu Picchu and his twelve-canto poem evoking not Peru's Inca princes but the Quechua slaves who built that city of stone. Though the Indians of his own childhood had "lived totally apart," he came to merge Araucania's demise with his own genesis, declaring himself a poet of "those somber woods" and "obscure fallen lives." Chile's native people resisted for centuries. Finally in 1881 a treaty was signed on Ñielol Hill, where a generation later a boy went catching spiders and dodging doves. At Cuzco, Peru, in 1943, embedded between Andean peaks high in the cordillera, the Quechua poet Kilko Warak'a told Neruda the very stones

Awoke from their centuries' sleep
And opened their frozen breasts
When they knew you had arrived.

The next day he went north along the Urubamba River and climbed on horseback to Machu Picchu, perched on a saddle two thousand feet above the river.

Begun around 1440, this remote outpost of the Inca empire escaped Spanish conquest. Back in Cuzco you're hardly aware of the smooth, slow-curving, yellowish-gray stones of the ancient Temple of the Sun, because they've long formed the foundation of a Dominican monastery. But Machu Picchu appears pure, arrested in time, a people latent within it. In 1911 a Yale archaeologist discovered the finest stonework he'd ever seen, "partly covered with trees and moss, the growth of centuries, but in the dense shadow, hiding in bamboo thickets and tangled vines, appeared here and there walls of white granite ashlars carefully cut and exquisitely fitted together." When Neruda went there the ruins were only half cleared, as in the Quechuan Martín Chambi's 1928 photograph.

Welcomed home as a poet of the people, Neruda composed *Alturas de Macchu Picchu* in autumn 1945 at his home on the Pacific, Isla Negra. Bombs had dropped on Hiroshima and Nagasaki. In a hemisphere dominated by the superpower to the north, a radical voice would have to call on deep resources for Latin America to speak through him.

Martín Chambi, Machu Picchu, 1928.
Courtesy Teo Allein Chambi, Martín Chambi Family Archives, and Edward Ranney.

"This was the dwelling, this is the place," frozen in time. *Este es el sitio.*
Neruda first links city to earth via the surreal imagination of his early lyrics:
"Mother of stone, spume of condors," he names the place (though hunting,
habitat loss, and pollution had long threatened the Andean condor),

> High reef of the human dawn.
> Spade lost in primal sand.

The boy who'd lost his way in Arauco's teeming maternal forest now reaches
this lost and found American site, an origin now a goal.

> I plunged my turbulent and gentle hand
> into the genital quick of the earth.

> I bent my head into the deepest waves,
> dropped down through sulfurous calm
> and went back, as if blind, to the jasmine
> of the exhausted human spring.

On one recording, Neruda misspeaks *jazmín* / jasmine as *jardín,* as if seeking a garden, a lost Eden like his wooded, flowery childhood. And though *gastada primavera humana* speaks of an exhausted human season, the chance pun on "spring" in English taps a source, a fountainhead for this quest.

Machu Picchu arises integral to rock and earth, its masonry walls, towers, lintels, stairs, water conduits, stepped plazas meld with terracing beneath, which falls away "into blue-green abysses," says an architectural historian, while the "rush of the river waters rises to the ear on all sides" along with "Chinese washes of fog and mist." To build the great city, he notes casually, may not have cost "more than a generation or two" of labor. "Stone upon stone, and man, where was he?" *Hambre, coral del hombre,* Neruda cries, for nothing keeps *hambre* from *hombre,* hunger from man, but one small vowel.

> Hunger, coral of humankind,
> hunger, hidden plant, woodcutter's root,
> hunger, did your reef-edge climb
> to these high and ruinous towers?

Root and reef make hunger organic to this site, this "high reef of the human dawn."

> I question you, salt of the paths,
> show me the trowel. Architecture, let me
> grind stone stamens with a stick,
> climb every step of air up to the void,
> scrape in the womb till I touch man.

Now he grasps not the city's heights but *la entraña.* Saying "womb" rather than "entrails" or "core" marks the lost son's sexual embrace of nature—and with good cause, since Neruda once translated "womb" in William Blake as *entraña.* What's more, his own handwork will dig to the city's human base.

A tension holds death and life together at Machu Picchu. In canto nine a litany of seventy-two images, half from wild nature, names the lost site. *Madrépora del tiempo sumergido,* "Coral of sunken time," sees it gone under yet growing durably. Two other images catch the city's energy arrested in time, like Wordsworth's "stationary blasts of waterfalls" and Coleridge's "Motionless torrents":

> *Vendaval sostenido en la vertiente.*
> *Inmóvil catarata de turquesa.*
> Gale sustained on a slope.
> Immobile turquoise cataract.

An elemental force still not spent, a torrential energy in cut-stone beauty: three-beat cadences holding nature and history in a single breath.

Ending his epic with a stroke of honesty seldom heard, Neruda urges the

Edward Ranney, Machu Picchu, Torreón Complex.
© Edward Ranney.

forgotten workers, such as "Jack Stonebreaker, son of Wiracocha" the Incan creator god,

> Rise to be born with me, brother.
> Give me your hand out of the deep
> region seeded by all your grief.

Then abruptly he turns:

> You won't come back from bottom rock.
> No coming back from time under ground.

No volverán . . . No volverán. Earth and time won't release them, so echoing Whitman's "Through me many long dumb voices," Neruda takes on the burden: "Hasten to my veins to my mouth. / Speak through my words and my blood."

After *Alturas de Macchu Picchu*, his finest work, Neruda went on writing and traveling for a quarter-century. No less popular than his love poems are the odes to everything under the sun, such as the "Ode to Laziness," rendered by William Carlos Williams. *Stones of Chile, Where the Rain Is Born, Art of Birds, Bestiary, House in the Sand, Grapes and the Wind, Isla Negra Notebook, Winter Garden, The Sea and the Bells* and more flowed from his green felt-tip pen. He can't get enough of his native land.

When the brutal coup struck on September 11, 1973, sponsored by the United States, Neruda was ill and dying—not in Araucania's "wooded and rainy land" but on his other true soil, the seaside house at Isla Negra, still near that "precious spume the waves lay down and break up."

"the wild / braid of creation / trembles"
Stanley Kunitz—His Nettled Field, His Dune Garden

"S"wimming in Lake Chauggogagogman-chauggagogchabunagungamaugg" meant a lot to Stanley Kunitz (1905–2006). "When I was a boy in Massachusetts one of my favorite haunts was Lake Webster." He'd made "a thrilling discovery" in the public library: "Indians who once lived on the shores of Lake Webster had a word of their own for it,"

Chauggogagogmanchauggagogchabunagungamaugg.

Wonderfully, "this fantastic porridge of syllables" meant something: "I-fish-on-my-side, you-fish-on-your-side, nobody-fishes-in-the-middle." The boy practiced uttering it. Since "the beginning of the human adventure a word" can pack in "subterranean electric feelings."

This thrill started a lifetime of discoveries. Late one September, for instance, Kunitz was "chopping weeds in the field behind my house" in rural Pennsylvania. "Toward sunset I heard a commotion in the sky and looked up, startled to observe wedge after wedge of wild geese honking downriver, with their long necks pointing south. I watched until the sun sank and the air turned chill." He went inside with this vision and "tried until dawn to get the words down on paper."

After five days and hundreds of lines, he saw he shouldn't be describing the migration—"it was the disturbance of the heart that really concerned me and that insisted on a language." Then with a rush of three- and four-beat lines came "End of Summer."

An agitation of the air,
A perturbation of the light
Admonished me the unloved year
Would turn on its hinge that night.

I stood in the disenchanted field
Amid the stubble and the stones,
Amazed, while a small worm lisped to me
The song of my marrow-bones.

Blue poured into summer blue,
A hawk broke from his cloudless tower,
The roof of the silo blazed, and I knew
That part of my life was over.

Already the iron door of the north
Clangs open: birds, leaves, snows
Order their populations forth,
And a cruel wind blows.

Nature's doings fill each stanza, while a few words pack in subterranean feelings. But why "perturbation," someone asked him, rather than "commotion"
or "flurry"? Because "There's more wingbeat in 'perturbation'," with its
beating stresses. And how can a field be disenchanted, or a silo blaze without
burning?

This sort of craft is "closer to biology than to mechanics" in the way a poem
sounds, "the way it lives from word to word, the way it breathes." For instance,
"the *unloved year*" gets a startling stress on "un-," then quickens a bit "on its
hinge" toward winter. Conjuring this poem "in the disenchanted field," Kunitz
felt a need to leave his wife and young daughter to work abroad. So "the stubble
and the stones" sounds harsh, boring rhymewise into "my marrow-bones."

With the geese gone, but not their perturbation, sharp change occurs. A
hawk broke out, in late sunlight a silo "blazed," answering "amazed." And
change, in him as in the weather, prompts a present tense: "the iron door of the
north / Clangs open." "End of Summer" ends on its briefest line, held onto by
his spoken voice, "blo-o-o-ows." Have the geese really gone? No, "their wings
keep beating, from the first word to the last."

Wild geese and wild swans gripped Yeats, a "great master" for Kunitz, and an
earlier spirit hovers over "End of Summer." Keats's stubble fields and gathering swallows bode loss and leaving in "To Autumn," where Kunitz hears even
more: "Many poems, like the medlar pear, get rotten before they are ripe; this
one stays golden and does not turn." Maybe he felt as much in getting "End of
Summer" written.

"Even in grade school I was rhyming—doggerel, mainly." Kunitz was born in Worcester, Massachusetts, to Russian Jewish immigrants. His father, committing suicide just before his birth, haunted him. When he was thirteen, his mother built a big house "beyond the last trolley-stop," with "acres of woods behind us" and a disused quarry, and he spent "long summers" on a farm in Quinnapoxet. Many decades later, naming a poem for that vanished backwater village, he dreams of fishing in an "abandoned reservoir" where "snapping turtles cruised" and a bullhead catfish "gashed my thumb / with a flick of his razor fin." Within the dream his parents appear "on the Indian road, / evenly stepping / past the apple orchard."

> "Why don't you write?" she cried
> from the folds of her veil.
> "We never hear from you."
> I had nothing to say to her.
> But for him who walked behind her
> in his dark worsted suit,
> with his face averted
> as if to hide a scald,
> deep in his other life,
> I touched my forehead
> with my swollen thumb
> and splayed the fingers out—
> in deaf-mute country
> the sign for father.

Folded into this agony is a feel for place: "abandoned" reservoir, tree stumps, dusty Indian road—signposts to an otherwise mute emotion.

Memory recovers what "set me on the track of poetry." Kunitz's signature poem, "The Testing-Tree," returns to these woods to find nostalgia blunted by loss and worse. "I went back to Worcester and looked for the old house at the city's edge and those Indian woods. It was a most depressing adventure. The place had turned into a technological nightmare . . . an express highway running through my childhood. On the site of my nettled field stood a housing development ugly enough for tears." Yes, though highways and housing have a use, however unbeautiful.

Why he had to write it, "The Testing-Tree" doesn't say outright. Its thirty-seven stanzas begin as classic storytelling: "On my way home from school . . ." He's scuffing in a drainage ditch, "hunting for perfect stones / rolled out of glacial time / into my pitcher's hand." Triplets fetch back to a time when "dawdling came natural" and he could walk

> across a nettled field
>   riddled with rabbit-life
>   where the bees sank sugar-wells

in the trunks of the maples
　　and a stringy old lilac
　　　　more than two stories tall
blazing with mildew
　　remembered a door in the
　　　　long teeth of the woods.

The indents move memory step by step, but it's no jaunt, what with "riddled," "sank," "stringy," that visionary "blazing" again, and a magical door in the woods' "long teeth." Along this trail, "flickering presences" meet a child following "in the steps / of straight-backed Massasoit / soundlessly heel-and-toe / practicing my Indian walk."

His quest, like Frost's "Directive" moving through woods back to a childhood source, takes a fatherless boy "Past the abandoned quarry" and

on to the clearing
　　with the stones in my pocket
　　　　changing to oracles . . .
There I stood in the shadow,
　　at fifty measured paces,
　　　　of the inexhaustible oak . . .
that locked King Philip's War
　　in its annulated core
　　　　under the cut of my name.

Much is happening here. Massasoit, a Wampanoag sachem, befriended the Pilgrims, but the native inhabitants were soon threatened. In 1675 his son "King Philip" led a revolt against the colonists—with devastating losses. Of course the Jewish child of immigrants wouldn't have known that an oak he carved his name in had rings stemming from this core history. As a boy in 1918, "My life hinged on the three throws permitted me . . . If I hit the target-oak once, somebody would love me; if I hit it twice, I should be a poet; if I scored all three times, I should never die."

Along with tribal tragedy, a ritual of sacred groves and trees touches the loyal son, then (and now) calling

Father wherever you are
I have only three throws
*　　bless my good right arm.*

Now the poet finds no trail but a highway, and tanks maneuvering where Model A Fords once sputtered. It's "a murderous time," with Vietnam in mind and Martin Luther King's assassination. An ache ends this journey.

It is necessary to go
　　through dark and deeper dark

and not to turn.
I am looking for the trail.
Where is my testing-tree?
Give me back my stones.

Childhood, semi-wild terrain, a lost trail and special tree pull Kunitz back to test himself within America's scarred history.

His task, he says, is making life into legend, in poems from which "fire breaks each time you turn to them." Both fire and legend break from "The Wellfleet Whale," about a stranded finback.

You have your language too,
an eerie medley of clicks
and hoots and trills,
location-notes and love calls,
whistles and grunts. Occasionally,
it's like furniture being smashed,
or the creaking of a mossy door,
sounds that all melt into a liquid
song with endless variations.

That eerie song or language does not much interest Japan, which every year kills fifty humpbacks with their incredible songs, plus hundreds of whales from other species, for "scientific research"—never mind that they find their way to festive tables.

Since the Lord God challenged Job's pettiness in face of Leviathan, the question is, Can we grasp Creation's hugest creature? And since Roger Payne's discovery in the late 1960s, what of their singing? Is it "like furniture being smashed"? Kunitz hedges, calling it also "a sorrow without name," "both more / and less than human."

Years after what happened off Cape Cod in 1966, he does justice to it. The sixty-three-foot whale had "coasted into sight,"

All afternoon you swam
tirelessly round the bay,
with such an easy motion . . .
And when you bounded into air,
slapping your flukes,
we thrilled to look upon
pure energy incarnate
as nobility of form.

"That night we watched you / swimming in the moon," and then a single line caps the tragedy: "At dawn we found you stranded on the rocks."

Trouble starts as men come running, "schoolgirls in yellow halters," a house-

Stanley Kunitz, Wellfleet Whale, 1966.
Stanley Kunitz, *The Wellfleet Whale and Companion Poems*
(New York: Sheep Meadow Press, 1983).

wife in curlers, "beach buggies with assorted yelping dogs." Against that motley
crew, and still speaking to the whale, Kunitz gives his attentiveness:

> crushed by your own weight, . . .
> you bared your fringework of baleen,
>   a thicket of horned bristles.

Despite its "hoarse and fitful bleating" he won't moralize.

> Somebody had carved his initials
>   in your flank. Hunters of souvenirs
>   had peeled off strips of your skin.

Another dawn brings "your unearthly outcry,"

as you swung your blind head
toward us and laboriously opened
a bloodshot, glistening eye,
in which we swam with terror and recognition.

Terror greets things that stagger knowing, but such recognition locks us into contact, like Ted Hughes when an immense pike "rose slowly towards me, watching." Several years earlier Kunitz had said of poetry, "what we strive for is to move from the world of our immediate knowing . . . into the unknown."

A bitter thought ends "The Wellfleet Whale": "You have become like us, / disgraced and mortal." And yet the poet's voice reaches out to generations of whales

edging between the ice-floes
through the fat of summer,
lob-tailing, breaching, sounding,
grazing in the pastures of the sea
on krill-rich orange plankton
crackling with life.

Writing a poem, he said, "I have the sense of swimming underwater towards some kind of light and open air that will be saving."

Human carelessness always angered Kunitz. "The War Against the Trees" sees "bulldozers, drunk with gasoline," attack

the great-grandfathers of the town . . .
They struck and struck again,
And with each elm a century went down.

That striking resounds from a century earlier, the "strokes of havoc" in "Binsey Poplars":

O if we but knew what we do
When we delve or hew—
Hack and rack the growing green!

No wonder his discovery of Gerard Manley Hopkins "overwhelmed me during my college years." Wherever possible—Blake, Wordsworth, Coleridge, Whitman—Kunitz finds a "root-purity of wonder" at the unspoiled world.

Most of all, Theodore Roethke showed him that purity. Around 1935 a "battered jalopy" arrived at Kunitz's Pennsylvania home, and "a perfectly tremendous raccoon coat emerged." They talked all night, and until Roethke died in 1963. This dear comrade's poems brought him "news of the root, of the minimal, of the primordial": "the stretching and reaching of a plant, its green force, its invincible Becoming."

Even in America's backyards, Kunitz has an ear and eye for invincible Becoming.

Raccoons! I can hear them
confabulating on the porch,
half-churring, half-growling,
bubbling to a manic hoot
that curdles the night air.
Something out there appalls.
On the back door screen
a heavy furpiece hangs,
spreadeagled, breathing hard,
hooked by prehensile fingers,
with its pointed snout pressing in,
and the dark agates of its bandit eyes
furiously blazing.

Once again there's "blazing," this time hellish, though language this wild, this joyous, outdoes what's appalling.

He's never far from "the creature world" around him. "In my bad times they've sustained me." A talisman poem, "The Snakes of September," follows on Coleridge's Ancient Mariner blessing the flashing water snakes, Dickinson stunned by "a narrow Fellow in the Grass," and Lawrence awestruck by a sinuous gold snake in his water trough.

All summer I heard them
rustling in the shrubbery,
outracing me from tier
to tier in my garden.

They shelter in Kunitz's Cape Cod garden, mating

in the dense green brocade
of a north-country spruce,
dangling head-down, entwined
in a brazen love-knot.
I put out my hand and stroke
the fine, dry grit of their skins.

And you know he did that—how else the deftness of "fine, dry grit"?

At my touch the wild
braid of creation
trembles.

In Whitman this might sound arrogant. Here it feels like radical innocence, thanks to a light touch: pausing "wild" at the break, slant-rhyming "braid," marveling as "creation / trembles," tapering and quieting. "In a poem, what's real *happens*!" says poet-survivor Paul Celan.

In his ninety-eighth year, Kunitz was taking on strenuous engagements across the country, among them a talk on Celan and the Holocaust. At one point he fell terribly ill. Friends from all over came to his Greenwich Village apartment to say goodbye—but miraculously he recovered. What mattered then was the seaside garden. With Genine Lentine he completed a gathering of garden words and images that came out on his centennial: *The Wild Braid*.

Years earlier his front yard had been a steep dune with patches of witch grass: "when I was looking at that sloping sand, I had a vision . . . a garden that seems to have taken over a steep hillside, something at rest and in motion at the same time"—at rest on the slope, in motion inwardly with "plants growing and blooming and fading and falling away. And there is the natural motion that comes from the wind itself." "Mad about gardening," Kunitz eventually planted sixty-nine species in tiers from gate to house. "I'm disappearing," he said once, walking into the thick of his garden. (plate 14)

The Wild Braid blends gardening with poetry. Both are "a passionate effort to organize a little corner of the earth, which I want to redeem." Both harbor wildness. Think about stroking the entwined snakes, then about the word "trembles."

> At my touch the wild
> braid of creation
> trembles.

1. William Blake, *Creation*, from *Europe, a Prophecy*. P.127-1950.pt.19.
The Ancient of Days, frontispiece of *Europe, A Prophecy*, ca. 1821
(relief etching with pen and watercolor on paper) by William Blake.
© Fitzwilliam Museum, University of Cambridge, UK / The Bridgeman Art Library.

2. John James Audubon, *Osprey*, 1829. 1863.17.081.
Collection of The New-York Historical Society.

3. "Western Wind," sixteenth-century MS.
The British Library Board.

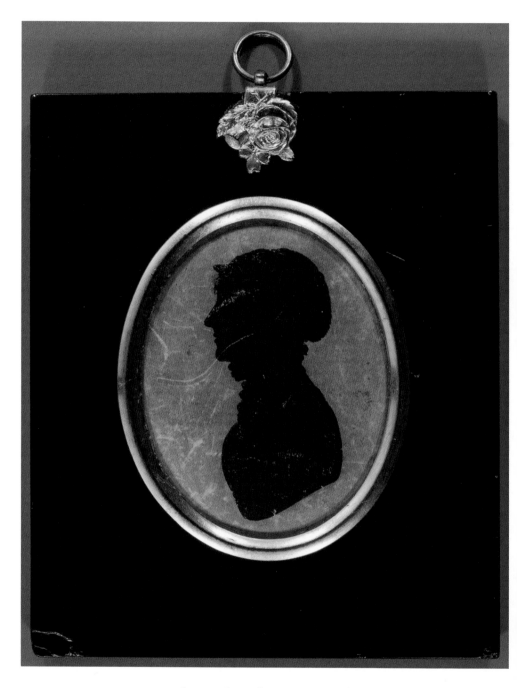

4. Dorothy Wordsworth, anonymous silhouette.
Dove Cottage, Wordsworth Trust.

5. Simplon Pass.
Courtesy of Edward Boenig.

6. *A Cloud Study, Sunset,* ca. 1821 (oil on paper on millboard) by John Constable.
Yale Center for British Art, Paul Mellon Collection, USA / The Bridgeman Art Library.

7. Lapis Lazuli stone, front.
Courtesy of A. P. Watt Ltd. and the National Library of Ireland.

8. Lapis Lazuli stone, front.
Courtesy of Susan Felstiner Thomas.

9. Cellar-bin, Robert Frost Farm, Derry, New Hampshire.
Courtesy of The Trustees of the Robert Frost Homestead and
John Felstiner.

10. Cover design by D. H. Lawrence, *Birds, Beasts and Flowers!*
From *Birds, Beasts and Flowers!*
(New York: Thomas Seltzer, 1923).

Not Man Apart

LINES FROM
ROBINSON JEFFERS

PHOTOGRAPHS OF THE BIG SUR COAST

11. Cover, *Not Man Apart*. From *Not Man Apart: Lines from Robinson Jeffers, Photographs of the Big Sur Coast*, by Ansel Adams, edited by David Brower
(San Francisco: Sierra Club/Ballantine Books, 1965).

12. "Oh, Lovely Rock," Ventana, California.
Courtesy of Scott Slovic.

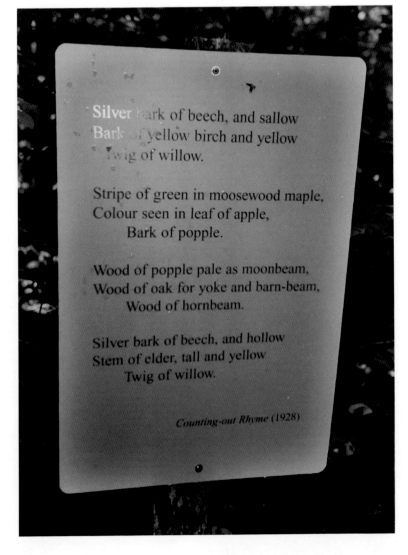

Silver bark of beech, and sallow
Bark of yellow birch and yellow
   Twig of willow.

Stripe of green in moosewood maple,
Colour seen in leaf of apple,
   Bark of popple.

Wood of popple pale as moonbeam,
Wood of oak for yoke and barn-beam,
   Wood of hornbeam.

Silver bark of beech, and hollow
Stem of elder, tall and yellow
   Twig of willow.

Counting-out Rhyme (1928)

13. Edna St. Vincent Millay, "Counting-out Rhyme."
Elizabeth Barnett, Literary Executor, The Edna St. Vincent Millay Society.
Courtesy of John Felstiner.

14. Stanley Kunitz. Marnie Crawford Samuelson, from Stanley Kunitz, Genine Lentine, Marnie Crawford Samuelson, *The Wild Braid: A Poet Reflects on a Century in the Garden* (New York: W. W. Norton, 2005).

15. Deer.
Photographer unknown. Courtesy of John Felstiner.

16. *Great Village, Nova Scotia*, George Hutchinson. Actual size.
Courtesy of Alice Methfessel, Estate of Elizabeth Bishop.

"Focuses the spotlight on the most fascinating
ornithological mystery of a bird that once rivaled
the passenger pigeon."—*Richard H. Pough*

Last of the
CURLEWS
BY FRED BODSWORTH
ILLUSTRATED BY T. M. SHORTT

17. Cover, Fred Bodsworth, *The Last of the Curlews*,
illustrated by T. M. Shortt
(New York: Dodd Mead, 1955).

18. Cover, Donald Hall, *Ox-Cart Man*. From *Ox-Cart Man* by Donald Hall, illustrated by Barbara Cooney. Illustrations copyright © 1979 by Barbara Cooney Porter. Used by permission of Viking Penguin, A Division of Penguin Young Readers Group, A Member of Penguin Group (USA) Inc., 345 Hudson Street, New York, NY 10014. All rights reserved.

19. Derek Walcott, *Breakers, Becune Point*, 1995. From Derek Walcott, *Tiepolo's Hound* (New York: Farrar, Straus and Giroux, 2000). Copyright © by Derek Walcott.

20. *Islands, Mountains, Houses, Bridge,*
Guan Huai, eighteenth century.
Seattle Art Museum, Eugene Fuller Memorial Collection.

21. *Islands, Mountains, Houses, Bridge,* detail,
Guan Huai, eighteenth century.
Seattle Art Museum, Eugene Fuller Memorial Collection.

22. *Yucky Pollution*, *Shiny Pretty*, 2001. Sunlight Room, Hilltop Children's Center, Seattle. Courtesy of Sarah Felstiner.

"Bright trout poised in the current"
Things Whole and Holy for Kenneth Rexroth

"Tu Fu has been without question the major influence on my own poetry ... In some ways he is a better poet than either Shakespeare or Homer. At least he is more natural and intimate." So says Kenneth Rexroth (1905–1982) about the eighth-century T'ang Dynasty poet whose life's work blended nature, transience, and war. Here is Rexroth voicing Tu Fu, "Brimming Water."

> Under my feet the moon
> Glides along the river.
> Near midnight, a gusty lantern
> Shines in the heart of night.
> Along the sandbars flocks
> Of white egrets roost,
> Each one clenched like a fist.
> In the wake of my barge
> The fish leap, cut the water,
> And dive and splash.

Natural in the shape and gist of each sentence, intimate but not self-absorbed, the poem lays out four things: moon, lantern, egrets, fish. Tu Fu's and his translator's touch liven them: the moon "glides," the lantern's "gusty," egrets are "clenched," fish "cut the water." Drama, but no moralizing. "No ideas but in things," said William Carlos Williams. Here, ideas arise from "the heart of night," "like a fist," "cut the water."

At eighteen Rexroth's life changed when "an hour's conversation in a sun-baked patio" with an older poet in Taos, New Mexico, turned him toward Tu Fu. From then on he brought many classical poets to American consciousness. As a conscientious objector during World War II, for instance, he calls his version of a loaded Tu Fu poem "The War Is Permanent."

> Tumult, weeping, many new ghosts.
> Heartbroken, aging, alone, I sing
> To myself. Ragged mist settles
> In the spreading dusk. Snow skurries
> In the coiling wind. The wineglass
> Is spilled. The bottle is empty.
> The fire has gone out in the stove.
> Everywhere men speak in whispers.
> I brood on the uselessness of letters.

Graphic mist, dusk, snow, and wind (Rexroth liked drawing Chinese calligraphy for his poems) bring home war's everpresence, via nature. While he says his versions came mainly from the Chinese, this is a slight stretch. He's tuning up an Englishwoman's 1929 paraphrase of Tu Fu. "Ragged mist" was her *Clouds, torn in confusion,* "spreading dusk" *prevailing twilight,* "Snow skurries" *Hurrying snowflakes,* "coiling wind" *whirling wind.* "I sing / To myself" was Tu Fu *humming poems in a deep low voice*—her "humming poems" is good, but Rexroth manages to echo Whitman's *Song of Myself.* In 756 Tu Fu, captive and craving news of a disastrous rebellion, actually said *Verily it is futile to send a letter.* "I brood on the uselessness of letters" bends the ancient poem toward Rexroth's own wartime, his pun on "letters" as literature putting a life's vocation in question.

Born in Indiana and orphaned at thirteen, Rexroth was colorfully self-raised in Chicago, Ohio, Michigan, the Southwest, and Greenwich Village. He was precocious in matters of intellect, politics, sexuality, and especially nature. He recalls a boy

> Coming home from swimming
> In Ten Mile Creek,
> Over the long moraine in the early summer evening,
> My hair wet, smelling of waterweeds and mud.
> I remember a sycamore in front of a ruined farmhouse,
> And instantly and clearly the revelation
> Of a song of incredible purity and joy,
> My first rose-breasted grosbeak,
> Facing the low sun, his body
> Suffused with light.

From his 1940 vantage point Rexroth adds, "Thirty factories empty their refuse into the creek. / The farm has given way to an impoverished suburb."

With his first wife he moved to California in 1927, and for more than fifty years worked at galvanizing American culture. What Li Po gave Ezra Pound during World War I, Tu Fu gave Rexroth: a spur for renewing consciousness with precise images from the surrounding world, pared-down verse, straight syntax, startling turns of mind. "Toward an Organic Philosophy" tries it all out on his favorite terrain, the Sierra Nevada.

> All day cloud shadows have moved over the face of the mountain,
> The shadow of a golden eagle weaving between them
> Over the face of the glacier.

Nearer his campsite, things pass from visual to visionary.

> The wiry clumps of dwarfed whitebark pines
> Are smoky and indistinct in the moonlight,
> Only their shadows are really visible.
> The lake is immobile and holds the stars
> And the peaks deep in itself without a quiver.

Immobile lake, peaks sunk in water: despite the shadows, moonlight makes a reflection Ansel Adams would have waited days for. Then wildness passes even nearer.

> All night the eyes of deer shine for an instant
> As they cross the radius of my firelight.

On their own, the deer in this "organic philosophy" shine for only an instant within the human circle.

Camping meant rapture for Rexroth and his wife Andrée. Her death in 1940 sparked a lament echoing Milton's *Lycidas*—"Yet once more, O ye Laurels . . ."—on their cherished ground at Mount Tamalpais, north of San Francisco.

> Now once more gray mottled buckeye branches
> Explode their emerald stars,
> And alders smoulder in a rosy smoke
> Of innumerable buds.
> I know that spring again is splendid
> As ever, the hidden thrush
> As sweetly tongued, the sun as vital—
> But these are the forest trails we walked together,
> These paths, ten years together.
> We thought the years would last forever,
> They are all gone now, the days
> We thought would not come for us are here.
> Bright trout poised in the current—
> The raccoon's track at the water's edge—

A bittern booming in the distance—
Your ashes scattered on this mountain—
Moving seaward on this stream.

Sorrow brightens with the music given to nature, "alders smoulder in a rosy smoke," and there's more: "Bright trout poised in the current." Spring again is splendid but those years are gone, so these trout, poised and shining, hold still against the current carrying her ashes downstream. For Tu Fu, Rexroth once said, "Values are the way we see things"—the emphasis falling on *see*.

Several years later he wrote a longer elegy, starting at Tamalpais where life still thrives around her ashes: waterfalls, birds, "Ripe toyon and madrone berries." Deer and raccoon abound, "A bittern / Calls from the same rushes." Then moving to Kings River Canyon in the Sierra, we find the trout have migrated. It's autumn, the couple lie among "turning and falling leaves," with

Bats from the caves, dipping
Over the odorous pools
Where the great trout drowsed in the evenings.

Maybe that's the most we get, balancing what's human with what is not, youth and loss held like Keats's gathering swallows in this autumn "Where the great trout drowsed." Rexroth nursed a "Chinese sense of the unbreakable wholeness of reality."

Nature and Love have run together for millennia. The beloved is like a young hart in the Song of Songs, "Western Wind" and "small rain" bring my love in "my arms again," Shakespeare's Juliet is the sun, and so on. For Rexroth, Eros flourishes outdoors, bound up with the "holiness of the real": the lake immobile with stars and peaks, the bright trout poised. And sometimes passion in the grass leaves no time for holiness.

The sweet virile hair of thunderstorms
Brushes over the swelling horizon.
Take off your shoes and stockings.
I will kiss your sweet legs and feet
As they lie half buried in the tangle
Of rank scented midsummer flowers.
Take off your clothes. I will press
Your summer honeyed flesh into the hot
Soil, into the crushed, acrid herbage
Of midsummer.

It bothers a bit to see "woman" bound to Nature, molded by man. Though Rexroth finds "summer in our twined bodies" and celebrates Sappho, the ancient Greek lesbian poet, he sounds more like Pablo Neruda than Sappho, pressing summer flesh into hot soil.

Shortly after emceeing San Francisco's landmark 1955 event at which Allen Ginsberg first chanted *Howl*, Rexroth translated Spanish love poems for Lawrence Ferlinghetti's City Lights Books, snugly fitting Neruda's manner:

> You are the delirious youth of the bee,
> The drunkenness of the wave . . .
> When I lie on the earth you come into being
> Like the flowing dust, the river deepening its bed.

The question is, Will the real woman please step forward? Rexroth praised and helped publish women such as Muriel Rukeyser and Denise Levertov. Then late in life he invented a woman to voice his *Love Poems of Marichiko*. She offers—or Rexroth has her offer—her lover "the dew / Of the first morning of the world," she blazes "like the inside of a vast expanding pearl," and holds "the perfumed dusk" in her hair.

One way or another we come back gratefully to Rexroth's bounding energy —erotic, poetic, political, philosophic, religious, environmental. *In Defense of Earth* gives his daughters an aardvark-to-zebra bestiary, and for the older girl, "Mary and the Seasons" overflows with open-air life and the "completely open nervous system" Tu Fu had.

The wholeness of life, for Rexroth, means finding holy within bodily events, the supernatural within nature, and doing this through poems. So, weaving seven- with eight-syllable lines, he begins "Incarnation" in the mountains, as ever.

> Climbing alone all day long
> In the blazing waste of spring snow,
> I came down with the sunset's edge
> To the highest meadow, green
> In the cold mist of waterfalls,
> To a cobweb of water
> Woven with innumerable
> Bright flowers of wild iris.

Then sunset, blazing snow, waterfall mist, wild iris weave into his wife's "touch and smell" to bring on incarnation.

> Forever the thought of you,
> And the splendor of the iris,
> The crinkled iris petal,
> The gold hairs powdered with pollen,
> And the obscure cantata
> Of the tangled water, and the
> Burning, impassive snow peaks,
> Are knotted together here.

"I swayed out on the wildest wave alive"
Theodore Roethke from Greenhouse to Seascape

"They were to me," says Theodore Roethke (1908–1963), recalling the greenhouses of his childhood, "both heaven and hell, a kind of tropics created in the savage climate of Michigan." Roethke's father and his grandfather, who'd been head forester to the German chancellor Bismarck, had wild timberland outside Saginaw and greenhouses on a twenty-five-acre clearing in the city. These humid glass enclosures for growing flowers on a huge scale became "my symbol for the whole of life, a womb, a heaven-on-earth."

"Cuttings," close and sensuous, dreams of an Eden astir with organic beginnings.

> Sticks-in-a-drowse droop over sugary loam,
> Their intricate stem-fur dries;
> But still the delicate slips keep coaxing up water;
> The small cells bulge;
>
> One nub of growth
> Nudges a sand-crumb loose,
> Pokes through a musty sheath
> Its pale tendrilous horn.

Visceral, visual, palpable, with "sugary" taste, "musty" smell, and gut *u*-sounds in every line. This prehuman yet sexual plant life—sticks, loam, stem, slips, cells, crumb, sheath, tendril, horn—actually grows across the stanza break, quickened by Roethke's terse verbs: drowse, droop, dry, coax, bulge, nudge, poke.

In "Cuttings (*later*)" the speaker's become a spellbound child.

> This urge, wrestle, resurrection of dry sticks,
> Cut stems struggling to put down feet,
> What saint strained so much,
> Rose on such lopped limbs to a new life?
>
> I can hear, underground, that sucking and sobbing,
> In my veins, in my bones I feel it,—
> The small waters seeping upward,
> The tight grains parting at last,
> When sprouts break out,
> Slippery as fish,
> I quail, lean to beginnings, sheath-wet.

From vaginal "beginnings, sheath-wet," a self emerges, kin to the vegetal birth around him. And holy dread clings to the verse: "wrestle . . . resurrection . . . struggling . . . saint . . . strained . . . lopped limbs . . . sobbing . . . I quail." Some mystery draws him down into a world that clasps his turbulent inner world too.

No wonder William Carlos Williams cheered these poems when Roethke sent them—Williams, whose "Spring and All" has things "enter the new world naked," where "rooted, they / grip down and begin to awaken." Roethke had darker leanings than Williams. His greenhouse lyrics, published in *The Lost Son*, owe their turbulence partly to a gardener father with a "palm caked hard by dirt." Overbearing if also nurturing, he died when Roethke was fourteen, a son not yet sure of his manly standing.

"Root Cellar," for instance, scours memory—"My memory, my prison," he once said—for a threatening growth, his hellish roots of life.

> Nothing would sleep in that cellar, dank as a ditch,
> Bulbs broke out of boxes hunting for chinks in the dark,
> Shoots dangled and drooped,
> Lolling obscenely from mildewed crates,
> Hung down long yellow evil necks, like tropical snakes.
> And what a congress of stinks!—
> Roots ripe as old bait,
> Pulpy stems, rank, silo-rich,
> Leaf-mold, manure, lime, piled against slippery planks.
> Nothing would give up life:
> Even the dirt kept breathing a small breath.

Flower bulbs, but lolling like a dog's tongue, obscenely? Long yellow necks, but evil? "It was a jungle, and it was a paradise," Roethke said of his teeming youth. Tapping into a child's fascination, every line emits words like reeking compost. Organic and sexual, this decay in the same breath ferments with growth.

Rampant verbs generate a changing changeless biosystem of uncannily human plant life: "breathing . . . pulsing . . . swelling . . . creaking . . . crawling . . . swaying . . . stretching . . . winding and unwinding . . . shooting up . . . devouring."

Talking about growth of any kind, Roethke insists it's not naïve but primitive, in the best sense, to see soul animating all of nature. Animism, we call this, and "Why not? Everything that lives is holy." "I mean *all* living things," he says, "including the sub-human," though subhuman implies a hierarchy he denied, so let's say nonhuman. Scanning his early verse, we don't find Wordsworthy daffodils or Frosty birches but Roethke revering every kind of lowlife: sand, stones, dirt, dust, dead leaves, weeds, thistle, thorn, straw, moss, fern, fungus, mold, muck, manure, dung, ground bones, lime, loam, scum, algae, marrow, marl, marsh, bog, puddle, husk, seed, bulb, bud, pod, stem, slip, shoot, sprout, tendril, and then some. Think of Whitman in *Song of Myself,* spanning "the peace and knowledge that pass all the argument of the earth" on down to "mossy scabs of the worm fence, heap'd stones, elder, mullein and poke-weed."

So much for the so-called inanimate world. As for animals, literature has given us the Bible's Leviathan, Beowulf's dragon, Christopher Smart's cat Geoffry, Milton's, Coleridge's, Dickinson's, Lawrence's, Kunitz's snakes, Blake's Tyger, Melville's whale, Whitman's eagles copulating in air, Yeats's "rough beast," Rilke's panther, Elizabeth Bishop's moose, Ted Hughes's fox, pike, and otter. Roethke leans toward the slug, worm, fly, moth, midge, wasp, bee, grub, beetle, cicada, caterpillar, shrew, lice, rat, field mouse, bat, toad, newt, crab, eel, spider, mollusk, and "small birds" too, the swallow, finch, towhee. He welcomes "The small! The small! I hear them singing clear."

The world's singing fuses with his own, just as he heard cut stems sucking "In my veins, in my bones." If Keats hears a nightingale "pouring forth thy soul" and Shelley a skylark "That panted forth a flood of rapture so divine," Roethke finds in minnow or snail "A small thing, / Singing." For his friend Stanley Kunitz's daughter, he danced thumped and chanted a children's poem.

> There Once was a Cow with a Double Udder.
> When I think of it now, I just have to Shudder!
> She was too much for One, you can bet your Life:
> She had to be Milked by a Man and His Wife.

The little girl burst into tears and crawled under the sofa.

When later it comes to love poems, nature still pervades but with a freer lilt.

> Love, love, a lily's my care,
> She's sweeter than a tree.
> Lovingly I use the air . . .

She *is* a lily, somehow "sweeter than a tree," and the poet's caring is happy to rhyme on "air." Taking after "Western Wind," these "Words for the Wind" weave weather into loving.

> The wind's white with her name,
> And I walk with the wind. . . .
> She sways, half in the sun.

Roethke alliterates himself and her into the elements.

A spell of loneliness also exposes this bond. "The shoal rocks with the sea" in a supple line learned from Yeats, then Roethke tests his own voice,

> I sing the wind around
> And hear myself return
> To nothingness, alone,

and ends "His Foreboding" on an elemental omen:

> I sniff the darkening air
> And listen to my own feet.
> A storm's increasing where
> The winds and waters meet.

Shot through by nature's light and dark, the lover sounds like Thomas Hardy, writing as if life depended on getting all this into verse.

"How wonderful the struggle with language is," Roethke tells his notebook. "The words grappling across my tongue, things never said coming across the lip's threshold." Carolyn Kizer, once his student, recalls Roethke's compassion and attentiveness: "He was fanatic about active verbs" and distrusted adjectives. Drafts for "Cuttings" show more than twenty prunings and graftings to get a line right. We need "sensory sharpness," he would say, "the eye close on the object," like Dickinson perusing a hummingbird. Then we need "a speech so flexible . . . we're alive to every nuance that the language has." Always the "rhythm must move as a mind moves," must have a "psychic energy" that re-creates reality.

"Every sentence a cast into the dark," says Roethke. "Make the language take really desperate steps." At forty-four, "in that particular hell of the poet: a longish dry period . . . I thought I was done," a washout, a fraud. Suddenly, in one evening, he composed "The Dance." "I felt, I *knew,* I had hit it. I walked around and I wept; and I knelt down," he tells us, and "I wept for joy."

Mental breakdowns dogged Roethke, who said he'd be content in heaven "If they let you eat and swear / With the likes of Blake, / And Christopher Smart, / And that sweet man, John Clare." Yet he never wavers from nature. Small things help him pray at his father's grave:

Snail, snail, glister me forward,
Bird, soft-sigh me home.
Worm, be with me.
This is my hard time.

His happy marriage in 1953 buoyed the spirit—"I knew a woman, lovely in her bones"—yet later poems from the northwest pursue a "long journey out of the self" into "raw places / Where the shale slides dangerously." His line lengthens:

The arroyo cracking the road, the wind-bitten buttes, the canyons,
Creeks swollen in midsummer from the flash-flood roaring into the narrow valley.

Moving into these straits, his lines can close in too:

The way blocked at last by a fallen fir-tree,
The thickets darkening,
The ravines ugly.

In the Michigan greenhouse poems, things germinating matched his own growing pains. Now the west holds out a starker psychic landscape.

North American Sequence enters place after place to "move as the mind moves": to "be a stream, winding between great striated rocks in late summer"; to "rock with the motion of morning, / . . . By the lapping of water"; to "rise and fall in the slow sea of a grassy plain"; to "live with the rocks, their weeds, / Their filmy fringes of green"; to "sway outside myself / Into the darkening currents." The Pacific Northwest, Puget Sound, Olympic Peninsula become an existential test site. Roethke's terrain, "half-land, half-water," blends life and death for him, "becoming and perishing, / . . . Gathering to itself sound and silence— / Mine and the sea-wind's."

As Roethke pushes from small things and greenhouse fleshliness toward the mind's "far field," contraries coexist. A Yeatsian poem intones prophetically,

In a dark time, the eye begins to see,
I meet my shadow in the deepening shade . . .
A man goes far to find out what he is—
Death of the self in a long, tearless night.

Then he seizes the rhyme to see "All natural shapes blazing unnatural light," like Blake. Yet unlike Blake he never abhors the physical world in favor of pure vision. Roethke's late poems cleave to some topographic "place of my desire."

His landscapes and seascapes are anything but idyllic, with daffodils glistening beside a breezy lake. Often dusty and scraggly, they stay touchable: rocks, waters, plants, animals. Sooner than most poets, Roethke's eye caught man-made waste and spoilage. When a boy digging moss to line cemetery baskets,

"afterwards I always felt mean" for "pulling off flesh from the living planet."
He notices "young rabbits caught in the mower," a "ravaged hillside," "sluggish water running between weeds, broken wheels, tires, stones," or "sulfurous
water" where "A fish floats belly upward."

"The Longing" does more. Starting from a landscape's "sensual emptiness"
of "cockroaches, dead fish, petroleum," fuming "slag heaps . . . garbage,"
Roethke turns up fresh scenes, "the blackening salmon . . . the branch singing."
But after "delighting in the redolent disorder of this mortal life," jarringly he
recalls early frontier slaughter.

> On the Bullhead, in the Dakotas, where the eagles eat well,
> In the country of few lakes, in the tall buffalo grass at the base of the
>   clay buttes,
> In the summer heat, I can smell the dead buffalo,
> The stench of their damp fir drying in the sun,
> The buffalo chips drying.

In his day it wasn't much known that Indians also practiced mass slaughter.
Shortly before his death, Roethke was reading up for a dirge on our injustices: "it
behooves us to be humble before the eye of history." He knelt before the grave
of Chief Seattle, who surrendered his territory in 1854, saying (as remembered
by a witness, thirty years later), "There was a time when our people covered
the land as the waves of a wind-ruffled sea cover its shell-paved floor. . . . The
very dust upon which you now stand responds more lovingly to their footsteps
than to yours."

Like William Stafford—"I place my feet / with care in such a world," and
Gary Snyder cobbling a mountain trail—"Lay down these words / Before your
mind like rocks," Roethke ties his craft to nature's process.

> God bless the Ground! I shall walk softly there,
> And learn by going where I have to go.

His gut sense of earthly closeness tallies with Native American belief, the Yokuts
Indian chanting "My words are tied in one / With the great mountains, / With
the great rocks, / With the great trees."

At the same time a need, part anguish part joy, drives Theodore Roethke
"out of the self" toward ecstasy, a kind of dance:

> The spirit moves,
> Yet stays:
> Stirs as a blossom stirs.

In *North American Sequence*, "The Rose" closes on another dancelike motion
and stillness, whose verses also move and stay,

As if I swayed out on the wildest wave alive,
And yet was still.
And I rejoiced in being what I was.

River water rushing over hollowed stone shows Coleridge a steady rose-shape, Frost sees a white wave flung back forever on a rock, "Not gaining but not losing." Steeped as a Midwestern child in damp drooping roots, Roethke in the Pacific Northwest discovers a wild grace, the dancelike energy we crave and poems give us.

"That they are there!"
George Oppen's Psalm of Attentiveness

"It's . . . a lyric reaction to the world,"
says George Oppen (1908–1984), "a sense of awe, simply to feel that the thing
is there and that it's quite something to see." Casual as it sounds, this bracing
view goes to the core of modern American poetry. William Carlos Williams had
reawakened us to "the New World that rises to our windows" every day:

> Now the grass, tomorrow
> the stiff curl of wildcarrot leaf
> One by one objects are defined—
> It quickens . . .

And before that, as if out of nowhere, Walt Whitman's native tongue tapped
"Nature without check with original energy."
   Simply to sense "that the thing is there and that it's quite something to see"
is not simple, when it comes to making language actual, immediate. Again Williams: "So much depends" upon seeing afresh and saying anew

> a red wheel
> barrow
>
> glazed with rain
> water
>
> beside the white
> chickens

if we're to come through sanely. Just that rain-glazed wheelbarrow has a cleansing effect, what's mundane glistens a little.

"We awake in the same moment to ourselves and to things." Oppen prized this notion, from the philosopher Jacques Maritain. Though no human self, no "I" enters the scene, his title poem from a 1965 collection catches such an awakening. This wild scene's biblical title and Latin epigraph dawn on us line by line.

PSALM

Veritas sequitur . . .
In the small beauty of the forest
The wild deer bedding down—
That they are there!

Their eyes
Effortless, the soft lips
Nuzzle and the alien small teeth
Tear at the grass

The roots of it
Dangle from their mouths
Scattering earth in the strange woods.
They who are there.

Their paths
Nibbled thru the fields, the leaves that shade them
Hang in the distances
Of sun

The small nouns
Crying faith
In this in which the wild deer
Startle, and stare out.

A kind of psalm, but no figures of speech as in the Hebrew Psalms: "Like as the hart desireth the water brooks, so longeth my soul after thee, O God." Nor any praise of divine providence: "Thou makest the darkness that it may be night, wherein all the beasts of the forest do move." Yet Oppen will earn his title.

Veritas sequitur . . . Knowing "verity" in English and "non sequitur," we grasp his epigraph: "Truth follows . . ." But truth follows what? Or follows from what? What sort of truth, and why those dots holding suspense? Few of us will recognize Saint Thomas Aquinas: *Veritas sequitur esse rerum,* "Truth follows the being of things." Maybe this jibes with Williams, "No ideas but in things"? Whatever we make of its openness, the epigraph comes alive in Oppen's lines.

Along with gratitude for Creation, the Psalms cry out in estrangement. Oppen passes somewhere between those two voices. First comes a quiet awe at "the small beauty of the forest." His small word "small" trips the clichéd "beauty of the forest" into an alert, a bit of news about where true beauty occurs, much as Theodore Roethke praised "The small! The small!" Then an ongoing verb, "bedding down," and a dash arrest the action. It's not: "In the forest the wild deer bed down," or "The wild deer bedding down are beautiful."

> In the small beauty of the forest
> The wild deer bedding down—
> That they are there!

In other words (though a poem shuns other words), it's enough "That they are there!"

Right then something rare happens. Beginning his next stanza deeply indented, just under an exclamation point, Oppen pronounces a quiet echo: "That they are there! / / Their eyes . . ." These *th*-sounds merge "there," an adverb of place, with "Their," a pronoun of possession. Across a space they link forest to deer, a place to its creature. Now it's *their* "there." And they're *there*, not *here* where we or the speaker may be.

"Their eyes / Effortless." Just how close is this, to spot effortless eyes, soft lips, small teeth? Thirty feet? Three feet?—to see their "soft lips / Nuzzle," their "alien small teeth / Tear at the grass"? Surprising us over line breaks, "Nuzzle" and "Tear" zoom in on what our naked eye never witnesses. And why "alien"? Given such extreme focus, have we entered the mind of grass?

Then as if the grass weren't close enough, again deeply indented,

> The roots of it
> Dangle from their mouths
> Scattering earth in the strange woods.

Grass roots and bits of earth magnify and slow things down, greatening their impact. But "strange" woods? Strange to the deer? Not likely. To a human beholder? The scene shows none. Oppen is staking out unfamiliar terrain, wilderness as in medieval "wild-deer-ness," a place protected from farming, from human (peasant) footprint.

The same taut cadence as "That they are there!" underpins this stanza too, now a touch quieter—"They who are there"—and still with no platitude or piety about animals and wilderness. Again a short line prompting an indent produces the mysterious echo.

> They who are there.

> Their paths
> Nibbled thru the fields, the leaves that shade them
> Hang in the distances
> Of sun

Our distant closeness in which the wild deer appear, eyes effortless and lips nuzzling, gives way to cosmic "distances / Of sun."

Here a long pause opens, a whiteness, the poem's forest clearing with no punctuation as shading leaves "Hang in the distances"

> Of sun
>
> The small nouns

Small beauty—this the forest has. And small nouns, a baker's dozen of them: deer, eyes, lips, teeth, grass, roots, mouths, earth, woods, paths, fields, leaves, sun. A loving wordsmith has been speaking all along.

The small nouns are "Crying faith," for Oppen wants to place that sacred term and task in poetry's care,

> Crying faith
> In this in which the wild deer
> Startle, and stare out.

It's easy now to circle back, finding faith in the forest's "small beauty." The forest is simply where wild deer abide, and as Dickinson once said, "Beauty is Nature's fact." But "this in which" they "Startle, and stare out" must be something and somewhere else—if only because Oppen oddly entitled his entire book not *Psalm* but *This in Which*, setting that much store by the phrase.

Where the deer bed down, where they feed, roots dangling and paths nibbled —that would be forest, woods, fields. But they startle and stare out only at some sudden strangeness, otherness. So "this in which the wild deer / Startle, and stare out" must contain the alien presence they've just now noticed. Crying faith in this new dimension, this wild wholeness—woods, deer, witness—creates a poet's Psalm.

If you've ever slowly stalked deer just to get as close as possible, you know how at one moment suddenly becoming aware, they look over at you, but in poising they don't yet bolt. Bob Hass sees it this way:

> What I want happens
> not when the deer freezes in the shade
> and looks at you and you hold very still
> and meet her gaze but in the moment after
> when she flicks her ears & starts to feed again.

Oppen only has them "Startle, and stare out" in a tense balance, here and now. Meshing the poetry of nature with the nature of poetry, his lines stop right then.

Stopped, poised, the deer "stare out." These words acknowledge ourselves, our human selves, at the last possible moment. Now it could go either way. The

Deer.
Photographer unknown. Courtesy John Felstiner.

deer might flee, their eyes no longer effortless, or might quietly admit us. Within "Psalm" there's no knowing which. "Truth follows . . . ," but (those three dots imply) can never quite capture "the being of things." (plate 15)

From a wholly other time comes a Navajo hunting song with its (translated) refrain, "Comes the deer to my singing / Comes the deer to my singing." Oppen couldn't own such mutual empathy, or the artist's instinctual touch in Lascaux cave drawings of deer. As Gary Snyder says, "Hunting magic is designed to bring the game to you—the creature who has heard your song, witnessed your integrity, and out of compassion comes within your range." Nor would Oppen sign on to God's majesty in Psalms: "The voice of the Lord maketh the hinds to calve, and discovereth the forests."

Would even such tact as Oppen's, or William Stafford's "I place my feet / with care in such a world," impinge too much? Is "Psalm" too human-centered in a time when we need to be letting animal, vegetal, and mineral worlds alone?

If the wild deer will not stay for us, that's fair enough. For this moment at least, a poem helps us "feel that the thing is there and that it's quite something to see."

"surprised at seeing"
Elizabeth Bishop Traveling

A scream, the echo of a scream, hangs over that Nova Scotian village. No one hears it; it hangs there forever, a slight stain in those pure blue skies . . . Flick the lightning rod on top of the church steeple with your fingernail and you will hear it.

The five-year-old daughter heard it, never forgot it, and years later begins this story-memoir with an echo, as if she were gazing at a watercolor, blue skies and church steeple you can reach out and touch.

Elizabeth Bishop (1911–1979), the most beloved of postwar American poets, had a harder start than most. Her father's death when she was eight months old, in Worcester, Massachusetts, shattered her mother. They went up to live with the mother's parents in a fishing village on the Bay of Fundy. Elizabeth bonded to the place, but in 1916 her mother broke down and was committed to an asylum. The daughter never saw her again. Her father's parents took her back to Worcester from that loved "home of the long tides," sunset sea, herring boats, churches, farmhouses, blacksmith shop, one-room school, old elms, water meadows, red soil, blue fir, salt marsh. Unhappy and sick with asthma, the girl luckily went on to spend summers back in her "very small" village.

A good few poems, and one painting she had, call up Bishop's early years, with their skies' slight stain and church's lightning rod. Any twentieth-century rural childhood, any childhood at all, may become a lost paradise. This loss meant all the more to an orphan exiled at five.

Sixty years later Bishop published "The Moose," which she'd "written in bits and pieces over a number of years." Starting out from "narrow provinces" back in 1946, it recounts a bus journey west from Nova Scotia down to Boston

—"a dreadful trip," she told Marianne Moore. The poem's first sentence, winding through six six-line stanzas, gathers a lifetime of familiar things seen and recalled.

> From narrow provinces
> of fish and bread and tea,
> home of the long tides
> where the bay leaves the sea
> twice a day and takes
> the herrings long rides,
>
> where if the river
> enters or retreats
> in a wall of brown foam
> depends on if it meets
> the bay coming in,
> the bay not at home;
>
> where, silted red,
> sometimes the sun sets
> facing a red sea,
> and others, veins the flats'
> lavender, rich mud
> in burning rivulets;

"From . . . where . . . where . . . where": small words retrace this topography, this verse journey varied yet channeled—four to six syllables pacing each line, two rhyme sounds tuning each stanza. The language, duly plainspoken, blends humankind with nature: bread and tea with tides, bay, sea, and river, with silt, sun, and mud. No single word slows or speeds our attention until sun lavishes the land with lavender rivulets.

How things look trade off with how she looks at them, in Bishop's take on the world around her. And her observance needs turns of speech: "long tides" taking the herrings "long rides," tidal force making the river "a wall of brown foam," a "silted" sun that "veins" the "burning" mud. To look back this way is to re-present, turning then and there into the poem's here and now.

"The Moose" moseys along (the poem, that is—no creature's in sight), taking two or three beats per line through small words that move us "on . . . down . . . past . . . past . . . through," but still no main verb for this place and way of life.

> on red, gravelly roads,
> down rows of sugar maples,
> past clapboard farmhouses
> and neat, clapboard churches,
> bleached, ridged as clamshells,
> past twin silver birches,

through late afternoon
a bus journeys west,
the windshield flashing pink,
pink glancing off of metal,
brushing the dented flank
of blue, beat-up enamel;

down hollows, up rises,
and waits, patient, while
a lone traveller gives
kisses and embraces
to seven relatives
and a collie supervises.

Signs of human dwelling turn up. A local sea image, "ridged as clamshells," sharpens our glimpse of the church more than a bus would allow. We're moving in time, too, "through late afternoon." Maybe this travelogue means a second leaving-behind, and some sort of pilgrimage past maple and birch, farmhouse and church. Then like a Canterbury pilgrim, "a lone traveller" joins the beat-up bus that must also contain our Chaucer, our guide.

Now goodbye and "The bus starts"—such a short sentence! Landscape resumes, maritime and domesticated.

Goodbye to the elms,
to the farm, to the dog.
The bus starts. The light
grows richer; the fog,
shifting, salty, thin,
comes closing in.

Its cold, round crystals
form and slide and settle
in the white hen's feathers,
in gray glazed cabbages,
on the cabbage roses
and lupins like apostles;

the sweet peas cling
to their wet white string
on the whitewashed fences;
bumblebees creep
inside the foxgloves
and evening commences.

Bishop's homegrown rhyming fits her scene: "dog / fog," "cling / string." We half notice as the dog gives way to "thin" fog that "comes closing in."

Then with no warning, our bus window turns visionary in richer light. How else could we see the fog's crystals "slide and settle / in the white hen's feathers"? And spot white string along with whitewashed fences? A painter's eye catches that pure color, and a child's gaze whose mother left her back where the journey began. For crystals to settle upon "lupins like apostles," light must be supernatural. Praise of a sort, Hopkins tempered by Dickinson, magnifies the things of this world: sweet peas cling to string on fences, and as "bumblebees creep / inside the foxgloves," quietly "evening commences."

After stops at quaint but true places—Lower, Middle, and Upper Economy, "Five Houses, / where a woman shakes a tablecloth / out after supper"—our invisible guide spots odd omens. "A pale flickering. Gone" over marshes could be will-o'-the-wisp. "An iron bridge trembles / and a loose plank rattles." A ship's red running light "swims through the dark," a dog barks. This land-and-sea outlook breaks when "A woman climbs in / with two market bags," then it returns.

> Moonlight as we enter
> the New Brunswick woods,
> hairy, scratchy, splintery;
> moonlight and mist
> caught in them like lamb's wool
> on bushes in a pasture.

Loath to show nature mimicking human concerns, Bishop favors actual and local imagery: mist caught "like lamb's wool on bushes." And finally no "I" but "we" enter, a first-person speaking for passengers, poet, maybe reader as well.

Afternoon, evening, now night has fallen as we enter the woods. For Dante it was a *selva oscura*, his journey's dark wood as in myth, fable, fairytale. Here "The passengers lie back. / Snores. Some long sighs." We hear "an old conversation / . . . back in the bus: / Grandparents' voices." Making "Grandparents" her own, Bishop drifts back to childhood eavesdropping on talk of marriage, childbirth, sickness, drink, "who got pensioned," "She went to the bad," a "son lost / when the schooner foundered."

> "Yes . . ." that peculiar
> affirmative. "Yes . . ."
> A sharp, indrawn breath,
> half groan, half acceptance,
> that means "Life's like that.
> We know *it* (also death)."

It took a yearning ear to tune these lines to drowsy fitful gab.

Confiding to us inside this southbound, nightbound bus, our guide says

> Now, it's all right now
> even to fall asleep
> just as on all those nights

overhearing the adults. Then mid-stanza, as if in dream vision,

> —Suddenly the bus driver
> stops with a jolt,
> turns off his lights.

> A moose has come out of
> the impenetrable wood
> and stands there, looms, rather,
> in the middle of the road.
> It approaches; it sniffs at
> the bus's hot hood.

The title has turned up, a bit threatening like Frost's "great buck" in "The Most of It," Ted Hughes's huge old "Pike," the snake whose "notice sudden is" for Emily Dickinson.

It's taken twenty-three stanzas with as many hours journeying past sea, bay, tide, mudflats, river, roads, farms, and lived-on landscape, plus their endearing, enduring populace, to arrive at something unlooked-for. Rhyming "impenetrable wood" with "bus's hot hood" doesn't domesticate this wild critter "Towering, antlerless, / high as a church, / homely as a house"—nor do those likenings. The old folks' country lingo,

> "Sure are big creatures."
> "It's awful plain."
> "Look! It's a she!"

only heightens and distances the beast.

> Taking her time,
> she looks the bus over,
> grand, otherworldly.

Not so inhuman as Lawrence's "Snake" or Jeffers's "Hurt Hawks"—after all, she's a mammal, like us, and female.

Such surprise in the drowsing night. United now, "we" sense something more:

> Why, why do we feel
> (we all feel) this sweet
> sensation of joy?

Because the strange creature is grand yet homely, towering yet mild? Comes out of the dark wild but stands right "in the middle of the road," our road? Why joy? Maybe everlasting tides and human vicissitudes are eased by this communal "jolt" of pure animal presence. In a poem "You should be surprised at seeing something new and strangely alive," Bishop said. So "the moose" needs to be half animal, half poem.

Surprised somehow by joy, with childhood left behind, we feel our driver shift into gear as an awkward stanza break sends us on our way.

> For a moment longer,
>
> by craning backward,
> the moose can be seen
> on the moonlit macadam;
> then there's a dim
> smell of moose, an acrid
> smell of gasoline.

This whole poem arcing through life and memory has meant a "craning backward," which now rhymes slackly with "acrid." Looking for what "can be seen," we end with "gasoline." Life's like that, too true to prettify. As Bishop said about "The Moose": "It was all true."

"I'd like to be a painter most, I think." Indeed she was one, with a knack for line, shape, color, and detail. Elizabeth Bishop's seemingly naïve watercolors slightly skew perspective, always surprising.

Shortly after "The Moose" she wrote "Poem," about a great-uncle's oil painting handed down by her aunt (and restored for this book), depicting the village and landscape sometime before Bishop's childhood. Her title hints that "Poem" touches on the essence of what poetry can do.

> About the size of an old-style dollar bill,
> American or Canadian,
> mostly the same whites, gray greens, and steel grays
> —this little painting (a sketch for a larger one?)

Every verse has its doubts: the painting's "about" the size, American "or" Canadian, "mostly" the same colors, and maybe a sketch. Right away her longing enters the painting.

> It must be Nova Scotia; only there
> does one see gabled wooden houses
> painted that awful shade of brown.
> The other houses, the bits that show, are white.
> Elm trees, low hills, a thin church steeple
> —that gray-blue wisp—or is it?

That steeple again, from the child's echoing memory. Surmising, unsentimental, she's aware that art only fakes reality ("the bits that show"), and that a "gray-blue wisp" might give us what we wish to see. After decades of grime cleaned away, and magnified five times, maybe, just maybe that steeple wisp appears.

Still and all, a pastoral emerges, line by line reminding us how paint, illusion, imagination bring the world alive. (As William Carlos Williams said, "it's what you *put* on the canvas and *how* you put it on . . . *words! pigment! put on!*") Peering back into this scene, Bishop finds white above all—the houses, now geese and iris.

> In the foreground
> a water meadow with some tiny cows,
> two brushstrokes each, but confidently cows;
> two minuscule white geese in the blue water,
> back-to-back, feeding, and a slanting stick.
> Up closer, a wild iris, white and yellow,
> fresh-squiggled from the tube.

Actually there are several iris squiggles, the geese aren't all that white, and they're on the meadow not in the water. Then "Poem" adds more of its own imagination, divining even the picture's weather, memory's bonus sensation.

> The air is fresh and cold; cold early spring
> clear as gray glass; a half inch of blue sky
> below the steel-gray storm clouds.
> (They were the artist's specialty.)
> A specklike bird is flying to the left.
> Or is it a flyspeck looking like a bird?

You can even take Bishop's doubts—"specklike" and "Or" and the question mark—as deeper sight, and take accident as truth. (Plate 16)

Now "Heavens!"—and "I" leaps in bodily, leading us back. This "must be" the church of her hymn-singing upbringing.

> Heavens, I recognize the place, I know it!
> It's behind—I can almost remember the farmer's name.
> His barn backed on that meadow. There it is,
> titanium white, one dab. The hint of steeple,
> filaments of brush-hairs, barely there,
> must be the Presbyterian church.

Exploring brush hairs that hint at what's there, she can "almost remember" a lost place, set even deeper because "Those particular geese and cows / are naturally before my time."

Bishop once called herself "a Nature Lover" (to Robert Lowell), a "minor female Wordsworth." But "Tintern Abbey" has nothing on this surge of memory. At first "It must be Nova Scotia," then later, "I recognize the place!" Musing how she and her artist forebear coincide, as do life and art, nature and people, her mind now digs back through the painting's surface into time and memory.

> I never knew him. We both knew this place,
> apparently, this literal small backwater,
> looked at it long enough to memorize it,
> our years apart. How strange. And it's still loved,
> or its memory is (it must have changed a lot).

She never knew him, George Hutchinson (1852–1942), who long ago won a British Royal Academy prize, so memory's vital. So much depends on her hedging "or": Do we love what's changed and lost, or our memory of it? Maybe both, for the painter-poet.

> Our visions coincided—"visions" is
> too serious a word—our looks, two looks:
> art "copying from life," and life itself,
> life and the memory of it so compressed
> they've turned into each other. Which is which?

Uncannily, as scientists found out recently, when we remember a long-gone event, the neurons firing are the same ones that acted back then. Immersing herself in a small painting, Bishop reclaims the reality of her childhood terrain, makes it present again.

"Poem" toward the end verges on tragic, the cadence deepening with each breath, while reminding us this is only artwork.

> Life and the memory of it cramped,
> dim, on a piece of Bristol board,
> dim, but how live, how touching in detail
> —the little that we get for free,
> the little of our earthly trust. Not much.
> About the size of our abidance
> along with theirs: the munching cows,
> the iris, crisp and shivering, the water
> still standing from spring freshets,
> the yet-to-be-dismantled elms, the geese.

Our earthly trust—what a stirring phrase! As on Keats's Grecian urn this landscape is forever young, these munching cows, crisp iris, spring freshets—not much, but free, and about as much life as we can bear. Art gives us what, being mortal, we can take, what's

> About the size of our abidance
> along with theirs . . .

She fetches up an antique term, "abidance," then lets her line run on, sharing our predicament with other life on earth. We can't go back and save those yet-to-be-dismantled elms, but "how live" they are, "still standing" in Uncle George's painting as in "Poem." This is what art, what memory, what words can do.

"I wish I knew as much . . . as she does," said Hemingway the great angler about "The Fish," seventy-six taut verses from another geography of hers, Key West, Florida. Wedged amid marine and piscine data, our hero marks her way without explaining anything: "I caught a tremendous fish . . . I thought of the coarse white flesh . . . I looked into his eyes . . . I admired his sullen face . . . I saw that from his lower lip . . . I stared and stared . . . And I let the fish go."

Her mind's movement plays against the "grunting weight," the "battered and venerable" creature's barnacle-speckled, sea-lice-infested body, not in disgust but close-up gusto.

> Here and there
> his brown skin hung in strips
> like ancient wallpaper,
> and its pattern of darker brown
> was like wallpaper.

Wallpaper, whimsical, offsets nature's raw fact with a sort of beauty.

> While his gills were breathing in
> the terrible oxygen
> —the frightening gills,
> fresh and crisp with blood,
> that can cut so badly—
> I thought of the coarse white flesh
> packed in like feathers,
> . . . his shiny entrails,
> and the pink swim-bladder
> like a big peony.

Exactness plays with odd similes—like feathers, like a peony—making the fish both familiar and strange.

"I looked into his eyes" and found

> the irises backed and packed
> with tarnished tinfoil
> seen through the lenses
> of old scratched isinglass.

Preciseness, for Gerard Manley Hopkins, signals praise of God's Creation. For Bishop, not quite that, but a poet's, a painter's greeting of the spirit—a greeting unreturned, as "I admired his sullen face." She's nothing to him. From her catch's lower lip

hung five old pieces of fish-line,
or four and a wire leader
with the swivel still attached,

like Moby-Dick surfacing toward Ahab with a lance stuck in his back.

No moralizing blurs this event, as in D. H. Lawrence's longwinded "Fish."
Bishop's eye undercuts joyous with paltry, to admit them both—"victory" in a
"rented boat," a "rainbow" from bilge.   .

I stared and stared
and victory filled up
the little rented boat,
from the pool of bilge
where oil had spread a rainbow
around the rusted engine
to the bailer rusted orange,
the sun-cracked thwarts,
the oarlocks on their strings,
the gunnels—until everything
was rainbow, rainbow, rainbow!
And I let the fish go.

A fish's iris and oil's iridescence could give us God's saving covenant, "rainbow,
rainbow, rainbow!" Then any victory in this face-off flattens: "I let the fish
go." Sending her poem to Marianne Moore she called it a "trifle," yet it has
Moore's charged precision, and more. Bishop's flaying touch with the fish's
skin and the fisher's "victory" strains between beauty and rawness, human and
nonhuman nature. "Beauty is nature's fact," said Dickinson—here that wisdom
seesaws.

On Elizabeth Bishop's existential map, the vivid color belongs to Brazil,
a "different world" where she spent happy adult years living in dramatic
houses with a woman from Rio de Janeiro, traveling the Amazon and elsewhere, and translating from Portuguese. There too, inbred violence could challenge her sense of beauty. "The Armadillo," dedicated to Lowell and involving a Rio saint's-day carnival, begins with nighttime fire balloons climbing a
mountainside:

the paper chambers flush and fill with light
that comes and goes, like hearts.

Then "suddenly turning dangerous" they fall, dropping flames behind her
house. A pair of nesting owls "stained bright pink underneath . . . shrieked up
out of sight." Even "a glistening armadillo" fled, "rose-flecked, head down, tail
down." Clearly the rising human spirit can ravage nature.

> and then a baby rabbit jumped out,
> *short*-eared, to our surprise.
> So soft!—a handful of intangible ash
> with fixed, ignited eyes.

Surprise deflects from the armadillo to a rabbit, who turns into flat *a*-sounds as those last two lines purely horrify.

Was this what she stayed for in Brazil? Bishop can also be charmed. "Santarém," named for a town where the Amazon and Tapajós rivers meet, recalls a "watery, dazzling dialectic" one "golden evening."

> The street was deep in dark-gold river sand
> damp from the ritual afternoon rain,
> and teams of zebus plodded, gentle, proud,
> and *blue*, with down-curved horns and hanging ears,
> pulling carts with solid wheels.
> The zebus' hooves, the people's feet
> waded in golden sand,
> dampered by golden sand,
> so that almost the only sounds
> were creaks and *shush, shush, shush*.

Finding river sand in the streets, and balancing "zebus' hooves" with "people's feet," she paints this golden medley with no irony. Intriguingly,

> A river schooner with raked masts
> and violet-colored sails tacked in so close
> her bowsprit seemed to touch the church.

"Of course I may be remembering it all wrong," Bishop had begun "Santarém." That hardly weakens her surprise at seeing a magic schooner or oxlike zebus wading alongside people through deep gold sand. As in "The Moose" toward evening, truly "The light grows richer."

"Why is your mouth all green?"
Something Alive in May Swenson

"**M**aybe, somehow, after the New Year we can get together. We'd love to see the Blue-Footed Boobies on your slides, and hear about the Galápagos Islands. What luck to have been there!" The slides belong to Elizabeth Bishop, the "we" is May Swenson (1913–1989) and her partner Rozanne Knudson, the blue-footed boobies are gooselike tropical seabirds living on arid islands off South America's Pacific coast, with five-foot wingspan and powder-blue webbed feet.

It's no surprise these poets were friends, exchanging over 250 letters during thirty years. Enthusiasm for the makings of poetry kept them close, and for vivid flora and fauna. The blue-footed booby also signals their love of Marianne Moore's odd creatures and "audacious, hypnotic peacock display of language" (Swenson).

Professional candor marks these letters too. Swenson says about Bishop's recording of "The Fish," "You couldn't ruin it, even with that awful reading that sounded like a stock market report" (which is a fair description). Bishop cautions her against unorthodox punctuation and "low-brow" grammar. Their suggestions about unpublished poems are advanced firmly, gratefully acknowledged, and seldom taken.

In a house with no indoor plumbing and a boardwalk to the outhouse, Swenson was born in 1913, eldest among ten children of Swedish Mormon immigrants to Logan, Utah. Helping her mother with the kids and endless chores, she'd rather have been working in the orchard like her brothers. Her father, who taught woodworking at Utah State Agricultural College, at home would "Darn socks, peel pears, make rootbeer and cider, gather tomatoes, pick raspberries, dry apples and corn, prune fruit trees, keep bees." He made her a small desk and little books with blank pages she used for a diary, and she was her siblings' storyteller.

In 1936 Swenson left Mormon Utah to seek her own story in New York. Years later memory would send roots back and down to a Roethke-like vibrant world. "The Centaur" recalls the summer she was ten, creating her own half-horse, half-human creature. She'd start out barefoot to "a willow grove / down by the old canal." When,

> with my brother's jack-knife,
> I had cut me a long limber horse
> with a good thick knob for a head,
>
> and peeled him slick and clean
> except a few leaves for the tail,
> and cinched my brother's belt
>
> around his head for a rein,
> I'd straddle and canter him fast
> up the grass bank to the path,
>
> trot along in the lovely dust
> that talcumed over his hoofs,
> hiding my toes . . .

The head and neck were hers, though "My hair flopped to the side / like the mane of a horse in the wind."

> My forelock swung in my eyes,
> my neck arched and I snorted.
> I shied and skittered and reared,
>
> stopped and raised my knees,
> pawed at the ground and quivered.

As she galloped, "the leather I slapped to his rump / spanked my own behind." Once home, she tethered the horse, smoothed her skirt, and went in.

> *Where have you been?* said my mother.
> *Been riding,* I said from the sink,
> and filled me a glass of water. . . .
>
> *Go tie back your hair,* said my mother,
> and *Why is your mouth all green?*
> *Rob Roy, he pulled some clover*
> *as we crossed the field,* I told her.

To Bishop this poem felt overemphatic and too vernacular. Swenson had to defend "the constructions of 'cut me a long' and 'filled me a glass'—I used them as Westernisms, they came naturally, this being the way we used to talk out there when I was little (they still talk like that in my state). The knife is there to point up that she's doing something tomboyish, which her mother objects to." When "The Centaur" reached book form, nothing had changed. However Bishop heard the end, Swenson got it right, for a girl's nascent imagination: "*Rob Roy, he pulled some clover / as we crossed the field.*" She really had chomped some grass.

Emily Dickinson, a kindred spirit or feisty maiden aunt, spoke to May Swenson. For one thing, she took heart from Dickinson's skepticism. Swenson left religion behind, "It seems to me a redundancy for a poet." She also took Emily personally, deploring the retouched daguerreotype a 1924 editor had used for the Amherst recluse: curls displacing straight bound-back hair, bangs veiling the forehead, lips and eyebrows accentuated, white ruffles instead of the dark neckband, black bodice turned white, and the right hand that was resting on a book—totally cropped. All in all, robbed of her peculiar strength.

Robbed of her poems, too. Swenson fumes at the newspaper editor who printed "A narrow Fellow in the Grass" without Dickinson's consent, taming her "complex depths" with punctuation and slapping a title, "The Snake," on

Emily Dickinson, ca. 1847.
Amherst College Archives and
Special Collections, by permission of
the Trustees of Amherst College.

Emily Dickinson, retouched
daguerreotype, 1924.
By permission of the Houghton Library,
Harvard University MS Am 1118.15.a.

lines that wanted none. "When experiencing the full reality of something alive, one does not, to begin with, say its name"—good advice, dodging the mythic gift of naming to get a fresh sense of things. Just so, Dickinson's "A Route of Evanescence" presents "a revolving Wheel— / A Resonance of Emerald" (that turns out a hummingbird).

"When experiencing the full reality of something alive, one does not, to begin with, say its name." Swenson adopted an ancient form to catch that reality: Riddles. Anglo-Saxons made them for storm, fire, iceberg, barnacle goose. She called her first one "By Morning," wakening eye and ear:

> Some for everyone
>   plenty
>
> and more coming
>
> Fresh   dainty   airily arriving
>   everywhere at once . . .
>
> Each building will be   a hill
>   all sharps made round . . .
>
> Streets will be   fields
>   cars be   fumbling sheep . . .
>
> By morning we'll be   children
>   feeding on manna
>
>   a new loaf on every doorsill

The *New Yorker*, to her distress, preferred to call this "Snow by Morning." It was her first appearance there, so she agreed, but switched back when the poem appeared in a book. Discovering reality within appearances fascinated her, as did our outward senses. All this a poem can capture, through inventive rhythm, shape, sound, wording, imagery, tone of voice, and surprise.

And all this happens in another kind of poem she favored: "shaped," "figured," or "concrete." She called hers "iconographs," graphic pictures. George Herbert, Shakespeare's contemporary, shaped the lines of poems into angel's wings or an altar. "A poem should not mean / But be," Archibald MacLeish once said, but the truest poems do both. In "How Everything Happens," Swenson's lines mimic the rise and fall of wave action. "I wanted to make my poems do what they say." Don't just talk the talk—walk the walk! It's our proof for the ideal oneness of that pesky dualism, form and content.

"Unconscious Came a Beauty," Swenson's finest iconograph, at once shows and tells something vital. Simply hearing this poem, with slight pauses at each line break, would alter us for good, and seeing does more. Our mind takes in the nameless reality of something alighting, while seeing what "it" must be.

Unconscious   **U**

came a beauty to my   **n**

wrist   **c**

and stopped my pencil,   **o**

merged its shadow profile with   **n**

my hand's ghost   **s**

on the page: **c**

Red Spotted Purple or else Mourning   **i**

Cloak,   **o**

paired thin-as-paper wings, near black,   **u**

were edged on the seam side poppy orange, **s**

as were its spots.   **C a m e   a   B e a u t y**

I sat arrested, for its soot-haired

body's worm

shone in the sun.

It bent its tongue long as

a leg

black on my skin

and clung without my

feeling,

while its tomb-stained

duplicate parts of

a window opened.

And then I

moved.

Why "arrested," at the poem's fulcrum? Fear of dislodging, awe at the shining? Thanks to Swenson's title splayed like antennae, this moment of arrest hinges two stanzas to shape a coming of consciousness, of beauty.

Between "stopped my pencil" and "then I moved" a long stillness occurs, though the creature's bending its tongue, clinging weightlessly, spreading window-wings. Was this poem the one being written when the pencil stopped, or another? Maybe human stillness, sensuously eyeing thin spotted wings, soot-tinted hairs, long black tongue, breeds full consciousness. "My eyes have been primal from the very beginning," says Swenson. Being nearsighted, "I look at everything more carefully close up and notice details." In George Oppen's "Psalm," the deer's "soft lips / Nuzzle" and "small teeth / Tear at the grass." Then just as his poem ends, "the wild deer / Startle, and stare out." Between stilling her pencil and finally stirring, Swenson's craft arrests us for a few seconds of sheer attentiveness.

In common with Dickinson, Swenson prized birds along with butterflies: "if I let myself, every poem would have a bird in it." An avid watcher who kept a life list of sightings, she bent her gaze on everything from Anna's hummingbirds to godwits, horned grebes, and the anhinga. Smaller but fiercer than a booby and flying underwater, spearing fish on its beak, the anhinga or snakefish drives her into reaches of language that wed Gerard Manley Hopkins with Marianne Moore:

> Her cry,
> a slatted clatter, inflates her chin-
> pouch; it's like a fish's swim-
> bladder. . . .
> She flaps up to dry on the crooked, look-
> dead-limb of the Gumbo Limbo, her tan-
> tipped wing fans spread, tail a shut fan dangled.

It's not—or not just—to fan her own wings that Swenson sounds like this. She liked Dickinson's "kinetic poetry" and allied herself with Hopkins, Clare, and Roethke. Poems that catch "the full reality of something alive" are bringing news that stays news.

For kinetic energy, take "The Willets," a sexual dance that Swenson watched in a Delaware salt marsh:

> He stamp-danced closer, his wings arose,
> their hinges straightened,
> from the wedge-wide beak the thin sound
> streaming agony-high . . .

As for "She,"

> The wings held off his weight.
> His tail pressed down, slipped off. She
> animated. And both went back to fishing.

So birds and also "Bees waft and hum through an extraordinary number of poems." Swenson is speaking of Emily, and her poem "A Couple" could almost be mimicking Dickinson.

> A bee rolls in the yellow rose.
> Does she invite his hairy rub?
> He scrubs himself in her creamy folds. . . .
> When he's done his honey-thieving
> at her matrix, whirs free, leaving,
> she closes, still tall, chill,
> unrumpled on her stem.

Dickinson too "was a skeptic," but "possessed intense emotional urges, her senses always sharp and at full pitch."

Poets' affinities speak also for themselves, as when we're told that reclusive Emily "was capable of . . . passionate love." Instinctively Swenson casts her love poems in moments from nature. She titles her remembrance of a college soulmate "Digging in the Garden of Age I Uncover a Live Root."

> The smell of wet geraniums. . . .
> A gleam of sweat in your lip's scoop.
> Pungent geranium leaves, their wet
> smell when our widening pupils met.

"Four-Word Lines" speaks as a flower, not at all skeptical.

> I'd let you wade
> in me and seize
> with your eager brown
> bees' power a sweet
> glistening at the core.

Well, we can never have too much of the birds and the bees.

One other element, lifegiving and destructive, runs through Swenson's poems. When Stanley Kunitz suggested a posthumous collection, *Nature,* its final section was reserved for "Waters": ocean's "purple heave," "glossy swells," "Wave after hissing / wave," "racing foam," "smooth-sucked stones," "the sound of water over stones." In 1938, new to the East Coast, she'd written of a woman "looking at the sea for the first time," standing in tidal surf and "watching in fascination the glossy green coil of water roaring upon her," then sucking back the sand from under her. Eventually she had homes in Sea Cliff, Long Island and Ocean View, Delaware, where the Atlantic pulled poem after poem from her.

Like Kunitz, whose sloping dune garden holds "something at rest and in motion at the same time," and A. R. Ammons's "dunes of motion," Swenson's "The Wave and the Dune" touches a mystery.

> The wave-shaped dune is still.

> Its curve does not break,
>   though it looks as if it will,
>
> like the head of the dune-
>   shaped wave advancing . . .

Flux takes shape here, waves can seem still and dunes may move. As Coleridge said of a stream rushing against a rock, throwing up a constant foam-rose constantly spent, *"It is the life* that we live." Thanks to hyphens, "wave-shaped dune" and "dune-shaped wave" interplay in poetry as in fact. Sand and sea, still and moving, losing and sustaining, make up a whole.

Facing the endlessly renewing ocean, the "overwhelming whale of water, mover and shaper," Swenson has mortal leanings. "I am pulled forward / . . . into her rough insane / annihilating grasp." She watches every "dark curl" of surf with its "hollows empty": "One of them is mine / and gliding forward, gaping wide."

Before Elizabeth Bishop died in 1979, Swenson's last letter had ended, "Please know that I love you—always will . . ." Her Bishop elegy, "In the Bodies of Words," starts as it must, outdoors.

> Tips of the reeds silver in sunlight. A cold wind
> sways them, it hisses through quills of the pines.
> Sky is clearest blue because so cold.

Even—or especially—in grief, music persists, in a poem's body language: sunlight, pines, and thin *i*-sounds, silver tips, wind hissing through quills. Then shock that the news didn't reach her on earth. "Why was there / no tremor of the ground or air?" Then this:

> I walk the shore. Scraped hard as a floor by the wind.
> Screams of terns. Smash of heavy waves. Wind rips
> the corners of my eyes. Salty streams freeze on my face.

Ocean salt blends with tears yet she won't, not now, foist feelings on the natural world. Her words, however harsh, bring the land's end alive, its touch, sight, sound, and cold taste.

"But vision lives!" Swenson promises her fellow-poet, "lives in bodies of words." "Ocean is gray again today," nothing to see

> Except, far out, low over sluggish waves, a long
> clotted black string of cormorants trails south.

Cormorant, "raven of the sea," ravenous. Their string "slips beyond the horizon. Vanished. / / But vision lives, Elizabeth," in that dark vanishing string that's just visible.

May Swenson.
Reprinted with permission of the Literary Estate of May Swenson.

A decade later May Swenson died. On a granite bench above her grave in Utah, hinting at a girl with "mouth all green," is carved "The Exchange": "I'll be the grass. / . . . My mouth, be moss." A fair exchange, after such a life in poems. This one ends,

> Wind, be motion.
> Birds, be passion.
> Water, invite me to your bed.

PART THREE

"care in such a world"
Earth Home to William Stafford

"The earth was my home; I would never feel lost while it held me." As a Kansas teenager, William Stafford (1914–1993) biked out of town one afternoon and spent a night alone above the Cimarron River. The slow, serene sunset, quail and coyote sounds, silence and "steady stars," later the sky brightening "yellow, gray, orange, and then the powerful sun," made for a "strange and fervent" lifelong vision. "The earth was my home; I would never feel lost while it held me."

Unlike another American of his generation, Robert Lowell, who dwelled on the eastern seaboard and found his poems there, or their dominant elder T. S. Eliot, who left Harvard for England and Europe, Stafford's sense of place kept him rooted in the Midwest and Northwest. He studied in Kansas and Iowa, then worked at soil conservation and forestry as a conscientious objector during World War II, for $2.50 a month. "The One who said 'No violence'," he wrote from the Sierra Nevada in 1944, "Said 'mountains', / And they are here, storm-violent, of stone." After teaching high school in California, he took a college job in Oregon, where he lived the rest of his life.

"The earth was my home." If this seems too true to bear saying, it's backed by Stafford's eye, ear, and voice for the down-to-earth places he dwelt in. They remain something other than himself, yet he stays responsive, with no agenda, no bardic tones, no hawklike perch like Jeffers or homespun persona like Frost.

Stafford takes the Midwest as a fortunate given, a home granted but never casually assumed. In that spirit his poems take care with place-names. "This is the hand I dipped in the Missouri / above Council Bluffs and found the spring," he says in "Witness," which often opened his public readings. "One Home" tells what might well ground a person to a locale.

> A wildcat sprang at Grandpa on the Fourth of July
> when he was cutting plum bushes for fuel,
> before Indians pulled the West over the edge of the sky . . .
>
> The sun was over our town; it was like a blade.
> Kicking cottonwood leaves we ran toward storms.
> Wherever we looked the land would hold us up.

In Stafford's company we're seldom unaware of this land's true natives. "Midwest," in his first book *West of Your City*, recalls seed corn the Indians held for generations and then "lost in stony ground / the gods told them to plant it in— / west of your city that corn still lies." For his own sake and ours, he stays in touch with native presence.

"Report to Crazy Horse" takes on the voice of a contemporary Indian reporting back to the Sioux chief who crushed Custer at Little Bighorn in 1876.

> The chokecherries along our valley
> still bear a bright fruit. There is good
> pottery clay north of here. I remember
> our old places. When I pass the Musselshell
> I run my hand along those old grooves in the rock.

And about Ishi, who survived by hiding as the last member of a northern California Stone Age people, Stafford writes with exact empathy.

> A rock, a leaf, mud, even the grass
> Ishi the shadow man had to put back where it was.
> In order to live he had to hide that he did.

In August 1911, this man staggered exhausted into a clearing and was harbored by the Berkeley anthropologist Alfred Kroeber, living until 1916 with a savvy the Golden State might gain from regaining.

"Our People," Stafford carefully titled one poem, tying these hunters into an ecologic story with low-key slant rhymes.

> Under the killdeer cry
> our people hunted all day
> graying toward winter, their lodges
> thin to the north wind's edge.
>
> Watching miles of march grass
> take the supreme caress,

they looked out over the earth,
and the north wind felt like truth.

Fluttering in that wind
they stood there on the world,
clenched in their own lived story,
under the killdeer cry.

As "our people" becomes "they," and each sentence metes out "their own" story, we feel Stafford's empathy, a deft word in each sentence—"thin," "caress," "clenched"—while verbs show this story has faded. Yet a later poem, "The Earth," extends Native American terrain under our feet today by reviving an ancient awe of the land. We may still "feel our own / shudder—the terror of having such a great / friend, undeserved."

Terror and closeness coexist in Stafford's sense of the wild, which is not all benign and can spring a wildness in language itself. Once, he says,

On the third finger of my left hand
under the bank of the Ninnescah
a muskrat whirled and bit to the bone.
The mangled hand made the water red.

Buckling him to land, water, and animal nature, this "Ceremony" imagines "the current flowing through the land, / . . . and the river richer by a kind of marriage."

Sometimes a sense of nature erupts with sacred force. "The Move to California," about uprooting and going west after World War II, starts at springs in Idaho, just over the continental divide, with something that nearly defies language:

Water leaps from lava near Hagerman,
piles down riverward over rock
reverberating tons of exploding shock
out of that stilled world.

Those *l*- and *v*- and *r*-sounds cascade through "leaps from lava," then "riverward over rock / reverberating," and those verbs arouse a geologic oracle. Water "leaps" and "piles down" over a wild verb "reverberating," then "exploding" springs from a "stilled world." The travelers stop to drink where violence joins stillness and a tribe could worship.

Of his several thousand poems, about one a day for fifty years, "The Well Rising" speaks perfectly for Stafford. Every act of speech counts in the body of this poem: title, verb form, sentences, punctuation, line breaks, rhyme, rhythm, repetition.

The well rising without sound,
the spring on a hillside,
the plowshare brimming through deep ground
everywhere in the field—

The sharp swallows in their swerve
flaring and hesitating
hunting for the final curve
coming closer and closer—

The swallow heart from wing beat to wing beat
counseling decision, decision:
thunderous examples. I place my feet
with care in such a world.

Clean, clear, quiet, yet decisive and thunderous.

His title's open-endedness, in a present participle, gives this poem's keynote: ongoing process and purpose. Since "The Well Rising" moves along with no main verb till the end, no explanatory voice, it calls for unscrolling line by line, drawing us into real time until its world grows whole.

The well rising without sound,

Wells betray human habitation but are silent, slow, more earthy than human. Listening closer we can even overhear the well "without sound" as unsounded, bottomless. Stafford's comma invites another such phrase, parallel and part of the same process:

the spring on a hillside,

For a moment, "-ing" almost signals another participle, or possibly the season covering an entire hillside. More likely this "spring" is the well's source higher up, a natural fountain like the Missouri River spring that Stafford once dipped his hand in. Then a comma and more ongoing,

the plowshare brimming through deep ground

Culture cuts in now on nature, but fruitful, agricultural, with peaceful overtones from Isaiah: "they shall beat their swords into plowshares." As it breaks and turns over soil, the share, the plow's curved blade, seems to be "brimming" like a lengthy breaker in deep sea as this line itself runs on with no comma, brimming

everywhere in the field—

Like "deep ground," a charmed notion has the plow working everywhere at once. One stanza's done but so far no verb has sealed the action—only a dash, carrying expectancy over the break.

The sharp swallows in their swerve

After the spring and all, new life strikes, those *sw*'s stirring tongue and lips. Swallows out of nowhere, bladelike pointed wings and tail, swerve to avoid things but unerringly go on seeking. A loaded word, "swerve" figures in Stafford's "Traveling through the Dark," when he finds a dead doe on a narrow canyon road. He could leave her there, but for the next traveler, "to swerve might make more dead." The doe carries an unborn fawn—can he salvage something? "I could hear the wilderness listen," he says, "I thought hard for us all—my only swerving—, / then pushed her over the edge into the river." In another poem, "The Swerve," Stafford's father dies in a car crash. So this word marks emergency, like the swallows

flaring and hesitating

Think of their wheeling flight path, flaring out like a flamenco skirt. Or like aircraft "flaring," as birds skimming turf or fresh-turned soil suddenly fan their wing and tail feathers to tilt and plunge *up* for a still moment,

hunting for the final curve

Do birds hesitate as we do? They hunt, our nerves can sense this. For them, the final curve captures an insect. To us, "final" feels foreboding,

coming closer and closer—

The birds' circlings and superhuman vision drive this *c . . . c . . . c* pulse, like a strobe going on and off at sixty cycles per second, which seems slow to swallows. In full flight they dart their heads to catch insects or falling raindrops. This predatory skill may threaten the felt-but-not-heard speaker. Meanwhile the stanza's four participles, unslowed by commas, still settle on no finite verb. A dash again keeps the energy open—as do this poem's curious rhymes. And instead of rhyming second and fourth lines, giving his stanza a solid stance, Stafford rhymes the odd lines one and three: "sound / ground," "swerve / curve." Each stanza leaves us leaning across a break, toward

The swallow heart from wing beat to wing beat

No sentence has ended yet, but again a new stanza capitalizes "The." We've focused in from "sharp swallows," something visible, to a single "swallow heart," a small creature's even tinier organ. After "coming closer and closer," more repetition stretches the poem's longest line into a heartlike pulse, "wing beat to wing beat"

counseling decision, decision:

Once again an ongoing participle with no closure in sight, plus another repeating pulse: "decision, decision." But now two changes occur. What's been a purely physical, nonhuman vocabulary so far, gives way to human reason. A colon buttressing the line, this poem's firmest punctuation, promises to sum up everything so far. Yet instead, after "decision, decision:" we get

> *thunderous examples. I place my feet*

Thunderous?—when the well, spring, plow, swallows, and swallow heart are silent? And they're examples of . . . what? Country living? Avian behavior? At least and at last the sentence stops, after "thunderous examples." Then a statement of the simplest sort: subject, verb, object—and not just any subject, but the poem's "I," till now invisible, the observant eye, the modest self entering this scene to say "I place my feet"

> *with care in such a world.*

Finally a decent sentence, with an iambic lilt familiar to us after centuries: Keats's "I cannot see what flowers are at my feet," Frost's "But I am done with apple-picking now." Stafford ends with his poem's only formal phrasing:

> *I place my feet / with care in such a world.*

Carefully breaking that news, he tells more by telling less than we expected. Thunderous silence, unexplained examples—those we'll have to realize for ourselves. That's his mode of generosity. "A part of the fun of writing," Stafford said shortly before his death, "is to have something that sounds so simple until later in the quiet of the night." "The Well Rising" offers thunderous examples of sheer being, of a careful footprint, of the clear, quiet attentiveness on which so much depends in "such a world."

"Everything excited me," when hunting as a young boy in Kansas with his father.

> On west was the salt marsh. Teal would be coming in, canvasbacks, buffle-heads. In the early dark we crept through tall weeds, past mysterious trees. At first light long scarfs of ducks came in talking to each other as they dropped. The seething cattails and grasses whispered and gushed in the shadows. And the river was there, going on westward, past islands, along groves, into the wilderness, an endless world for exploring. I stop now and worship those times. The air was clear and sharp; no one was ahead of us; all was like in the first days of creation. We could wander all day, try to get lost, always able to take care of ourselves.

One day "rambling the countryside" they saw a hawk landing in a cottonwood across the field. When they got there they couldn't spot it, and the boy stood waiting to be shown. "Bill, maybe your eyes are better than mine. Maybe you will be the one to see the hawk." His father did him this grace, as "The Well Rising" does us.

Listening to William Stafford speak his poems feels like walking with someone who'd like to let you see certain things, share them with you. At a reading, each brief poem gets a small sheet of paper, even if already published. A Midwestern music in his level voice blends the poems together with apt, brief, ego-free comments he makes in between. Sometimes you don't right away notice the transition from poem to comment, except as a poem's own rhythm distills what it moves.

"A writer is not so much someone who has something to say as he is someone who has found a process that will bring about new things he would not have thought of if he had not started to say them." He's "willing to go where the emergences come out of language," like going overland through new perspectives, perceptions. As Roethke put it, "I learn by going where I have to go."

Stafford likes "the surprise of action," not "worthy statements, but an experience of taking a roller coaster of offerings . . . that suddenly welds together what the whole poem has been tending toward." *Caminante, no hay camino, / Se hace camino al andar,* Antonio Machado wrote, "Wayfarer, there is no way, / You make a way as you go."

"I place my feet / with care in such a world." A good Stafford sentence speaks alike for dwelling and for writing in touch with this earth. So in his political moments, poetry and the land go hand in hand. Before the Vietnam war, "Watching the Jet Planes Dive" brought our threatening technologic power down to earth.

> We must go back and find a trail on the ground
> back of the forest and mountain on the slow land . . .
>
> We must go back with noses and the palms of our hands
> and climb over the map in far places, everywhere,
> and lie down whenever there is doubt and sleep there.

A half-century later, one wants to take this plea literally and broadcast it.

> The jet planes dive; we must travel on our knees.

Because the ways of the world, human greed and ingenuity and barbarity, can ride roughshod over such verse, its humility, its groundedness need hearing all the more.

Right after "The Well Rising" in *The Rescued Year,* Stafford placed another 1960 poem, "At the Bomb Testing Site."

> At noon in the desert a panting lizard
> waited for history, its elbows tense . . .
>
> There was just a continent without much on it
> under a sky that never cared less.

Ready for a change, the elbows waited.
The hands gripped hard on the desert.

As ever, attentiveness enlivens things seen and said: "its elbows tense." A pant-ing lizard knows no human designs, and eons separate it from us. A hope, a change would connect those hands gripping the desert with a youthful nightlong vision above the Cimarron River: "The earth was my home; I would never feel lost while it held me."

"The season's ill"
America's Angst and Robert Lowell's

"Pity the planet, all joy gone / from this sweet volcanic cone." It's summer 1965 on the Maine coast for America's classic twentieth-century poet Robert Lowell (1917–1977). Invited by Lyndon Johnson to a White House Arts Festival, Lowell publicly declines in anguish at the escalating Vietnam war. "Waking Early Sunday Morning" (from *Near the Ocean*), written in the Northeast at that troubled moment, begins just before dawn with a cry to our Northwest rivers.

> O to break loose, like the Chinook
> salmon jumping and falling back,
> nosing up to the impossible
> stone and bone-crushing waterfall—
> raw-jawed, weak-fleshed there, stopped by ten
> steps of the roaring ladder, and then
> to clear the top on the last try,
> alive enough to spawn and die.

This wild freedom would be something genuine, by human measure heroic and truly tragic (though another tragedy's occurred since then—chinook runs now endangered). Lowell habitually goes to nature to test his passion: spawning salmon, a hacked sperm whale, a mother skunk, or swinging oriole's nest.

When "my body wakes / to feel the unpolluted joy" of a Sunday morning, little is there to grace his life, as in Wallace Stevens's "Sunday Morning," where

> Deer walk upon our mountains, and the quail
> Whistle about us their spontaneous cries;
> Sweet berries ripen in the wilderness,

filling religion's void. For Lowell,

> Only man thinning out his kind
> sounds through the Sabbath noon, the blind
> swipe of the pruner and his knife
> busy about the tree of life,

driven by sinewy rhythms and bitter rhymes.

Stemming from New England's old Yankee families, Lowell grew up on a shabby-genteel branch of the tree, his Navy father ineffectual, his mother frustrated and overbearing. At eighteen he nurtured "the spiritual side of being a poet" as it faced "the actualities of the world," though it took years to steady that stance. Studying poetry and classics in college, he'd walk country roads with a friend, "talking every step of the way about ourselves or about our writing." The spring before graduating, Lowell married an aspiring novelist and converted to Catholicism. During the war, after trying to enlist, he declared himself a conscientious objector and served five months in jail, looking out "through sooty clothesline entanglements / and bleaching khaki tenements" at the Hudson River and yammering metaphysics with Abramowitz, "so vegetarian, / he wore rope soles and preferred fallen fruit."

"The Quaker Graveyard in Nantucket," begun in 1943, like Eliot's *The Waste Land* works myth, religion, history, geography and nature, literary and personal memory into Anglo-American prophecy. Lowell moves via Poseidon and Orpheus, Milton's Lycidas, Melville's Ahab and Moby-Dick, Thoreau's Cape Cod, Quaker sailors, Adam, Noah, Job, Jonah, Babylon, Psalms, Christ, the Lord God, and Nantucket surf. Dedicated to his cousin lost at sea in the war, the poem keeps surging in muscular passages and high language mixed with low. While working on it, Lowell spoke of Gerard Manley Hopkins's "inebriated exuberance."

"Why doesn't Bobby write about the sea?" Aunt Sarah asked from the deck of her yacht off the Massachusetts coast. "It's so pretty." But he did, wrestling its wild violence:

> A brackish reach of shoal off Madaket,—
> The sea was still breaking violently and night
> Had steamed into our North Atlantic fleet,
> When the drowned sailor clutched the drag-net.

Psalms now and then possess the sailors' cry:

This is the end of running on the waves;
We are poured out like water.

The whale draws a fury of words, Lowell's way of scathing human rapine and with it the war's:

Gobbets of blubber spill to wind and weather,
Sailor, and gulls go round the stoven timbers
Where the morning stars sing out together.

Beginning his poem with Genesis, man's "dominion" over earth and earth's creatures, Lowell echoes God's taunt to Job, "Where wast thou . . . When the morning stars sang together?" and ends by doubting God's covenant.

You could cut the brackish winds with a knife
Here in Nantucket, and cast up the time
the Lord God formed man from the sea's slime
And breathed into his face the breath of life,
And blue-lung'd combers lumbered to the kill.
The Lord survives the rainbow of his will.

Such a voice, turning Adam's dust into ocean slime, rolling waves into gaping whale-mouths, could be Melville's in *Moby-Dick*. The rhymes alone savage Creation—"slime" against "time," "knife" / "life," "kill" / "will," humankind hopeless after the Fall and Flood.

Though we don't think of Lowell as cleaving to nature, like Hopkins, Frost, and Roethke, ocean and above all animals gave him poet's plenty if not God's. Just as Yeats sees "Another emblem there!" in "sudden thunder of the mounting swan," Lowell finds nature acting out his own and the world's condition.

In college Lowell copied Hopkins into a notebook, "O the mind, mind has mountains; cliffs of fall / Frightful, sheer, no-man-fathomed." At thirty-two he suffered a first bout of manic depression, and later found images for it in "Skunk Hour." "The season's ill," he says, "A red fox stain covers Blue Hill." Nothing's authentic anymore in this Maine coastal town, at night "nobody's here,"

only skunks, that search
in the moonlight for a bite to eat.
They march on their soles up Main Street:
white stripes, moonstruck eyes' red fire.

Under the puritanic "spire of the Trinitarian Church" he spots lunatic, satanic "moonstruck eyes' red fire." To gain some purely physical clarity,

I stand on top
of our back steps and breathe the rich air—

a mother skunk with her column of kittens swills the garbage pail.
She jabs her wedge-head in a cup
of sour cream, drops her ostrich tail,
and will not scare.

In "my skunks," this creaturely force untroubled by existential angst, he saw "natural power" and called their march an "affirmation, an ambiguous one."

Lowell's pained stance in this world gives his Civil War elegy "For the Union Dead" a grip on 1950s America like no other. As if balking at homo sapiens, the poem abounds with wild animals. It centers on Boston's monument to Colonel Robert Shaw, who led the first African American regiment, half-slaughtered in 1863. Other history crowds in too, including the dinosaur age, World War II, civil rights years, Lowell's childhood, and the decaying South Boston aquarium.

The bronze weathervane cod has lost half its scales.
The airy tanks are dry.

Once my nose crawled like a snail on the glass;
my hand tingled
to burst the bubbles
drifting from the noses of the cowed, compliant fish.

Elementary life would be better than the havoc his language dramatizes.

My hand draws back. I often sigh still
for the dark downward and vegetating kingdom
of the fish and reptile. One morning last March,
I pressed against the new barbed and galvanized

fence on the Boston Common. Behind their cage,
yellow dinosaur steamshovels were grunting
as they cropped up tons of mush and grass
to gouge their underworld garage.

His verbs alone act out childlike malaise in face of urban mayhem.

Reaching for a sound heritage, Lowell looks to the bronze sculpture of the heroic "Shaw / and his bell-cheeked Negro infantry," though it's animal keenness that exposes our own lack.

Their monument sticks like a fishbone
in the city's throat.
Its Colonel is as lean
as a compass-needle.

He has an angry wrenlike vigilance,
a greyhound's gentle tautness.

Crouching at his TV, Lowell watches "the drained faces of Negro school-children."

> The Aquarium is gone. Everywhere,
> giant finned cars nose forward like fish;
> a savage servility
> slides by on grease.

No animal tautness here but human excess, slavishness to the machine.

With Berlin divided, Soviet against American, and nuclear tensions sky-high, "Fall 1961" filters Lowell's anxiety through nursery sing-song, grating rhymes, odd figures of speech, upended proverbs, and exemplary animals.

> Back and forth, back and forth
> goes the tock, tock, tock
> of the orange, bland, ambassadorial
> face of the moon
> on the grandfather clock.

> All autumn, the chafe and jar
> of nuclear war;
> we have talked our extinction to death.
> I swim like a minnow
> behind my studio window.

> Our end drifts nearer,
> the moon lifts,
> radiant with terror.
> The state
> is a diver under a glass bell.

> A father's no shield
> for his child.
> We are like a lot of wild
> spiders crying together,
> but without tears.

> Nature holds up a mirror.
> One swallow makes a summer.
> It's easy to tick
> off the minutes,
> but the clockhands stick.

> Back and forth!
> Back and forth, back and forth—
> my one point of rest
> is the orange and black
> oriole's swinging nest!

In this man's psychic imbalance, off rhymes scrape the ear, however slight: "jar" / "war," "minnow" / "window," "nearer" / "terror," "shield" / "child," plus troublous unrhymed words in every stanza. Like Yeats in "The Stare's Nest by My Window," from Ireland's civil war, Lowell yokes private predicament with public, present with past, nature with history in a casual mode open to breakdown at any moment.

The clock—an heirloom, maybe from his great-great-uncle James Russell Lowell, poet and ambassador to England—this ticking time bomb clock alongside U.N. blather unnerves someone still peering out at the watery world. For Lowell as father of a four-year-old child, proverbial wisdom's upset. Hamlet says art should "hold the mirror up to nature," and the old saw has it, "One swallow doesn't make a summer." But with Cold War heating up, language like nature is going askew. At the last minute his inane heirloom gives way to an oriole's nest outside the window, rhyming easily on "rest" and swinging in nature's rhythm.

A year later, symptoms from Lowell's malaise within the American scene seep through "The Mouth of the Hudson"—"scuffles . . . discarded . . . condemned . . . jar . . . junk . . . trouble . . . drifts . . . wild . . . blank . . . puncture . . . Chemical" —and all this is seen from a hospital overlooking the river. Here the same spirit that culls nature to write historical and illness poems, writes these bitter environmental lines.

> A single man stands like a bird-watcher,
> and scuffles the pepper and salt snow
> from a discarded, gray
> Westinghouse Electric cable drum.
> He cannot discover America by counting
> the chains of condemned freight-trains
> from thirty states. They jolt and jar
> and junk in the siding below him.
> He has trouble with his balance.
> His eyes drop,
> and he drifts with the wild ice
> ticking seaward down the Hudson,
> like the blank sides of a jig-saw puzzle.
>
> The ice ticks seaward like a clock.
> A Negro toasts
> wheat-seeds over the coke-fumes
> of a punctured barrel.
> Chemical air
> sweeps in from New Jersey,
> and smells of coffee.

Across the river,
ledges of suburban factories tan
in the sulphur-yellow sun
of the unforgivable landscape.

A solitary man (if only he *could* be a bird-watcher!) and "A Negro," the poet's proxies, cannot discover America like Columbus and Walt Whitman. Wastage, pollution, leave "wild ice" the only genuine sight. We're left in an "unforgivable," unforgiving landscape.

"that witnessing presence"
Life Illumined Around Denise Levertov

"So a poet, although often impelled . . . to write poems of pure celebration, is driven inevitably to lament, to anger, and to expression of dread." Driven, says Denise Levertov (1923–1997), because "although we humans are a part of nature ourselves, we have become . . . an increasingly destructive element within it, shaking and breaking the 'great web'—perhaps irremediably."

Shortly before she died, Levertov gathered nature poems from her career in *The Life Around Us.* "I decided not to group them separately—praise-poems in one clump, laments and fears in another," but to let poems in one vein or the other follow along with "those in which celebration and the fear of loss are necessarily conjoined. I believe this flux and reflux echo what readers also feel in their response to 'the green world'."

Join celebration to lament, like the Psalms, as Levertov knew well. Sited at Stanford where she taught for twelve years, "In California" tests praise with anger, dawn light "emblazoning" palm and pine with pesticide "poking" at weeds and moss. Posing "deep oakshadow, airy / shadow of eucalyptus" against bulldozers, "babel of destructive construction," she finds a phrase for it all: "Fragile paradise."

> Who can utter
> the poignance of all that is constantly
> threatened, invaded, expended,

and constantly
nevertheless
persists in beauty,

she asks at the end,

Who can utter
the praise of such generosity
or the shame?

Her poem has already answered that psalmlike question.

"My mother was descended from the Welsh tailor and mystic Angel Jones of Mold, my father from the noted Hasid, Schneour Zalman, 'the Rav of Northern White Russia'." Levertov herself, born in Essex outside London, attended only ballet school, did lessons at home, and was greatly read to in "a house full of books." She traces her spiritual, earthly, verbal fervency to that Christian-Judaic legacy, as in "Illustrious Ancestors": "thinking some line still taut between me and them," she summons up the mystical Russian rabbi who understood the language of birds, and the Welsh tailor whose meditations "were sewn into coats and britches."

I would like to make . . .
poems direct as what the birds said,
hard as a floor, sound as a bench,
mysterious as the silence when the tailor
would pause with his needle in the air.

Another poem, "The 90th Year," credits her mother:

It was she
who taught me to look;
to name the flowers when I was still close to the ground,
my face level with theirs.

Under "the roar / of mowers / cropping the already short / grass of lawns," "In California" looks close at "miner's lettuce, / tender, untasted."

Paul Levertoff, Denise's father, had broken with his parents and Judaism "to be, as he believed, the more fully a Jew," she says. Ordained an Anglican priest, he published a book when she was five, *St. Paul in Jewish Thought,* which at one point focuses on a certain Jewish quality: "This union of a deep faith in God with the highest concentration of human energy." He goes on, uncannily in 1928, to as much as foretell Denise Levertov's poetic creed: "Jewish materialism is *religious* materialism, or, rather, realism. For every idea and every ideal the Jew demands a visible and touchable materialization." Given "the highest spiritual truth," he must "see and feel its real working. He believes in the invisible . . . but he desires that this invisible should become visible and reveal its power; that it should permeate everything material."

This desire, which so impressed Paul Levertoff, would permeate poem after poem by his daughter. "For Instance," opening *The Life Around Us,* recalls to herself those instants when something gleams not at you but "through you," a

> fragment
> of lichened stone, or some old shed
> where you took refuge once from pelting rain
> in Essex, leaning on wheel or shafts
> of a dusty cart, and came out when you heard
> a blackbird return to song though the rain
> was not quite over; and, as you thought there'd be,
> there was, in the dark quarter where frowning clouds
> were still clustered, a hesitant trace
> of rainbow; and across from that the expected
> gleam of East Anglian afternoon light, and leaves
> dripping and shining. Puddles, and the roadside weeds
> washed of their dust. Earth,
> that inward cry again—
> *Erde, du liebe* . . .

Those dots are hers, letting one of Levertov's guiding spirits, the poet Rainer Maria Rilke, seal her gratitude for "Earth, you belovèd."

A "gleam of East Anglian afternoon light, and leaves / dripping and shining" —that's what her father meant. The "real working" of spirit illumines poem after poem.

> Trunk in deep shade, its lofting crown
> offers to each long day's
> pale glow after the sun
> is almost down, an answering gold—

> *   *   *

> Small town, early morning.
> No cars. Sunlit
> children wait for the green light.

> *   *   *

> Pale, then enkindled,
> light
> advancing,
> emblazoning
> summits of palm and pine

> *   *   *

all night the glitter
of all that shines out of itself
crisps the vast swathes of the current.

These glints and glimpses, giving the world around us "that attention to detail which is a species of love" (Bill Alfred), become more and more vulnerable, more shadowed, throughout her career.

Precarious thus precious moments begin and end "An English Field in the Nuclear Age," as in her handwritten draft, working "To render it!" by deep indents and abrupt line breaks, italics, spacings, parentheses.

To render it!—this moment,
haze and haloes of
sunbless'd particulars . . .

What fends off desperation are "centuries furrowed in oakbole, *this* oak, / *these* dogrose pallors." Finally she notices

how among
thistles, nettles, subtle silver
of long-dried cowpads,

gold mirrors of buttercup satin
assert eternity as they reflect
nothing, everything, absolute instant,
and dread

holds its breath, for
this minute at least was
not the last.

Sheer craft proves these lines: the half-rhymed texture of "thistles, nettles" met rhythmically by "subtle silver," the run-on buckling "subtle silver" to "long-dried cowpads." Her late revision added a stanza break, so that "dread / / holds its breath" while an exquisite timing metes out one more moment saved.

"Only connect": Levertov prized E. M. Forster's motto. Connect the illumined pines with the pesticide, an English field with the nuclear age. In that intolerable dimension where greed and carelessness violate earth's integrity, her mentor was not Rilke but the Jesuit poet Gerard Manley Hopkins:

My aspens dear, whose airy cages quelled,
Quelled or quenched in leaves the leaping sun,
All felled, felled, are all felled.

This, in 1879, when wasting of the land was not recognized.

Denise Levertov, "An English Field in the Nuclear Age" manuscript.
Courtesy of Department of Special Collections and University Archives,
Stanford University Libraries, and of Trustees of the Denise Levertov Literary Trust,
Valerie Trueblood and Paul Lacey.

And for all this, nature is never spent;
There lives the dearest freshness deep down things.

With Hopkins she shared a faith that the freshest language for God's created world might possibly begin reclaiming it.

To bear that faith through a time of war, as Levertov unflaggingly did, makes for poignant political poetry. Her earliest published verse, "Listening to Distant Guns," stems from 1940 when she was sixteen and the Germans attacked British troops at Dunkirk.

The roses tremble; oh, the sunflower's eye
Is opened wide in sad expectancy.
Westward and back the circling swallows fly,
The rooks' battalions dwindle near the hill.

And in "Christmas 1944," "Who can be happy while the wind recounts / its long sagas of sorrow?" Her rhymed and measured stanzas would vanish soon after the war. So would the humanizing of nature, but not its witness to human ill.

Wherever calamity takes place, nature holds out someplace to turn. Yeats counters the violent Irish rebellion with a "living stream," moorhens calling moorcocks. Edward Thomas tracks a kestrel overhead the week German shells kill him in 1917. From World War I trenches, Isaac Rosenberg hears "night ringing with unseen larks." If you ask "why his poems / don't tell us of dreams, and leaves, / and great volcanoes in his native land," writes Pablo Neruda (another inspiration for Levertov), "Come see / the blood in the streets" of Spain's civil war. Robert Lowell fearing nuclear war gazes at an "orange and black / oriole's swinging nest." An Arab woman's "kilo of ripe figs" counterbalances the day's crushing news in Shirley Kaufman's Jerusalem.

Levertov's Vietnam-era collection *The Sorrow Dance* struggles to imagine how once, "water buffalo stepped surely along terraces" and "peaceful clouds were reflected in the paddies." Then "bombs smashed those mirrors."

Yes, this is the knowledge that jostles for space
in our bodies along with all we
go on knowing of joy, of love.

Honesty taking on the brunt of awareness—a form of responsibility.

"The Pulse," seaside and intimate, barely seems to concern Vietnam.

Sealed inside the anemone
in the dark, I knock my head
on steel petals
curving inward around me.

Her sense of peril stuns us all the more, lodged in a colorful invertebrate. Then the "petals," really tentacles, open onto radiant images,

> the air they call *water*,
> saline, dawngreen over its sands,
> resplendent with fishes.
> All day it is morning,
>
> all night the glitter
> of all that shines out of itself
> crisps the vast swathes of the current.
> But my feet are weighted:
>
> only my seafern arms
> my human hands
> my fingers tipped with fire
> sway out into the world.

Free for just this moment, she says "I sing." But

> the petals creak and
> begin to rise.
> They rise and recurl
> to a bud's form
>
> and clamp shut.
> I wait in the dark.

Rather than blatant horror, she shuts her anemone bud on what can't be expressed.

"Insofar as poetry has a social function it is to awaken sleepers by other means than shock." Levertov in 1959 says that poems, no matter if driven by dread or outrage, must keep an "inner harmony." She held to a basic principle for poetry, organic form, passing from Coleridge and Emerson through Whitman, Hopkins, and others. Poems of environmental awakening give that much more weight to the word "organic." Robert Frost's apple-picking, William Stafford's "sharp swallows in their swerve," Levertov's anemone petals evolve a growth of their own: "form is never more than a *revelation* of content."

Here we see "the most powerful influence on my poetry," William Carlos Williams. In his "Young Sycamore," a single free-verse sentence exfoliates from trunk to tip, shaping a new sense of this tree. "Spring and All" moves through "dried weeds" until newly rooted plants "grip down and begin to awaken." Arriving in the United States in 1948, Levertov came to value the idiomatic speech in Williams's poems, his local (New Jersey) inspiration, and "a Franciscan sense of wonder" at common things that "deepened for me . . . some latent capacity in myself to see the world more freshly." Meanwhile the older poet welcomed in her writing an "energy and chained power," plus her American standpoint as against expatriates like Ezra Pound and T. S. Eliot.

After Williams died, Levertov composed "a kind of flower-sketch of Bill" for his widow, Flossie, set by a river near his home.

> Brown and silver, the tufted
> rushes hold sway
> by the Hackensack
>
> and small sunflowers
> freckled with soot
> clamber out of the fill.

Amid "crude industrial debris" these sunflowers carry "in each disk / of coarse yellow" a smile, "almost / a boy's grin." She also had in mind the "Sunflower Sutra" of another Williams protégé, Allen Ginsberg chanting his holy golden sunflower "poised against the sunset, crackly bleak and dusty with the smut and smog and smoke." Tenacious like sunflowers, her dogrose and buttercup, oakshadow and summits of palm and pine resist a more and more denatured world. That "flux and reflux" of celebration and dread, as she put it, kept her voice sane.

In her mid-sixties Levertov moved to Seattle, living near a large semi-wild park on Lake Washington. She continued to teach and help younger poets, while working against war, nuclear proliferation, environmental wastage. When local citizens "daylighted" a suffocated urban stream, she wrote how "fish and waterbugs swim again in its ripples." Her poem is posted there. Settling into the terrain, she greeted its "generous" presence with crisp verse: dark silent woods under "winter sunlight favoring / here a sapling, there an ancient snag, / ferns, lichen," the lake "always ready to change its skin / to match the sky's least inflection," and above all, the mountain.

Mount Rainier's 14,400-foot volcanic peak south of the city, seldom fully visible, astonished her. Like Hokusai's "Thirty-Six Views of Mount Fuji," Levertov in many poems, while never naming Rainier, records its changing aspects.

> The mountain comes and goes
> on the horizon,
> > a rhythm elusive as that of a sea wave
>
> *   *   *
>
> The mountain absent,
> a remote folk-memory

> the mountain revealing itself unclouded, its snow
> tinged apricot as it looked west

Far but not too far from Marianne Moore's octopus Rainier, Levertov sees an "Animal mountain" of clefts and creases, a "snowwhite foam mirage," "obdurate, unconcerned," sensing too its "slopes of arid scree" and "scarring roads."

Throughout her chronicle runs a sense that revealed or hidden, massive stone and snow or ethereal vapor, this everpresent mountain has a more-than-natural reality. Her own awareness reflects its silent witness to human transience, like the gazing grain along Dickinson's path toward eternity. Sometimes,

> I forget or refuse to go
> down to the shore or a few yards
> up the road, on a clear day

so as to see Rainier. Mindful of nature, religion, politics, personhood, Denise Levertov must go see Rainier

> to reconfirm
> that witnessing presence.

"the tree making us / look again"
Shirley Kaufman's Roots in the Air

"American *hyphen* Israeli" seems the way to describe her, says Shirley Kaufman (b. 1923) in a talk called "Roots in the Air." Born in Seattle to immigrants from eastern European villages that crop up in her poetry, Kaufman lived in San Francisco, had three daughters, and at forty-six published her first book. In 1973 she moved to Jerusalem with her new husband, a South African who'd immigrated during Israel's war of independence. "The little line that has become a bridge between America and Israel, has begun to sway and swing like the Golden Gate Bridge suspended on cables between San Francisco and Marin County, and even though the wind is strong coming in from the ocean and over the bay, I begin to find my balance on it. I discover that, after all, it does connect me. I am not rootless . . . That hyphen—that bridge and what it connects me to—is my place in the world."

My place in the world—a vexed enough question for anyone nowadays, and all the more so for Kaufman. Seattle, California's gold country, Bayshore Freeway, Big Sur, Watts, Taos, Brest Litovsk, Ulanov, Lake Como, Mycenae, Ganges, Cairo: her poems range wherever some viewpoint if not foothold may be found. Eventually they come back to the adopted landscape: Ramallah, Rosh Hanikra, Dead Sea, Mount Sinai, City of David and Mount of Olives, Western Wall and Dome of the Rock, Mount Moriah and Via Dolorosa, places that surge up against the soles of anyone keeping her balance in the Holy Land.

"What are you doing in Jerusalem?" Kaufman asks herself in "Stones."

When you live in Jerusalem you begin
to feel the weight of stones.
You begin to know the word
was made stone, not flesh. . . .

There's a huge rock lying on my chest
and I can't get up.

And in a collection called *From One Life to Another*,

You can't learn two
landscapes in one
life he said
or a language
to put them in.

She couldn't speak with her Yiddish grandparents, her mother's tongue is not
her mother tongue, and the Hebrew "holy tongue" comes hard. Yet Kaufman
has translated Israeli poets, with their help, naturalizing their strangeness into
English: Amir Gilboa, Abba Kovner, Dan Pagis, themselves émigrés and survivors from eastern Europe to Palestine, and Meir Wieseltier. Meanwhile "I
have fallen in love with the landscapes, the wooded mountains of the north,
and the stark mountains of the Judean wilderness . . . But I'm always reminded
of my marginality."

Inevitably she finds another divide, as much geopolitical as personal, in the
city built upon a hill.

When I stand on this ridge,
the earth slides helpless
in two directions. There's only
Jerusalem on my left, everyone
climbing over the corpses,
on my right the frozen wilderness,
black goats looking for something green.

The terrain lays bare a history that "slides helpless / in two directions": everyone's losses littering Jerusalem, and goats as ever, David's or any nomad people's "looking for something green." A later poem ends with Jewish Sarah and
Egyptian Hagar,

two halves
of an ancient slippage
split
on the fault lines.

The land is biblical, political, personal.

This countryside offers up metaphors without a poet's having to invent them.

From *Claims*, "Chosen" begins not with nature imaging history but imaged by history, for once.

> Leaves are the color of burned-out
> trucks on the road to Jerusalem. Obsolete
> armor. Grapes in the market
> already smell of wine,
> and the flies tap sugar
> from their overstuffed skins.
>
> We think we can smell the rain too,
> smashing its tiny mirrors in the north
> as if what we waited for
> might come.
>
> Chosen for what? The live carp
> flap in their vats. They think
> they should be flying.
> I take one home in a plastic bag.

Trucks left as they fell along the Tel Aviv–Jerusalem road lend their color to autumn leaves, though any rusted metal would do—barrel hoop, plowshare. Since 1948 it took flame, then rain and sun to make a rough dark russet now a figure of speech.

In Israel, as elsewhere, Kaufman finds nature closely, sometimes corrosively touched by history. So is human nature, of course. While the poem's and a people's title word "Chosen" lingers over this poem, there's still shopping to do. Get close enough to smell wine in the grapes and the flies dismay you. You're too close, a heartbeat from "armor" to "Grapes," then flies "tap" sugar from "overstuffed skins." Waiting for Messiah and something sooner, we look north for rain "smashing its tiny mirrors"—a split-second image, rain smashing what might have shown us something.

Kaufman's title has been ticking away on the road to Jerusalem, in the market, through a parched summer, the word "chosen" a nagging question. Now it surfaces: "Chosen for what?" Instead of an answer, "The live carp / flap in their vats." Messianic, Chagallesque, they dream of flying, while she's of the chosen people in a promised land and can "take one home in a plastic bag." A vapid music undercuts the dream: flap, vats, plastic, bag.

Those late rains everyone waits for sound a litany throughout Kaufman's poems. In "Déjà Vu," a story of Sarah and Hagar,

> The air ticks slowly. It's August
> and the heat is sick of itself
> waiting all summer for rain.

In "Waiting," on the Day of Atonement,

> . . . the rains are late, we're not forgiven,
> and autumn won't come.
> A few blurry showers in the north,
> not in Jerusalem. No loosening.
> No green rinsing of the trees.

No "green rinsing," unless that verbal music brings a grace of its own. In the hot dry wind of "HAMSIN Breaking After Five Days,"

> Something flutters the ivy on the walls
> across the street . . .

> Blessed be whatever sprinkles
> a little water on the dust
> to make it settle.

Like the "small rain" craved in England's anonymous "Western Wind," Eliot's sunken Ganges where "the limp leaves / waited for rain," and like earlier religions, Judaism needs a blessing for rain, news of release and a fresh start. In Kaufman's writing, always seasonally alert and weather-wise, waiting for rain gives a local presence to no-less-present political and spiritual longings.

If wherever you walk in Jerusalem is holy ground, it's political as well and physical, fruitful earth. "Autumn Crocus" moves like Breughel and Van Gogh into the fields, "I go . . . I watch," eking out ecologic news fraught with overtones.

> I go to the center of the world
> near the edge of Jerusalem
> where the grapes are all picked
> and the men are climbing
> into the olive trees.

> I watch how they beat the branches
> and the dark fruit drops to the ground.
> The families move in and out
> of the dust to gather them.

> October again.
> The rains are coming, the steep cold
> and the festering idleness.

> The women are sorting the bitter crop.
> In the empty fields small
> clusters of lavender petals
> explode from the soil
> without any warning, not even
> a stem or a single leaf.

A kind of privilege. As if
they earned the right
through the exacting summer.

Look! They say for a moment.

"It is difficult to get the news from poems," Williams warns us, "yet men die
miserably every day for lack of what is found there."

Old maps putting Jerusalem at the center of the world still serve today,
though storm center is more like it. "Autumn Crocus" offers personal witness.
While "The families" are Arab, this year's rains bring cold and festering for
everyone. "The women," all this land's women, "are sorting the bitter crop,"
the Mediterranean's biblical fruit in need of curing. Then comes the season's
gift: "clusters of lavender petals / explode from the soil / without any warning."
Figures of speech are fair game, as in "leaves the color of burned-out / trucks."
Here as in the day's news a verb explodes over a line break, almost blotting out
these lavender petals. Yet they do what poems can do. "Look! They say for a
moment."

In the Prologue to *Claims,* Kaufman's tact, phrasing, and surprise find anxiety in the promised land along with resurgences of life—here, a tree outside
her door.

JACARANDA
Because the branches hang down with blossoms
for only a few weeks, lavender clumps
that let go quickly
and drop to the ground,

because the flowers are so delicate
even their motion through the air
bruises them,
and they lie where they fall
like tiny pouches of shriveled skin,

because our lives are sagging with marvels
ready to fail us,
clusters of faces drifting away,

what's settled for is not nearly
what we are after, claims
we keep making or are made on us.
But the recurrence of change
can still surprise us, lilac
that darts and flickers
like the iridescent head of a fly,
and the tree making us
look again.

"Because . . . because . . . because": what's to come of this hanging, dropping, bruising, sagging, drifting away, and the "claims" these causes frustrate? The sentence beginning "But" bears a saving or at least hopeful logic, veering this poem toward *change*.

In Jerusalem a clause spans beauty and hurt, flowers "so delicate / even their motion through the air / bruises them." Line by line freeze-frames their fall, catching what we can barely imagine much less see. On top of this, surprise: the blossoms "lie where they fall / like . . ."—like what? Like bonny curls of a newborn babe? Like tiny sachets of crumpled silk? No, "like tiny pouches of shriveled skin." The decrepit figure risks a lot, and is not the last to do so.

A third "because" moves from botany to the human condition. Where branches "hang down with blossoms," our lives in like rhythm are "sagging with marvels," God's unfulfilled promises and miracles. And where "lavender clumps . . . drop to the ground," now "clusters of faces" drift away—family and friends gone with the 7 A.M. news.

Because of all this, the "claims / we keep making or are made on us" go wanting. *But* "the recurrence of change," hanging on a line break, "can still surprise us." After such fallings and failings, is this enough? At least we have late spring "lilac / that darts and flickers," explosive as autumn crocus ("Look! They say for a moment"). What's this lilac flicker like? Another surprise: "like the iridescent head of a fly." Skirting disgust, the image quickens to radiance: iris, rainbow, a rainwashed covenant after the flood. Then back home to jacaranda, "the tree making us / look again." So much depends on looking again at things and people, on heeding their claims.

A later poem, from *Threshold*, is still waiting:

> No rain yet
>   good news doesn't come
> through the window
>   but the jacaranda
> is more ferny than ever
>   filling
> with so many birds
> I don't even know the names of

Nature's good news can outdo our grasp, and in this poem it's finally a jaybird rasping *countthedead countthedead*.

With her contemporary Denise Levertov, Shirley Kaufman shares the lineage of William Carlos Williams. His "Spring and All" brings dried weeds, but "sluggish / dazed spring approaches—"

> Now the grass, tomorrow
> the stiff curl of wildcarrot leaf

Much American poetry, such as Kaufman's lavender petals and jacaranda clumps, stems from that "stiff curl of wildcarrot leaf" in 1923. And his poem's last line break, "rooted, they / grip down and begin to awaken," fosters her "tree making us / look again."

Roots, putting down roots—the choice for an exile, expatriate, anyone. Yehuda Amichai ends "Jews in the Land of Israel" this way:

> Spilled blood is not the roots of trees,
> but it's the closest to them that we have.

In "Deathfugue" Paul Celan, who survived but whose parents did not survive Nazi genocide, says "we shovel a grave in the air." Another poem of his points

> In the air, there's where your root is, there,
> in the air.

"Roots in the Air," Shirley Kaufman calls a poem from *Claims*, thinking not of crematorium smoke but of any dogged nationhood.

"At Kibbutz Ein Hahoresh," she explains, "where many survivors of the Holocaust, including Vitka and Abba Kovner, have started their lives again, I saw a Bengal ficus tree, transplanted from India. In India the tree propagates itself by roots that grow from the branches of a single tree downward into the soil, rerooting itself. In Israel, fleshy white tubers dangle from the branches, *but never reach the earth*." "Roots in the Air" gets the tree's hard news and an open question.

> Over my head
> the Bengal ficus
> dangles its roots like seaweed
> out of the sea, licking
> the ashes from the air.
>
> Sure of which way is down
> but unable to get there,
> one tree makes a hundred
> out of the steaming soil it comes from,
> replanting itself.
>
> Not here.
> The roots are shaggy
> with trying in this land.
> No earth, no water,
> what are they doing
> in the light?

"Not here"—or possibly, Not yet.

"that the rock might see"
News of the North from John Haines

*A*L VERO LETTORE. With this dedication "To the True Reader," John Haines (b. 1924) begins his memoir of twenty-five years in the northern wilderness, *The Stars, the Snow, the Fire*. Ah, but if you haven't followed a wolverine's "loping, toed-in track" through Alaskan snow "uphill for two miles one spring morning, until it finally dropped away into another watershed," can you still be Haines's true reader? Or haven't trekked six miles (and back) in a cold wind, chiseled a three-foot-deep hole in pond ice, built a spruce tripod to sink an aspen-baited trap below the ice, then returned days after the hole has frozen over to chop it open and pull up a drowned forty-pound beaver? And this is not to mention rabbit, marten, fox, lynx, deer, moose, caribou, and grizzly bear.

Haines felt troubled over his first killings, and fearful at times, but meat and pelts meant a living. Unlike Native Americans "a long time gone" who matter so much to him, unlike the "quiet hunter" who carved or painted on cave walls "an image of the thing he followed," Haines *chose* this elemental life. We can be grateful he did.

No other poet has brought such news of a stark locale where "I could walk north . . . all the way to the Arctic Ocean and never cross a road nor encounter a village."

> Last night I heard wolves howling,
> their voices coming from afar
> over the wind-polished ice.

Alaskan glacier.
From John Haines, *News from the Glacier: Selected Poems, 1960–1980* (Middletown,
Conn.: Wesleyan University Press, 1982), courtesy of John Haines.

For his heartland habitat the poet finds a steady tempo and tone:

> The land gave up its meaning slowly,
> as the sun finds day by day
> a deeper place in the mountain.

Simplicity, here, embraces mystery. You can see that happen in his own black-and-white photos for *News from the Glacier.* Half are detailed close-ups: a deep-grained section of dead tree trunk, a rotting log beside a flower sprig, oak leaves just settled on a pool. The others show far-reaching terrain: a glacier across a lake, a road rolling across plains below huge sky, and near his homestead, the Tanana River up toward the Alaska Range.

Before all this, as a naval officer's son, Haines was shifted around the country. "I never had a home." After seeing combat during World War II, and a year on the GI Bill in art school, he chose to root himself, homesteading southeast of Fairbanks in daunting wilderness and weather, absorbing old-timers' lore of the land: "they'd begin telling stories, and I'm just sitting there listening to them."

Haines went back to painting and sculpture but returned to the north, clearing forest, building cabins, making his own stove and boats, planting gardens, chopping wood, cutting trails, moving by snowshoe and dogsled, hunting, trapping, weaving nets for salmon fishing, often alone and sometimes with his wife. Home and wilderness the same, he forged a life little different from generations ago, close to an "American grain" his much-admired William Carlos Williams once imagined. His wife, like Dorothy Wordsworth, kept a journal. Winter 1961, November 29: "John skinned two more marten . . . Dark at 2 P.M. . . . John wrote tonight." December 22: "up to -44° for a little while . . . John got two sleds of wood."

Now does this make someone a stronger poet? Not necessarily, any more than Thoreau choosing to live alone at Walden Pond or climb Katahdin could have written as he did without rare literary and spiritual wherewithal. Haines:

> I came to this place,
> a young man green and lonely.
>
> Well quit of the world,
> I framed a house of moss and timber,
> called it a home . . .
>
> I made my bed under the shadow
> of leaves, and awoke
> in the first snow of autumn,
> filled with silence.

That spareness of word and rhythm make his low-keyed phrase "filled with silence" even more mind-bending.

By the time Haines published his first collection, *Winter News,* at forty-two, he'd read and written much poetry, all the while keeping his foothold on a "hillside overlooking the Tanana River" in central Alaska. "To one who lives in the snow and watches it day by day, it is a book to be read." Or put largely,

Building the homestead, ca. 1961.
Courtesy of John Haines.

"I have often felt that we write at our best . . . out of an ancient and durable
sense of our earthly life and experience." That way "our everyday lives and
events may at times return us to an older mythological source." He thanks Pablo
Neruda's *Heights of Macchu Picchu* for retracing *la gastada primavera humana*,
our "exhausted human spring"—not as an Eden but a fresh source.

Like Wordsworth, Hardy, Yeats, Frost, Jeffers, and others, Haines as poet
was born from his chosen milieu. "The trails I made led outward into the hills
and swamps, but they led inward also." Finding plain words for the ways of
weather, plant life, animals, and himself, his poems and prose still verge on
dream, his dreams, taking us down and back toward myth and the totems we
live with. In "Horns,"

> I went to the edge of the wood
> in the color of evening,
> and rubbed with a piece of horn
> against a tree,

believing the great, dark moose
would come, his eyes
on fire with the moon.

He fell asleep, the moose "came roaring,"

His horns exploded in the brush
with dry trees cracking
and falling.

When the dreamer called to him, the moose "gently rubbed / his horns against
the icy willows," then "soundlessly he walked away."

I stood there in the moonlight,
and the darkness and silence
surged back, flowing around me,
full of a wild enchantment,
as though a god had spoken.

Haines's respect for the nonhuman world doesn't mean staying detached, like
Elizabeth Bishop from her Nova Scotia moose, or so restrained as Gary Snyder
in Washington's North Cascades:

   unseen
Cold proud eyes
Of Cougar or Coyote
Watch me rise and go.

He rubs a piece of horn, sees eyes on fire with the moon, hears horns exploding,
finds wild enchantment and pagan godlike presence. Stopping short of Romantic
overkill, Haines stands before the supernatural as a shaman sensing "the inmost
human experience on this earth," his dream of that earth.

A poem conjuring "shaggy tribesmen" listens for prehistoric animals tram-
pling the grass—"this is how it all began"—and ends, "We are still kneel-
ing / and listening." "Prayer to the Snowy Owl" begins, "Descend, silent
spirit." Our food and drink, culture, religion, art, poetry, thought itself, "are
all part of the one process at work." From the earliest, so-called primitive cave
and rock drawings to modern poems, from the classical Chinese poetry Haines
prizes to his Alaskan story, humankind is enmeshed within nature at large,
drawing sustenance and imagination both.

He values this "ancient dialogue":

Among the Dogon in West Africa, an individual gifted in divination will go
outside the village in the evening, and on a space of clean, raked sand will
draw certain signs in a more or less geometrical pattern. When he is done,
he will carefully and strategically scatter peanuts or other food scraps over
his table of signs. During the night a jackal, lured from the nearby bush, will

come out to eat the food. At sunrise the diviner will return, and by noting where the tracks of the jackal enter, cross, or seem to communicate between the signs, he will read and interpret their meaning.

Any poet needs this "creative flow between the inner and the outer worlds."

To absorb the "elements of rock and water, of night and dawn" where Robinson Jeffers lived, Haines at one point moved to a redwood barn near the Carmel River in California. The older poet's presence spurred him "like a spring in the desert." Even if Jeffers's soaring hawks, if "the very rocks of the shoreline disappear and the cypresses are displaced by the restless engineers of our world," his words and verse like "the beat of the ocean . . . will survive."

When times turned drastic, during the Vietnam years, Haines like Denise Levertov and Galway Kinnell did not offer self-righteous polemic. He trusts his own psyche and environs to gauge war's impact. "Smoke" makes no pretense of depicting but instead dreams home the overseas disaster as a wild presence.

> An animal smelling
> of ashes
> crossed the hills
> that morning. . . .
>
> All day that animal
> came and went,
> sniffing at trees
> still vaguely green,
> its fur catching
> in the underbrush.
>
> At sundown, it settled
> upon the house,
> its breath
> thick and choking.

The war in Southeast Asia "mingles with smoke / from moss fires / in the homesteader's clearing." In dire times we can only, and we must, connect outer to inner world.

Because Alaska taught him a wholeness of earth and spirit he saw lacking in twentieth-century America, California's Indian past grips Haines.

> A girl, half Indian, seated
> on a floor of beaten clay,
> threading beads,
> little knots of green fire
> on a strand of sinew.

Though "the wilderness vanished," he says, "Wilderness survives at the camp / we have made within us"—a striking thought. Yet "the green circle is broken" (shades of Black Elk after Wounded Knee: "the nation's hoop is broken"). This poem's simple question shivers on a line break. "Will we ever again be at home / on earth?"

Perhaps not, in the age-old way. Haines touches that question's core in a nine-hundred-year-old rock painting above a Montana lake.

> The late morning was calm, the sun bright and warm. As we approached from offshore, the rockface came into view, and what appeared from a distance to be rusty splashes of lichen, or patches of a reddish mineral color in the rock, resolved into a scattered arrangement of small painted figures. Roughly vertical, rising thirty to forty feet above the lake, and with numerous faults and planes, the rockface with its red-painted figures dispersed among the gradations of rock color, was like a weathered mural, faded from its original brilliance but, in full sun, still glowing and subtly dappled with light from the water below.

This encounter brought about "The Eye in the Rock."

> A high rock face above Flathead Lake,
> turned east where the light
> breaks at morning over the mountain.
>
> An eye was painted here by men
> before we came, part of an Indian face,
> part of an earth
> scratched and stained by our hands.
>
> It is only rock, blue or green,
> cloudy with lichen,
> changing in the waterlight.
>
> Yet blood moves in the rock,
> seeping from the fissures;
> the eye turned inward, gazing back
> into the shadowy grain,
> as if the rock gave life.
>
> And out of the fired mineral
> come these burned survivors,
> sticks of the wasting dream:
>
> thin red elk and rusty deer,
> a few humped bison,
> ciphers and circles without name.
>
> Not ice that fractures rock,
> nor sunlight, nor the wind
> gritty with sand has erased them.
> They feed in their tall meadow,
> cropping the lichen a thousand years.

> Over the lake water comes this light
> that has not changed,
> the air we have always known . . .

What matters with this and all poems, says Haines, is how *"craft* turns into *vision,"* his own and the tribal artists' craft.

Thanks to the day's mission starting early, morning sun on the rock and a break where "the light / breaks" create a mythic scene "before we came"—"we" including all white latecomers scarring the earth. Now the poet's craft and vision enter the painters': this rock could be "blue or green," seems "cloudy with lichen," "changing" before our divining eyes in "waterlight," an apt coinage. "Yet blood moves in this rock," bright rust or brick pigment, maybe simply the available coloring. Then why blood? Just as the rock's fissures and grain "gave life" to the pictographs, so "the rockface took on life from those painted figures," he notes, and we recall how "Every accidental crack or dent" in Yeats's carved lapis lazuli stone "Seems a water-course or an avalanche." Fed by changing sunlight and lakewater, an uncanny eye sees into the rock, bringing it alive.

By shifting angles of view and later examining his photos, Haines saw that the Indians had used irregular rockface to set a "many times life-size" eye within facial contours, an eye gazing *back into* the rock. Given a sign of such conscious art, his language sharpens: "fired" mineral, "burned" survivors, "wasting" dream evoke centuries of sunlight and human doings as well. Only "thin red elk and rusty deer, / a few humped bison" remain of a rockbound myth.

Haines won't leave it at that. "Not ice . . . / nor sunlight, nor the wind / gritty with sand has erased them." On Keats's urn the lovers and heifers are still in motion, and for Haines, the game on this naturally carved surface still feed "in their tall meadow"—tall on the rock face, and abundant. Spirit-creatures "cropping the lichen a thousand years" remain fused with geologic time. Despite our scratch and stain, Haines leaves this vision open for us with his three dots: "the air we have always known . . ."

Then turning from "we" to "They," "The Eye in the Rock" brings human spirit then and now in face of elemental nature.

> They who believed that stone,
> water and wind might be quickened
> with a spirit like their own,
> painted this eye that the rock might see.

Haines once asked, "Will we ever again be at home / on earth?" Will our words be "tied in one," quickening "the great rocks," as a Yokuts shaman once prayed?

"asking for my human breath"
Trust in Maxine Kumin

"I am writing in my journal in the blackness of the barn while waiting for a mare to foal." Is this Tolstoy working up a farm scene for *Anna Karenina*? "Sawdust bedding is heaped in a bin roughly fifteen by six feet parallel to the last stall on the south side. This week I am sleeping in the bin on the levelled-out pile." Not a very favorable spot for the creative spirit? "Although her milk-bag is full and hard, night after night she resists dropping her foal. . . . I overhear every rustle, munch and snore." Perhaps the worthy Russian is losing valuable time? "If the mare lies down, I wake up."

New England readers and many others will recognize not Count Leo Tolstoy but New Hampshire's and the nation's onetime poet laureate, Maxine Kumin (b. 1925). One journal entry speaks in the third person: "A woman creeps on all fours through a squash patch in mid-September seeking out the late bloomers." Another records tapping maples in February: "Putting in the spiles [spigots] I lean on the brace and bit, heaving to use all my weight to keep the metal spiral angling upward into the tough tree. How astonishing, after the hole is bored, that the sap glistens, quivers, begins to run freely." Months later, "All in a one-day seizure, cattails, fiddlehead ferns, and nettles up for the foraging. Nettle soup for supper."

What with all this, knowingly described—"foal" as a verb, "dropping," "spiles," fresh nettle soup—plus "daily hauling water, mucking stalls [removing dung], paring hoof abscesses," it's a wonder Kumin manages to write at all.

But that's just the point: "you can console yourself with the thought that come May, come June, you're going to have new life in the barn." The two sides prime each other, poetry and farming, "my writing depends on the well-being" from "chores undertaken and completed."

Nature of several kinds, animal and plant and weather, glistens and runs freely through "Credo," in the *New York Times* on New Year's Day 1991. Reaching out to a budding year, "I believe in the resurrected wake-robin," says Kumin, naming not a bird but a flower, the "first wet knob of trillium." Raised Jewish, Calvinist in her work ethic or "Hebrew Puritan," and an atheist believer in natural process, she cites "the black crumbles / of ancient manure that sift through my fingers" in her credo, "wet strings of earthworms," the bear "still denned up"—"I cede him a swale of chokecherries in August."

Ever since she and her husband settled in 1976 on a two-hundred-acre New Hampshire farm, Kumin believes in "the gift of the horse," and gives horses her keenest language.

> their deep fear-snorts in play when the wind comes up,
> the ballet of nip and jostle, plunge and crow hop,
>
> I trust them to run from me, necks arched in a full
> swan's S, tails cocked up over their backs
> like plumes on a Cavalier's hat. I trust them
> to gallop back, skid to a stop, their nostrils
>
> level with my mouth, asking for my human breath
> that they may test its intent, taste the smell of it.
> I believe in myself as their sanctuary
> and the earth with its summer plumes of carrots,
>
> its clamber of peas, beans, masses of tendrils
> as mine.

A fine balance, this belief in herself within the world at large. The horses run off yet come back trusting, she trusts earth's clambering fruits "as mine." So she may, after decades of work carving out pasture, bringing in produce, splitting cordwood, breeding, training, caring for horses because "We've taken them out of their wild state."

We're a long way from Jeffers and his soaring hawks, Lawrence's mythic snake, Bishop's armadillo, Hughes's crow and pike, Oppen's deer who "startle, and stare out" at human presence. In Kumin's hands, a harmony of species occurs as the horses "skid to a stop, their nostrils / / level with my mouth, asking for my human breath." Her encounter seems to flout God's chiding of Job: "Hast thou given the horse strength? Hast thou clothed his neck with thunder? Canst thou make him afraid as a grasshopper? The glory of his nostrils is terrible. He paweth in the valley . . . and he smelleth the battle afar off." For her and the Bible both, a poet's touch makes the encounter genuine: "fear-snorts," "crow hop," then the surprises of "skid," "level," "asking."

To Make a Prairie (Emily Dickinson's phrase), her book on poetry and country living, describes riding an eleven-month-pregnant mare she's fitted with a gauze ear-bonnet against black flies. After giving birth the mare rejects her foal, and Kumin recalls her own cracked bleeding nipples years before. Four days of bottle-feeding follow, then weaning to a formula of gruel to be mashed and stirred at two in the morning. Thirteen years later, now a prize-winning trail horse, it's *this* mare the poet attends to, sleeping "in the blackness of the barn."

Another poet comes to mind, practicing and writing animal husbandry. Off a narrow lane in Devon, Ted Hughes fumbles a cow's teat into her struggling calf's mouth, "Stuffing its slippery muscle into his suction." When a lamb strangles during birth, Hughes has to cut off the head and then help the ewe, "timing my effort / To her birth push groans." His Anglo-Saxon word hoard works more strenuously, but Kumin's working voice, no less strong and sure, gives the lie to any gender clichés.

"Splitting Wood at Six Above":

> I open a tree.
> In the stupefying cold
> —ice on bare flesh a scald—
> I seat the metal wedge
> with a few left-handed swipes,
> then with a change of grips
> lean into the eight-pound sledge.

Her rhymes come rough and ready—"cold . . . scald," "swipes . . . grips," "wedge . . . sledge"—like her hardy lines. The next section, figuring weather and wood as a householder might, takes our breath away.

> It's muslin overhead.
> Snow falls as heavy as salt.
> You are four months dead.
> The beech log comes apart
> like a chocolate nougat.

She means her dearest friend Anne Sexton, a fierce poet who like Hughes's wife Sylvia Plath took her own life by gas. Kumin's closing lines stretch their sinews across a tough syntax of emotion.

> It is the sound
> of your going I drive
> into heartwood. I stack

> my quartered cuts bark down,
> open yellow-face up.

Instead of fluency, as in "It's muslin overhead," she bears down on her work, stacking rough-cut lines as she must.

"Allegiance to the land is tenderness," she says in "Hay," "defying the chrome millennium" by celebrating the old way of haying in her youth and now her present, "trundling hay in my own barn." Close as she keeps to the land, animal nature rivets her concern. The poems in *Nurture* speak out for threatened or endangered creatures: caribou, penguin, manatee, killer whale, arctic fox, Aleutian goose, trumpeter swan.

And horses, who claim her most, even when the subject is "A Bangkok Gong." Kumin's daughter has brought as a gift this "circle of hammered brass."

> When barely touched it imitates
> the deep nicker the mare makes
> swiveling her neck
> watching the foal swim
> out of her body.

As Shakespeare puts it, "my nature is subdued / To what it works in, like the dyer's hand." A gong's lightest resonance sends Maxine Kumin straight to the stable for metaphor and the unique word for a mare's soft neighing. Then that familiar moment of a horse's "swiveling" turns up the surprise of "swim." With this thought, she says, you can console yourself.

"What are you doing out here / this windy"
Wind in the Reeds in the Voice of A. R. Ammons

*T*he *Really Short Poems of A. R. Ammons,* by A. R. Ammons (1926–2001), begin,

> A day without rain is like
> a day without sunshine

A light pause at the line break, so we expect "a life without pain" or some such, veers elsewhere. Days have their way with us, we gather, and any day matters, any weather.

"Small Song" touches off ecologic revelation.

> The reeds give
> way to the
>
> wind and give
> the wind away

While an oak breaks in the wind, says the old parable, reeds bend. They have much to say, like the moves that words can make. Shorter than "Western Wind," this pun of a poem turns simple to subtle, "give / way to the / / wind" flips to "give / the wind away," hinging an invisible force onto human awareness. As Ammons gives away his own gaze, an (in)verse wordplay proves the two events belong to one whole.

Another windy hinging poem has the limber rhythms of William Carlos Williams.

ENOUGH
I thought the
woods afire
or some
house behind the
trees
but it was
the wind
sprung loose
by a random
thunderstorm
smoking pollen fog
from the
evergreens

Strike a branch in the right season and a puff of pollen bursts out. Ammons calls it fog, coming as it does from acres of trees in slanting light. Looking for fire, he finds a pun on "smoking": to smoke out, force out of hiding, give away, plus the smoke he thought he saw. One jolt of perception is event "enough" for a poem—just to recognize the actual, the thing itself, gold-yellow pollen clouds, without lifting off into conjecture.

Archie Randolph Ammons was born near the town of Whiteville, North Carolina, in a farmhouse built by his grandfather on fifty acres, half woods, half cleared for tobacco. During the Depression his family was dirt poor. He never brought more than a penny to Sunday school, "And we were lucky if we had a penny to bring." In early spring the boy was excused from his one-room schoolhouse to help with plowing and chores. The adult recalls he'd hitch up his mule Silver

and go out, wrench in my hip pocket for later adjustments,
        down the ditch-path
by the white-bloomed briars, wet crabgrass, cattails,
        and rusting ferns,
riding the plow handles down.

Riding the plow handles—a fine recollection, but going home again takes its toll.

The sap is gone out of the trees
in the land of my birth
and the branches droop
    The rye is rusty in the fields
and the oatgrains are light in the wind . . .
The wind whipped at my carcase saying
How shall I
    coming from these fields
water the fields of earth

Well, now he knows how, writing a poem, though it was "a time of tremendous economic and spiritual deprivation, even loneliness . . . the only book we had in our house was the Bible . . . But all this privation was compensated for by a sense of the eternal freshness of the land itself," a "sense of identity with the things around me."

His seventh-grade teacher, a first cousin, says Archie wrote a poem then, and in tenth grade "I wrote one about Pocahontas—it was a beauty." After high school he worked in a shipyard and at eighteen joined the Navy, a destroyer in the South Pacific. There his off hours went into poems. In college he studied biology, then ran a grammar school in North Carolina, went to grad school at Berkeley where the poet Josephine Miles encouraged him, and for twelve years was vice president for a New Jersey glass manufacturer. The state's landscape and southern shore imprinted his poems, but his first book, selling sixteen copies in five years, earned royalties so small that "one year I got two four cent stamps."

Yet the book's first poem, written at twenty-five, sounds a keynote to his work, speaking through the priest-scribe who brought the Bible and its people out of Babylonian exile.

> So I said I am Ezra
> and the wind whipped my throat
> gaming for the sounds of my voice

The Bible tells us Ezra, in Jerusalem, read from the law of God "distinctly, and gave the sense, and caused them to understand." Ammons naturally sets him on the seashore,

> but there were no echoes from the waves
> The words were swallowed up
>   in the voice of the surf
> or leaping over the swells
> lost themselves oceanward

Walt Whitman, declaiming "Homer or Shakspere to the surf and sea-gulls by the hour," loved the "words of my voice loos'd to the eddies of the wind." He also felt Nature rebuffing him "Because I have dared to open my mouth to sing at all." Ammons too feared immersing his voice "in the voice of the surf."

But wind and water are his elements, and voice his very being. "Somers Point" has "bay water thrashing" the New Jersey shore.

> What are you doing out here
> this windy on the headland
> said the bay reeds bent inland.

From the beginning he asks how to reach out, respond to the sea's endless surging and dissolving, "the yielding resistances / of wind and water." That reedlike paradox, "yielding resistances," happens again in "Expressions of Sea Level."

> Peripherally the ocean
> marks itself
>   against the gauging land
> it erodes and
> builds.

Erodes *and* builds? Ammons was spared the spectacle of Nantucketers dredging the sea bottom (and fish habitat) to replenish beaches below their bluff-top homes.

Erodes and builds. The dunes themselves do as much, while the poet gauges what changes changelessly, the "tide-held slant of grasses / bent into the wind." He's riveted to "yielding resistance," the converse between seashore grasses and the elements.

If for an instant we could spot "a point of rest where / the tide turns," then we'd have something, be somewhere. Ammons merges nature's loss and gain with poetry's:

> is there an instant when fullness is,
> without loss, complete: is there a
> statement perfect in its speech.

This question might even touch on puns, that instant union of contraries—loss and gain, reality and speech. "Expressions of Sea Level," Ammons calls his poem. Only a level conversation, words tied to things, mind to matter, will find out fullness—fullness suspending loss for a moment, a dynamic fullness embodying loss, change, motion.

Motion! It holds his attention, when the "motion of mind and thought correspond to natural motions," meandering like "winds or streams." "A poem is a walk," taking us through turns and returns. Poems are like ice-skating too, "inexhaustibly fresh and surprising," always "an action." And like surfing, "shooting the curl," when "one 'dwells' in an ongoing, onbreaking wave," finding "immobility in motion."

"Motion," a poem of his, admits that "The word is / not the thing," but "the music / in poems" can make it so. Decades later, in "Motion's Holdings," Ammons grasps a visual marvel with the zest of Gerard Manley Hopkins.

>   boulders, their green and white
> moss-molds, high-held in moist
> hill woods, stir hum with
>
> stall and spill.

Their music, moss-molded, at once stalls and spills moisture, like a scooped rock

Hopkins found constantly splaying up streamwater. Words are not things, yet "things are slowed motion," says Ammons. Otherwise why would an artist over and over sketch hovering clouds, or paint surf endlessly breaking and forming?

What grips him are "dunes of motion, organizations of grass"—in a word, ecology. A serious amateur natural scientist, Ammons swore by the term in 1963:

> *ecology* is my word: tag
> me with that.

He likes "disorderly orders of bayberry," "manifold events of sand," biosystems reckless of the square grids Jefferson's 1785 Land Ordinance decreed for ruling our western lands.

All these unions of order with flux, stillness with motion, occur in an autumn poem from the Jersey shore. "Corsons Inlet" has one of those classic openings,

> I went for a walk over the dunes again this morning
> to the sea . . .

Like any beach walk, this 128-line, three-sentence poem pauses then moves on, noticing things, freely indented, again and again, in the root sense experimental.

> the news to my left over the dunes and
> reeds and bayberry clumps was
> fall: thousands of tree swallows
> gathering for flight:
> an order held
> in constant change:

Since "Poetry is news that stays news" (Ezra Pound), we note those colons: "just connect and connect and connect," Ammons said about colons, "the world is so interpenetrated." Dunes with gathering swallows, as in Keats's "To Autumn," equal "an order held / in constant change."

"Corsons Inlet" tracks a walk "*again* this morning," a fresh motion of mind, moving and staying like the dunes so dear to Stanley Kunitz and May Swenson. Ammons writes (and we read) not for reportage, "you don't want the poem to amount to no more than what you already knew when you began to write." So "Corsons Inlet," poem and place alike, stays open to action, discovery, knowing nothing final except "that tomorrow a new walk is a new walk."

"I have been for a / walk:" Ammons tells us years later in "Easter Morning,"

> the wind is tranquil: the brook
> works without flashing in an abundant

tranquility: the birds are lively with
voice:

He's come from his home in Ithaca, New York, "back to my home country" and the graveyard holding parents, teachers, "trinket aunts who always had a little / something in their pocketbooks, cinnamon bark / or a penny or nickel."

> I stand on the stump
> of a child, whether myself
> or my little brother who died, and
> yell as far as I can, I cannot leave this place, for
> for me it is the dearest and the worst,
> it is life nearest to life which is
> life lost:

Into this place of origin his lines move as far as they can, then withdraw, at least holding onto a bleak childhood. Those last two lines have hope going for them.

Tranquil, Ammons sees "something I had never seen before": two bald eagles going north, "oaring the great wings steadily," circling, coasting, resting. One veers away and circles again, "looking perhaps for a draft," then comes back, and flying off together "they broke across the local bush and trees." Seeing their patterns of exploring and returning, he ends by calling this

> a dance sacred as the sap in
> the trees, permanent in its descriptions
> as the ripples round the brook's
> ripplestone: fresh as this particular
> flood of burn breaking across us now
> from the sun.

The birds' "descriptions": punwise we say their flight "describes" a circle, much as the poet describes it. And always particulars—ripplestone!—otherwise what's the point? Permanent as ripples, fresh as sunburst. And why "us," in this solitary venture? The aunts and parents, maybe his little brother, himself with that penny for Sunday school, the piping birds, the migrating eagles in their (and his poem's) sinuous movements?

"Sunday Morning," by Wallace Stevens, ends as quail

> Whistle about us their spontaneous cries;
> Sweet berries ripen in the wilderness;
> And, in the isolation of the sky,
> At evening, casual flocks of pigeons make
> Ambiguous undulations as they sink,
> Downward to darkness, on extended wings.

Ammons too finds sacredness on earth not in heaven, though his "Easter Morning," part homage to Stevens, stays more personal and self-questioning. Both poets thrive along the bind between words and things—Stevens outdoing his Snow Man's "mind of winter" by tracking the pigeons' ambiguous undulations, Ammons walking along watching the eagles' circlings, tracing earth's changes with his changing lines.

> The reeds give
> way to the
>
> wind and give
> the wind away

"between the earth and silence"
W. S. Merwin's Motion of Mind

"His words convey a sense that he is not standing outside the world he is portraying but is an intimately and endlessly concerned part of it, as it in turn is a part of the ceaselessly attentive motion of his own mind."

This could speak for John Clare the peasant poet, Thoreau, and many others. Instead it's W. S. Merwin (b. 1927) in "The Blind Seer of Ambon," saluting a seventeenth-century German naturalist who came to Ambon, one of the South Pacific Spice Islands, and stayed for fifty years. Rumphius wrote about plants and animals but not with technical possessiveness, classifying so as "to occupy a commanding position in a pattern of existence." Instead he was "a wondering presence," even humorous, as with hermit crabs carrying off some "beautiful shells" he'd laid out to bleach. "These little quarrelsome creatures have caused me much grief."

Rumphius lost his wife and daughter to earthquake, his flower drawings to fire, manuscripts to the sea, and finally his sight.

> I take a shell in my hand
> new to itself and to me
> I feel the thinness the warmth and the cold
> I listen to the water
> which is the story welling up
> I remember the colors and their lives
> everything takes me by surprise
> it is all awake in the darkness

Not standing outside, the poet takes the naturalist's part in earth's oldest story, life we can't really know but whose truth takes us by surprise, "all awake in the darkness."

Through many decades, William Merwin has become a wondering presence, not so much knowing and naming as trusting the world, while questioning his language for it. Moving away early from rhyme and orderly stanzas, he begins "The Bones,"

> It takes a long time to hear what the sands
> Seem to be saying, with the wind nudging them,
> And then you cannot put it in words nor tell
> Why these things should have a voice.

Likewise the blind seer of Ambon admits, "I continue to arrive at words,"

> but the leaves
> and the shells were already here
> and my fingers finding them echo
> the untold light and depth

Untold. "Language is well after the fact," Merwin says, but poetry "reconnects us" to the natural world. Like blind Rumphius, the poet taps a sixth sense, the "motion of his own mind" toward depth and openness. Merwin also moved this way in translating Pablo Neruda, Osip Mandelstam, Provençal and other poetry.

Born to a pacifist mother and a severe Presbyterian minister, "I tried to write hymns when I was four or five," but they didn't get used in church. Merwin's father, "a bully," made his childhood "very, very restricted." Going for mountain hikes near his Pennsylvania home was "one of the things I could do," he recalls. "I suppose those places came to represent freedom, beauty, and some sort of exhilaration." Sixty years later he calls up "The Wild."

> First sight of water through trees
> glimpsed as a child
> and the smell of the lake then
> on the mountain
> how long it has lasted
> whole and unmoved and without words
> the sound native to a great bell
> never leaving it

—that childhood sense like a Buddhist monastery bell still resonating in air.

Without words: Merwin's gesture toward "untold light and depth" as in his twenty books of poetry, plus translations, essays, fables, plays, fiction, travel and history writing. In his early book, *Green with Beasts*, "Leviathan" seethes with words.

This is the black sea-brute bulling through wave-wrack,
Ancient as ocean's shifting hills, who in sea-toils
Traveling, who furrowing the salt acres
Heavily, his wake hoary behind him,
Shoulders spouting, the fist of his forehead
Over wastes grey-green crashing, among horses unbroken
From bellowing fields, past bone-wreck of vessels,
Tide-ruin, wash of lost bodies bobbing
No longer sought for, and islands of ice gleaming,
Who ravening the rank flood, wave-marshalling,
Overmastering the dark sea-marches, finds home
And harvest.

Here the Bible's Job and Jonah, Melville's *Moby-Dick*, Hopkins's windhover rebuffing the big wind, Lowell's Atlantic where the "fat flukes arch and whack," take on the pagan beat of Anglo-Saxon alliterative verse—*Beowulf*, "The Seafarer," Ted Hughes's "Hawk in the Rain." And this is only its first sentence. So much surging wordage feels like Adam going hog-wild when God brought the beasts "to see what he would call them." Otherwise humankind is absent from this wrack and waste—"no gardens . . . no eye of man moving." As "Leviathan" closes, a breath-spirit hovers over the deep, the wild whale "soothes to stillness" and, a day before Adam, "waits for the world to begin."

A decade later Merwin returned to whales. By then Rachel Carson's *Silent Spring* had jolted awareness, Roger and Katy Payne had recorded the humpback's forty-minute eight-octave songs, and "endangered species" entered our vocabulary. "For a Coming Extinction" needs no maelstrom of words to speak prophetic irony.

Gray whale
Now that we are sending you to The End
That great god . . .

When you will not see again
The whale calves trying the light
Consider what you will find in the black garden
And its court
The sea cows the Great Auks the gorillas . . .

Join your word to theirs
Tell him
That it is we who are important

Another poem speaks of our "eating the earth" and ends, "If I were not human I would not be ashamed of anything." As of 2008, some gray whales are endangered, and humpbacks, manatees, and gorillas are barely hanging on.

Learning one day about a creature far closer to extinction, Merwin did a rare thing. He'd happened on Fred Bodsworth's *The Last of the Curlews* (1955), which re-creates an Eskimo curlew's fall and spring nine-thousand-mile migrations and mating search. Well into the nineteenth century, these shorebirds with incredible endurance flew between arctic tundra and Patagonia in mile-long V-formations. But clubs and guns wasted them away. A Hudson's Bay Company store in Labrador would kill two thousand a day, sometimes twenty-five at a shotgun blast. In March 1945 a pair was spotted in Texas, then another pair twenty years later. Since then, virtually none. So Merwin fostered a new edition, warning against our "unending growth" and "the greed and indifference of a species that considers its own withering arrival an improvement." (plate 17)

Breaking from his native land, Merwin in 1963 took a long-empty stone farmhouse in southwest France. He found there an ecology of landscape, Lascaux caves, village, workers, animals. Affection and attention run through unpunctuated poem after poem chronicling blackberry brambles, oak and walnut, wildflowers, wine, plums and potatoes, fox, cicada, a snake's "empty skin like smoke on the stone," fishermen's "low voices," "the red-haired boy whose father / had broken a leg parachuting into Provence / to join the Resistance" and been killed by the Germans.

While keeping his Dordogne terrain, Merwin began refurbishing a house in Chiapas, Mexico, and translated Indian poems from that region. Then in 1975, encountering another world (and a woman) in Hawaii, he moved to Maui island where he still lives, tending an abandoned pineapple plantation on the slopes of Haleakala volcano, reintroducing native palms and restoring original rainforest.

This venture prompted a biting satire, "Questions to Tourists Stopped by a Pineapple Field," a 102-line quasi-questionnaire with a relentless, unnerving grip.

> Did you like your piece of pineapple   would you like a napkin
> who gave you the pineapple   what do you know about them

The "broken back" line, as he calls it, helps quash the heedlessness left over from colonialism.

> did you ever imagine   pineapples growing somewhere . . .
> do you know whether pineapple   is native to the islands
> do you know whether the natives   ate pineapple
> do you know whether the natives   grew pineapple
> do you know how the land was acquired   to be turned into pineapple
>   fields
> do you know what is done to the land   to turn it into pineapple fields . . .
> what do you think was here   before the pineapple fields

Do you know, he's asking, do you think at all?

Cover, Fred Bodsworth, *The Last of the Curlews*, illustrated by T. M. Shortt
(New York: Dodd Mead, 1955).

> what is your opinion   of those square miles of black plastic
> where do you think the plastic   goes when the crop is over
> what do you think becomes of the land   when the crop is over
> do you think the growers know best   do you think this is for your own
>   good

And so it goes, politely harassing.

Adopting Hawaii as home ground, he wrote *The Folding Cliffs*, a verse novel
Hughes called "the tragic history of Hawaii . . . told almost as if by a native."
Merwin and his poems quietly, urgently work to save what once was a bioregion
of native birds, plantlife, languages. From "Rain at Night":

> after an age of leaves and feathers
> someone dead
> thought of this mountain as money

and cut the trees
that were here in the wind
in the rain at night
it is hard to say it
but they cut the sacred 'ohias then
the sacred koas then
the sandalwood and the halas
holding aloft their green fires
and somebody dead turned cattle loose
among the stumps until killing time

Unlike those dead men, "the trees have risen one more time."

Ohia, koa, sandalwood, hala: Hawaii tempers Merwin's sense that naming exposes human arrogance. Other poems point to the native ohia, first tree to grow on new lava, and the sandalwood. "Chord" begins with a dissonance from the 1820s.

While Keats wrote they were cutting down the sandalwood forests
while he listened to the nightingale they heard their own axes echoing
    through the forests,

and ends on a deeper chord:

while he groaned on the voyage to Italy they fell on the trails and were
    broken
when he lay with the odes behind him the wood was sold for cannons
when he lay watching the window they came home and lay down
and an age arrived when everything was explained in another language

Keats's great odes knew nothing of this ravage. Now "another language," colonial arrogance, confronts the human tongue of poetry.

Whatever his concern—memory, history, nature, love, loss—Merwin never stops questioning, as in "Utterance," the word spoken or unspoken

still spinning its one syllable
between the earth and silence

The Rain in the Trees, its cover photo showing mist in Ohia Forest, contains "Losing a Language."

A breath leaves the sentences and does not come back
yet the old still remember something that they could say

As languages go extinct, week after week, what gets lost?

many of the things the words were about
no longer exist

the noun for standing in mist by a haunted tree
the verb for I

Did Hawaii once *have* such a verb, lying "between the earth and silence"?

In "Hearing the Names of the Valleys," the poet free of colonial or missionary motive wants to hear if not learn them.

> Finally the old man is telling
> the forgotten names
> and the names of the stones they came from . . .
>
> I have lived without knowing
> the names for the water
> from one rock
> and the water from another
> and behind the names that I do not have
> the color of water flows all day and all night
> the old man tells me the name for it
> and as he says it I forget it

Still his years spent on limber verse have bred the tact of such lines and breaks—and tact goes a long way toward consciousness.

"When you hear a poem," Merwin told Bill Moyers, "you hear something that you always knew, but it's completely new!" News that stays news—we crave it in times of need. During the war in Vietnam, Merwin began translating from Vietnamese tradition (using literal English versions). Here is a medieval poem of place:

> I will choose a place where the snakes feel safe.
> All day I will love that remote country.
> At times I will climb the peak of its lonely mountain
> to stay and whistle until the sky grows cold.

The war's turning point, winter 1964–65, found Merwin in France, whose imperial grip on Vietnam had led to America's. "The Asians Dying" takes the brunt of war's brutal news on a rural landscape.

> When the forests have been destroyed their darkness remains
> The ash the great walker follows the possessors
> Forever
> Nothing they will come to is real
> Nor for long
> Over the watercourses
> Like ducks in the time of the ducks
> The ghosts of the villages trail in the sky
> Making a new twilight

Phrasings and images grope to imagine a scorched earth ten time zones away. Ash "the great walker," smoke like ghost villages, like ducks migrating, "a new twilight." Nature turns witness, almost accomplice, as

> Rain falls into the open eyes of the dead
> Again again with its pointless sound
> When the moon finds them they are the color of everything

An uncanny accuracy pierces the verse, rain falling into eyes of the dead. Their eyes are also open with some claim on us. What do we make of eyes "the color of everything"?

Rumphius the blind seer of Ambon says "everything takes me by surprise," and Merwin says in an interview, "We don't just look, we see. We don't just listen, we hear." If anything in poems can make us really see and hear, it will be—what Merwin saw in Rumphius speaks for himself as well—that "ceaselessly attentive motion of his own mind."

"bear blood" and "Blackberry Eating"
Zest of Galway Kinnell

"I know half of my life belongs to the wild darkness," says Galway Kinnell (b. 1927). Whatever those halves contain—indoor and outdoor, body and spirit, conscious and unconscious—we see them merging in "How Many Nights," from 1965.

> How many nights
> have I lain in terror,
> O Creator Spirit, Maker of night and day,
>
> only to walk out
> the next morning over the frozen world
> hearing under the creaking of snow
> faint, peaceful breaths . . .
> snake,
> bear, earthworm, ant . . .
>
> and above me
> a wild crow crying '*yaw yaw yaw*'
> from a branch nothing cried from ever in my life.

Echoing the Catholic hymn *Veni Creator Spiritus,* "Come, Creator Spirit," this also calls up Job facing God's rebuke: "Hast thou commanded the morning since thy days? . . . Who provideth the raven his food?" Kinnell's revelation is "of the earth, earthy," as the Bible says. And like the Psalms, "How Many

Nights" moves between solitary terror and—what? How do we get from holy speech to *yaw yaw yaw?*

Starting in deep, Kinnell can't explain why we might lie in terror, at night in northern winter. Possibly Vietnam encroaching. Thank goodness for the stanza break, because come morning we're out walking, alert to hibernating bear breaths. But snake, earthworm, ant—can we hear them inside his three dots? Life is stirring, waiting beneath us to awaken. Then crying from above—some raucous spirit. Since tame crows are uncommon, the wild must really matter. Nature, being indifferent, greets the poem's prayer with a rawness caught in roughhewn verse: "a wild crow crying *'yaw yaw yaw'* / from a branch nothing cried from ever in my life." Desolation? Consolation? Both in one?

Frost's perfect anecdote now sounds a bit tame.

> The way a crow
> Shook down on me
> The dust of snow
> From a hemlock tree

only changes "some part" of a bad day. His bleakest moment occurs in "The Most of It," when "a great buck" stumbles past him into the underbrush "—and that was all."

Bypassing platitude and piety, Kinnell runs awestruck into raucousness. What convinces is his compact, concrete, startling touch. Swayed in his late teens by Yeats, like Roethke and countless others, he worked away from lush language, rhyme, and meter. Take "The Gray Heron":

> It held its head still
> while its body and green
> legs wobbled in wide arcs
> from side to side. When
> it stalked out of sight,

the speaker followed and found only a large lizard

> watching me
> to see if I would go
> or change into something else.

Like George Oppen facing "the wild deer" in "Psalm," Kinnell denies "we can do whatever we wish with the other creatures." We're "only one among the many animal species," each with "their intricate ways of living on earth."

"Let the cow, the horse, the mussel, eel, the sting-ray, and the grunting pig-fish—let these, and the like of these, be put on a perfect equality with man and woman!" Whitman's demand sounds right for Kinnell. Even pigs get the gift of his gab, in "Saint Francis and the Sow,"

from the earthen snout all the way
through the fodder and slops to the spiritual curl of the tail.

"The Porcupine" sports everything physical, nothing human mixed in.

> Fatted
> on herbs, swollen on crabapples . . .
> the porcupine
> drags and bounces his last meal through ice,
> mud, roses and goldenrod, into the stubbly high fields.

Eventually the voice turns first-person and is "beat dead with a locust club / on the bare snout." Kinnell ends in empathy.

> And tonight I think I prowl broken
> skulled or vacant as a
> sucked egg in the wintry meadow, softly chuckling, blank
> template of myself, dragging
> a starved belly through the lichflowered acres.

Jagged lines break any smug standpoint, but where does "softly chuckling" come from? Maybe our porcupine-poet, saying "tonight *I think* I prowl," knows something we do not. "I awaken I think," we hear in "The Bear," when the poem has dreamt of lumbering in the carcass of a hunted bear. Without an empathy for other living things, Kinnell warns, "we'll never save ourselves or the earth."

The "I" in "The Bear," an Eskimo hunter, step by step turns bearlike, searching long sentences past mythic way-stations along the "fairway of the bears"— all this heard in Kinnell's husky precise speaking voice.

> 1
> In late winter
> I sometimes glimpse bits of steam
> coming up from
> some fault in the old snow
> and bend close to see it is lung-colored
> and put down my nose
> and know
> the chilly, enduring odor of bear.
>
> 2
> I take wolf's rib and whittle
> it sharp at both ends
> and coil it up
> and freeze it in blubber and place it out
> on the fairway of the bears.
>
> And when it has vanished
> I move out on the bear tracks,

roaming in circles
until I come to the first, tentative, dark
splash on the earth.

And I set out
running, following the splashes
of blood wandering over the world.
At the cut, gashed resting places
I stop and rest,
at the crawl-marks
where he lay out on his belly
to overpass some stretch of bauchy ice
I lie out
dragging myself forward with bear-knives in my fists.

3
On the third day I begin to starve,
at nightfall I bend down as I knew I would
at a turd sopped in blood,
and hesitate, and pick it up,
and thrust it in my mouth, and gnash it down,
and rise
and go on running.

Present tense—"glimpse . . . bend close . . . put down . . . know . . ."—drives a
skilled hunt, which tallies with Eskimo practice: the frozen baited rib, the turd's
nourishing blood. Yet strange moments nudge this tale toward another dimension. What would it mean to follow blood-traces "over the world"?
    Suddenly it's a biblical day seven.

4
On the seventh day,
living by now on bear blood alone,
I can see his upturned carcass far out ahead, a scraggled,
steamy hulk,
the heavy fur riffling in the wind.

I come up to him
and stare at the narrow-spaced, petty eyes,
the dismayed
face laid back on the shoulder, the nostrils
flared, catching
perhaps the first taint of me as he
died.

I hack
a ravine in his thigh, and eat and drink,
and tear him down his whole length

and open him and climb in
and close him up after me, against the wind,
and sleep.

Fur "riffling in the wind" takes a sharp eye, and the "face laid back on the shoulder."
But "petty" eyes, "dismayed" face? Humanness seems to have seeped in with "perhaps the first taint of me as he / died"—*just* as he died, that odd line break implies.

Hints not of conquest but possession, man by bear, have been emerging. "At
the . . . resting place / I stop and rest," "where he lay out . . . / I lie out." For
a moment, human "taint" points up the creature's separate animality. Then
hacking into the thigh our hunter-poet begins to "eat and drink" in flesh-and-
blood communion, "and tear . . . and open . . . and climb . . . and close . . . and
sleep." This ritual cadence turns wilderness survival technique into a kind of
metamorphosis, a vision quest.

Right here the tale pivots on a stanza break: "and sleep. / / And dream . . ."
Doubling back to the animal's ordeal in strongest language, "I" turns prey, not
hunter.

5
And dream
of lumbering flatfooted
over the tundra,
stabbed twice from within,
splattering a trail behind me,
splattering it out no matter which way I lurch,
no matter which parabola of bear-transcendence,
which dance of solitude I attempt,
which gravity-clutched leap,
which trudge, which groan.

6
Until one day I totter and fall—
fall on this
stomach that has tried so hard to keep up,
to digest the blood as it leaked in,
to break up
and digest the bone itself: and now the breeze
blows over me, blows off
the hideous belches of ill-digested bear blood
and rotted stomach
and the ordinary, wretched odor of bear,

blows across
my sore, lolled tongue a song
or screech, until I think I must rise up
and dance. And I lie still.

If the blood-sopped turd thrust in and gnashed down wasn't already enough, here some readers lose it in hideous belches. Yet this dream creature, lying in a charged stillness, wants to rise, dance, sing.

Finally, half dream half waking, the poem opens to a new reality. "I awaken I think" and spring has come, as we know from "*re*appear" and "trailing *again*."

> 7
> I awaken I think. Marshlights
> reappear, geese
> come trailing again up the flyway.
> In her ravine under old snow the dam-bear
> lies, licking
> lumps of smeared fur
> and drizzly eyes into shapes
> with her tongue. And one
> hairy-soled trudge stuck out before me,
> the next groaned out,
> the next,
> the next,
> the rest of my days I spend
> wandering: wondering
> what, anyway
> was that sticky infusion, that rank flavor of blood, that
>   poetry, by which I lived?

Is he still dreaming? Marshlights, from methane gas, we call will-o'-the-wisp that flickers deceptively over damp terrain. But a mother bear is licking her newborn cubs.

Then midway through a line where her tongue shapes new life, the ordeal resumes, trudging toward a question. What's this last-ditch saving flavor? The bear-poet's song? Perhaps, says Kinnell, but "whatever allows us to flourish, *that* is the poetry" in our lives.

Hunt, ordeal, quest, legend, ritual, dream, with overtones of Creation and the Eucharist, plus Faulkner's novella *The Bear*, whose hero hunts then refrains from killing his prey: Kinnell's "The Bear" is all that and something more. Gauging the task of a poet's imagination and its cost, he enters a primitive place of men and animals. Like it or not, says Kinnell, we're "creatures of nature," too often thwarting "our deepest desire, which is to be one with all creation."

Lots more has come from his pen. An oratorio to lower Manhattan, "The Avenue Bearing the Initial of Christ into the New World," teems with urban sounds, sights, people, creeds, and trades in verse that smacks of Pablo Neruda, his favorite foreign poet.

> In the pushcart market, on Sunday,
> A crate of lemons discharges light like a battery.
> Icicle-shaped carrots that through black soil
> Wove away like flames in the sun,

and so on. Wild nature dwindles here,

> The smelts draped on each other, fat with roe,
> The marble cod hacked into chunks on the counter,
> Butterfishes mouths still open, still trying to eat.

Sewage leaks into the East River with dead fish in a rash of verbal music, call it "that rank flavor," half-redeeming the squalor.

> Even the gulls pass them up, pale
> Bloated socks of riverwater and rotted seed,
> That swirl on the tide, punched back
> To the Hell Gate narrows, and on the ebb
> Steam seaward, seeding the sea.

"I recall getting a little thrill from writing those sounds to match their meaning."

Kinnell may have lacked that thrill when Vietnam barged in on nature and our stateside selves, much as for other poets—Stafford, Levertov, Haines, Merwin, Hass. "Vapor Trail Reflected in the Frog Pond" starts honestly, at home in Vermont. He's watching tadpoles overflown by bombers in the innocence of "immaculate ozone." A middle section mimics Whitman's democratic joy,

> And I hear,
> coming over the hills, America singing,
> her varied carols I hear,

but ousts Walt's singing carpenter with "sput of cattleprod" (homeland protests) and "curses of the soldier" (battlefield anguish). The last section reaches beyond reach, arcing over to "rice paddies in Asia" where "the flesh that is upthrown in the air / shall be seized by birds," and crinkled eyes

> gaze up at the drifting sun that gives us our lives,
> seed dazzled over the footbattered blaze of the earth.

Speaking his poem at rallies back then, Kinnell kept changing these closing lines, struggling to imagine and voice war's impact on our sunbathed planet.

Just that, the struggle to imagine, was crucial during the Vietnam years. And a good few American combatants, young men shocked into poetry, hardly had to imagine—they told what they saw. Frank A. Cross, Jr., a California farmer, found himself spotting (for artillery) a woman in blue with rice-filled baskets springing from a yoke on her shoulders. Later, "near An Trang August 14, 1969," he wrote "Gliding Baskets." "Her face was hidden by her / conical rice

Galway Kinnell, ca. 1966.
Photographer unknown.

straw hat." Hidden from us her foreign enemies, yes, and what else but rice straw among rice paddies? Next we hear the slur of army lingo, "I have Fire Mission. / Dink in the open," while the baskets she carries,

> The two heavy baskets
> balanced on tips

of the springing Chogi stick
glided close to the hard smooth path.

Then "Shot, on the way, out," and "shrapnel catches the gliding baskets, / and they crumple with the woman in blue." Slantways, painfully, we're getting ecologic news. It took long practice to load those baskets just so they'd glide close to the path, a path made hard and smooth over many native generations.

A closeness to earth comes down through Whitman to Galway Kinnell, and a zest that language passes along. "It just seems the more ordinary and close at hand is often the more true and real," he once said. The interviewer asked, "Can you go on a little more with that idea?" "Well no. I think that's enough."

BLACKBERRY EATING
I love to go out in late September
among the fat, overripe, icy, black blackberries
to eat blackberries for breakfast,
the stalks very prickly, a penalty
they earn for knowing the black art
of blackberry-making; and as I stand among them
lifting the stalks to my mouth, the ripest berries
fall almost unbidden to my tongue,
as words sometimes do, certain peculiar words
like *strengths* or *squinched*,
many-lettered, one-syllable lumps,
which I squeeze, squinch open, and splurge well
in the silent, startled, icy, black language
of blackberry-eating in late September.

"Kicking the Leaves"

Donald Hall and Jane Kenyon at Eagle Pond Farm

> The sun goes in and out
> of the grand clouds, making the air alive
> with golden light, and then, as if heaven's
> spirits had fallen, everything's somber again.
>
> After music and poetry we walk to the car.
> I believe in the miracles of art, but what
> prodigy will keep you safe beside me . . . ?

Few coupled American poets, or European either, had such interlaced sympathies as Donald Hall (b. 1928) and Jane Kenyon (1947–1995). Here Kenyon speaking to her husband, who's fighting liver cancer, asks what marvel beyond poetry can save him. Soon after, she herself came down with leukemia and died fifteen months later.

> no snowdrop or crocus rose no yellow
> no red leaves of maple,

Hall wrote then,

> no spring no summer no autumn no winter
> no rain no peony thunder no woodthrush . . .

He called this poem "Without."

Three years into their marriage, in 1975, they settled where he'd always wanted to be, on a central New Hampshire farm his mother's grandparents bought in 1865. At first, Kenyon would "move from room to room, / a little dazed," but soon she "fit in with the furniture / and the landscape." On a shelf in the root cellar, after moving in, the poets found a quart of maple syrup made by Hall's grandfather decades before. They used it but poured the last drops into a store-bought gallon, then did the same next time and so on, sustaining the ancestral strain.

Eagle Pond Farm, within sight of Mount Kearsarge, meant "attachment to the soil of one particular spot by generation after generation." At eleven Hall began spending summers there, writing poems and reading in the morning, in the afternoon working with his grandparents at haying and other tasks. Since that early idyll, Hall has written again and again on the countryside's seasons and rhythms of work: chopping wood, cutting ice, tapping sap, milking cows, manuring, plowing, weeding, harvesting, mowing and gathering hay, canning fruits and vegetables, and always, keeping house. He remembers "watching my grandfather's practiced rhythm with the fork" in pitching hay: "plunge in, turn, heave, swing, shake loose, and back for more."

That rhythm runs through "Ox-Cart Man," his short poem turned much-loved children's story with Barbara Cooney's folk-art illustrations. Imagine a kindergarten teacher reading this slim book aloud, holding it up for kids to see and flipping the pages every few lines as a year comes round in the tempo of its nouns and verbs. (plate 18)

> In October he backed his ox into his cart
> and he and his family filled it up
> with everything they made or grew all year long
> that was left over.
>
> He packed a bag of wool
> he sheared from the sheep in April.
>
> He packed a shawl his wife wove on a loom
> from yarn spun at the spinning wheel
> from sheep sheared in April.
>
> He packed five pairs of mittens
> his daughter knit
> from yarn spun at the spinning wheel
> from sheep sheared in April.
>
> He packed candles the family made.
> He packed linen made from flax they grew.
> He packed shingles he split himself.
> He packed birch brooms his son carved
> with a borrowed kitchen knife.
>
> He packed potatoes they dug from their garden
> —but first he counted out potatoes enough to eat all winter
> and potatoes for seed next spring.
>
> He packed a barrel of apples
> honey and honeycombs
> turnips and cabbages
> a wooden box of maple sugar

from the maples they tapped in March
when they boiled and boiled the sap away.

He packed a bag of goose feathers that his children collected
from the barnyard geese.

When his cart was full, he waved good-bye to his wife,
his daughter, and his son
and he walked at his ox's head ten days
over hills, through valleys, by streams
past farms and villages

until he came to Portsmouth
and Portsmouth Market.

There, in the same cadence each thing had while being made, he sold it—with one favorite moment not in the shorter, original poem: "Then he sold his ox, and kissed him good-bye on his nose."

In the market he bought essentials for his household, wife, daughter, and son, plus something added for the children's book: two pounds of wintergreen peppermint candies. "Then he walked home," past the same farms and villages, over the same hills, to his waiting family, who took up their implements and went back to work,

and that night the ox-cart man sat in front of his fire
stitching new harness
for the young ox in the barn

and he carved a new yoke
and sawed planks for a new cart
and split shingles all winter,

while his wife made flax into linen all winter,
and his daughter embroidered linen all winter,
and his son carved Indian brooms from birch all winter,
and everybody made candles,

and in March they tapped the sugar maple trees
and boiled the sap down,

and in April they sheared the sheep,
spun yarn,
and wove and knitted,

and in May they planted potatoes, turnips, and cabbages,
while apple blossoms bloomed and fell,
while bees woke up, starting to make new honey,

and geese squawked in the barnyard,
dropping feathers as soft as clouds.

The poem's drafts say "I pack wool . . . I sell the ox." By changing tense and standpoint—"He packed . . . He sold"—by distancing that world, Hall keeps us in touch with a way of life that used to be.

Rural New England around 1800 comes alive in these rhythms. The seamless round of family and work and earth and weather, the seasons' cycle outdoors and in, where nature's yield prompts a family's tasks—all this evolves in the simple trends, the economies and concreteness of Hall's verse: "In October . . . He packed . . . When his cart was full . . . he walked . . . until he came . . . He sold . . . Then he sold . . . He bought . . . Then he walked home . . . until he came . . . and his daughter . . . and his son . . . and he carved . . . and . . . and . . . and . . . while his wife . . . and in March . . . and in April . . . and in May . . ." "But how come he didn't sell the linen?" a clever schoolchild noticed. "The ox got hungry on the way to Portsmouth," Hall improvised, "so the man fed it to him."

Generation and regeneration, in nature and livelihood alike, drives *Ox-Cart Man*. When Hall's elderly cousin Paul was a boy, "an old man told him this tale, and the old man told Paul that he had heard it from an old man when *he* was a boy." For the working poet "It's a tale of work, work, work, of total dispersal and starting again." Like human life, the ox-cart man "is a perennial plant." Hall tells things plainly, though music turns up now and then: "yarn spun at the spinning wheel" yields "a shawl . . . from sheep sheared in April." Frugal like what's depicted, and lovingly attentive, he does without figures of speech until the very end, when geese are "dropping feathers as soft as clouds." And why not, as on the page we're seeing light clouds above rolling hills, the fairest of spring days.

Of course *Ox-Cart Man* purifies the scenario, a pastoral minus crushing cold, sucking mud, wasting heat, draining weariness. What's more, this holistic life and much of its landscape were gone or going by the time Hall came to Eagle Pond Farm as a child in World War II. And what if you're not fortunate like the boy in Hall's storybook *The Farm Summer 1942*, whose "great-great-great-grandfather . . . fought in the American Revolution against the King of England!"? Or like the author, whose grandmother "played the organ seventy-eight years" in the nearby church?

Ox-Cart Man, like *Ishi, the Last of His Tribe*, has something to teach us. Back then, Hall says, "Work was holy." In this day and age perhaps it still can be. Various people or events "connect us to the past." Even without long-dwelling ancestors, we might "connect, joyously, with a place and a culture." Almost anywhere, almost anyone can catch "the gorgeous cacophony of autumn."

Seasons. The Fall from Eden's eternal spring brought toil into the world "by the sweat of thy brow," brought the seasons, and death. "In October" our hero packs his cart with fruits of nature and of work. Then winter, spring, and summer the family brings them forth again. The year pivots on fall, a harvest tending toward winter. Not spring but fall animates Hall's poetry, written "in defiance of death." Thus "Ox-Cart Man": "It's a tale of . . . starting again."

No surprise, then, that when "Wesley Wells, old man I loved," died in March 1953, the poet saw his grandfather's half-century of work in light of how fall might strike Eagle Pond Farm.

> When next October's frosts harden the ground
> And fasten in the year's catastrophe,
> The farm will come undone—
> The farmer dead, and deep in his ploughed earth.

Decades later Hall again calls up the hard season.

> Late in October after the grass freezes
> and cattle remain in their stalls, twice a day loosed
> to walk stiff-legged to the watering trough
> from which the old man lifts a white lid of ice.

Robert Frost's "October" prayer comes to mind, and his New Hampshire "apple-picking" with the "pane of glass / I skimmed this morning from the drinking trough." But Hall keeps a light humor, spelling out the cattle's swelling moo, *mm-mmm-mmmmm-mmmmmmmm-ugghwanchhh*.

His years have brought a horn of plenty: stories, essays, criticism, memoirs, honors, and poetry coming in all forms modern and classical. Since settling at Eagle Pond Farm with Kenyon, Hall's core, his physical, ethical, spiritual, aesthetic touchstone, remains the place's round of life, binding humankind to nature. In "Maple Syrup,"

> we take my grandfather's last
> quart of syrup
> upstairs, holding it gingerly,
> and we wash off twenty-five years
> of dirt, and we pull
> and pry the lid up, cutting the stiff,
> dried rubber gasket, and dip our fingers
> in, you and I both, and taste
> the sweetness, you for the first time,
> the sweetness preserved, of a dead man
> in the kitchen he left
> when his body slid
> like anyone's into the ground.

This homely ritual lets a startling line break trigger conjugal sweetness, "dip our fingers / in, you and I both," a moment's paradise regained on ancestral terrain.

Another durable presence, crossing New England pastures long since overgrown to woods, crops up in "Stone Walls," an anthem to what emerges in late fall:

> everything gray and brown, against the dark evergreen,
> everything rock and silver, lichen and moss on stone,
> strong bones of stone walls showing at last.

Hall's vocal music owes a lot to the "joy of leaves falling."

> In October the leaves turn . . .
> purples, greens, reds, grays, oranges, weaving together
> this joyful fabric,
> and I walk in the afternoon sun, kicking the leaves

as he had in the same place forty years before.

"Kicking the Leaves," title poem of a 1978 volume, finds Hall in Michigan walking with his new wife in October "as the leaves swirl upward from my boot." He fetches back to his boyhood in Connecticut "wearing corduroy knickers that swished / with a sound like leaves," then to a New Hampshire cider stand and Massachusetts college. Even if wilderness and animal wildness at the heart of things, as for Lawrence, Jeffers, Haines, Hughes, Snyder, don't mark the work of Donald Hall, still a wildness in words can surprise us. One Saturday before the war, his father came home from work

> and tumbled in the leaves with me,
> laughing, and carried me, laughing, my hair full of leaves.

Now, years after this so memorable moment,

> Now I fall, now I leap and fall
> to feel the leaves crush under my body, to feel my body
> buoyant in the ocean of leaves, the night of them,
> night heaving with death and leaves, rocking like the ocean.
> Oh, this delicious falling into the arms of leaves,
> into the soft laps of leaves!
> Face down, I swim into the leaves.

Exuberance worthy of Whitman stirs the verbs here, and leaves, leaves, leaves. Before the poem ceases we'll have heard that tocsin word thirty-five times.

The dying perennial season returns in a poem by Jane Kenyon, bringing her husband home from his operation.

> He dozed in the car,
> woke, and looked with astonishment
> at the hills, gold and quince
> under October sun, a sight so
> overwhelming that we began to cry,
> he first, and then I.

He recovers, only to see her struck by leukemia in 1994. *Without,* four years later, chronicles her dying in an exact, reserved voice that testifies all the more poignantly to her medical ravages.

> Daybreak until nightfall,
> he sat by his wife at the hospital
> while chemotherapy dripped
> through the catheter into her heart.

This poem closes,

> . . . They pushed the IV pump
> which she called Igor
> slowly past the nurses' pods, as far
> as the outside door
> so that she could smell the snowy air.

This will be her last opening to nature.

Over a year and forty-five indoor clinical pages later comes *Without*'s title poem, devoid of punctuation: "no snowdrop or crocus rose no yellow / no red leaves of maple without october." Now the wounded distancing of "he" and "she" dissolves, and earth returns.

> Your daffodils rose up
> and collapsed in their yellow
> bodies on the hillside
> garden above the birches
> you laid out in sand.

Letter poems follow the seasons, bringing her news of Eagle Pond Farm,

> here where I sat each fall
> watching you pull your summer's
> garden up.

"Letter in the New Year" reports the weather, as

> I walk over packed snow
> at zero, my heart quick
> with joy in the visible world.

As they both know, the Bible promises we are not left comfortless.

"Weeds and Peonies," ending *Without,* finds this world mixed. Before Kenyon's illness her peonies were "whiter than the idea of white as big as basketballs." Now there's another simile, "Your peonies burst out, white as snow squalls."

> Your peonies lean their vast heads westward
> as if they might topple. Some topple.

Speaking this poem, Hall pauses deeply before his last, briefest sentence.

Several years later another book dwells on Kenyon and loss. *The Painted Bed* (where his forebears slept, she died, and he still sleeps) brings back humor. "'What will become of Perkins?' / Jane asked" (for some reason she called him that). Now

> I miss her teasing voice
> that razzed my grandiloquence:
> "Perkins, dim your lights."
> "Somebody cover Perkins's cage."

Hall's gift to her comes as homage to Thomas Hardy, whose wife's death released a spate of laments. One of these begins, "Hereto I come to view a voiceless ghost." In another, Hardy speaks of "Leaves around me falling, . . . / And the woman calling." So Hall's "The Wish" begins, "I keep her weary ghost inside me," and echoes Hardy's falling rhymes with his own: "crying . . . dying," "colder . . . hold her." Hardy: "We stood by a pond that winter day." Hall: "We spent green afternoons / . . . Beside dark Eagle Pond." Greater love hath no man for a woman than to give her his favorite poet.

"Ordinary days were best," Hall writes, "when we worked over poems / in our separate rooms." Even more closely than his, Jane Kenyon's poetry gets its bearings from the world around her. In "Depression in Winter," a sun-heated stone renders her "chastened and calm." "Twilight: After Haying" finds "dusty stubble" and "long shadows," but "soul's bliss / and suffering are bound together / like the grasses," so

> The last, sweet exhalations
> of timothy and vetch
> go out with the song of the bird;
> the ravaged field
> grows wet with dew.

In the vein of Psalms, "The grass resolves to grow again, / . . . but my disordered soul thirsts / after something it cannot name." "Gettysburg: July 1, 1863" enters into a dying soldier—"How good the earth smelled, / as it had when he was a boy."

Whether nature's everpresence brings on joy or depression, Kenyon mints one perception after another: "the low clovery place / where melt from the mountain / comes down in the spring, and wild / lupine grows"; a wood thrush "singing in the great maples; its bright, unequivocal eye." How is it such touch for language lifts the heart no matter what? "At the Winter Solstice" gives that longest night a breathtaking, breathgiving turn of thought: "While we slept an inch of new snow / simplified the field."

"Let Evening Come," as fine as it gets in our time and often set to music, turns close to prayer in turning close to nature. Its first quiet modulation, "Let ... light ... late," Kenyon's eight-syllable lines, and the mystery of afternoon light "moving / up the bales as the sun moves down," let us this once at least "believe in the miracles of art." She times her phrasings so as to weigh mortality in the scales with sunlight, crickets, stars, wind. A biblical litany moves down her page with the sun—"Let the light ... Let dew ... Let the fox ... Let the wind"—until new verbs assure us, "don't / be afraid. God does not leave us," bringing her title home forever. "Let Evening Come."

> Let the light of late afternoon
> shine through chinks in the barn, moving
> up the bales as the sun moves down.
>
> Let the cricket take up chafing
> as a woman takes up her needles
> and her yarn. Let evening come.
>
> Let dew collect on the hoe abandoned
> in long grass. Let the stars appear
> and the moon disclose her silver horn.
>
> Let the fox go back to its sandy den.
> Let the wind die down. Let the shed
> go black inside. Let evening come.
>
> To the bottle in the ditch, to the scoop
> in the oats, to air in the lung
> let evening come.
>
> Let it come, as it will, and don't
> be afraid. God does not leave us
> comfortless, so let evening come.

"I dared not cast / / But silently cast"
Ted Hughes Capturing Pike

There are all sorts of ways of capturing animals and birds and fish. I spent most of my time, up to the age of fifteen or so, trying out many of these ways and when my enthusiasm began to wane, as it did gradually, I started to write poems. . . .

My pursuit of mice at threshing time when I was a boy, snatching them from under the sheaves as the sheaves were lifted away out of the stack and popping them into my pocket till I had thirty or forty crawling around in the lining of my coat, that and my present pursuit of poems seem to me to be different stages of the same fever. In a way, I suppose, I think of poems as a sort of animal. They have their own life, like animals, by which I mean that they seem quite separate from any person, even from their author, and nothing can be added to them or taken away without maiming or perhaps even killing them. And they have a certain wisdom. They know something special . . .

Finally . . . my attitude to animals changed. I accused myself of disturbing their lives. I began to look at them, you see, from their own point of view.

$\mathbf{T}$his notion of "capturing," from Ted Hughes (1930–1998), begins his fine primer *Poetry Is*. Many would welcome his changed attitude, such as the nineteenth-century peasant poet John Clare. Gerard Manley Hopkins, saying "I caught this morning" the windhover or kestrel, means a sighting, not a hunter's catch. Leaving it as they found it, poems like photos also "catch" something.

"My first six years shaped everything," Hughes said toward the end of his life. In his rural Yorkshire childhood, some fox cubs he'd tried to keep alive were killed by a farmer. Recalling this years later, "late one snowy night in dreary lodgings in London," he tried his first animal poem. Poemless for a year, in a sort of fever he wrote "The Thought-Fox." As he said of Emily Dickinson conjuring a cloudburst, "every phrase is a fresh event."

I imagine this midnight moment's forest:
Something else is alive
Beside the clock's loneliness
And this blank page where my fingers move.

Through the window I see no star:
Something more near
Though deeper within darkness
Is entering the loneliness:

Cold, delicately as the dark snow,
A fox's nose touches twig, leaf;
Two eyes serve a movement, that now
And again now, and now, and now

Sets neat prints into the snow
Between trees, and warily a lame
Shadow lags by stump and in hollow
Of a body that is bold to come

Across clearings, an eye,
A widening deepening greenness,
Brilliantly, concentratedly,
Coming about its own business

Till, with a sudden sharp hot stink of fox
It enters the dark hole of the head.
The window is starless still; the clock ticks,
The page is printed.

While Hughes's clipped angular twang projects an odor of fox, this poem's keynote sounds at the outset: "I imagine."

A predator—nose, eyes, prints, wary, concentrated—moves through the poem's landscape fitting the fox's pace: ongoing stanzas with flexible line lengths rhyming like trees along a trail, constant but no two alike. Hughes later wanted even livelier words for his creature's movements, "the twitch and craning of its ears, the slight tremor of its hanging tongue and its breath making little clouds, its teeth bared in the cold, the snow-crumbs dropping from its pads as it lifts each one in turn." Such a zoom lens would only sharpen the mystery of a "Thought-Fox . . . deeper within darkness." As both fox and spirit it "enters the dark hole of the head," the fox's "own business" becomes the poet's. This midnight creation myth also undermines Britain's pastoral tradition, including its foxhunt mystique.

Hughes's contemporary Adrienne Rich has something of the same creative impulse. Her "fox, panting, fire-eyed, / gone to earth in my chest," enters an early poem. And in the title poem of *Fox* (2001), "I needed fox   Badly I needed /

a vixen" to fire the dissenting spirit in trying times. "For a human animal to call for help / on another animal / is the most riven the most revolted cry on earth / . . . it blurts / into the birth-yell of the yet-to-be human child / pushed out of a female."

A long trail of animals winds through British and American poetry. Some are fabulous: Melville's Moby-Dick, Poe's Raven, Lewis Carroll's Snark, Hughes's Crow. Most are capturings, seen then reseen: Clare's badger (a Hughes favorite), Whitman's hermit thrush and "beetles rolling balls of dung," Dickinson's "narrow Fellow in the Grass," Lawrence's snake, pike, mountain lion, mosquito (another favorite), Eliot's hermit thrush, Jeffers's hawks, Kunitz's raccoon and Wellfleet whale, Oppen's deer, Roethke's slug, Stafford's "sharp swallows in their swerve," Lowell's skunk, Bishop's moose, fish, armadillo, Swenson's butterfly, Kumin's horses, Kinnell's bear, Snyder's Cougar and Coyote, and they go on and on, a virtual Noah's ark.

Why such fascination? Pure wonder and strangeness? Catching them in words? They're potent models, other than human yet not entirely so—and that's their force as metaphors too. Animals wild or domestic compel us by difference and kinship both. As Hughes says, "they have a certain wisdom. They know something special."

Something special happens, a stunning poem, when Hopkins catches the windhover "in his riding / Of the rolling level underneath him steady air, and striding / High there." As the hawk rebuffs the wind, "My heart in hiding / Stirred for a bird." Then like Christ this "Brute beauty" turns mortal. Falling, it shines even more, the way "blue-bleak embers" when they break apart "gash gold-vermillion." Hopkins, nineteenth-century Jesuit priest, in his turn spurred Hughes toward his first book's title poem, "The Hawk in the Rain."

> I drown in the drumming ploughland, I drag up
> Heel after heel from the swallowing of the earth's mouth,
> From clay that clutches my each step to the ankle
> With the habit of the dogged grave, but the hawk
>
> Effortlessly at height hangs his still eye.
> His wings hold all creation in a weightless quiet,
> Steady as a hallucination in the streaming air.
> While banging wind kills these stubborn hedges,
>
> Thumbs my eyes, throws my breath, tackles my heart,
> And rain hacks my head to the bone, the hawk hangs
> The diamond point of will that polestars
> The sea drowner's endurance: and I,
>
> Bloodily grabbed dazed last-moment-counting
> Morsel in the earth's mouth, strain towards the master-

Fulcrum of violence where the hawk hangs still.
That maybe in his own time meets the weather

Coming the wrong way, suffers the air, hurled upside down,
Fall from his eye, the ponderous shires crash on him,
The horizon trap him; the round angelic eye
Smashed, mix his heart's blood with the mire of the land.

So much charges these words, exciting every visceral verb and noun. Where Hopkins reels with Catholic spirit, Hughes struggles for sheer survival.

Instinctually he mimics the alliteration in Old English poetry, such as the Anglo-Saxon "Seafarer" (Ezra Pound's version): "Hung with hard ice-flakes, where hail-scur flew, / There I heard naught save the harsh sea." Half the lines in "The Hawk in the Rain" go that way—"drown . . . drumming . . . drags," "clay . . . clutches," "height hangs," "wings . . . weightless." This archaic vision thrusts back and forth from drumming plowland to quiet height, streaming air to stubborn hedges, diamond polestar to earth's mouth, lurching between "I" and the hawk till its "angelic eye" mires in earth.

Despite a speaker, all the poem's passion comes from earth, sky, weather. Then a mayhem of syntax at the end, all "I" gone, hurls the hawk upside down and he feels the air "fall" from his eye as England's shires crash against him. The poetry itself strains our grasp and jars complacence, barely poising stillness against violence.

Wildlife encounters don't usually explode this way, in mind or in fact, but they carry a sense of risk. A "sudden sharp" fox enters the head, a hawk hangs above the dazed speaker. As a "very keen angler for pike," Hughes tells how once, unable for a while to go fishing, he dredged up memories of his childhood fishing hole, a deep pond holding more than he knew. For him, poems can outdo life, they're "continually trying to displace our experience." So "Pike" got him fishing again—with a vengeance. "One of my prize catches," he calls this poem.

Pike, three inches long, perfect
Pike in all parts, green tigering the gold.
Killers from the egg: the malevolent aged grin.
They dance on the surface among the flies.

Or move, stunned by their own grandeur,
Over a bed of emerald, silhouette
Of submarine delicacy and horror.
A hundred feet long in their world.

In ponds, under the heat-struck lily pads—
Gloom of their stillness:
Logged on last year's black leaves, watching upwards.
Or hung in an amber cavern of weeds.

The jaws' hooked clamp and fangs
Not to be changed at this date;
A life subdued to its instrument;
The gills kneading quietly, and the pectorals.

Much data packs these opening stanzas, sentence fragments shaping an ominous legend.

The pike (from Anglo Saxon *pic*, pickax), three inches but "perfect / Pike in all parts," spawn an animal-on-animal verb to sharpen their menace, "green tigering the gold," and seem hundred-foot submarines in our world too. Hughes's fragments sketch a primordial scene where rational human sentences have no hold. "Killers from the egg . . . The jaws' hooked clamp and fangs"—no further evolution needed. What's scarier, the pike are "watching upwards."

Yet homo sapiens may cultivate them.

Three we kept behind glass,
Jungled in weed: three inches, four,
And four and a half: fed fry to them—
Suddenly there were two. Finally one

With a sag belly and the grin it was born with.
And indeed they spare nobody.
Two, six pounds each, over two feet long,
High and dry and dead in the willow-herb—

One jammed past its gills down the other's gullet:
The outside eye stared: as a vice locks—
The same iron in this eye
Though its film shrank in death.

As "we" (Hughes's Yorkshire family or his wife Sylvia Plath, an equally trenchant poet) enter this story, it turns tame only briefly. Any breath of empathy for pike stifles on "the grin it was born with" and the iron "vice." Yet attentiveness to detail—"gills kneading quietly," "sag belly," the eye whose "film shrank in death"—may breed a kind of love.

Now a personal voice summons up remembrance: his pond, huge pike, trancelike casting in a super- or subnatural encounter.

A pond I fished, fifty yards across,
Whose lilies and muscular tench
Had outlasted every visible stone
Of the monastery that planted them—

Stilled legendary depth:
It was as deep as England. It held
Pike too immense to stir, so immense and old
That past nightfall I dared not cast

But silently cast and fished
With the hair frozen on my head
For what might move, for what eye might move.
The still splashes on the dark pond,

Owls hushing the floating woods
Frail on my ear against the dream
Darkness against night's darkness had freed,
That rose slowly towards me, watching.

Not a large pond, but more than meters deep "It was as deep as England," some pre-Christian place and time akin to childhood.

At this depth Hughes's writing mutates from crude fragments into layers of uncanny experience. A drawn-out sentence holds immense pike past nightfall, through hypnotic casting and terrific alertness. Within this sentence a stanza gap, a gaping between "I dared not cast" and "But silently cast," deepens the reluctance of a dream descent. Like the thought-fox's "deepening" eye and the hawk's "still eye," the pike's eye "watching upwards" and now simply staring confronts a once-young angler.

Finally a quiet wildness seizes his language. Still splashes and owls hooting actually deepen night's stillness into what looks like "dream Darkness." But this key line break compresses the sentence: not exactly "dream / Darkness," though the words say as much, but "the dream [that] Darkness beneath night's darkness had freed." Freed how, from where, and why? We're left in the dark with an ongoing verb. Like the fox emerging "deeper within darkness," a pike-like poem-dream "rose slowly towards me, watching."

"Pike" came out in *Lupercal*, named for a Roman fertility festival honoring the wolf. Later *Wodwo* featured "some sort of goblin creature . . . half-man half-animal spirit of the forests." Then came *Crow*, a barbarous whimsical bird indelible in Leonard Baskin's drawings for the book. For children (first) Hughes wrote *Moon-Whales*, *Ffangs the Vampire Bat*, and *Nessie, the Mannerless Monster*. In a jolly lunar exercise, *The Earth Owl and Other Moon-People* has foxes hunting "that noble rural vermin," a country squire. With *Remains of Elmet* (an ancient Celtic place-name) Hughes goes back to the West Yorkshire moorland of his childhood and its wildlife: weasel, cormorant, loach, snipe, curlew. Elegizing a "spirit of the place" but without nostalgia, he conjures "mad heather and grass," "wild rock," "misty valleys," "crumbling outcrop," "sour hills," "blown water" (and sometimes he sounds just a bit overblown).

Even as a child, Hughes felt this landscape polluted: "the only life" in the River Calder was a "bankside population of brown rats." He played "by the River Don, which drained the industrial belt between Sheffield and Doncaster: a river of such concentrated steaming, foaming poisons that an accidental ducking was said to be fatal." One day nearby "I saw all the fish in this lake bobbing their mouths at the surface." Anger surfaces, always in sensuous speech, when he revisits the fishing grounds of Tarka, England's much-loved fictional otter.

> The river is suddenly green—dense bottle green.
> Hard in the sun, dark as spinach.
> Drought pools bleach their craters.
> The river's floor is a fleece—
> Tresses of some vile stuff
> That disintegrates to a slime as you touch it
> Leaving your fingers fouled with a stink of diesel.

Thunderbolts flush through, "But never a flood enough to scour a sewer, / Never enough to resurrect a river."

Remembering his forebears' saying, "Back to the land in three generations," Hughes and his wife in the 1970s bought a farm in Devon, where ancient ways and "high-banked, deep-cut lanes" survive and "the financial nightmares, the technological revolution and international market madness" were only just beginning to devastate local farming. There they practiced animal husbandry, raising sheep and cattle. At night Hughes would note down details in "improvised verses," staying "close to what is going on." He published these as *Moortown Diary*.

Many have to do with nursing and birthing cows and calves, ewes and lambs—not a famous subject for lyric poetry. The pages bristle with life and death too. They're so steeped in earthy pastoral, that when someone staying at Moortown cottage left behind his copy of the book, Hughes sent it along inscribed, "The sheep that was lost is found again." Without an ounce of fakery or self-regard, he wields exact lingo for what's going on and for his hand in all that, thanks to a muscling Anglo-Saxon word hoard. A "dumb calf" can't manage the "tight hard bag of stiff teats."

> He nuzzled slobbering at their fat sides
> But couldn't bring one in. They were dripping,
> And as he excited them they started squirting.
> I fumbled one into his mouth—I had to hold it,
> Stuffing its slippery muscle into his suction.

Like Maxine Kumin on her New England farm, Hughes's animal touch shapes his verse lines too.

On "17 February 1974,"

> A lamb could not get born. Ice wind
> Out of a downpour dishclout sunrise. The mother
> Lay on the mudded slope. Harried, she got up
> And the blackish lump bobbed at her back-end
> Under her tail. After some hard galloping,

Some manoeuvring, much flapping of the backward
Lump head of the lamb looking out,
I caught her with a rope. Laid her, head uphill
And examined the lamb. A blood-ball swollen
Tight in its black felt, its mouth gap
Squashed crooked, tongue stuck out, black-purple,
Strangled by its mother. I felt inside,
Past the noose of mother-flesh, into the slippery
Muscled tunnel, fingering for a hoof,
Right back to the port-hole of the pelvis.
But there was no hoof. He had stuck his head out too early
And his feet could not follow. He should have
Felt his way, tip-toe, his toes
Tucked up under his nose
For a safe landing. So I kneeled wrestling
With her groans. No hand could squeeze past
The lamb's neck into her interior
To hook a knee. I roped that baby head
And hauled till she cried out and tried
To get up and I saw it was useless. I went
Two miles for the injection and a razor.
Sliced the lamb's throat-strings, levered with a knife
Between the vertebrae and brought the head off
To stare at its mother, its pipes sitting in the mud
With all earth for a body. Then pushed
The neck-stump right back in, and as I pushed
She pushed. She pushed crying and I pushed gasping.
And the strength
Of the birth push and the push of my thumb
Against that wobbly vertebra were deadlock,
A to-fro futility. Till I forced
A hand past and got a knee. Then like
Pulling myself to the ceiling with one finger
Hooked in a loop, timing my effort
To her birth push groans, I pulled against
The corpse that would not come. Till it came.
And after it the long, sudden, yolk-yellow
Parcel of life
In a smoking slither of oils and soups and syrups—
And the body lay born, beside the hacked-off head.

Overmuch for the squeamish, but it happened, and happens again here in bone-true language astir with music and lifelike timing at the line breaks. Whatever awe freezes man versus creature in "Pike," here it's deadlock at first, then an impassioned wrestling. Some saving grace comes through, a life for a life, as the ewe joins the poet "timing my effort / To her birth push groans."

"the still pond and the egrets beating home"
Derek Walcott, First to See Them

How quickly it could all disappear! And how it is beginning to
drive us further into where we hope are impenetrable places, green
secrets at the end of bad roads, headlands where the next view
is not of a hotel but of some long beach without a figure and the
hanging question of some fisherman's smoke at its far end.
The Caribbean is not an idyll, not to its natives. They draw their
working strength from it organically, like trees, like the sea
almond or the spice laurel of the heights.

Toward the climax of his 1992 Nobel Prize
acceptance speech, Derek Walcott (b. 1930) fends off any touristic image of
his native islands. He means to reclaim their selfhood, their genius, and if sea
almond and spice laurel can't be found in an unabridged dictionary, that too
speaks for a special place. You can see Walcott, a fine naturalist painter, visually
calling up a landscape he cherishes: "the next view . . . some long beach without
a figure," "the hanging question of some fisherman's smoke."

"I have felt from my boyhood that I had one function and that was somehow
to articulate, not my own experience, but what I saw around me," he says about
his West Indian childhood. "I'm the first person to look at this mountain and
try to write about it. I'm the first person to see this lagoon, this piece of land.
Here I am with this enormous privilege of just being someone who can take
up a brush." He could be Adam or Columbus, this "first person to see" those
"green secrets." Yet Walcott's homeland is no Eden for working Caribbeans,
whose precursors saw the land long before Columbus.

So what has a poet to do with his culture's endangered survival?

There is a force of exultation, a celebration of luck, when a writer finds himself
a witness to the early morning of a culture that is defining itself, branch by
branch, leaf by leaf, in that self-defining dawn.

That "self-defining dawn" comes after long colonial status. Of course the West

Indies are as old as America, far older if we slough off their European colonial namings. That's his predicament and his strength alike, in this new morning: to be striking clear of America and Europe both, without denying their deep place in him.

"Where shall I turn, divided to the vein?" asks the early poem "A Far Cry from Africa." Born in the onetime British colony of St. Lucia to parents who themselves were of mixed West Indian and English parentage, Walcott has never stopped exploring exile, testing his mulatto standpoint "Between this Africa and the English tongue I love." This Africa, for him, sends calypso spirit into many of Walcott's plays, while two dialects he's absorbed, Creole English and French Creole, color the tone of his writing—the local flora, fauna, place-names, the vivid hues of land and sea, town and harbor. He likes the island patois of *ciseau* or *scisour la mer,* for the scissor-tailed tern or frigate-bird cutting the air.

As for "the English tongue I love," he claims a full tradition: the Bible, Shakespeare on through Keats, Clare, Whitman, Dickinson, Hardy, Yeats, Frost, Williams, Eliot, Edward Thomas, Auden, Robert Lowell, Ted Hughes, plus Melville, Joyce, Faulkner, Hemingway. Walcott prizes these Anglo and American voices while clinging to another lineage, French West Indian, the white "patrician" Saint-John Perse and black "proletarian" Aimé Césaire. He calls these men, along with Pablo Neruda the Whitman of Chile, New World poets, bypassing that term's colonial taint. Their faith goes to "elemental man," a "second Adam" renaming, with some bitterness, the tropical cityscape, country-side, and wild surroundings he stems from. Like his Robinson Crusoe in "The Castaway," Walcott finds on empty Caribbean beaches "a green wine bottle's gospel choked with sand," and "In our own entrails, genesis." That choked gut comes from his inner split, the "African" seeking pure green origins via western culture.

Digging deeper than he had before, Derek Walcott composed his own Gene-sis in *Omeros* (1990). Revamping Homer's Odyssey and the Bible, with hints of the Babylonian epic *Gilgamesh,* the poet's quest starts on his Caribbean island and ends there after three hundred pages of Dantean triplets. In Book One the first chapter's first section begins with origins. "This is how, one sunrise, we cut down them canoes"—a Creole voice telling tourists how the natives felled trees to make pirogues, dugout canoes. "Once wind bring the news"

> to the *laurier-cannelles,* their leaves start shaking
> the minute the axe of sunlight hit the cedars,
> because they could see the axes in our own eyes.

A native integrity shows up in *laurier-cannelles,* whose French West Indian name Walcott won't translate, like W. S. Merwin with Hawaii's native trees: "they cut

the sacred 'ohias then / the sacred koas then / the sandalwood and the halas."
"Do I have to explain?" Walcott has said. "I think not." Since he grew up with
it, *laurier-cannelles,* though a colonial naming and not native Aruac, would lose
truth and tone in English as cinnamon laurel.

Gilgamesh too centers on violence, as the king destroys the Cedar Forest
for a gate in his capital and a raft to return there. Walcott's native voice, from
under a sea-almond tree, tells how we "murderers" first "killed" West Indian
cedar for the dugouts that mean their livelihood. "I lift up the axe and pray for
strength in my hands / to wound the first cedar." Not just "wound" but "pray"
looks for a primal oneness, a violence tenderly, sacredly done.

This genesis in *Omeros* ties nature's loss to human need.

> Wind lift the ferns. They sound like the sea that feed us
> fishermen all our life, and the ferns nodded "Yes,
> the trees have to die."

When huge new power saws wounded these trees, "the Aruacs' patois crackled
in the smell / of a resinous bonfire . . . and their language was lost." Yet the
logs, still feeling "eagerness to become canoes," entered the surf "and their
nodding prows / agreed with the waves to forget their lives as trees"—as if
nature already forgave the original sin.

Walcott reaches back before colonial time to the iguana (an Aruac word the
tribe's name stems from) that watched "for centuries . . . till a new race / unknown to the lizard stood measuring the trees." Even "nettles guard the holes
where the laurels were killed," and Nature itself wants in on the storytelling:
"garrulous waterfall," "talkative brooks."

Now the epic moves out on pirogues with Hector and Achilles by way of
contemporary Africa, Europe, and America—places that have drawn Walcott
himself away from home. Following "the American dream," he discovers a
ripe Indian summer marred by history: "a New England / / that had raked
the leaves of the tribes into one fire / on the lawn back of the carport," and the
Union Pacific Railroad, "A spike hammered / into the heart of their country as
the Sioux looked on."

As this modern odyssey heads home, Achilles meets strange weather, bursting
seas that mean "somewhere people interfering / with the course of nature." If
once that sea could "feed us / fishermen all our life," now the seabed is scoured by
thirty-mile nets, "steely blue albacore / / no longer leapt to his line," "man was
an endangered / / species now." Only Achilles' return redeems this wandering
along "the rift in the soul." His own cove and village "held all I needed of paradise," with "no other laurel but the *laurier-cannelle*'s." Mooring his dugout "ribbed
in our native timber," he recalls the story's "green sunrise of axes." To square

that violence with paradise, Walcott ends on the constant changing nature of things: "the sea was still going on."

"Sea-light on the cod barrels," "the blue, gusting harbour," "the cobalt bay," "the schooners in their stagnant smells," "racing bitterns": West India colors the opening stanzas of another book-length poem, *Tiepolo's Hound*, published when Walcott was seventy. What was still driving him, after seventeen poetry books, twenty-nine plays, essays and conversations, journalism and teaching, a lifetime of painting, much travel, the Nobel Prize? First and last a primal urge to get things said, "the fevered bliss that shook John Clare": "it lies in the small spring of poetry everywhere." That bliss spurs a "freshness of detail" he says "should be true of the remembered life":

> the almond's smell from a torn almond leaf,
> the spray glazing your face from the bursting waves.

Our word-sense renews a place on earth that's long been unrecognized for itself.

In freshening memory Walcott knows a need—historical, political, spiritual—to redeem his birthright rooted in a specific place, a slender archipelago, the Lesser Antilles, a chain of islands settled by Spain, the Netherlands, Denmark, France, England, America. Here as in *Omeros*, "The empire of naming colonised even the trees." (Like the "gusting harbour," "colonised" insists on British spelling, still loyal to the poet's mother tongue despite a New York publisher.) Titling his Nobel Prize speech "The Antilles: Fragments of Epic Memory," he could be echoing Eliot's *The Waste Land*, "These fragments I have shored against my ruins," or Neruda's epic recovery of the pre-Columbian Andean sanctuary Machu Picchu: "This was the dwelling, this is the place," *el sitio*. Stemming from, dwelling in St. Lucia and Trinidad, Walcott will bring those places vibrantly into the present, however fragmented their past. Poetry "conjugates both tenses simultaneously." Through time and memory, poems go about remaking place.

Before introducing Tiepolo's hound, Walcott's verse makes clear that *place*, St. Thomas in the West Indies—that reclaiming a place of his desire has everything to do with wordcraft, art, light. On page one we meet a family strolling past a synagogue, past "small island shops / / quiet as drawings" toward "the blue, gusting harbour" where gulls mark the waves "like commas." "Sea-light" strikes the cod barrels of St. Thomas, "the salt breeze brings the sound of Mission slaves / / chanting deliverance from all their sins / in tidal couplets of lament and answer." Before we know it, these pentameters with their rhymes—"like commas" / "St. Thomas," "waves" / "slaves"—weave sea light into city trade, salt breeze into forced religion, while coupling waves with both writing and slavery, tides with couplets and lament, and letting Van Gogh-like gulls offset Catholic dogma. The painter's eye, the writer's ear can do all this, bonding human acts to nature's.

Strolling with his family here is a now-famous artist, born one hundred years before Walcott. Camille Pissarro's ancestors, Sephardic Jews, had fled the Spanish Inquisition to France, then settled in St. Thomas where Pissarro was born. Now the later, West Indian poet bonds with the earlier painter, who left the islands for Paris, taught Cézanne for a while, joined the great Impressionists, and died abroad. Walcott questions his own affinities via the arc of Pissarro's life. "You could have been our pioneer," he tells him, in your "archipelago, where / hues are primal, red trees, green shade, blue water." Has Walcott, living partly in the United States, also betrayed Caribbean roots? The verse itself of *Tiepolo's Hound* gives body to this dual quest: paired couplets casually rhymed, "civilising" with "egrets rising," "torn almond leaf" with "remembered life," "thigh" with "Levi."

And Tiepolo's hound? Early on, Walcott finds himself in New York's Metropolitan Museum, stunned by a painting's Renaissance feast.

> Then I caught a slash of pink on the inner thigh
> of a white hound entering the cave of a table,
>
> so exact in its lucency at *The Feast of Levi*,
> I felt my heart halt.

This one detail gives him "sacred shock," and "even as I write,"

> paused on a step of this couplet, I have never found
> its image again, a hound in astounding light.

His pulsing lines jump-start a quest, tying "as I write" to "astounding light," "one stroke for a dog's thigh!" Painting and poetry alike offer an "art of seeing," while "The Feast of Levi" signals Pissarro's Jewish otherness behind Walcott's alienated search for what art can do.

Ultimately we don't know whether the painting is by Tiepolo or maybe Veronese, and Walcott never does find that white hound. What counts is light, ecstasy, "the stroke, the syllable, planted in the furrows / of page and canvas," and the venture of two kindred artists—a half-African at home in English, a French-speaking Jew in and out of exile. Following Pissarro away from home toward Gauguin and Van Gogh, Giotto and Botticelli, Walcott as painter aches for what's left behind: "tossing green bananas / and the prongs of the ginger lily," "bright wind on water," "tints beneath black skin,"

> the wet light moving down the ebony fissure
> of a fisherman's shoulders as he hauled in a seine,

a black dog panting for entrails near a pirogue
on sand so white it blinded, a sea so blue

it stained your hand,

cobalt from the harbor of St. Thomas.

Once in Paris with the city's river, cafés, and boulevards, Walcott's keen eye,
within Pissarro's, filters them all through homegrown vision, images of the sea
around their islands: "along the Seine / an oceanic surging in the trees," "The
surge of summer lifted the park trees / like breakers cresting." Even Prussia's
crushing 1870 invasion of France, seen through Walcott's alter ego, roils with
nature's tropical palette: "Staccato chrysanthemums, like bursts of gunfire,"
"tubes of red like disembodied entrails, / and the gamboge pus of wounds."
Gamboge, a yellow-orange pigment, turns up elsewhere—a Caribbean memory
of "gamboge cliffs"—along with leaf-yellow, laburnum-yellow, gold, orange,
ocher, and most often saffron, whenever bright or deep earth coloring enters
Walcott's poem, as in his oils and watercolors interleaving this book.

Beneath its quest through time and place, every page in *Tiepolo's Hound* finds
the artist bringing land and sea alive to us: "brush-point cypresses," "the impasto
indigo bay," "wriggles for tree trunks, charred twigs for figures," "light that
can gladden / the mind like the flash of a hound's thigh in Veronese." Think of
Elizabeth Bishop's "Poem" on a small painting, giving us

some tiny cows,
two brushstrokes each . . .

a wild iris, white and yellow,
fresh-squiggled from the tube.

Scanning a canvas, we accept such tricks unconsciously. For Walcott they mate
with a writer's touch. "Studying his *paysages*," he says of Pissarro, "you feel the
fevered bliss that shook John Clare / and Edward Thomas." In memory or exile
it *must* come down to the mind's eye, "brushstroke and word." Possessing the
painter's imagination, the poet points it back home: "the same sun is yours . . .
the same silvering birches of approaching rain, / if this pen were a brush."

Pissarro's betrayal and loss, "what it means / to leave the fading Eden where
you were," embitters Walcott's own quest "back to the original, where one
stroke caught / the bright vermilion of the white hound's thigh." He summons
the whole "Antillean isthmus," the strip of islands bridging New World to Old.
"The ochre shallows of the lagoon reflect / the setting empire of an enormous
sky." Colonial destiny troubles "the world around me,"

Dusk burrows into the roots from the egret's scream
as it launches itself across the brightened water;

the fraying banner of the dishevelled stream
reddens the reeds from some invisible slaughter.

A rhyme grinds history against nature with an artist's touch, "slaughter" against "brightened water," reddened reeds.

Opposing empire he creates homeward scenes,

the still pond and the egrets beating home
through the swamp trees, the mangrove's anchors.

Mangroves send their exposed roots down into the ground. So should the islands' artists. Their early poets echoed Wordsworth and painters copied Constable, yet the Caribbean gum tree, "The gommier in flower did not mimic the dogwood," a northern growth—"they were, like the breadfruit, true to their sense of place."

About certain namings, little can be done. Walcott the "West Indian" bridles at "American" christening of the "New World." What Columbus, "What the Genoan did,"

fingering our rocks on his rosary, was to seal,
rubbing finger and thumb, the indelible christening

of St. Thomas, Santa Lucia, Trinidad, the unreal
baptism of roofs beaded with rain and glistening.

Perhaps what's misdone by language, language can undo or redo. Walcott's eye for light and ear for rhyme recoup a pre-Christian reality of glistening roofs, like the red wheelbarrow William Carlos Williams "glazed with rain / water." What's more, behind his mercantile, imperial, religious, and personal aims, Columbus did feel ecstasy at the prolific world he found. His voice begins Williams's *In the American Grain*: "Bright green trees, the whole land so green it is a pleasure to look on it."

Still tracking Pissarro's retreat to the Old World, Walcott wonders about the 1892 Dreyfus affair, where a French-Jewish army captain was falsely accused of treason. Did this scandal taint the painter? "Examined closely, his foliage could be read / as Hebrew script." Like a spy, "Had he not copied with Sephardic eyes / those fields . . . ?" Ironically, Dreyfus was banished to Ile du Diable, France's Caribbean penal colony.

Finally Walcott journeys back home.

Then one noon where acacias shade the beach
I saw the parody of Tiepolo's hound

in the short salt grass, requiring no research,
but something still unpainted, on its own ground.

This was no "lapdog in its satin seat" but an "abandoned, houseless thing," so Walcott "set it down in the village to survive / like all my ancestry. The hound was here." Here on home ground again, he imagines himself and Pissarro watching "a windmill's / vanes grind to a halt with slavery." Not idyllic, but it seals them both within a climate and calling.

Toward the end of *Tiepolo's Hound* we come across the poet's self-portrait, an up-front colorful presence after 150 pages of free-flowing, wide-reaching, time-changing inward and outward experience. He's standing at an easel, looking straight out at us—and likely *into* a mirror, because his left hand's holding a brush to the canvas, whereas the book's back cover photo shows him right-handed. In the poetry opposite this portrait his fine brush, as it were, gives us couplets with "leaf-glued autumn pavements" from Pissarro's France and "a crescent fringe / of rustling yellow fronds on a white shore" in Walcott's homeland. Yet another bifocal view of their environs.

An astonishing sight begins the poem's closing section.

> The swallows flit in immortality,
> moving yet motionless on the canvas roofs.

Whether in Paris or St. Thomas, in fact or in art, Walcott has all along been tracking this singular thought. Young West Indians were impressed by European art, "the fountaining elation / of feathery palms in an engraving's stasis." Veronese's "bright rotunda riots / with fury that is motionless but moves"—"O turbulence, astounding in its stasis." And now come the swallows, "moving yet motionless."

Call this moment spellbinding, this paradoxical sight and image. The swallows exist in and out of time. Surging with life they're stayed by art, like the lovers on Keats's Grecian urn, and that Autumn ode keeps its swallows gathering in the skies. Neruda grasps Machu Picchu's potency:

> Gale sustained on a slope.
> Immobile turquoise cataract.

On the page as on canvas, Walcott catches West Indian life "moving yet motionless," like the surf's "exploding spray."

Poetry like painting holds still the "gusting harbour" of St. Thomas and "egrets rising." The still motion in these ordinary miracles, to borrow his term, also warps time as he brings Pissarro into his own day and "we stand doubled in each other's eyes." Through memory, *Tiepolo's Hound* conjugates past with present, and history with art. At the outset Pissarro's family strolled past a synagogue. The last section will "bring the occasional pilgrim to St. Thomas / to find the synagogue on its small street." Derek Walcott's pilgrimage, "a search that will lead us / where we began," has caught two artists wandering from the

Caribbean to Europe and pictured them lovingly, attentively enough to make their New World—"the still pond and the egrets beating home"—a home now, no exile any more.

The book's beginning saw "a white herring gull over the Mission / droning its passages from Exodus." In the end,

> This is my peace, my salt, exulting acre:
> there is no more Exodus, this is my Zion,
>
> whose couplets race the furrowing wind, their maker,
> with those homecoming sails on the horizon.

And happily, standing opposite these lines, a Walcott seascape done years earlier shows two tiny white sails on the horizon. Like the Native American prayer, *My words are tied in one / With the great mountains,* Walcott ties couplets into coastal waves, their poet into a homeland acre, and thus Sephardic / West Indian exile into Zion. (plate 19)

Finally he speaks for humankind through Pissarro and himself, for "we, as moving trees, must root somewhere."

"It looks just like the Cascades"
Gary Snyder's Eye for the Real World

When I was eleven or twelve, I went into the Chinese room at the
Seattle art museum and saw Chinese landscape paintings; they blew
my mind. My shock of recognition was very simple: "It looks just
like the Cascades." The waterfalls, the pines, the clouds, the mist
looked a lot like the northwest United States. The Chinese had an
eye for the world that I saw as real.

Washington's North Cascades mountains
never faded for Gary Snyder (b. 1930), wherever his paths between nature and
poetry took him: South America and the Persian Gulf as a working seaman, San
Francisco and the Beat Movement, the Northwest on logging teams, trail crews,
fire lookout, Japan for Zen practice and mountain climbing, Reed College and
Berkeley studying American Indian anthropology and East Asian languages,
California's Sierra Nevada where he's lived sustainably since 1970.

"Mid-August at Sourdough Mountain Lookout" opens his first book, *Riprap*,
with a keen sense for what the poet now "saw as real."

> Down valley a smoke haze
> Three days heat, after five days rain
> Pitch glows on the fir-cones
> Across rocks and meadows
> Swarms of new flies
>
> I cannot remember things I once read
> A few friends, but they are in cities.
> Drinking cold snow-water from a tin cup
> Looking down for miles
> Through high still air.

Noting nothing but what's present, these "small nouns / Crying faith" (as Oppen
put it) take no needless adjectives, and one verb draws us close, illumining an

Islands, Mountains, Houses, Bridge, Guan Huai, eighteenth century.
Seattle Art Museum, Eugene Fuller Memorial Collection.

immense vista: "Pitch glows." No "I" so far, the scene does without oneself—though "down valley" and the glow hint at an observer.

On second hearing, more comes to mind. Everything seems still, but the poet's on alert, fire-watching in high summer. Smoke started this poem, maybe left over from a lightning-struck dead tree. It took smokechasers eighteen hours to reach one such burn he called in. Pitch glows, so it must be clear, if hazy down below. Now a voice enters, his own person, "I cannot remember." The solitary Zen practicer then dissolves in "Drinking . . . Looking," his ongoing verbs scanning a very present landscape traced in the simplest syllables.

Frugality guides this poem. "It's like backpacking. I don't want anything that's unnecessary." Think of John Muir roaming Yosemite with blanket, bread, and cheese. Snyder would rather have no mark after "cities," but his friends aren't "in cities / Drinking cold snow-water." Far from San Francisco, the poem ends in silence, clarity, or doesn't end, as "Looking" drifts "for miles / Through high still air." These "plain poems," he said, "run the risk of invisibility." They do "the work of seeing the world *without* any prism of language, and to bring that seeing *into* language." An arc of tension connects words to the world.

All's not blissful mindlessness in still air. Summer of 1952, Snyder kept a journal at Crater Mountain lookout, 8,149 feet—icicles frozen upward in July wind, a few midsummer weeks without snow. "Really wretched weather for three days now—wind, hail, sleet, snow . . . hit my head on the lamp, the shutters fall, the radio quits . . . Outside wind blows, no visibility." After a week the weather clears onto three million acres of forest. 28 July his "pressing need" is "to look within and adjust the mechanism of perception." That same day sees a small "dead sharp-shinned hawk, blown by the wind against the lookout." So even man's bare lookout on the world can cause damage. "To write poetry of nature," Snyder says, "to articulate the vision," means a conflict between one thing and the other:

> (reject the human; but the tension of
> human events, brutal and tragic, against
> a non-human background? Like Jeffers?)

The hawk and rock at Crater lookout set him thinking of Robinson Jeffers, who'd "sooner, except the penalties, kill a man than a hawk." Admiring the California poet since high school, now he wonders "if, to take as strong a stance in and around nature as Jeffers does required such an alienated attitude towards human beings." One last entry on 28 July: "Pair of eagles soaring over Devil's Creek canyon."

Like Keats at Ambleside Falls thinking of Milton's Eden, Snyder carries a poet's knapsack. He amused the grizzled firewatchers by hauling in Zen Buddhist

Gary Snyder at Sourdough Mountain, Summer 1953.

From John Suiter, *Poets on the Peaks: Gary Snyder, Philip Whalen and Jack Kerouac in the Cascades* (Washington, D.C.: Counterpoint Press, 2002).

Gary Snyder at Crater Mountain Lookout, Summer 1952.
Photo © Harold Vail. All rights reserved. From John Suiter, *Poets on the Peaks:
Gary Snyder, Philip Whalen and Jack Kerouac in the Cascades* (Washington, D.C.:
Counterpoint Press, 2002).

readings to his lookout along with a sack of brown rice, a gallon of soy sauce, Japanese green tea, and Chinese calligraphy brushes. At Sourdough Mountain lookout, above the Skagit River, his journal sounds like an ancient scroll painting: "wind blowing mist over the edge of the ridge, or out onto the snowfield . . . Clumps of trees fading into a darker and darker gray." He stuffs the stove "with twisted pitchy Alpine fir limbs" and in mid-August comes on William Blake's proverb, "If the doors of perception were cleansed, everything would appear to man as it is, infinite."

An eighteenth-century Chinese scroll, much like the view from his Cascades lookout, has been in Seattle's Asian Art Museum since he was a boy. This vertical landscape, unlike the horizontal one joined to Snyder's *Mountains and Rivers Without End,* recedes upward through peaks, pines, and waterfalls into clouds and mist. He thinks this may well be the source for his youthful shock of recognition, and thanks Chinese landscape painters for their "vision of earth surface as organism, in which water, cloud, rock, and plant growth all stream through each other." Near the base of this three-foot scroll, the eye barely spots two figures sitting outside an open pavilion, doubtless sipping tea and talking philosophy like the Chinamen in Yeats's "Lapis Lazuli." Scarcely visible, they mark human presence in wild nature. We're present alright, though a far cry from the Romantics' first-person singular—"I wandered lonely as a cloud." (Plates 20 and 21)

Not mindlessness but Zen emptiness, alert, attentive, clear of clutter and

Islands, Mountains, Houses, Bridge, detail, Guan Huai, eighteenth century.
Seattle Art Museum, Eugene Fuller Memorial Collection.

anxiety, opens perception for Snyder: glowing fir-cones, new flies swarming,
fresh water chilling a tin cup. Call it mindfulness, immersion until the surrounding wildness finds a kindred ecosystem in us, in the cup of our own wild mind.
"Shall I not have intelligence with the earth?"—Snyder was reading Thoreau's
Walden in 1953. His journal for 14 August says, "Don't be a mountaineer, be
a mountain," though he hadn't yet come across Aldo Leopold's land ethic in
Sand County Almanac (1949), "Thinking Like a Mountain."

That autumn Snyder met Kenneth Rexroth, a generation older and long since
primed for California's high country by the classical Chinese and Japanese poets.
Holding salons at his home, Rexroth spotted a poet in the making. Snyder,
pursuing his way within a tradition, began studying East Asian languages at
Berkeley. He translated the Cold Mountain poems of Han-shan, a seventh-
century T'ang dynasty hermit and his Chinese alter ego, smacking also of the
American Indian Coyote trickster, scratching poems on bamboo, wood, stones,
cliffs, house walls.

> Cold Mountain has many hidden wonders,
> People who climb here are always getting scared.
> When the moon shines, water sparkles clear
> When wind blows, grass swishes and rattles.

On the bare plum, flowers of snow
On the dead stump, leaves of mist.
At the touch of rain it all turns fresh and live
At the wrong season you can't ford the creeks.

A wry turn at the outset, then a crisp straight sense of time and place, bringing that way of seeing and saying things into twentieth-century American poetry.

Soon it became plain: Snyder must follow Zen Buddhism in Japan. He did, between 1956 and 1968. "Kyoto: March," from *Riprap,* has a "tight and chill" voice.

A few light flakes of snow
Fall in the feeble sun;
Birds sing in the cold,
A warbler by the wall. The plum
Buds tight and chill soon bloom.
The moon begins first
Fourth, a faint slice west
At nightfall. Jupiter half-way
High at the end of night-
Meditation. The dove cry
Twangs like a bow.
At dawn Mt. Hiei dusted white
On top; in the clear air
Folds of all the gullied green
Hills around the town are sharp,
Breath stings.

Light flakes, weak sun, birdsong, plum buds—What *of* it? What's the point?— new moon, dove cry, dawn snow on the peak, the gullied green's clear air. But maybe *they're* the point: clean nouns, fresh verbs, beginnings, all in the day's first breath. So much depends—he'd heard William Carlos Williams in college— upon seeing and saying, upon "the world that I saw as real."

Riprap was printed in Kyoto, five hundred copies on fine paper folded and sewn Japanese-style. Snyder glosses his title word, "a cobble of stone laid on steep slick rock to make a trail for horses in the mountains." The title poem begins like a trail crew chief:

Lay down these words
Before your mind like rocks.
　　　　　placed solid, by hands
In choice of place, set
Before the body of the mind
　　　　　in space and time:
Solidity of bark, leaf, or wall
　　　　　riprap of things.

Robert Frost gets the sound of sense in an ax-helve's lines "native to the grain," Paul Celan finds his "unannullable witness" "Deep / in the time-crevasse, / by / honeycomb ice," Ted Hughes tracks a fox across "dark snow" till the poem is done. So in *Riprap*, "each rock a word / a creek-washed stone" lays down mountain trail. Snyder's economy and ecology make his way through steep terrain using native materials, fitting words. Saying "Lay down these words . . . *like* rocks," something more than likeness drives him. Physically, psychically part of nature, as we all are, he wants the same source of energy and design in his poems as he finds in the world they speak for.

At a volcano on a Japanese island, looking down to "red molten lava in a little bubbly pond" in 1967 at the new moon, Snyder married Masa Uehara, and when a son was born, they settled in the States. There all the segments of his life and work have made up a whole: rural youth, avid hiker-climber, redneck (his word) logger, seaman, and firewatcher, Amerindian anthropologist, Zen Buddhist adept, erotic lyricist, teacher, traveler, translator, Beatster in Jack Kerouac's *Dharma Bums*, social critic, environmental guru and activist, essayist, speaker, interviewee, inheritor of Hopkins, Whitman, Thoreau, Yeats, Eliot, Pound, Williams, Lawrence's *Birds, Beasts and Flowers*, after Jeffers and Rexroth the American West's leading twentieth-century poet.

But "America" and our carved-out "States" don't identify his native country for Gary Snyder. What does is "Turtle Island—the old/new name for the continent, based on many creation myths of the people who have been living here for millennia," myths of the earth sustained on the back of a great turtle. His *Turtle Island* (1974), changing the stories our culture lives by, starts with a section called "Manzanita"—that tough Pacific Coast shrubby tree with crooked slick red-brown peeling branches, glossy green leaves, early-blooming pinkish-white flowers favored by hummingbirds, and "little-apple" fruit eaten by bear, coyote, deer.

"Manzanita," published first in the Sixties enclave of Bolinas, California, opens with "Anasazi"—ancient Southwest pueblo people, ancestors to the Hopi, who migrated mysteriously, leaving grand desert dwellings, pictographs and petroglyphs, including the humpback flute-playing fertility figure Kokopelli or Kokopilau much loved by Snyder among others.

> Anasazi,
> Anasazi,
>
> tucked up in clefts in the cliffs
> growing strict fields of corn and beans
> sinking deeper and deeper in earth
> up to your hips in Gods
>   your head all turned to eagle-down

         & lightning for knees and elbows
your eyes full of pollen

        the smell of bats.
        the flavor of sandstone
        grit on the tongue.

        women
        birthing
at the foot of ladders in the dark.

trickling streams in hidden canyons
under the cold rolling desert

corn-basket   wide-eyed
        red baby
        rock lip home,

    Anasazi

The way of the words makes an ongoing whole of Anasazi dwellings cornfields religion animals mothers children and watershed desert homeland. Meanwhile "growing . . . sinking . . . birthing . . . trickling" hold a people in their own present, or maybe caught back then—which poses a challenge, if we want their ways open to us now.

It's still not quite known why the Anasazi vanished after flourishing for centuries—drought, erosion, deforestation, religious or political hostility. Today we see a far-removed people, each in their "energy-pathways that sustain life," Snyder tells us. "Hark again to those roots, to see our ancient solidarity, and then to the work of being together on Turtle Island."

Being together. On a 1950 visit to Reed College, William Carlos Williams treated three young poets as writers, not hicks. Snyder recalls one thing the elder man said, "Art is about conviviality"—"And that stuck in my mind!" Living together joyously. We can hear and see as much when Snyder performs his poems, moving from a deep voice to a tenor, varying speed, volume, tone, intensity, emphasis, with sudden enunciations, hands gesturing, fingers pointing, often with a comical shrug, facial turns and shakes and glances. Poetry jogs us together with other peoples, with our own and other species.

During the Sixties a fresh urgency moved him, just before Rachel Carson's wake-up call *Silent Spring*: "As poet I hold the most archaic values on earth. They go back to the late Paleolithic: the fertility of the soil, the magic of animals . . . the common work of the tribe. I try to hold both history and wilderness in mind, that my poems may approach the true measure of things and stand against the unbalance and ignorance of our times."

Moving his family in 1970 to a hundred acres in the Sierra Nevada foothills,

Snyder began shaping a life by those values—not trapping and hunting for his food, like John Haines in Alaska, but building a home among like-minded neighbors, treating the forest sustainably, working locally for good governmental practices. That year he spoke out: "I wish to bring a voice from the wilderness, my constituency. I wish to be a spokesman for a realm that is not usually represented either in intellectual chambers or in the chambers of government." To be an "ecological conscience."

"To speak of wilderness is to speak of wholeness," for Snyder, thinking of deep ecology. "Human beings came out of that wholeness." More so than not, the continent's early peoples lived in that spirit. Snyder also speaks for places set apart, groves and waterholes held sacred. These began as "optimal habitat," such that reckless mining, digging, drilling, logging, damming, draining, and grazing risk the wildland we call "resources." We see through that risk in growing alert to our dwelling place—ecology stems from Greek *oikos*, "house."

Turtle Island sites one poem near his new home. "By Frazier Creek Falls" finds room for dimming vistas, as in the scrolls, as well as glittering, rustling detail and now, a generation after Sourdough lookout, a heartening human presence.

> Standing up on lifted, folded rock
> looking out and down—
>
> The creek falls to a far valley.
> hills beyond that
> facing, half-forested, dry
> —clear sky
> strong wind in the
> stiff glittering needle clusters
> of the pine—their brown
> round trunk bodies
> straight, still;
> rustling trembling limbs and twigs
>
> listen.
>
> This living flowing land
> is all there is, forever
>
> We *are* it
> it sings through us—

In a breathtaking moment those "limbs and twigs / / listen" to the wind, just as that pause asks us to listen too. We *are* the land and it sings through us.

All his life Gary Snyder has pledged himself to holding both wilderness and history in mind. *Danger on Peaks* (2004) arcs back to August 1945, when he

Gary Snyder, Mount St. Helens, 1945.
Photograph taken by Gary Snyder, August 1945. Copyright 2004 by Gary Snyder
from his work *Danger on Peaks*. Reprinted by permission of Shoemaker & Hoard.

climbed Mount St. Helens in southern Washington. The next day came news
of Hiroshima, and a scientist saying "nothing will grow there again for seventy
years." "I swore a vow to myself, something like, 'By the purity and beauty
and permanence of Mount St. Helens, I will fight against this cruel destructive
power and those who would seek to use it, for all my life'." The fifteen-year-
old took a photo, looking across the calm reflective expanse of Spirit Lake
toward a mountain that would later erupt with five hundred times the force of
the atomic bomb.

"Just imagine"
Can Poetry Save the Earth?

"We must go back and find a trail on the ground," says William Stafford in "Watching the Jet Planes Dive." Blazing that trail toward environmental sanity is the English peasant John Clare, least known of the Romantics, who told his children, "I usd to drop down under a bush & scribble the fresh thoughts on the crown of my hat as I found nature then." Our own children will depend on that alertness, that freshness.

It's said that kids today suffer from "nature-deficit disorder," exploring the Web not the woods. But listen to a Seattle preschool's Sunlight Room, writing to the city council: "We hate pollution. Stop it! You should ride bikes, or walk, or go on roller skates or rollerblades. You should do recycling. . . . Send this to another people, and then they read it, and then they give it to another person, and they give it around to the whole wide city, and Africa. Pass it until it comes in the whole wide world." (plate 22)

Bringing news to the world has been a task of poets. Bob Hass, poet laureate in 1995, set out bringing poetry close to the American grain. A kind of Johnny Appleseed, he alerted folks across the country, schoolchildren as well as fraternal groups, to our indispensable environment, and founded the River of Words project, inviting children to write poems on the watershed they dwell in. El'Jay Johnson, age eight, from River Terrace Elementary School in Maryland, whose teacher was Patricia Ann Goodnight, won the Watershed Prize for his poem on the Anacostia River, where sewage from the houses of Congress flows through Washington's black neighborhoods.

> Just imagine
> Waking up one day,
> Looking out your window starting to say . . .
> No dead birds because of
> No dead trees because of
> No dead people because of

El'Jay hits on poetry's primal impulse: "Just imagine." So did William Carlos Williams: "imagine the New World that rises to our windows" every day.

Of course environmental sanity requires more than imagination. It needs fieldwork, science, journalism, activism, and policy to make life livable for us all. "Looking out your window," though, reacting to a poem's pulse and images, may strike deeper than policy pronouncements. No wonder Joe Knight's "Observations from a Penitentiary Window" reaches out to "a bright waterfall running / down the leaf-green hills," and "bumblebees / loping above the wild roses / along the shoreline."

Few people spend their days among leaf-green hills, but in cities, where other sorts of news reach us. Urban environment, before it was called that, abounds in poems like El'Jay Johnson's: Blake on London's "blackening street," Coleridge pent up "In the great city," Hopkins deploring Oxford's "base and brackish skirt," Yeats fleeing "pavements gray," Eliot in "rats' alley," Millay rhythmically "Sick of the city, wanting the sea," Neruda's "streets frightful as gullies," Lowell gaping at Boston's "giant finned cars," Levertov's "babel of destructive construction."

Just as often, despite any bitterness, poems of urban nature turn up joyous, bolstering sights: Whitman's "still excitement" leaning over "swift current" on the Brooklyn ferry, Williams's young sycamore thrusting "between the wet / pavement and the gutter," Neruda greeting the Inca city of Machu Picchu—"Mother of stone, spume of condors," Elizabeth Bishop charmed by Santarém, an Amazonian town whose "street was deep in dark-gold river sand," May Swenson welcoming snow to Manhattan, where

> Streets will be   fields
>   cars be   fumbling sheep . . .
> By morning we'll be   children
>   feeding on manna
>   a new loaf on every doorsill,

Lowell's "mother skunk" parading Main Street, Shirley Kaufman's autumn crocus exploding from Jerusalem soil—"Look! They say for a moment," Kinnell's pushcart market where a "crate of lemons discharges light like a battery," Walcott's Paris "along the Seine / an oceanic surging in the trees," Allen Ginsberg's sunflower "poised against . . . smut and smog and smoke."

Poised—that's the point. Bitter or joyous, honest poetry will poise nature along with society, wilderness with civilization, nonhuman with human. Separate them, and damage in both realms becomes likelier.

How then to find a way of living on earth? Our animal bodies are "of the earth, earthy," as the Good Book says, yet in experiencing nonhuman nature we don't truly know it. We sense but can't really grasp stone or tree, let alone stream or bird. Still, at times, the saving grace of attentiveness, and the way poems hold things still for a moment, make us mindful of fragile resilient life.

Poems have been doing this since well before environmentalism became a watchword. In fact, the tradition enables what came later. To muse over our place on this planet, we can always recall the Book of Job's rolling cadences for "rain . . . on the wilderness, wherein there is no man." In their heads, today's poets hear Coleridge and Clare, Whitman and Dickinson, Frost and Williams, Jeffers and Bishop, Stafford and Levertov, and on through Gary Snyder. These presences back up more recent figures, such as Scott Momaday and Wendell Berry, Mary Oliver and William Heyen, Pattiann Rogers and Alice Walker, Les Murray, Homero Aridjis, and Don McKay, Simon Ortiz and Joseph Bruchac, Linda Hogan, James Welch, Bob Hass, Alison Deming, John Daniel, among many others.

Like many of us, contemporary poets want to survive in touch with things without harming them. Scott Momaday, of Kiowa origin, touches the nerve and verve of earth in his verbs: "the earth glitters . . . the sky glistens with rain . . . eagles / hie and / hover" within an indigenous Creation poem he calls "New World," reclaiming that word "new" from Columbus. In midnight fear of the Vietnam war, Wendell Berry has to "go and lie down where the wood drake / rests in his beauty on the water, and the great heron feeds. / I come into the peace of wild things."

Emily Dickinson told a friend, "Earth's most graphic transaction is placed within a syllable." Earth's transaction, she said, and it's ours too, happening within a human syllable. We can have it both ways, like the Yokuts shaman's prayer: "My words are tied in one / With the great mountains . . ."

Can poetry save the earth? For sure, person by person, our earthly challenge hangs on the sense and spirit that poems can awaken.

Sources

Introduction

Alfred Kroeber, *The Yokuts Language of South Central California* (Berkeley, Calif., 1907).

Kroeber, *Handbook of the Indians of California* (Berkeley, Calif., 1925).

Bruce Chatwin, *The Songlines* (London, 1987).

Gilgamesh: A New Rendering in English Verse, trans. David Ferry (New York, 1992).

The Bible, King James Version.

The Hebrew Bible.

William Carlos Williams, *Selected Poems* (New York, 1968, 1976).

Williams, *Paterson* (New York, 1963).

Ezra Pound, *ABC of Reading* (London, 1934).

Max Oelschlager, *The Idea of Wilderness: From Prehistory to the Age of Ecology* (New Haven, 1991).

Gary Snyder, *The Practice of the Wild* (San Francisco, 1990; Washington, D.C., 2004).

William Cronon, ed., *Uncommon Ground: Toward Reinventing Nature* (New York, 1995).

John Winthrop, "Conclusions for the Plantation in New England" (1629; Boston, 1896).

Daniel Boone, in John Filson, *The Discovery and Settlement of Kentucke* (1784; Ann Arbor, 1966).

William Cronon, George Miles, Jay Gitlin, eds., *Under an Open Sky: Rethinking America's Western Past* (New York, 1992).

Charles C. Mann, *1491: New Revelations of the Americas Before Columbus* (New York, 2005).

Ben Brantley, "150th Anniversary: 1851–2001; Fool or Prophet? No, Just a Critic," *New York Times,* November 15, 2001.

L. J. Campbell, *A Concise School History of the United States Based on Seavey's Goodrich's History* (Boston, 1871).

Theodore Taylor Johnson, *Sights in the Gold Regions* (1849; New York, 1935).

John G. Neihardt, *Black Elk Speaks: Being the Life Story of a Holy Man of the Oglala Sioux* (1932; Lincoln, Neb., 1961).

George Perkins Marsh, *Man and Nature: Or, Physical Geography as Modified by Human Action*, ed. David Lowenthal (1864; Cambridge, Mass., 1965).

Sharon Begley, "Cry of the Wild," and Scott Johnson, "Gorilla Warfare," *Newsweek*, August 6, 2007.

Natalie Angier, "Slow Is Beautiful," "Though Sturdy Survivors, Turtles Prove to Be Ill Equipped for Human Threat," *New York Times*, December 12, 2006.

Linda Lear, *Rachel Carson: Witness to Nature* (New York, 1997).

"Where It All Began," *Audubon*, December 2004.

Thomas Cole, "Essay on American Scenery," *American Monthly* 1 (January 1836).

Rachel Carson, *The Sense of Wonder* (New York, 1965).

The Essential Haiku: Versions of Bashō, Buson, and Issa, ed. Robert Hass (Hopewell, N.J., 1994).

Singing Ecology unto the Lord

The Bible, King James Version.

The Hebrew Bible.

The Book of Common Prayer.

Francis Bacon, "The Great Instauration: Preface" and "Aphorisms," in *Selected Writings Of Francis Bacon*, ed. Hugh G. Dick (New York, 1955).

William Bradford, from *Of Plymouth Plantation*, in *The American Tradition in Literature*, 10th ed., ed. George Perkins and Barbara Perkins (New York, 2002).

Henry David Thoreau, "Walking," in *The Norton Book of Nature Writing*, 2nd ed., ed. Robert Finch and John Elder (New York, 2002).

George Perkins Marsh, *Man and Nature: Or, Physical Geography as Modified by Human Action*, ed. David Lowenthal (1864; Cambridge, Mass., 1965).

Wallace Stegner, "Wilderness Letter," in *The Norton Book of Nature Writing.*

Ralph Waldo Emerson, "The Poet," in *The American Tradition in Literature.*

F. O. Matthiessen, *American Renaissance; Art and Expression in the Age of Emerson and Whitman* (New York, 1941).

John Hollander, "Adam's Task," in *Spectral Emanations: New and Selected Poems* (New York, 1978).

Gershom Scholem, *Major Trends in Jewish Mysticism* (1941; New York, 1961).

Denise Levertov, *The Life Around Us: Selected Poems on Nature* (New York, 1997).

George Oppen, *This in Which* (New York, 1965).

Anon Was an Environmentalist

John Frederick Nims, *Western Wind: An Introduction to Poetry* (New York, 1974).

Virginia Woolf, *A Room of One's Own* (London, 1929).

Igor Stravinsky, *Cantata* (1952): On Anonymous Fifteenth- and Sixteenth-Century English Lyrics.

Blake, the Wordsworths, and the Dung

William Blake, *Poetry and Prose of William Blake*, ed. Geoffrey Keynes (London, 1935).

William Wordsworth, *The Norton Anthology of English Literature*, 7th ed., vol. 1, ed. M. H. Abrams (New York, 1999).

Dorothy Wordsworth, *Journals*, ed. Helen Darbishire (New York, 1958).

Dorothy Wordsworth's Illustrated Lakeland Journals, intro. Rachel Trickett (London, 1987).

Jonathan Bate, *Romantic Ecology: Wordsworth and the Environmental Tradition* (London, 1991).

Harriet Ritvo, "Fighting for Thirlmere—The Roots of Environmentalism," *Science* 300 (June 6, 2003), 5625.

Thomas Cole, "Essay on American Scenery," *American Monthly* 1 (January 1836).

Samuel Taylor Coleridge, *The Portable Coleridge*, ed. I. A. Richards (New York, 1950).

Coleridge Imagining

Samuel Taylor Coleridge, *The Portable Coleridge*, ed. I. A. Richards (New York, 1950).

The Poems of Samuel Taylor Coleridge, Including Poems and Versions of Poems . . ., ed. Ernest Hartley Coleridge (London, 1912).

Dorothy Wordsworth, *Journals*, ed. Helen Darbishire (New York, 1958).

Humphry House, *Coleridge* (London, 1953).

John Keats Eking It Out

John Keats, *The Complete Poems of John Keats* (New York, 1994).

Keats, *The Odes of Keats and Their Earliest Known Manuscripts*, ed. Robert Gittings (Kent, Ohio, 1970).

Keats, *The Letters of John Keats, 1814–1821*, ed. Hyder Edward Rollins (Cambridge, Mass., 1958).

Keats, "Winander Lake and Mountains, and Ambleside Falls," *Western Messenger*, Louisville, Ky., June 1836, pp. 772–777, ed. James Freeman Clarke.

William Gilpin, *Observations Relative Chiefly to Picturesque Beauty, Made in the Year 1772, on Several Parts of England; Particularly the Mountains, and Lakes of Cumberland, and Westmoreland* (London, 1786).

Walter Jackson Bate, *John Keats* (Cambridge, Mass., 1963).

Michael Rosenthal, *Constable: The Painter and His Landscape* (New Haven, 1983).

John Clare at Home in Helpston

"I Am": The Selected Poetry of John Clare, ed. Jonathan Bate (New York, 2003).

The Prose of John Clare, ed. J. W. and Anne Tibble (London, 1951).

Sketches in the Life of John Clare by Himself, ed. Edmund Blunden (London, 1931).

The Essential Clare, ed. Carolyn Kizer (Hopewell, N.J., 1992).

William Howard, *John Clare* (Boston, 1981).

Jonathan Bate, *John Clare* (New York, 2003).

John Barrell, *The Idea of Landscape and the Sense of Place, 1730–1840: An Approach to the Poetry of John Clare* (London, 1972).

Seamus Heaney, "John Clare's Prog," in Heaney, *Finders Keepers: Selected Prose, 1971–2001* (London, 2002).

Jonathan Bate, *The Song of the Earth* (London, 2000).

James Fenton, "John Clare's Genius" and "Getting Clare Clear," *New York Review*, September 23 and October 7, 2004.

Franco Moretti, *Graphs, Maps, Trees: Abstract Models for a Literary History* (London, 2005).

Adamic Walt Whitman

Walt Whitman, *Leaves of Grass*, ed. Sculley Bradley and Harold W. Blodgett (New York, 1973).

Whitman, *Specimen Days in America* (1882; New York, 1935).

F. O. Matthiessen, *American Renaissance; Art and Expression in the Age of Emerson and Whitman* (New York, 1941).

Justin Kaplan, *Walt Whitman: A Life* (New York, 1980).

Ralph Waldo Emerson, *Selected Essays* (New York, 1982).

The Norton Book of Nature Writing, 2nd ed., ed. Robert Finch and John Elder (New York, 2002).

John Muir, *The Yosemite*, with photographs by Galen Rowell (1912; San Francisco, 1989).

Lawrence Buell, *The Environmental Imagination: Thoreau, Nature Writing, and the Formation of American Culture* (Cambridge, Mass., 1995).

Gustav Janouch, *Conversations with Kafka*, trans. Goronwy Rees (1953; New York, 1971).

Parodies on Walt Whitman, ed. Henry S. Saunders (New York, 1923).

Syllables of Emily Dickinson

The Poems of Emily Dickinson, ed. Thomas H. Johnson, 3 vols. (Cambridge, Mass., 1955).

The Letters of Emily Dickinson, ed. Thomas H. Johnson (Cambridge, Mass., 1958).

Open Me Carefully: Emily Dickinson's Intimate Letters to Susan Huntington (Ashfield, Mass., 1998).

The Years and Hours of Emily Dickinson, ed. Jay Leyda, 2 vols. (New Haven, 1960).

Richard B. Sewall, *The Life of Emily Dickinson*, 2 vols. (New York, 1974).

James H. McIntosh, *Nimble Believing: Dickinson and the Unknown* (Ann Arbor, Mich., 2000).

David Porter, *Dickinson: The Modern Idiom* (Cambridge, Mass., 1981).

Cynthia Griffin Wolff, *Emily Dickinson* (New York, 1986).

Christopher Benfey, "The Mystery of Emily Dickinson," *New York Review*, April 8, 1999.

Roger Shattuck, "Emily Dickinson's Banquet of Abstemiousness," *New York Review*, June 20, 1996.

Mary Elizabeth Kromer Bernhard, "Lost and Found: Emily Dickinson's Unknown Daguerreotypist," *New England Quarterly* 72, no. 4 (December 1999), 594–601.

Nature Shadowing Thomas Hardy

Collected Poems of Thomas Hardy (London, 1962).
Thomas Hardy, *The Return of the Native*, *Mayor of Casterbridge*, *The Woodlanders*.
Florence Hardy, *The Life of Thomas Hardy*, 2 vols. (London, 1930).

The World Charged by Gerard Manley Hopkins

Gerard Manley Hopkins, *Poems and Prose* (New York, 1995).
The Journals and Papers of Gerard Manley Hopkins, ed. Humphry House, completed by Graham Storey (London, 1959).
Gerard Manley Hopkins, By the Kenyon Critics (New York, 1944).
Robert Bernard Martin, *Gerard Manley Hopkins: A Very Private Life* (New York, 1991).
Robert Lowell, "Hopkins's Sanctity" (1944), in Lowell, *Collected Prose*, ed. Robert Giroux (New York, 1987).
Robert Pinsky and Maggie Dietz, eds., *An Invitation to Poetry: A New Favorite Poem Project Anthology* (New York, 2004).

Nature Versus History in W. B. Yeats

W. B. Yeats, *Selected Poems and Three Plays of W. B. Yeats*, ed. M. R. Rosenthal, 3rd ed. (New York, 1986).
Yeats, *Mythologies* (New York, 1959).
Yeats, ed., *Irish Fairy and Folk Tales* (1888; New York, 1918).
Joseph Hone, *W. B. Yeats* (London, 1942).
David Parker, "Yeats's Lapis Lazuli," *Notes and Queries* 24, no. 15 (October 1977), 452–454.
Donald D. Stone, "Sailing to Cathay," *Ex/Change* 2 (2005), Centre for Cross-Cultural Studies, City University of Hong Kong.

Robert Frost

Robert Frost, *The Poetry of Robert Frost*, ed. Edward Connery Latham (New York, 1979).
Frost, *Collected Poems, Prose, and Plays* (New York, 1995).
Frost, *Selected Letters*, ed. Lawrance Thompson (New York, 1964).
"Robert Frost and Helen Thomas: Five Revealing Letters," ed. William R. Evans, *Dartmouth Library Bulletin*, November 1989.
Lawrance Thompson, *Robert Frost: The Early Years, 1874–1915* (New York, 1966).
Thompson, *Robert Frost: The Years of Triumph, 1915–1938* (New York, 1970).
Thompson, *Robert Frost: The Later Years, 1938–1963* (New York, 1976).
Richard Poirier, *Robert Frost: The Work of Knowing* (New York, 1977).
William Stafford, "The Terror in Robert Frost," *New York Times Magazine*, August 18, 1974.
Marie Borroff, "Sound Symbolism as Drama in the Poetry of Robert Frost," *PMLA* 107, no. 1 (January 1992), 131–144.

England Thanks to Edward Thomas, 1914–1917

The Collected Poems of Edward Thomas, ed. R. George Thomas (Oxford, 1978).

The Poems of Edward Thomas, ed. Peter Sacks (New York, 2003).

Edward Thomas, *The South Country* (London, 1909).

Thomas, *Keats* (London, 1916).

Thomas, *In Pursuit of Spring* (London, 1914).

A Language Not to Be Betrayed: Selected Prose of Edward Thomas, ed. Edna Longley (Manchester, England, 1981).

Edward Thomas, *Selected Letters*, ed. R. George Thomas (Oxford, 1995).

Thomas, *Letters to Helen*, ed. R. George Thomas (Manchester, England, 2000).

Elected Friends: Robert Frost and Edward Thomas to One Another, ed. Matthew Spencer (New York, 2004).

Robert Frost, "War Thoughts at Home" (1918), *Virginia Quarterly Review* (Fall 2006), with Robert Stilling, "Between Friends: Rediscovering the War Thoughts of Robert Frost."

R. George Thomas, *Edward Thomas: A Portrait* (Oxford, 1985).

Andrew Motion, *The Poetry of Edward Thomas* (London, 1980).

Elected Friends: Poems for and About Edward Thomas, ed. Anne Harvey (London, 1991).

Jon Silkin, "Introduction," *The Penguin Book of First World War Poetry*, 2nd ed. (New York, 1981).

Clare: The Critical Heritage, ed. Mark Storey (London, 1973).

Isaac Rosenberg, "Returning, We Hear the Larks," in *The Collected Works of Isaac Rosenberg*, ed. Ian Parsons (New York, 1979).

Wings of Wallace Stevens

Wallace Stevens, *Collected Poems* (New York, 1954).

Stevens, *The Necessary Angel: Essays on Reality and the Imagination* (New York, 1951).

Stevens, *Opus Posthumous*, ed. Samuel French Morse (New York, 1957).

Joan Richardson, *Wallace Stevens: The Early Years, 1879–1923* (New York, 1986).

Richardson, *Wallace Stevens: The Later Years, 1923–1955* (New York, 1988).

William Carlos Williams

William Carlos Williams, *The Collected Earlier Poems* (New York, 1951).

Williams, *Collected Later Poems* (1950; New York, 1963).

Selected Essays of William Carlos Williams (New York, 1954).

The Selected Letters of William Carlos Williams (New York, 1957).

The Autobiography of William Carlos Williams (New York, 1951).

Williams, *Spring and All* (Paris, 1923).

Williams, *In the American Grain* (New York, 1925).

Williams, *Paterson* (New York, 1963).

Williams, *I Wanted To Write a Poem*, ed. Edith Heal (Boston, 1958).

Writers at Work: The Paris Review Interviews, 3rd series, ed. George Plimpton (New York, 1976).

Paul Mariani, *William Carlos Williams* (Chicago, 1975).

Denise Levertov, "On Williams' Triadic Line," in Levertov, *New and Selected Essays* (New York, 1992).

The Journal of Christopher Columbus (During His First Voyage, 1492–93) . . . , trans. Clements R. Markham (London, 1893).

D. H. Lawrence in Taormina and Taos

D. H. Lawrence, *Birds, Beasts and Flowers* (New York, 1923).

Lawrence, *Mornings in Mexico* (New York, 1927).

Lawrence, *Studies in Classic American Literature* (New York, 1923).

Peter Matthiessen, *The Snow Leopard* (1936; New York, 1978, 1996).

Ocean, Rock, Hawk, and Robinson Jeffers

The Selected Poetry of Robinson Jeffers, ed. Tim Hunt (Stanford, Calif., 2001).

James Karman, *Robinson Jeffers: Poet of California* (Brownsville, Ore., 1995).

Robinson Jeffers, *Rock and Hawk: A Selection of Shorter Poems*, ed. Robert Hass (New York, 1987).

Donnan Jeffers, "The Stones of Tor House" (Carmel, Calif., 1985).

James Karman, ed., *Critical Essays on Robinson Jeffers* (Boston, 1990).

"Coastal Clash," KQED-TV (PBS), August 3, 2006.

Marianne Moore's Fantastic Reverence

The Complete Poems of Marianne Moore (1967; New York, 1982).

The Complete Prose of Marianne Moore, ed. Patricia C. Willis (New York, 1986).

Charles Molesworth, *Marianne Moore: A Literary Life* (New York, 1990).

Bonnie Costello, *Shifting Ground: Reinventing Landscape in Modern American Poetry* (Cambridge, Mass., 2003).

Patricia Willis, *Marianne Moore: Vision into Verse* (Philadelphia, 1987).

John Muir, "An Ascent of Mount Rainier," in *Steep Trails*, ed. William Frederick Badè (Boston, 1918), 261–270.

To Steepletop and Ragged Island with Edna St. Vincent Millay

Edna St. Vincent Millay, *Collected Poems*, ed. Norma Millay (New York, 1956).

Letters of Edna St. Vincent Millay, ed. Alan Ross Macdougall (Camden, Me., 1952).

Nancy Milford, *Savage Beauty: The Life of Edna St. Vincent Millay* (New York, 2001).

Daniel Mark Epstein, *What Lips My Lips Have Kissed: The Loves and Love Poems of Edna St. Vincent Millay* (New York, 2001).

Vincent Sheean, *The Indigo Bunting: A Memoir of Edna St. Vincent Millay* (New York, 1951).

Arnold T. Schwab, "Jeffers and Millay: A Literary Friendship," *Robinson Jeffers Newsletter* 59 (September 1981), 17–33.

Pablo Neruda at Machu Picchu

Pablo Neruda, *Obras completas,* 3rd ed., 2 vols. (Buenos Aires, 1967).

Neruda, *Obras completas,* 4th ed., 3 vols. (Buenos Aires, 1973).

Kenneth Rexroth, *Thirty Spanish Poems of Love and Exile* (San Francisco, 1956).

John Felstiner, *Translating Neruda: The Way to Macchu Picchu* (Stanford, Calif., 1980).

Stanley Kunitz—His Nettled Field, His Dune Garden

Stanley Kunitz, *The Collected Poems* (New York, 2000).

Stanley Kunitz, Genine Lentine, Marnie Crawford Samuelson, *The Wild Braid: A Poet Reflects on a Century in the Garden* (New York, 2005).

Kunitz, *A Kind of Order, A Kind of Folly: Essays and Conversations* (Boston, 1975).

Stanley Moss, ed., *Interviews and Encounters with Stanley Kunitz* (Riverdale-on-Hudson, N.Y., 1993).

Kunitz, Interview with Chris Busa, *Paris Review* 83 (1982).

Christopher Busa, Introduction, *A Celebration for Stanley Kunitz: On His Eightieth Birthday* (Riverdale-on-Hudson, N.Y., 1986).

Marie Hénault, *Stanley Kunitz* (Boston, 1980).

Gregory Orr, *Stanley Kunitz: An Introduction to the Poetry* (New York, 1985).

Dana Goodyear, "The Gardener," *New Yorker,* September 1, 2003.

Things Whole and Holy for Kenneth Rexroth

Kenneth Rexroth, *The Collected Shorter Poems* (New York, 1966).

Rexroth, *Selected Poems,* ed. Bradford Morrow (New York, 1984).

Rexroth, *In Defense of the Earth* (New York, 1956).

Rexroth, "Tu Fu, *Poems,*" in *Classics Revisited* (Chicago, 1968).

The Rexroth Reader, ed. Eric Mottram (London, 1972).

Rexroth, *Thirty Spanish Poems of Love and Exile* (San Francisco, 1956).

Linda Hamalian, *A Life of Kenneth Rexroth* (New York, 1991).

Florence Ayscough, *Tu Fu: The Autobiography of a Chinese Poet,* A.D. *712–759* (London, 1929).

Ayscough, *Travels of a Chinese Poet: Tu Fu, Guest of Rivers and Lakes,* A.D. *759–770* (New York, 1934).

Ling Chung Odell, *Kenneth Rexroth and Chinese Poetry: Translation, Imitation, and Adaptation,* Ph.D. thesis (University of Wisconsin, Madison, 1972).

Sam Hamill, "The Poetry of Kenneth Rexroth," *Jacket* 23 (August 2003).

Steve Bradbury, "Reading Rexroth Rewriting Tu Fu in the 'Permanent War,'" *Jacket* 20 (August 2003).

Theodore Roethke from Greenhouse to Seascape

Theodore Roethke, *Words for the Wind* (New York, 1958).

Roethke, *The Far Field* (New York, 1964).

Ralph J. Mills, *Theodore Roethke* (Minneapolis, 1963).

Don Bogen, *Theodore Roethke and the Writing Process* (Athens, Ohio, 1991).
On Poetry and Craft: Selected Prose of Theodore Roethke, ed. Carolyn Kizer
(Port Townsend, Wash., 2001).
Lars Nordström, *Theodore Roethke, William Stafford, and Gary Snyder:
The Ecological Metaphor as Transformed Regionalism* (Uppsala, Sweden, 1989).

George Oppen's Psalm of Attentiveness

George Oppen, *This in Which* (New York, 1965).
Oppen, *The Collected Poems of George Oppen, 1929–1975* (New York, 1975).
Oppen, *New Collected Poems*, ed. Michael Davidson, pref. Eliot Weinberger
(New York, 2002).
The Selected Letters of George Oppen, ed. Rachel Blau DuPlessis (Durham, N.C.,
1990).
Robert Hass, *Praise* (New York, 1979).
Jerome Rothenberg, ed., *Shaking the Pumpkin: Traditional Poetry of the Indian
North Americas* (New York, 1972).
"Poetry and the Primitive," in *The Gary Snyder Reader: Prose, Poetry, and
Translations, 1952–1998* (Washington, D.C., 1999).

Elizabeth Bishop Traveling

Elizabeth Bishop, *Questions of Travel* (New York, 1965).
Bishop, *North and South* (Boston, 1946).
Bishop, *Geography III* (New York, 1977).
Bishop, *The Complete Poems, 1927–1979* (New York, 1983).
Elizabeth Bishop: The Collected Prose, ed. Robert Giroux (New York, 1984).
One Art: Letters, ed. Robert Giroux (New York, 1994).
Guy Rotella, *Reading and Writing Nature* (Boston, 1991).

Something Alive in May Swenson

May Swenson, *Another Animal: Poems*, in *Poets of Today*, ed. John Hall Wheelock
(New York, 1954).
Swenson, *Nature: Poems Old and New* (Boston, 1994).
Swenson, *May Out West* (Logan, Utah, 1996).
Swenson, *Made with Words*, ed. Gardner McFall (Ann Arbor, Mich., 1998).
R. R. Knudson and Suzanne Bigelow, *May Swenson: A Poet's Life in Photos*
(Logan, Utah, 1996).

Earth Home to William Stafford

William Stafford, *West of Your City* (Los Gatos, Calif., 1960).
Stafford, *Traveling Through the Dark* (New York, 1962).
Stafford, *The Rescued Year* (New York, 1966).
Kim Stafford, *Early Morning: Remembering My Father* (2003).

America's Angst and Robert Lowell's

Robert Lowell, *Collected Poems*, ed. Frank Bidart and David Gewanter (New York, 2003).

Lowell, *Collected Prose*, ed. Robert Giroux (New York, 1987).

William Carlos Williams, "These," in *Collected Earlier Poems* (New York, 1938).

Sarah Payne Stuart, *My First Cousin Once Removed: Money, Madness, and the Family of Robert Lowell* (New York, 1998).

Steven Gould Axelrod, *Robert Lowell: Life and Art* (Princeton, N.J., 1978).

Ian Hamilton, *Robert Lowell: A Biography* (New York, 1982).

Life Illumined Around Denise Levertov

Denise Levertov, *Collected Earlier Poems, 1940–1960* (New York, 1979).

Levertov, *Poems, 1960–1967* (New York, 1983).

Levertov, *Poems, 1968–1972* (New York, 1987).

Levertov, *The Life Around Us: Selected Poems on Nature* (New York, 1997).

Levertov, *The Poet in the World* (New York, 1973).

Levertov, *Light Up the Cave* (New York, 1981).

Levertov, *New and Selected Essays* (New York, 1992).

Levertov, *Tesserae* (New York, 1995).

The Letters of Denise Levertov and William Carlos Williams, ed. Christopher MacGowan (New York, 1998).

Shirley Kaufman's Roots in the Air

Shirley Kaufman, *The Floor Keeps Turning* (Pittsburgh, 1970).

Kaufman, *Gold Country* (Pittsburgh, 1973).

Kaufman, *Looking at Henry Moore's Elephant Skull Etchings in Jerusalem During the War* (Greensboro, N.C., 1979).

Kaufman, *From One Life to Another* (Pittsburgh, 1979).

Kaufman, *Claims* (New York, 1984).

Kaufman, *Rivers of Salt* (Port Townsend, Wash., 1993).

Kaufman, *Roots in the Air: New and Selected Poems* (Port Townsend, Wash., 1996).

Kaufman, *Threshold* (Port Townsend, Wash., 2003).

Kaufman, "Roots in the Air," *Judaism* 186 (Spring 1998), 161–168.

Kaufman, "Sky-Space and Stone," *Mānoa* 9, no. 1 (1997), 109–112.

Translations: Abba Kovner, Amir Gilboa, Judith Herzberg, Meir Wieseltier, *The Defiant Muse: Hebrew Feminist Poems from Antiquity to the Present* (New York, 1999).

News of the North from John Haines

John Haines, *At the End of This Summer: Poems, 1948–1954* (Port Townsend, Wash., 1997).

Haines, *News from the Glacier: Selected Poems, 1960–1980* (Middletown, Conn., 1982).

Haines, *The Owl in the Mask of the Dreamer* (St. Paul, Minn., 1993).

Haines, *For the Century's End: Poems, 1990–1999* (Seattle, 2001).

Haines, *Of Your Passage, O Summer: Uncollected Poems from the 1960s* (Boise, Id., 2004).

Haines, *Fables and Distances: New and Selected Essays* (St. Paul, Minn., 1996).

Haines, *The Stars, the Snow, the Fire: Twenty-Five Years in the Northern Wilderness* (St. Paul, Minn., 1989).

Haines, *Living Off the Country* (Ann Arbor, Mich., 1982).

"Certain Things Intruding on the Wilderness: A Three-Cornered Conversation with John Haines," interview, Wooster College, 1998, *Artful Dodge* 1998 (online).

The Wilderness of Vision: On the Poetry of John Haines, ed. Kevin Bezner and Kevin Walzer (Brownsville, Ore., 1996).

Trust in Maxine Kumin

Maxine Kumin, *Selected Poems, 1960–1990* (New York, 1997).

Kumin, *Our Ground Time Here Will Be Brief* (New York, 1982).

Kumin, *Looking for Luck* (New York, 1992).

Kumin, *To Make a Prairie: Essays on Poets, Poetry, and Country Living* (Ann Arbor, Mich., 1979).

Kumin, *Women, Animals, and Vegetables: Essays and Stories* (New York, 1994).

Kumin, *In Deep: Country Essays* (New York, 1997).

Hilde Raz, "Maxine Kumin's Sense of Place in Nature," in *Telling the Barn Swallow: Poets on the Poetry of Maxine Kumin,* ed. Emily Grosholz (Hanover, N.H., 1997).

Alicia Ostriker, "Making the Connection: The Nature Poetry of Maxine Kumin," in *Telling the Barn Swallow.*

Steven Ratiner, "Maxine Kumin: New Life in the Barn" (interview), in *Conversations with Contemporary Poets* (Amherst, Mass., 2002).

Wind in the Reeds in the Voice of A. R. Ammons

A. R. Ammons, *Collected Poems, 1951–1971* (New York, 1972).

Ammons, *The Really Short Poems of A. R. Ammons* (New York, 1990).

Ammons, *Set in Motion: Essays, Interviews, and Dialogues,* ed. Sofia Burr (Ann Arbor, Mich., 1996).

Ammons, Interview, *Poets in Person,* Conversation with Alice Fulton and Joseph Parisi (Chicago, 1991).

Alan Holder, *A. R. Ammons* (Boston, 1978).

Harold Bloom, ed., *A. R. Ammons: Modern Critical Views* (New York, 1986).

Robert Kirschten, *Critical Essays on A. R. Ammons* (New York, 1997).

W. S. Merwin's Motion of Mind

W. S. Merwin, *Migrations: New and Selected Poems* (Port Townsend, Wash., 2005).

Merwin, *Selected Translations, 1948–1968* (New York, 1975).

Merwin, foreword to Fred Bodsworth, *The Last of the Curlews* (1955; Washington, D.C., 1995).

Edward J. Brunner, *Poetry as Labor and Privilege: The Writings of W. S. Merwin* (Urbana, Ill., 1991).

Cheri Davis, *W. S. Merwin* (Boston, 1981).

Jane Frazier, *From Origin to Ecology: Nature and the Poetry of W. S. Merwin* (Cranbury, N.J., 1999).

Elizabeth Lund, "A Master Gardener of Verse," *Christian Science Monitor,* April 24, 2003.

Dinitia Smith, "A Poet of Their Own," *New York Times,* February 19, 1995.

Zest of Galway Kinnell

Galway Kinnell, *The Avenue Bearing the Initial of Christ into the New World: Poems, 1946–1964* [*What a Kingdom It Was, Flower Herding on Mount Monadnock*] (Boston, 1974).

Kinnell, *Body Rags* (Boston, 1968).

Kinnell, *Mortal Acts, Mortal Words* (Boston, 1980).

Kinnell, *Imperfect Thirst* (Boston, 1994).

Kinnell, *When One Has Lived a Long Time Alone* (New York, 1990).

Kinnell, *Walking Down the Stairs: Selections from Interviews* (Ann Arbor, Mich., 1978).

"An Interview with Galway Kinnell," by Daniela Gioseffi, *Hayden's Ferry Review,* Fall–Winter 2002–03 (poetsusa.com).

Kinnell, "Poetry, Personality, and Death" (1971), in *A Field Guide to Contemporary Poetry and Poetics,* ed. Stuart Friebert and David Young (New York, 1980).

Donald Hall and Jane Kenyon at Eagle Pond Farm

Donald Hall, *Old and New Poems* (New York, 1990).

Hall, *Without* (Boston, 1998).

Hall, *The Painted Bed* (Boston, 2002).

Hall, *The Farm Summer 1942* (New York, 1994).

Hall, *Ox-Cart Man,* illustrated by Barbara Cooney (New York, 1979).

Hall, *String Too Short to Be Saved: Recollections of Summers on a New England Farm* (1961; Boston, 1979).

Hall, *Seasons at Eagle Pond* (New York, 1987).

Hall, *Here at Eagle Pond* (New York, 1990).

Hall, *Life Work* (Boston, 1993).

Hall, *The Pleasures of Poetry* (New York, 1971).

Hall, *Remembering Poets—Reminiscences and Opinions: Dylan Thomas, Robert Frost, T. S. Eliot, Ezra Pound* (1978; New York, 1992).

Hall, *To Keep Moving: Essays, 1959–1969* (Geneva, N.Y., 1980).

Jane Kenyon, *Otherwise: New and Selected Poems* (New York, 1996).

Ted Hughes Capturing Pike

Ted Hughes, *The Hawk in the Rain* (London, 1957).

Hughes, *Lupercal* (London, 1960).

Hughes, *Crow* (New York, 1971).

Hughes, *Moortown Diary* (London, 1979).

Hughes, *Remains of Elmet*, photographs by Fay Godwin (New York, 1979).

Hughes, *Three Books: Remains of Elmet, Cave Birds, River* (London, 1993).

Hughes, *Poetry Is* (New York, 1967).

Hughes, 1996 interview by Eilat Negev, *Daily Telegraph* (London), November 2, 1998.

Adrienne Rich, "Abnegation," from *Leaflets: Poems, 1965–1968* (New York, 1969).

Rich, "Fox," from *Fox* (New York, 2001).

Derek Walcott, First to See Them

Derek Walcott, *Collected Poems, 1948–1984* (New York, 1986).

Walcott, *Omeros* (New York, 1990).

Walcott, *Tiepolo's Hound* (New York, 2000).

Walcott, *What the Twilight Says: Essays* (New York, 1998).

Conversations with Derek Walcott, ed. William Baer (Jackson, Miss., 1996).

"Talking with Derek Walcott," interview by Carroll Fleming, *Caribbean Reader* 7 (1993).

Gary Snyder's Eye for the Real World

The Gary Snyder Reader: Prose, Poetry, and Translations, 1952–1998 (Washington, D.C., 1999).

Gary Snyder, *The Back Country* (New York, 1968).

Snyder, *Turtle Island* (New York, 1974).

Snyder, *Riprap* (Ashland, Mass., 1959).

Snyder, *Danger on Peaks* (San Francisco, 2004).

Snyder, *Riprap and Cold Mountain Poems* (San Francisco, 1966).

Snyder, "Afterword," *Riprap and Cold Mountain Poems* (San Francisco, 1990).

Snyder, *Myths and Texts* (New York, 1960).

Snyder, *Six Sections from Mountains and Rivers Without End* (San Francisco, 1965).

Snyder, *Earth House Hold: Technical Notes and Queries to Fellow Dharma Revolutionaries* (New York, 1969).

Snyder, *The Real Work: Interviews and Talks, 1964–1979*, ed. William Scott Mclean (New York, 1980).

Snyder, *Mountains and Rivers Without End* (Washington, D.C., 1996).

Snyder, *The Practice of the Wild* (San Francisco, 1990; Washington, D.C., 2004).

John Felstiner, interview with Gary Snyder, Berkeley, October 27, 2006 [www.poetryfoundation.org].

Bob Steuding, *Gary Snyder* (Boston, 1976).

David Kherdian, *Six Poets of the San Francisco Renaissance: Portraits and Checklist* (Fresno, Calif., 1967).

Critical Essays on Gary Snyder, ed. Patrick D. Murphy (Boston, 1991).

Anthony Hunt, *Genesis, Structure, and Meaning in Gary Snyder's Mountains and Rivers Without End* (Reno, Nev., 2004).

Bernard Quetchenbach, "Gary Snyder," in *Back from the Far Field: American Nature Poetry in the Late Twentieth Century* (Charlottesville, Va., 2000).

John Suiter, *Poets on the Peaks: Gary Snyder, Philip Whalen and Jack Kerouac in the Cascades* (Washington, D.C., 2002).

Can Poetry Save the Earth?

Sarah Felstiner, Pollution Project, Hilltop Children's Center, Seattle.

Robert Hass, interview, *Mother Jones*, March–April 1997.

John Felstiner, "'Just Imagine': Robert Hass, Poet Laureate and the Watershed Project," Stanford University English Department Newsletter, 2001 (http://english.stanford.edu/newsletters); www.riverofwords.org/poetry.

Scott Momaday, "New World," in *In the Presence of the Sun: Stories and Poems, 1961–1991* (New York, 1992).

PEN American Center, Prison Writing poetry prizes, 2005.

Camille T. Dungy, "Black Nature: A Poetry Anthology" (Athens, Ga., forthcoming, 2009).

Text Credits

I thank the copyright holders for permission to reprint the following poems or poem extracts.

A. R. Ammons: "Easter Morning," Copyright © 1979 by A. R. Ammons. "Expressions of Sea Level," Copyright © 1964 by A. R. Ammons, from *The Selected Poems, Expanded Edition* by A. R. Ammons. Used by permission of W. W. Norton & Company, Inc. "Small Song," copyright © 1969, 1986, 1972 by A. R. Ammons. "Corsons Inlet," copyright © 1963 by A. R. Ammons, from *Collected Poems, 1951–1971* by A. R. Ammons. Used by permission of W. W. Norton & Company, Inc. "Motion's Holding," from *Sumerian Vistas* by A. R. Ammons. Copyright © 1987 by A. R. Ammons. Used by permission of W. W. Norton & Company, Inc. "Enough," from *The Really Short Poems of A. R. Ammons,* by A. R. Ammons. Copyright © 1990 by A. R. Ammons. Used by permission of W. W. Norton & Company, Inc. "The Sap Is Gone Out of the Trees" and "So I Said I Am Ezra," from *Ommateum: With Doxology* by A. R. Ammons. Copyright © 1955 by A. R. Ammons. Used by permission of W. W. Norton & Company, Inc.

Bashō: "Lightning Flash," from *The Essential Haiku: Versions of Bashō, Buson, and Issa*, edited and with an introduction by Robert Hass. Introduction and selection copyright © 1994 by Robert Hass. Unless otherwise noted, all translations copyright © 1994 by Robert Hass. Reprinted by permission of HarperCollins Publishers.

Elizabeth Bishop: "Poem" and excerpts from "The Moose," "The Fish," "The Armadillo," "Questions of Travel," and "Santarém," from *The Complete Poems, 1927–1979.* Copyright © 1979, 1983 by Alice Helen Methfessel. Reprinted by permission of Farrar, Straus & Giroux, LLC.

Buson: "Morning Breeze," from *The Essential Haiku: Versions of Bashō, Buson, and Issa,* edited and with an introduction by Robert Hass. Introduction and selection copyright © 1994 by Robert Hass. Unless otherwise noted, all translations copyright © 1994 by Robert Hass. Reprinted by permission of HarperCollins Publishers.

Shirley Kaufman: Excerpts from *Rivers of Salt* (Port Townsend, Wash., 1983) and *Roots in the Air: New and Selected Poems* (Port Townsend, Wash., 1996) reprinted with the permission of Copper Canyon Press.

Jane Kenyon: "Afternoon at MacDowell," "Chrysanthemums," "Twilight: After Haying," "Let Evening Come," copyright © 1996 by the Estate of Jane Kenyon. Reprinted from *New and Selected Poems* with the permission of Graywolf Press, St. Paul, Minnesota.

Galway Kinnell: Excerpt from "The Gray Heron," from *Mortal Acts, Mortal Words*, by Galway Kinnell. Copyright © 1980 by Galway Kinnell. "How Many Nights," "The Bear," "Blackberry Eating," "The Porcupine," "The Avenue Bearing the Initial of Christ into the New World," "Vapor Trail Reflected in the Frog Pond," excerpts from "The Gray Heron," from Galway Kinnell, *New Selected Poems*. Reprinted by permission of Houghton Mifflin Company. Copyright © 2000, 2001 by Galway Kinnell. Reprinted with the permission of Bloodaxe Books.

Maxine Kumin: "Splitting Wood at Six Above," copyright © 1978, 1996 by Maxine Kumin. "The Bangkok Gang," copyright © 1981, 1996 by Maxine Kumin, from *Selected Poems, 1960–1990*, by Maxine Kumin. Used by permission of W. W. Norton & Company, Inc. "Credo," from *Looking for Luck* by Maxine Kumin. Copyright © 1992 by Maxine Kumin. Used by permission of W. W. Norton & Company, Inc.

Stanley Kunitz: "End of Summer," copyright © 1953, 1958, 2000 by Stanley Kunitz, "Quinnapoxet," copyright © 1978, 2000 by Stanley Kunitz, "The Testing-Tree," copyright © 1968, 1995, 2000 by Stanley Kunitz, "The Wellfleet Whale," copyright © 1985, 1995, 2000 by Stanley Kunitz, "Raccoon Journal," copyright © 1985, 1995, 2000 by Stanley Kunitz, "The Snakes of September," copyright © 1985, 1995, 2000 by Stanley Kunitz, from *The Collected Poems* by Stanley Kunitz. Used by permission of W. W. Norton & Company, Inc.

D. H. Lawrence: "Snake" by D. H. Lawrence, "Fish" by D. H. Lawrence, "Mountain Lion" by D. H. Lawrence, from *The Complete Poems of D. H. Lawrence* by D. H. Lawrence, edited by V. de Sola Pinto and F. W. Roberts, copyright © 1964, 1971 by Angelo Ravagli and C. M. Weekley, Executors of the Estate of Frieda Lawrence Ravagli. Used by permission of Viking Penguin, a division of Penguin Group (USA) Inc. Reproduced by permission of Pollinger Limited and The Estate of Frieda Lawrence Ravagli.

Denise Levertov: Excerpts from "In California" and "For Instance" from *The Life Around Us: Selected Poems on Nature* (1997); excerpt from "Illustrious Ancestors," from *Selected Poetry* (2002); excerpt from "An English Field in the Nuclear Age," from *Poems 1972–1982* (1982); excerpts from "Listening to Distant Guns" from *Collected Earlier Poems, 1940–1960* (1979); excerpt from "Life at War," from *Poems 1968–1972* (1987); excerpts from "For Floss" and "The Pulse" from *Poems 1960–1967* (1983). Reproduced by permission of Pollinger Limited and the proprietor. Excerpts from "In California: Morning, Evening, Late January," and "For Instance," from *A Door in the Hive*, by Denise Levertov, copyright © 1989 by Denise Levertov; excerpt from "An English Field in the Nuclear Age," from *Candles in Babylon*, copyright © 1982 by Denise Levertov; excerpts from "Illustrious Ancestors" and "Listening to Distant Guns,"

Acknowledgments

My thanks go first to every poet, from King David on down, who literally made this book possible, including those who've been personally supportive: John Haines, Donald Hall, Bob Hass, Ted Hughes for a fortnight at Moortown Cottage, Shirley Kaufman, Galway Kinnell, Stanley Kunitz, Denise Levertov wintering annually across the green field behind my home, Gary Snyder, and Kim Stafford for his dad.

And second, to ASLE, the Association for the Study of Literature and Environment, and fellow-writers in this field of literature and environment, literary critics along with a growing legion of nature writers. Many are named among my sources.

To friends along the way, generous with their time and thought: Denise Banker, Peggy Bowers, Alek Felstiner, Adam and Arlie Hochschild, Nick Jenkins, Genine Lentine, Bob Lloyd, Randy Marks, Jim McIntosh, Linda Norton, Reeve Parker, Craig Segall, Cathy and Phred Short, Weixing Su, Murray and Roberta Suid, William Yaryan, and first and last Scott Slovic—student-friend two decades back, then mentor-colleague-consultant-reader and friend again from the moment this book took root.

To those who kindly came to my aid with images: Rick Ardinger, Edward Boenig, Chris Busa, Keith Ekiss, Sarah Felstiner, Camellia George, Joan Hendrickson, Jeff Henry and Paul Vee, Rozanne Knudson, David Parker, Edward Ranney, Scott Slovic, John Suiter, Susan Thomas, John Wronoski, Josh Yiu. I'm deeply grateful to Alice Methfessel for lending me the painting "behind" Elizabeth Bishop's "Poem," and glad that James Pennuto could restore it so well.

To Stanford friends: Rob Polhemus and Ramon Saldivar mightily chairing our department while minding my eight years of joyous travail, Alyce Boster genially, expertly managing permission payments, Ned Henningsen cheerfully steering me through the early crush of text permissions, Matt Jockers endlessly solving and salving technical cruxes, Emily Kopley keenly shooting digitals, Scobie Puchtler classily shopping them, Bryan Wolf heartfully responding to my crying need with a "color" subsidy from the Stanford Institute for Creativity and the Arts, and Stanford University Libraries as ever being there for me.

To Yale University Press: Jonathan Brent my once-again acquiring editor and squire, his assistant Annelise Finegan, John Kulka and his assistant Lindsay Toland, Donna Anstey for advice on permissions, my editor Jennifer Banks, who wisely and amicably saw me through, and her assistant Joseph Calamia, Margaret Otzel, my caring production editor, Noreen O'Connor-Abel, my copyeditor, Laura Moss Gottlieb, excellent indexer, and Justin Eichenlaub, who ably proofread. Also to the Press's two readers, whose graciousness and acumen encouraged and sharpened this book.

To the places that gave me time (and terrain) for writing: Djerassi Resident Artists Program, the Corporation of Yaddo, MacDowell Colony, Millay Colony for the Arts, Mesa Refuge in Point Reyes, California, Jentel Artist Residency Program in Banner, Wyoming, Stanford Humanities Center. And to friends who helped me get there: Geoffrey Hartman, Bob Hass, Scott Slovic.

To the magazines that harbored and editors who tended essay-chapters: *Parthenon West Review* (David Holler, Chad Sweeney), *Denver Quarterly* (Bin Ramke), *ISLE / Interdisciplinary Studies in Literature and Environment* (Scott Slovic), *Weekly Standard* (Philip Terzian), *American Poetry Review* (Steve Berg, Elizabeth Scanlon), *Iowa Review* (David Hamilton), *Michigan Quarterly Review* (Larry Goldstein), *Journal of American Studies* (Tbilisi, Georgia—Shelley Fisher-Fishkin), *Foreign Literature Studies* (Wuhan, China—Scott Slovic), *Seattle Review* (Andrew Feld), *World Literature in Translation* (Daniel Simon), *Jacket* (John Tranter).

To places that hosted presentations along the way: Stanford Sierra Camp, Stanford Quest Scholars Program, Stanford Humanities Center, Stanford Law and Environment Society, Stanford Alumni Association, Association for the Study of Literature and Environment, University of Nevada at Reno, Denver University, Sempervirens Fund, Puget Sound Community School, Sun Valley Writers Conference, Tor House Foundation, and of course the Stanford English Department curriculum.

Last and not least but most, to Mary Lowenthal Felstiner, who stood by me from start to finish while pursuing her own writing and teaching. Her spirit and savvy saved me countless times, from idiot moments like "I think I hit the wrong key" all the way to "Why am I writing this book?" In acknowledgments for my Paul Celan books, love poems to *his* wife gave me phrases I could translate toward mine. Now I borrow from William Carlos Williams's conjugal love poem, *Asphodel, That Greeny Flower:* "my sweet . . . My heart rouses / thinking to bring you news . . ." It *is* difficult to get the news from poems, the environmental news. Mary has kept me sane and true for the trying.

Index